To Martine
with compliments to a cherished
mentor and frie ...
the idea of put ...
this book.
Oral

The Quest for Regional Integration in the East African Community

EDITORS
Paulo Drummond, S. Kal Wajid, and Oral Williams

INTERNATIONAL MONETARY FUND

Cover design: IMF Multimedia Services Division

Cataloging-in-Publication Data
Joint Bank-Fund Library

The East African Community : quest for regional integration / editors: Paulo Drummond, Kal Wajid, and Oral Williams. – Washington, D.C. : International Monetary Fund, [2014].

p. ; cm.

Includes bibliographical references and index.

ISBN: 978-1-48436-441-3 (Paper)

1. East African Community. 2. Africa, East – Economic integration. 3. Monetary unions – Africa, East. 4. Customs unions – Africa, East. 6. Social integration – Africa, East. I. Drummond, Paulo Flavio Nacif, 1966- II. Wajid, Syed Khalid S. III. Williams, Oral. IV. International Monetary Fund.

HG1342.E32 2014

Please send orders to:
International Monetary Fund, Publication Services
P.O. Box 92780, Washington, DC 20090, U.S.A.
Tel.: (202) 623-7430 Fax: (202) 623-7201
E-mail: publications@imf.org
Internet: www.elibrary.imf.org
www.imfbookstore.org

Contents

Foreword

The East African Community (EAC) is a unique regional entity that was established in 2000 with a clear road map for establishing a Customs Union, Common Market, Monetary Union, and, ultimately, a political federation. The EAC Customs Union Protocol came into force in 2005 and the implementation of the Common Market Protocol commenced in 2010. The EAC Monetary Union (EAMU) Protocol comes into force in 2014. These stages of integration are being implemented in a progressive manner and major strides are being made to establish a political federation. The EAMU Protocol is a key milestone on the road to a single currency area in 2024 upon fulfilment of the key macroeconomic convergence targets.

Economic integration is benefiting the East African people through increased efficiency and productivity, and the entry into a single currency will eliminate bilateral foreign exchange risk, reduce transactions and accounting costs for intra-regional trade, and foster financial integration. This will facilitate the expansion of regional trade and investment, which will promote economic growth and cross-border financial transactions, resulting in lower interest rates.

This book is being produced at a time when critical economic reforms are being undertaken in fiscal, monetary, and exchange rate policies to achieve the EAC macroeconomic convergence criteria which are a major cornerstone in the EAC currency union arrangement. The book catalogs recent developments and presents ideas for the way forward on harmonization and coordination of fiscal, monetary, and financial policies, including strengthening and harmonizing the institutional framework underpinning these policies, as well as statistical harmonization and public financial management. It elaborates the framework for the formulation and implementation of monetary policy aimed at ensuring low and stable inflation and strong growth, discusses the alternative exchange rate arrangements in the transition to monetary union, and outlines the necessary regional financial stability framework. In doing so, it also draws on the different experiences of other currency unions.

The path to single currency will go hand in hand with sustainable and robust economic growth and undertaking the necessary investments in infrastructure. The EAC region has had recent discoveries in oil and natural gas, which, if well utilized through an EAC-wide coordinated revenue management framework complemented with robust macroeconomic policies, will raise the standard of living of the East African people. I appreciate the commitment of the authors in producing this book, which is an important contribution toward establishing a robust macroeconomic framework for the EAC region.

Ambassador Dr. Richard Sezibera
Secretary General
East African Community

CHAPTER 1

Overview

PAULO DRUMMOND, S. KAL WAJID, AND ORAL WILLIAMS

Under the Treaty for the Establishment of the East African Community (EAC), the signatory nations—Burundi, Kenya, Rwanda, Tanzania, and Uganda—have committed to regional integration across economic, social, and political spheres. The treaty explicitly emphasizes political federation as the ultimate goal underpinning regional integration efforts, which led to the ratification of the Customs Union Protocol in 2005 and the Common Market Protocol in 2010. Efforts toward a monetary union are well advanced and the member countries have adopted a Monetary Union Protocol.

Historically, countries in East Africa have at different times coalesced around forming some form of a currency union. In 1905 a currency board was established, creating a common currency for the East Africa Protectorate (which became the British colony of Kenya in 1922) and the Uganda Protectorate. Tanganyika joined after the First World War. A new currency board was constituted in 1919 by countries under British rule (Kenya, Uganda, and Tanganyika and, in 1936, Zanzibar) that adopted the East Africa shilling. The Blumenthal Report in 1963 recommended separate central banks, and an IMF mission in 1965 provided assistance with the introduction of a common currency and an East African Central Bank. After independence, local currencies were fully and freely convertible into sterling, and in 1966 the common currency became fully convertible legal tender in Kenya, Uganda, and Tanzania. The depreciation of sterling in the late 1960s and early 1970s led to the disintegration of the Sterling Area in 1972.[1] Following a period of divergence of inflation targets and interest rates, the East African Currency Area was formally ended in 1977. The recent efforts toward a monetary union therefore build on a long and fascinating history of monetary arrangements in the region.

This book focuses on regional integration in the EAC. It is motivated by ongoing initiatives in this direction that have significant sway over economic policymaking and economic outcomes in the region. The EAC countries are also among the fastest growing economies in sub-Saharan Africa since 2000 and have achieved average per capita income growth higher than that region. The EAC

[1] When the United Kingdom left the gold standard in 1931, many countries that had pegged their currencies to gold pegged them to sterling instead. After devaluation of the pound sterling in 1967, many countries in the sterling area did not also devalue, despite the imposition of exchange controls to minimize flight from sterling to the U.S. dollar.

countries are making significant progress toward financial integration, including harmonization of supervisory arrangements and practices and the modernization of monetary policy frameworks.

But much remains to be done. The removal of nontariff barriers is essential for the full functioning of the customs union. The establishment of a timetable for the elimination of the sensitive-products list and the establishment of a supranational legal framework for resolving trade disputes are also important reforms that should foster regional integration.[2]

The costs and benefits of regional integration and monetary union are well documented (such as in McCallum, 1995, and Frankel and Rose, 2002). It is argued that common markets and currency unions, by lowering tariffs and eliminating bilateral foreign exchange risk, reduce transactions and accounting costs for intraregional trade. Regional trade and investment expand under a monetary union, promoting economic growth and cross-border banking operations. This then boosts financial sector competition, integrates financial markets, and could help lower interest rates. Different studies have estimated the impact on the expansion of intraregional trade flows to be from 30 percent (Rose and Stanley, 2005) to as much as 200 percent (Rose and Frankel, 2000).

This book, as outlined in detail in the following, takes stock of key developments in EAC integration and sketches an agenda for reforms that could foster further integration. Although various factors determine the degree of integration, the book focuses on macroeconomic and financial aspects.

MAIN FINDINGS

Macroeconomic Setting

The EAC has been among the fastest growing regions in sub-Saharan Africa since 2005, its best performance since the 1970s. Indeed, at 3.5 percent per capita GDP growth during 2005–13, the EAC outpaced sub-Saharan Africa (3.3 percent) (Table 1.1).

Chapter 2 explores the basis of this strong growth by benchmarking performance with countries that have experienced sustained growth. A period of "catch up" partly explains this strong performance, making up for previous low growth. Favorable international commodity prices have also been an important contributing factor, as have a peace dividend following bouts of civil strife and sound macroeconomic policies. Rwanda, Tanzania, and Uganda have grown at rates comparable to countries that have sustained growth and share key characteristics such as periods of low inflation and small budget deficits. Improved business environments and government stability have also contributed to strong productivity gains and rising foreign direct investment (Figure 1.1).

---

[2]The EAC Exclusion List/List of Sensitive Products from export partnership agreements includes products that contribute to rural development, employment, livelihood sustainability, promotion of food security, and fostering infant industries.

TABLE 1.1

East African Community: Selected Economic Indicators

	2000	2005	2013
Nominal GDP (US$ billions)			
Burundi	0.9	1.1	2.7
Kenya	14.4	21.6	55.3
Rwanda	1.7	2.6	7.5
Tanzania	10.2	14.1	33.3
Uganda	6.1	10.0	22.9
GDP per capita (US$)			
Burundi	125.4	161.7	305.3
Kenya	426.3	546.6	1058.1
Rwanda	204.7	274.7	690.1
Tanzania	310.3	376.2	719.3
Uganda	274.0	361.9	621.5
Population (millions)			
Burundi	6.4	7.5	9.0
Kenya	29.5	33.8	41.8
Rwanda	8.4	9.4	10.8
Tanzania	32.4	37.1	45.6
Uganda	24.2	28.4	36.8
Inflation (period average, percent change)			
Burundi	14.1	1.1	9.0
Kenya	7.8	7.8	5.7
Rwanda	3.9	9.1	4.2
Tanzania	6.0	4.4	7.9
Uganda	3.4	8.6	5.0
Fiscal balance incl. grants (percent of GDP)			
Burundi	–1.5	–4.3	–2.4
Kenya	–0.3	–1.5	–5.5
Rwanda	0.8	0.6	–4.8
Tanzania	–0.9	–4.0	–5.9
Uganda	n.a.	n.a.	–4.2
Gross public debt (percent of GDP)			
Burundi	147.3	111.6	31.5
Kenya	51.5	46.6	40.0
Rwanda	82.5	58.3	20.9
Tanzania	—	56.0	40.5
Uganda	62.3	57.2	32.8
Gross reserves (in months of imports)			
Burundi	3.3	2.3	3.4
Kenya	2.7	2.7	4.0
Rwanda	5.3	6.2	4.8
Tanzania	4.4	6.1	4.1
Uganda	6.2	6.3	4.5
Credit to private sector (percent of GDP)			
Burundi	16.5	13.2	15.5
Kenya	23.2	22.1	32.4
Rwanda	10.5	9.1	15.7
Tanzania	3.7	8.9	19.4
Uganda	n.a.	7.7	14.6

(continued)

TABLE 1.1

East African Community: Selected Economic Indicators *(continued)*

	2000	2005	2013
Broad money (percent of GDP)			
Burundi	15.3	21.3	19.7
Kenya	32.8	34.2	41.9
Rwanda	17.5	15.2	21.3
Tanzania	15.4	22.2	30.3
Uganda	n.a.	17.3	22.4
Stock market capitalization (percent of GDP)[1]			
Burundi	—	—	—
Kenya	8.9	29.6	29.5
Rwanda	—	—	—
Tanzania	2.3	4.2	6.3
Uganda	—	1.0	34.3
Exports goods and services + imports goods and services (percent of GDP)			
Burundi	22.6	40.1	48.2
Kenya	45.7	56.0	52.5
Rwanda	34.7	37.3	48.5
Tanzania	34.0	51.5	66.7
Uganda	32.4	38.8	55.2

Sources: Country authorities; and IMF staff calculations.
[1] Final year data is 2012 in lieu of unavailable 2013 data.

Chapter 3 examines issues in macroeconomic convergence, which is critical to fostering economic growth that will support the eventual adoption of a single currency. The core, nominal convergence criteria are (1) a fiscal deficit of no more than 3 percent of GDP, (2) an inflation rate of no more than 8 percent, (3) international reserves at least equivalent to 4.5 months of imports, and (4) a public debt-to-GDP ratio of no more than 50 percent in net-present-value terms. While the convergence criteria on international reserves in months of imports and debt to GDP have invariably been met in recent years, in part because of sound macroeconomic policies as well as substantial debt relief, compliance with the deficit and inflation objectives has been more challenging. The former has been difficult because of the need for greater investment in infrastructure in these countries, and the latter because of the impact of food and fuel shocks. By contrast, differences in per capita incomes and productivity have narrowed over time, reflecting strong growth in the region.

Macrofiscal Situation and Monetary Union

Chapter 4 explores fiscal policy challenges and highlights a strengthening over time, with lower deficits and debt levels enabling EAC countries to respond effectively, for example, to the global financial crisis through countercyclical fiscal policy. That said, the crisis underscored the region's vulnerability to large external shocks. The chapter argues that a clause permitting relaxation for large economic shocks should accompany the fiscal deficit criterion. In light of the discovery of nonrenewable resources in several EAC countries, the case is made to commence

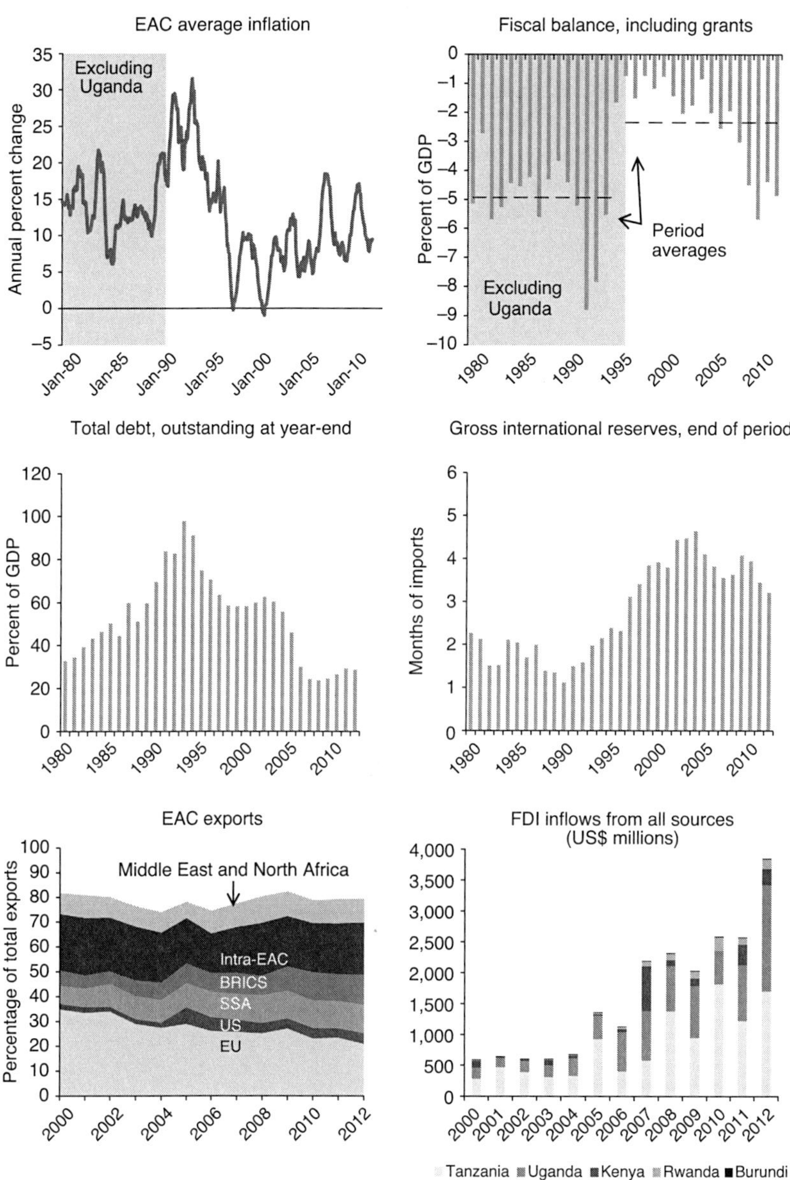

Figure 1.1 East African Community: Macroeconomic Stabilization

Sources: IMF, African Department database and World Economic Outlook database.

Note: Weighted by purchasing power parity GDP. Top panels exclude initial periods of hyperinflation and large fiscal balances in Uganda. BRICS = Brazil, Russia, India, China, and South Africa; EAC = East African Community; EU = European Union; FDI = foreign direct investment; SSA = sub-Saharan Africa; US = United States.

tracking nonresource primary balances to provide a more reliable measure of the impact of government policies on domestic demand. Chapter 5 covers topics related to strengthening and harmonizing the institutional framework underpinning fiscal policy, particularly data reporting and coverage and public financial management. It also draws on the experiences of other monetary unions in achieving harmonization of national fiscal practices and the need for the development of a national budget frameworks directive.

Monetary Policy Framework and Implementation

Chapter 6, in particular, lays out the rationale for harmonizing monetary policy, which is needed to cement credibility in the introduction of a monetary union, especially by ensuring low and stable inflation. Harmonization needs to be gradual given differences in the degree of exchange rate flexibility, the way monetary instruments are used, the weight given to monetary aggregates, and the role of policy interest rates in monetary operations. However, the chapter underscores that harmonization of monetary policy instruments should be undertaken first, during the transition to monetary union.

Chapter 7 explores the channels through which monetary policy is transmitted, that is, whether through interest rates or reserve money. A key finding is that, as in developed countries, there is a shift away from money-focused monetary aggregates as a result of, among other things, possible structural shifts in money demand and money multipliers because of a deepening of financial sectors and the openness of economies to international capital flows.

Chapter 7 also addresses EAC countries' response to the recent food and fuel shocks. Food inflation in all EAC countries peaked in the double digits in 2011, and higher nonfood inflation affected consumer price inflation in Burundi, Kenya, Tanzania, and Uganda. Higher transportation costs associated with rising global oil prices were particularly important in landlocked Burundi and Uganda, and power tariffs rose sharply in Tanzania. To curb potential second-round effects, Burundi, Kenya, Tanzania, and Uganda raised policy rates in late 2011. Tanzanian monetary authorities increased reserve requirements and reduced net open positions, causing both growth in broad money and credit to the private sector to slow and the exchange rate to stabilize, improving the outlook for inflation.

The chapter emphasizes that strengthening the monetary transmission mechanism would be enhanced by (1) ensuring that monetary targets and interest rate policy are consistent, (2) reducing the high share of currency in circulation, (3) deepening the financial sector and integrating money and foreign exchange markets, (4) reducing banks' excess reserves at the central bank, and (5) improving data quality and frequency.

Exchange Rate Arrangements and Management

Chapter 8 considers alternative exchange rate arrangements for the EAC countries in the transition to monetary union, underscoring three main considerations.

First, while exchange rate policies differ in important ways across the EAC, the member countries have expressed a desire to achieve a common exchange rate policy during the transition to union. Second, since the transition period will encompass several years, arrangements adopted during it should be consistent with macroeconomic stability and financial development on a country-by-country basis. Third, the transition process should be designed to avoid real exchange rate misalignment in the first few years of the monetary union.

The chapter concludes that, given the region's vulnerability to external shocks and the openness of its capital account, a managed float is the appropriate exchange-rate regime during transition to union. This should ensure that national inflation targets are consistent with community-wide convergence criteria for inflation, which would serve as the nominal anchor. The advantages of a managed float are underscored by the uncertain horizon during which union will occur.

Financial Integration and Framework for Financial Stability

Chapter 9 discusses the considerations for the EAC regarding responsibility for financial stability in the envisaged East African Monetary Union. Specifically, financial integration will necessitate the development of a regional financial stability framework—which should encompass a harmonized and a unified approach to supervision and regulation across the region—and appropriate legislation and methods for effective consolidated supervision and home-host cooperation. Financial stability analysis could also be undertaken, involving a review of data definitions and interpretations in order to assess the potential for cross-border contagion through regionally headquartered banks.

Several challenges will have to be addressed in the process of financial integration, including strengthening the capacity to monitor the nonbank financial sector and harmonization of supervision and regulation, and arrangements for crisis management and safety nets. These arrangements should be sequenced immediately after completion of the negotiation of the EAC Monetary Protocol.

Chapter 10 builds on the introductory issues raised in Chapter 9 by analyzing the degree of financial linkages and flows in the EAC region to understand the associated risks of greater interconnectedness and implications for supervision. Key findings are that while intraregional financial flows are limited, EAC banking systems are linked through cross-country ownership of banks. This makes the region vulnerable to crisis through contagion, if the regionally active banks are not properly supervised. Second, weaknesses in banking supervision in both home and host countries increase the risks of contagion. In particular, some home and host supervisors do not have the capacity to supervise complex financial institutions. Finally, the emergence of financial conglomerations requires closer cooperation among agencies supervising different financial sectors.

Chapter 11 empirically investigates whether actions taken under the EAC framework have succeeded in advancing financial integration. It assesses the degree of integration of the financial markets (treasury, interbank, and stock markets) of all five EAC countries, where possible, and examines whether integration has progressed. The empirical results on financial integration in the EAC are mixed but suggest that convergence of investment returns is taking place in all three financial markets assessed in this chapter—treasury bill, interbank, and stock markets. Moreover, the speed of convergence has increased in recent years in the treasury markets (and to lesser extent in the interbank markets). This suggests that financial integration efforts have reduced barriers to financial transactions across borders to some extent, creating incentives for financial institutions to take advantage of arbitrage opportunities across the markets.

Chapter 12 reviews recent financial sector assessment programs in the EAC countries from the perspective of regional financial integration, complementing Chapters 9, 10, and 11. It also summarizes the main findings of the regional financial sector assessment programs of 2012/13. Key findings include the need to link up the region's stock exchanges and depositories to advance capital market integration. The chapter underscores that greater effort is needed to strengthen and expand cross-border retail payments with supporting regulatory frameworks. As cross-border linkages become entrenched, it will be necessary to revisit rules governing the mandates of EAC institutions such as the EAC Secretariat in order to support decision making and delegation of responsibilities.

CHALLENGES AND THE WAY FORWARD

As EAC countries have become more integrated with the global economy, their increased interconnectedness will become a channel for spillovers from developments in both advanced and emerging market economies. The transmission of spillover effects of the Great Recession has slowed the pace of growth in emerging markets, in particular the BRICS (Brazil, Russia, India, China, South Africa), with whom EAC countries have increased trade linkages over the last decade.

Policy frameworks will need to be further strengthened as private capital flows, which tend to be more volatile than official flows, have increased in the context of excess global liquidity. Managing the volatility of private capital inflows and mitigating the macroeconomic impacts of "sudden stops" will increasingly test the robustness of monetary and fiscal policy toolkits. In this context, several EAC countries are moving toward using either the interest rate or inflation as a nominal anchor and have stepped up communications in signaling changes in the stance of monetary policy to the market. At the same time, the exchange rate has been permitted to act as an absorber of external shocks, as demonstrated during the recent food and fuel shocks in 2011 and the coordinated press release by EAC central bank governors.

Sustaining robust growth is a key objective and requirement for successful integration. This in turn will require substantial infrastructure investment. The associated financing needs are large and several countries have tapped bilateral nonconcessional financing from BRICS in meeting the demands for scaling up infrastructure investment. However, EAC countries will have to strike a delicate balance in meeting these needs and adhering to the primary convergence criterion on public debt.

The recent discovery of oil and gas in a number of EAC countries will have far-reaching implications for macroeconomic management and compliance with the macroeconomic convergence criteria. Deficits measured excluding natural resource incomes will need to be monitored carefully. Typically, natural resource incomes have a finite lifetime, based on the size of oil or mineral deposits. Exploiting these resources produces a period of high incomes (associated with license fees, royalties, and other taxes). While this can support a temporary period of higher expenditure, countries often save part of the income stream to extend the period over which higher expenditures can be sustained, and to avoid the sort of sharp rise and subsequent reversal of spending that poses the strongest risks of Dutch disease. Natural resource incomes are also subject to volatility, linked to changes in global commodity prices. Periods of high prices can strengthen fiscal performance, even where there is an underlying deterioration in the nonresource accounts. Given these considerations, EAC countries will need to carefully manage the proceeds from natural resources to avoid creating macroeconomic imbalances, which have been coined "the resource rich curse." In addition, differences in natural resource endowments will imply varying contributions of natural resources to fiscal revenues. This will pose challenges in the harmonization of the convergence criteria.

REFERENCES

Frankel, J., and A. Rose, 2002, "An Estimate of the Effect of Common Currencies on Trade and Income," *The Quarterly Journal of Economics*, Vol. 117, No. 2, pp. 437–466.

McCallum, J., 1995, "National Borders Matter: Canada-U.S. Regional Trade Patterns," *American Economic Review*, Vol. 85, No. 3, pp. 615–623.

Rose, A., and J. Frankel, 2000, "Estimating the Effect of Currency Unions on Trade and Output," NBER Working Paper No. 7857 (Cambridge, Massachusetts: National Bureau of Economic Research).

Rose, A., and T. Stanley, 2005, "A Meta-Analysis of the Effect of Common Currencies on International Trade," *Journal of Economic Surveys*, Vol. 19, No. 3, pp. 347–365.

CHAPTER 2

Sustaining Growth in the East African Community

CATHERINE MCAULIFFE, SWETA C. SAXENA, AND MASAFUMI YABARA

THE GROWTH RECORD

In the midst of sub-Saharan Africa's best decade of economic growth since at least the 1970s, the East African Community (EAC) is among the fastest-growing regions. Growth rates have picked up strongly since 2000, outpacing the rest of sub-Saharan Africa (Figure 2.1). During 2005–11, per capita income growth reached 3.6 percent a year in the EAC, compared with 3.0 percent for sub-Saharan Africa as a whole, quadrupling the rate achieved in the previous 15 years. Part of the recent high growth is "catching up" after years of very poor growth—in the last part of the 20th century, the region suffered periods of severe civil strife and bouts of economic instability. Since then, governments in EAC countries have been committed to strong policies.

However, growth has been uneven. Rwanda, Tanzania, and Uganda have had the longest periods of high growth. Uganda's growth started speeding up earlier than the others and has lasted more than 20 years, with per capita income growth averaging 3.4 percent a year during 1990–2011 (Figure 2.2). Growth in Rwanda and Tanzania has been strong since the early 2000s. After a period of stagnation, growth is picking up in Kenya—the largest of the EAC's five economies—averaging 1.9 percent per year since 2005 compared with -0.2 percent in 1990–2004. Output declined in Burundi in most of the period since 1990—reflecting periods of political conflict—but has shown signs of recovery in recent years.

Addressing Social Challenges

Some progress has been made toward the Millennium Development Goals. Most EAC countries are close to achieving universal primary education and child mortality rates have come down. Tanzania, Uganda, and Rwanda sharply have reduced poverty, driven by strong income growth (Figure 2.3). However, Kenya, despite having the lowest poverty ratio, and Burundi have not made much progress in the last decade. Poverty remains unacceptably high, especially in Burundi, Rwanda, and Tanzania. The region's high population growth (close to 3 percent per year over the last two decades) could constrain efforts to improve social indicators.

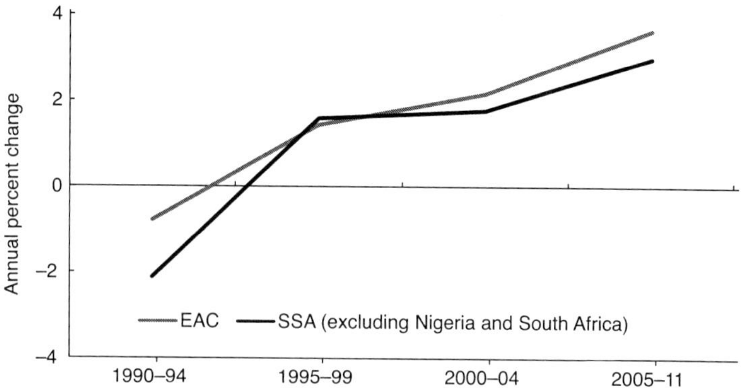

Figure 2.1 Real GDP Growth per Capita

Source: IMF, World Economic Outlook database.
Note: Weighted by population. EAC = East African Community; SSA = sub-Saharan Africa.

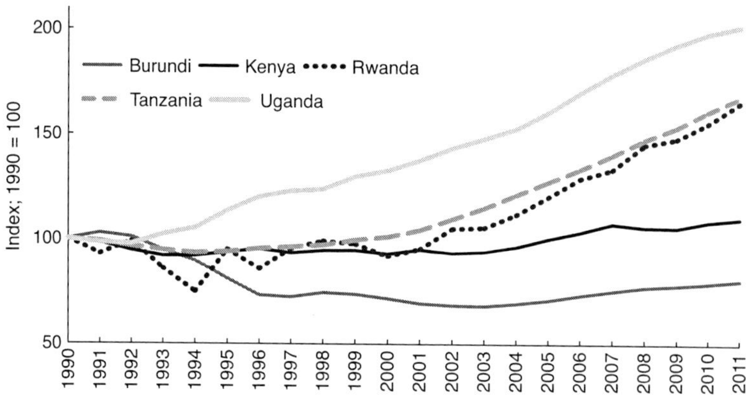

Figure 2.2 Cumulative Growth in Real GDP per Capita

Source: IMF, World Economic Outlook database.

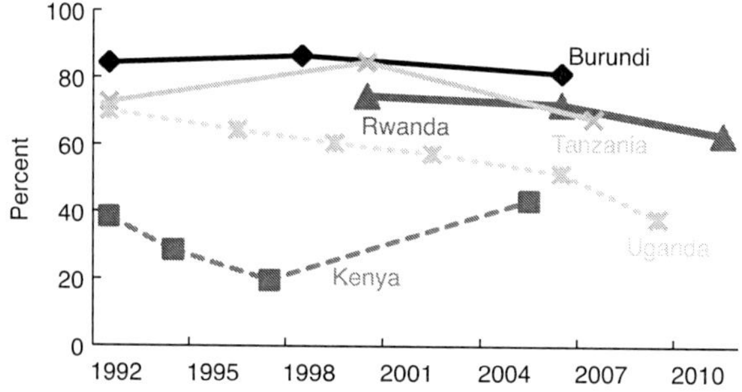

Figure 2.3 Poverty Headcount Ratio at $1.25 a Day (Purchasing Power Parity)

Source: World Bank, World Development Indicators database.

Achieving Middle-Income Status

The recent growth path will not be enough to achieve middle-income status and substantial poverty reduction by the end of the decade—the ambition of most countries in the region. To achieve these objectives, the region would need to grow at an average rate of about 5.5 percent in real per capita GDP per year for the rest of the decade, about 2 percentage points faster than in the last five years.[1] Rwanda, Tanzania, and Uganda, with per capita income somewhat below the regional average, would have to grow 7–8 percent per capita a year to meet that goal. Kenya is already close to middle-income levels and should achieve this earlier if it maintains current growth rates. Burundi—the poorest country in the EAC—will take much longer to reach that goal.

What Drives Growth?

There is no consensus on what it takes to initiate and sustain growth.[2] As a recent study puts it, there are "no recipes, just ingredients" (Commission on Growth and Development, 2008). The many factors vary from country to country, including macroeconomic policies, investment and trade, political and economic institutions, infrastructure and financial development, human capital, and income distribution. It is also widely recognized that the factors behind growth upturns are not necessarily the same as those that sustain growth, and that while starting growth is relatively easy, sustaining it is more difficult (Berg, Ostry, and Zettelmeyer, 2012; Hausmann, Pritchett, and Rodrik, 2004).

We look at the factors that have contributed to growth in the EAC and assess the prospects for translating the recent upturn into sustained high growth. To do this, we compare growth in the EAC countries with other countries that have achieved sustained growth by comparing levels and trends in certain indicators.[3] For example, are the EAC countries undergoing important shifts in growth patterns—similar to other sustained growth countries—that could underpin longer-term high growth? We also compare the record of sustained growth countries with countries that started to grow but failed to sustain it. And we look at the key factors that distinguish sustained and nonsustained growth and consider whether there are lessons for the EAC. Although this type of benchmarking cannot be used to make unconditional policy advice, it has been used with greater

---

[1]To illustrate, the calculation assumes a middle-income threshold of $1,000 GDP per capita in 2010 (close to the $1,006 threshold of middle-income status defined by the World Bank). We assume this threshold grows in nominal terms at about 3 percent a year—the observed growth of the middle-income threshold over the last decade—for the next decade to reach an estimated $1,331 in 2020.

[2]See Barro (2003) and Barro and Sala-i-Martin (2004) for comprehensive analysis.

[3]To support the benchmarking exercise, we also run regressions on drivers of growth, using models developed in the literature extended for additional variables relevant for the EAC, such as a peace dividend. We find that maintaining peace and liberalizing financial sectors improve the chances of both growth accelerations and sustained growth after some five to seven years. Persistence pays off. See McAuliffe, Saxena, and Yabara (2012) for more details.

frequency in the growth literature to help judge the growth potential of a country or region by identifying the types of strategies and policy interventions that have been successful, as well as identifying constraints to growth.

In the rest of this chapter, we explain the methodology used to identify growth accelerations and sustained growth episodes, and highlight factors contributing to sustained growth. We then provide a comparison of EAC growth with other growth episodes; the final section makes policy recommendations.

EXPLAINING GROWTH: THE EMPIRICAL FRAMEWORK

Identifying Growth Episodes

We identify countries where growth accelerated and was sustained, building on the methodology established in Hausmann, Pritchett, and Rodrik (2004); Johnson, Ostry, and Subramanian (2007); and Xu (2011). Our methodology modifies these earlier studies in two important areas. First, we extend the time series to 2009 (or 2006 depending on the explanatory variables), which covers the high growth period in sub-Saharan Africa, particularly in the EAC.[4] Second, our sample consists of commodity-exporting, low-income countries; that is, countries with similar economic characteristics to EAC countries.

According to the methodology, growth acceleration episodes must satisfy three criteria: (1) a period of rapid growth in per capita GDP of at least 3.5 percent a year for seven years, (2) an improvement in growth in per capita GDP of at least 2 percentage points (which captures the idea of acceleration), and (3) a higher postacceleration income level than the preacceleration peak (this requirement rules out cases in which accelerations are simply a rebound from a prior period of bad performance, owing to conflict or other shocks). On the basis of these criteria, and using the latest available data through 2009, we can identify growth acceleration episodes starting as late as 2002.[5]

Not all countries can sustain high growth. Therefore, to identify sustained high-growth episodes—that is, countries that not only exhibited accelerated growth but also sustained it—we add a fourth criterion: (4) that growth rates must stay above 3 percent for at least five years after the first seven years, similar to methodologies used in the literature. Given the end-year of 2009 in our data set, we can identify sustained growth episodes that started on or before 1997.[6] Some growth

[4]We use Penn World Tables 7.0 (May 2011) which covers 1950–2009 for 189 countries for identifying growth episodes. The International Monetary Fund's World Economic Outlook database and the World Bank's World Development Indicators database are used in benchmarking the EAC growth experience against identified growth episodes. They cover data starting in 1960.

[5]Since growth episodes must last for at least seven years to qualify as a growth acceleration (criterion 2), the latest year for the start of an acceleration is 2002 using Penn World Tables 7.0, which includes data through 2009.

[6]Countries that achieved growth acceleration in 1998 or after cannot meet the criterion for sustained growth simply because their episodes are too short and data are unavailable.

TABLE 2.1

Growth Episodes of Commodity Exporters

Sustained Growth (Meet all the criteria 1–4)		Nonsustained Growth (Meet only criteria 1–3)	
Brazil	1966	Afghanistan	1977
Cambodia	1994	Argentina	1989
Cameroon	1971	Benin	1976
Chile	1974* 1983	Chad	1997
China (Mainland)	1967 1976 1989	Haiti	1970
Colombia	1967 1991*	Honduras	1972
Congo, Republic of	1968 1976*	Jordan	1972
Dominican Republic	1965 1999	Lao P.D.R	1978 1988
Ecuador	1966	Lebanon	1978
Egypt	1958* 1972 1988*	Mali	1972 1983
Ghana	1964* 1997	Nicaragua	1958
Guatemala	1963	Papua New Guinea	1970 1989
Indonesia	1967 1985	Peru	1958
Iran	1964	Philippines	1969
Malawi	1961	Sri Lanka	1976 1991
Malaysia	1966 1986	Tunisia	1969
Mexico	1962	Uganda	1992
Morocco	1957 1970*	Uruguay	1972 1987
Mozambique	1994	Zambia	1962
Nigeria	1957* 1966* 1996		
Oman	1982		
Pakistan	1959		
Panama	1957 1974*		
Paraguay	1968		
Syria	1969 1989*		
Thailand	1957 1983		
Turkey	1964		
Vietnam	1988		

Sources: Penn World Tables Version 7.0; and authors' calculations.
Note: * denotes a nonsustained growth episode.

acceleration episodes did not meet the fourth criterion, although they started before 1997. We refer to these episodes as nonsustained growth episodes and use them to investigate factors distinguishing sustained and nonsustained growth.

We identify 34 episodes of sustained growth in 28 countries (SGs), as well as 35 nonsustained growth episodes in 28 countries (non-SGs). Table 2.1 shows all of the growth episodes and the years of acceleration (time *t*). The list of SGs includes most of the well-known growth episodes that followed significant policy changes or policy reforms. None of the EAC countries make this list. Uganda, Tanzania, and Rwanda have achieved growth accelerations (satisfying criteria 1–3, with acceleration in 1992 for Uganda, 1999 for Tanzania, and 2002 for Rwanda). However, they are not SGs and none meet criteria 4 (the growth episodes for Rwanda and Tanzania are too short, whereas Uganda fell just short of the threshold). In contrast, Burundi and Kenya, two countries with the lowest and highest per capita income in the EAC, respectively, have not yet registered a growth acceleration, failing to meet criteria 1–3.

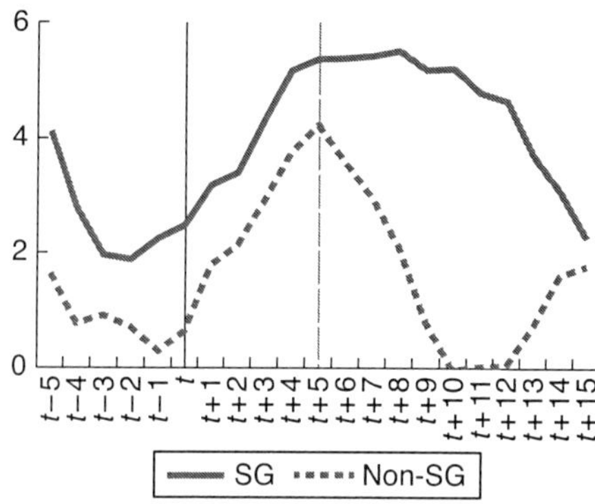

Figure 2.4 SGs versus Non-SGs: Real Gross Domestic Product per Capita (growth rate)

Sources: IMF, World Economic Outlook database; and authors' calculations.
Note: Five-year moving average. Non-SG = country with nonsustained growth; SG = country with sustained growth.

Differentiating Sustained and Nonsustained Growth

A simple review of the economic characteristics of countries with different growth experiences can be informative. The events that give rise to a growth acceleration may well be different from those that sustain an upturn, and contributory factors may be self-reinforcing or offsetting. In short, growth outcomes possibly reflect multifaceted processes that may be difficult to identify through econometric analysis alone. This section looks at possible lessons using a more low-tech approach to examine the evidence.

On average, growth tends to start stronger and last twice as long in SGs. For the sample of countries in Table 2.1, average real per capita growth in the first six years of growth acceleration was 4 percent for SGs, compared with just 1.8 percent for non-SGs (Figure 2.4). The growth upturn was also more durable. For SGs, growth remained at initial rates for a 10-year period, whereas for non-SGs, growth peaked after the first 5 years and subsequently slowed rapidly. This suggests that at least two different sets of growth-contributing factors may be at work. The first can be seen as contributing to the faster pace of growth in SGs during the initial expansionary period, whereas a second set may contribute to the collapse of growth rates in non-SGs around the five-year mark. Possible candidates for these roles are considered in the following.

Growth accounting analysis suggests important roles for both foreign direct investment (FDI) and productivity in explaining differences in growth performance. There is little evidence that domestic investment contributes to the faster initial growth of SGs because average investment rates during the first five-year period are very similar to non-SGs (Figure 2.5). Domestic investment declines beyond the five-year mark for non-SGs, but it is not clear whether this is a contributory factor to slow growth: most likely it is caused by the growth slowdown

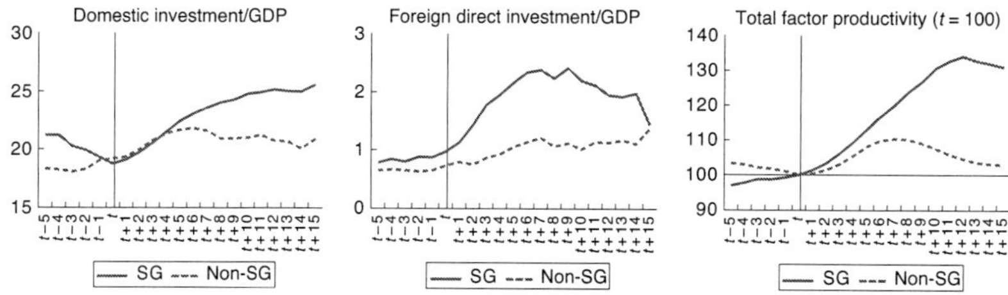

Figure 2.5 SGs versus Non-SGs: Investment and Productivity

Sources: IMF, World Economic Outlook database and *Regional Economic Outlook: Sub-Saharan Africa*; Johnson, Ostry, and Subramanian (2007); Bosworth and Collins (2010); Barro and Lee (2010); and authors' calculations.
Note: Five-year moving average. Non-SG = country with nonsustained growth; SG = country with sustained growth.

in these countries. The story is different for FDI, which rises much more sharply in SGs, paralleling the higher growth rates for this group. Similarly, total factor productivity rises faster for SGs and continues to grow beyond the five-year mark, in contrast to a slump in productivity for non-SGs.[7] These findings are consistent with other studies that find FDI is an important source for transferring technologies and enhancing productivity at firm levels, and is important for growth (Javorcik, 2004). The causalities are unclear, but it may be that sustained strong growth is closely linked to a successful and sustained upturn in productivity growth. And this may make SGs more attractive investment locations, reflected in higher FDI flows. We now turn to the factors thought to contribute to the favorable productivity trends associated with SGs.

Public Sector Finances and Institutions

On public sector finances, there are strong indications that large deficits are not helpful to growth. There is a striking and sustained difference between the size of fiscal deficits in SGs and those for non-SGs (Figure 2.6). This suggests that the macroeconomic instability that can arise from large deficits is a more important negative influence on growth than the possible benefits that larger deficits could offer in financing, say, higher public investments. There is little evidence in this sample that higher levels of official development assistance support productivity and growth. Overall, fiscal deficits appear to be a major risk factor for sustaining growth.

The quality of public institutions does not seem to help sustain growth upturns. Survey results on government stability are slightly higher in the first five years of the growth upswing for SGs, but the difference is not large. Moreover, government stability continues to improve in non-SGs through year 10, even as

---

[7]Total factor productivity for countries is estimated using a growth accounting methodology developed by Bosworth and Collins (2010) as follows:

$$\Delta\ln(Y/L) = 0.35[\Delta\ln(K/L)]) + (1 - 0.35)\Delta\ln H + \Delta\ln A,\ K_t = K_{t-1}(1 - d) + I_t, \text{ and } H = (1 + r)^s,$$

where Y denotes real GDP, L work force, K capital stock, A total factor productivity, I gross fixed investment, and H educational attainment or human capital. The d is a depreciation rate of capital, which is assumed to be 5 percent, whereas r, a return to each schooling year s, is assumed to be 7 percent.

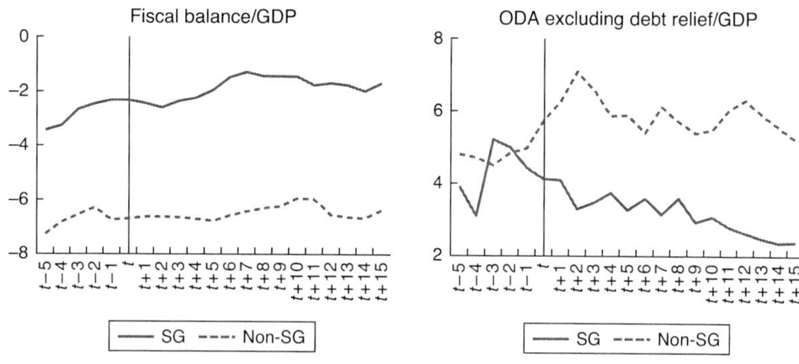

Figure 2.6 SGs versus Non-SGs: Public Sector Finance

Sources: IMF, World Economic Outlook database; Organization for Economic Cooperation and Development, OECD.Stat; and authors' calculations.
Note: Five-year moving average. Non-SG = country with nonsustained growth; SG = country with sustained growth; ODA = official development assistance.

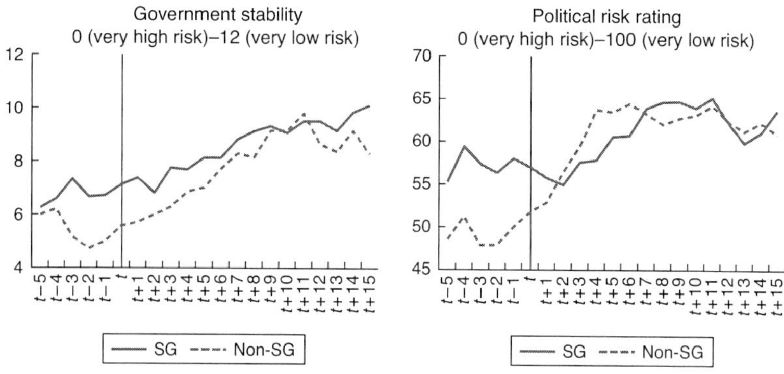

Figure 2.7 SGs versus Non-SGs: Quality of Institutions

Sources: International Country Risk Guide; and authors' calculations.
Note: Non-SG = country with nonsustained growth; SG = country with sustained growth.

growth weakens (Figure 2.7). And survey data on political risk is very similar across both types of countries. Overall, there is little here to suggest that the quality of public institutions makes a large difference in whether countries can sustain their growth accelerations.

Inflation Discipline

Inflation appears to be inversely related to growth performance. For the SGs, inflation averages about 11 percent in the decade after growth acceleration, compared with 18 percent for non-SGs (Figure 2.8). This may be linked to the higher fiscal deficits for non-SGs. Inflation, then, is another possible risk factor.

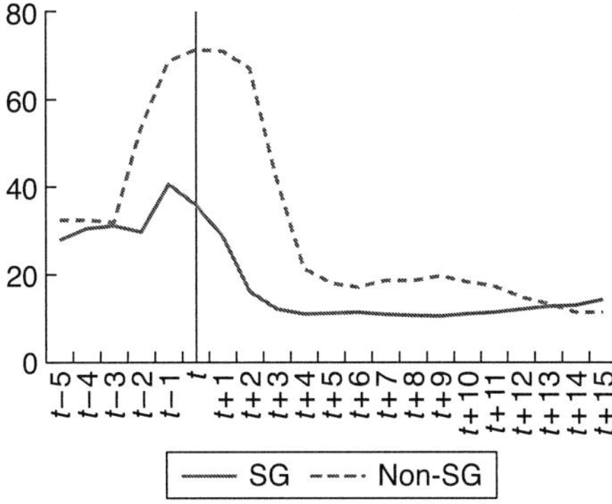

Figure 2.8 SGs versus Non-SGs: Consumer Price Index Inflation

Sources: IMF, World Economic Outlook database; and authors' calculations.
Note: Five-year moving average. Non-SG = country with nonsustained growth; SG = country with sustained growth.

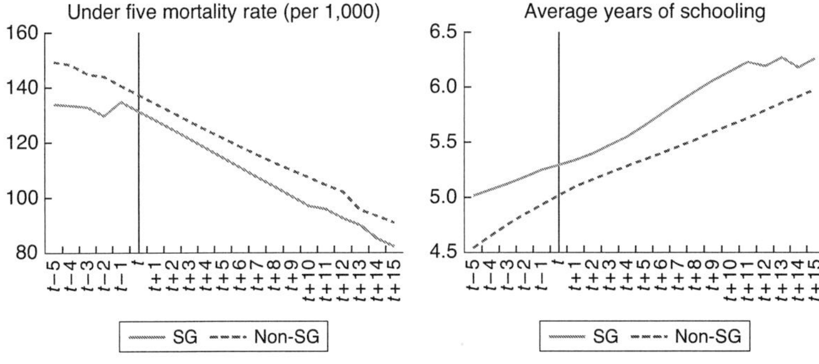

Figure 2.9 SGs versus Non-SGs: Human Capital

Sources: World Bank, World Development Indicators database; Barro and Lee (2010); and authors' calculations.
Note: non-SG = country with nonsustained growth; SG = country with sustained growth. Observations are linearly interpolated because source data are available only in increments of every five years. For average years of schooling, only observations whose *t* are after 1980 are included.

Health and Education

There is little evidence that superior health and education outcomes sustain growth upturns. Health and education indicators change only slowly over time, and there is little evidence that they either trigger growth upturns or make a difference on how long they last. Based on the country sample in this study, childhood mortality is lower and school attendance higher for SGs (Figure 2.9). Both samples show steady improvements largely unrelated to short-term growth performance, and the difference between SGs and non-SGs is broadly stable. Although investments in better health and education are important, especially in the long term, they appear to be unrelated to the chances of sustaining faster growth in the 5- to 10-year range.

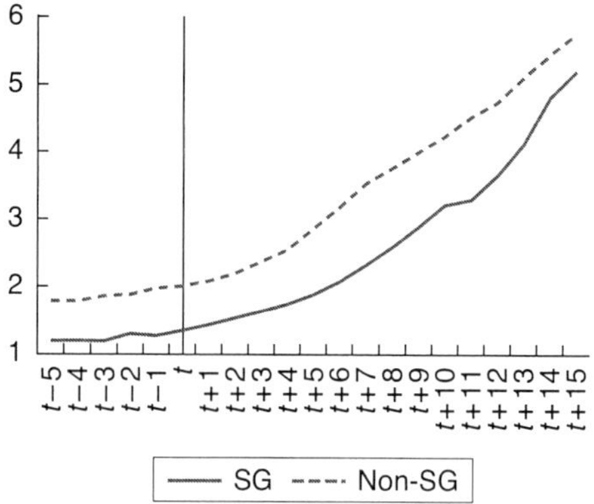

Figure 2.10 SGs versus Non-SGs: Infrastructure—Telephone Lines (per 100 people)

Sources: World Bank, World Development Indicators database; Barro and Lee (2010); and authors' calculations.
Note: non-SG = country with nonsustained growth; SG = country with sustained growth. Observations are linearly interpolated because source data are available only in increments of every five years.

Infrastructure

This chapter has only limited data on the quality of public infrastructure. Evidence of the density of telephone landlines suggests that infrastructure is, on average, worse for SGs, albeit improving (Figure 2.10). Although evidence for this assessment, it is difficult to make a case that the quality of infrastructure does not play a role in triggering and sustaining strong growth.

Financial Sector Depth

There is some evidence that the financial sector can make a difference to sustained growth. Domestic savings tend to be much higher, as a share of GDP, in SGs, though this may not entirely reflect financial sector performance (Figure 2.11). Smaller fiscal deficits also tend to increase domestic savings. Private sector credit tends to be higher in SGs, with credit picking up strongly in outer years in those countries that sustained high growth. SGs also typically made an earlier start in financial liberalization, although after five years, the head start in reforms relative to non-SGs is significantly narrowed. In sum, deep and efficient financial systems, providing access to finance, may play a role in triggering and supporting sustained strong growth.

External Competitiveness

External competitiveness appears to be critical to sustained strong growth. One of the largest differences between SGs and non-SGs is in terms of the more favorable real exchange rates of the former during growth upswings.[8] In the first

[8]Although the link between real exchange rates and growth is tenuous, Rodrik (1999) finds that undervalued real exchange rates stimulate economic growth.

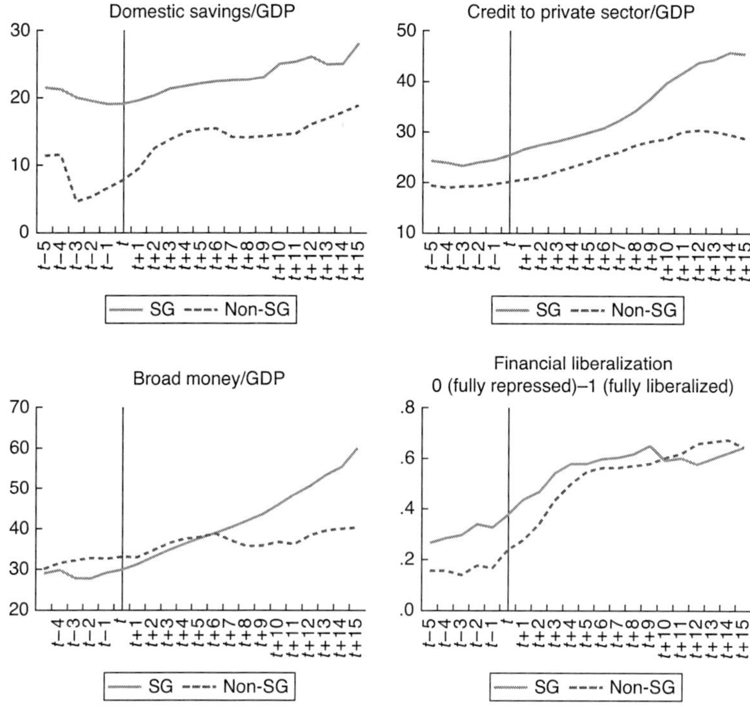

Figure 2.11 SGs versus Non-SGs: Financial Development

Sources: IMF, World Economic Outlook database; World Bank, World Development Indicators database; Abiad, Detragiache, and Tressel (2008); International Country Risk Guide; and authors' calculations.
Note: non-SG = country with nonsustained growth; SG = country with sustained growth. All the series besides financial liberalization are represented by five-year moving average.

five years, the real exchange rate depreciated by about 30 percent in SGs, compared with a slight appreciation for the non-SGs (Figure 2.12). For SGs, real exchange rates continued to depreciate during most of the period of sustained growth. More competitive currencies are associated with smaller current account deficits in SGs, and with higher export-to-GDP ratios. While competitiveness appears important, it likely reflects other contributory factors, rather than being a direct policy instrument for growth promotion. For instance, large fiscal deficits, higher inflation, and low domestic savings tend to appreciate real exchange rates and foster larger current account deficits.

Based on the previous review, a number of factors appear to be associated with differences in growth outcomes. The next section examines these in the context of EAC countries. In particular, we look at how these countries compare to sustained growth "benchmarks" for each variable, and whether this benchmarking exercise reveals important risk factors for sustaining strong growth in Rwanda, Tanzania, and Uganda. We also examine what the exercise shows for the prospects for initiating sustained strong growth in Kenya and, importantly, Burundi.

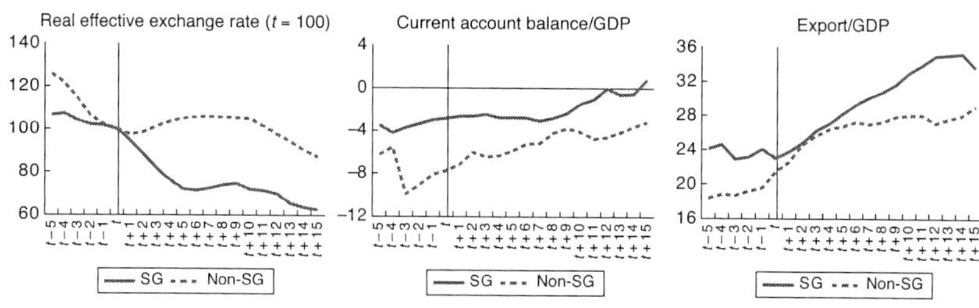

Figure 2.12 SGs versus Non-SGs: External Competitiveness

Sources: IMF, World Economic Outlook database; and authors' calculations.
Note: Five-year moving average. Non-SG = country with nonsustained growth; SG = country with sustained growth.

BENCHMARKING EAST AFRICAN COMMUNITY GROWTH AGAINST HIGH-GROWTH COUNTRIES

The growth performance of Rwanda, Tanzania, and Uganda in the initial phase of growth take-off is comparable to those experienced by SGs, whereas Burundi and Kenya are largely falling behind (Figure 2.13).[9] Rwanda, Tanzania, and Uganda achieved strong growth during the first five years of the take-off. Burundi and Kenya have been trending upward since 2000, but have not yet reached the growth experienced by SGs and Rwanda, Tanzania, and Uganda in their early take-off periods.[10] Despite a strong performance in the three countries, sustaining growth has been more difficult for them. Only Tanzania has sustained high growth beyond the critical five-year mark, when growth rates started to trend down in non-SGs. Growth rates in Uganda were sharply lower in the second five-year period, before rising in later years. In Rwanda, growth rates have been more erratic, but are recently trending downward, partly driven by the global financial crisis.

To identify areas that can help policymakers in Rwanda, Tanzania, and Uganda turn their growth take-offs into sustained growth—and help accelerate growth in Kenya and especially Burundi—the following section looks at factors that have contributed to the EAC's experience so far and benchmarks them against the group of SGs.

Investment and Productivity

Similar to the SGs, productivity gains have played an important role in explaining the recent growth performance in the EAC. For Rwanda, Tanzania, and Uganda, improvements in productivity have been rapid since the start of their growth episodes (Figure 2.14).[11] Productivity gains in Tanzania and Uganda outpaced

[9] In the rest of the chapter Rwanda, Tanzania, and Uganda are frequently referred to as a group.

[10] In the following benchmarking exercise, for illustration, we assume that time t is 2000 for Burundi and Kenya.

[11] Since the mid-1990s, sub-Saharan Africa has rebounded from low or negative total factor productivity growth and a corresponding decline in the contribution of factors of production to growth (IMF, 2008; Radelet, 2010).

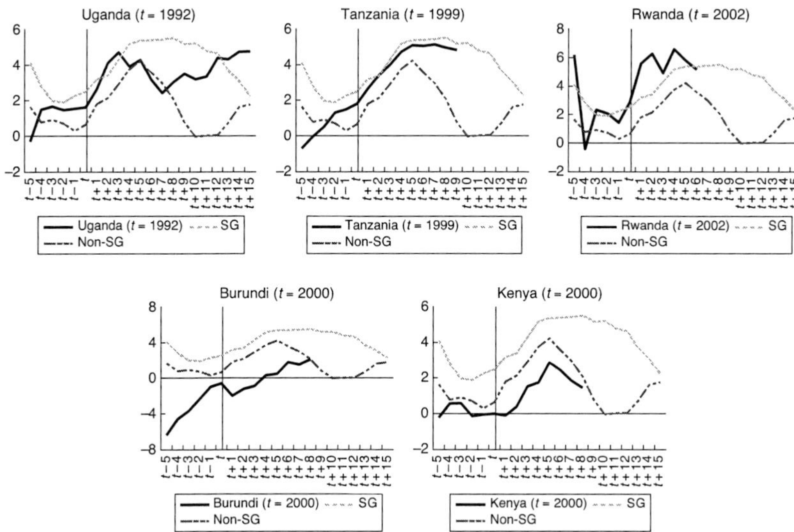

Figure 2.13 Real GDP per Capita (Growth rate, five-year moving average)

Sources: IMF, World Economic Outlook database; and authors' calculations.
Note: Non-SG = country with nonsustained growth; SG = country with sustained growth.

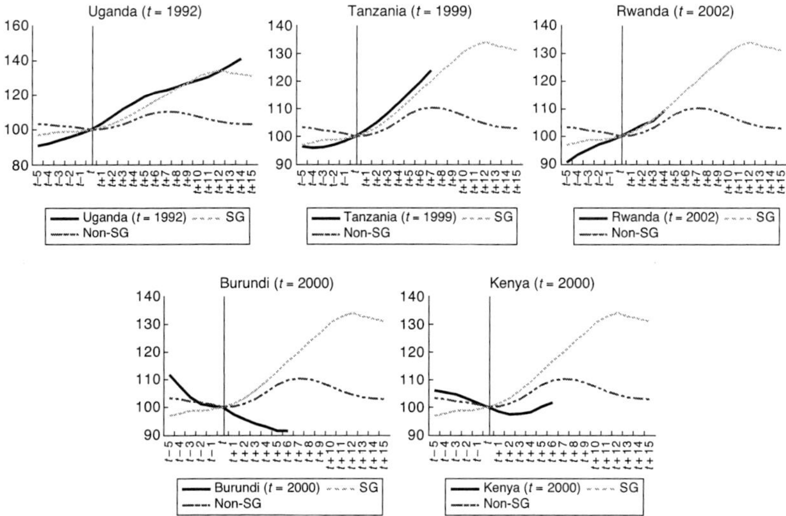

Figure 2.14 Total Factor Productivity (*t* = 100, five-year moving average)

Sources: Barro and Lee (2010); Bosworth and Collins (2010); IMF, *Regional Economic Outlook: Sub-Saharan Africa*; Johnson, Ostry, and Subramanian (2007); and authors' calculations.
Note: SG = sustained growth, Non-SG = non-sustained growth.

SGs during the take-off period, and Rwanda's productivity has closely tracked the SG's experience. In contrast, productivity has declined in Burundi and Kenya—where growth has stagnated—although there has been a turnaround in Kenya in recent years.

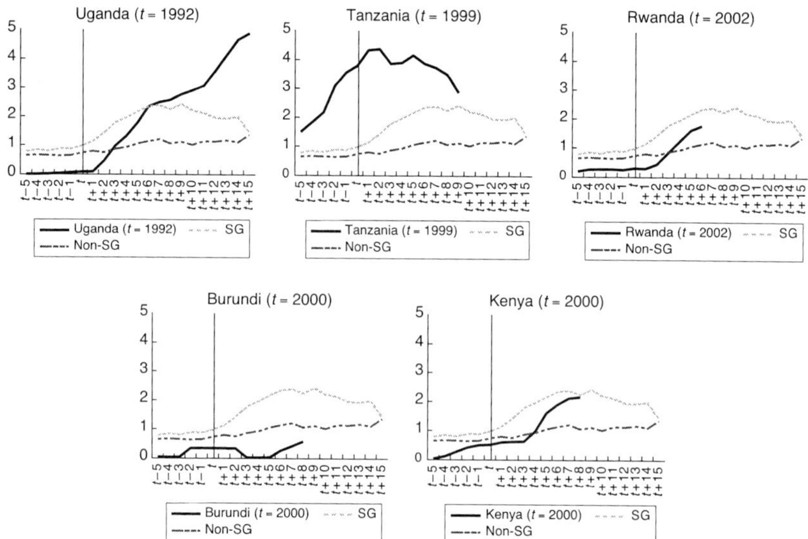

Figure 2.15 Ratio of Foreign Direct Investment to GDP (Five-year moving average)

Sources: IMF, World Economic Outlook database; and authors' calculations.
Note: Non-SG = country with nonsustained growth; SG = country with sustained growth.

FDI also surged in Rwanda, Tanzania, and Uganda during their growth take-off, similar to SGs. FDI rose strongly in Uganda for about 15 years after the start of its growth take-off, in contrast to SGs where FDI declined over time because they eventually relied more on domestic investment to sustain growth rates (Figure 2.15). Tanzania had sizeable FDI at the start of its growth episode—significantly higher than SGs and Rwanda, Tanzania, and Uganda at the start of their growth episodes. But Tanzania's has since been trending down, approaching levels in SGs. FDI increased sharply in Rwanda during the growth take-off and is trending toward SGs. After stagnating, FDI has recently picked up in Kenya, while FDI has remained low in Burundi.

Improved Macroeconomic Stability

Similar to SGs, sound macroeconomic management, especially in public finances, has coincided with stronger growth. For Rwanda, Tanzania, and Uganda, the period since their growth upturns has generally coincided with declining fiscal deficits (Figure 2.16). These declined in Uganda and Rwanda during the growth take-off, with Rwanda outperforming SGs and Uganda trending toward SGs. On the other hand, Tanzania has seen a steady deterioration in its budget deficit since its growth upturn, in sharp contrast to SGs. Budget deficits have also been growing in Kenya, while Burundi significantly improved its budget balance, thanks to substantial donor support. Inflation has generally been lower in the EAC compared with SGs during the initial growth take-off years. For Rwanda, Tanzania,

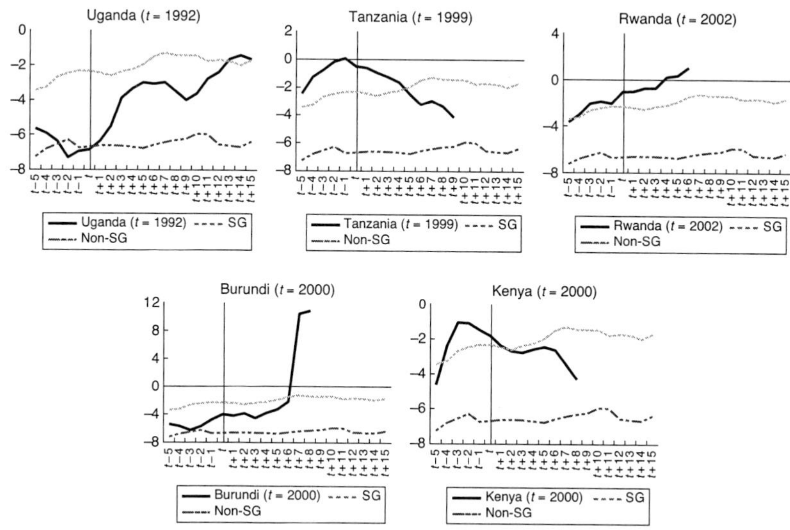

Figure 2.16 Ratio of Fiscal Balance to GDP (t = 100, five-year moving average)

Sources: IMF, World Economic Outlook database; and authors' calculations.
Note: Non-SG = country with nonsustained growth; SG = country with sustained growth.

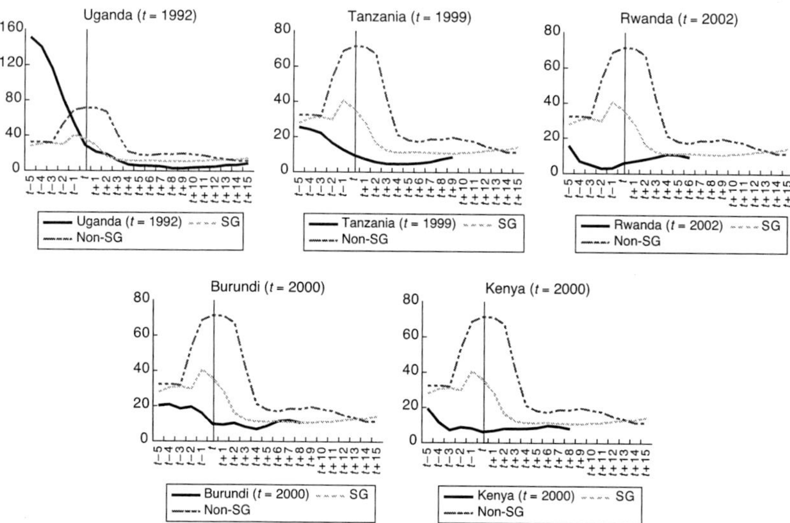

Figure 2.17 Consumer Price Index Inflation (Five-year moving average)

Sources: IMF, World Economic Outlook database; and authors' calculations.
Note: Non-SG = country with nonsustained growth; SG = country with sustained growth.

and Uganda, in particular, tighter fiscal and monetary policies led to significantly lower inflation—9.5 percent year-over-year on average during the seven years since the growth turnaround, down from 45 percent before the turnaround (Figure 2.17).

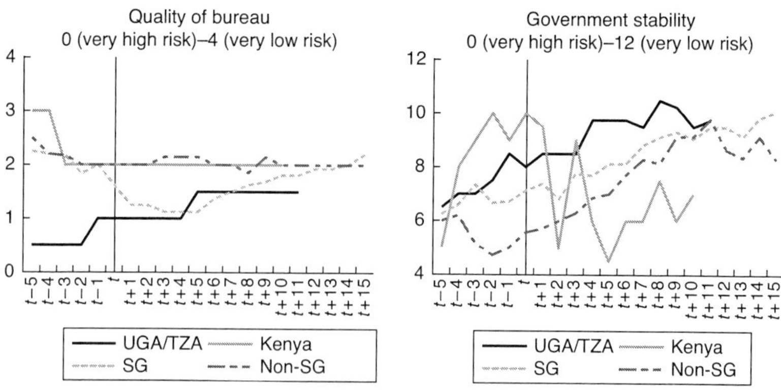

Figure 2.18 Quality of Institutions

Sources: International Country Risk Guide; and authors' calculations.
Note: Non-SG = country with nonsustained growth; SG = country with sustained growth; UGA/TZA = average of Uganda and Tanzania. For Kenya, *t* is set to be 2000. Rwanda and Burundi are not covered by the source data.

Quality of Institutions and Infrastructure

Contrary to the findings for SGs and non-SGs, the quality of public institutions matters for growth performance in the EAC. Since the mid to late 1990s, all EAC countries—albeit at different times—have introduced extensive liberalization and structural reforms. Rwanda, Tanzania, and Uganda, in particular, appear to have benefited from improved government stability (Figure 2.18). In contrast, in Kenya, less stable government conditions—at least during this period—may have contributed to lower productivity and lower growth, given the extent of the country's structural reforms and high capacity of labor and institutions.

Inadequate infrastructure is a constraint to accelerating and sustaining growth in the EAC, as in the rest of sub-Saharan Africa. Using the proxy of telephone lines for infrastructure, all EAC countries are at very low levels (Figure 2.19). Other anecdotal evidence also points to infrastructure constraints in the EAC. Electricity supply in the EAC lags far behind other sub-Saharan African countries (Ranganathan and Foster, 2011), and close to 60 percent of EAC businesses identified inadequate or poor electricity supply as one of the top problems for doing business in the EAC (World Economic Forum, 2010). Better provision of transportation and energy services is now high on the agenda of all EAC countries, and a number of projects have been initiated in these areas, including at the regional level. However, technical and financing difficulties have limited progress.

EAC countries have made continuous progress in improving human capital, but remain well below SGs, with the exception of Kenya. Health conditions in Rwanda, Tanzania, and Uganda have improved rapidly—catching up with SGs—and the pace at which school years are lengthening is similar to those of the comparators (Figures 2.20 and 2.21).[12] Kenya has consistently outperformed

[12] It should be noted that the data do not adjust for the quality of education.

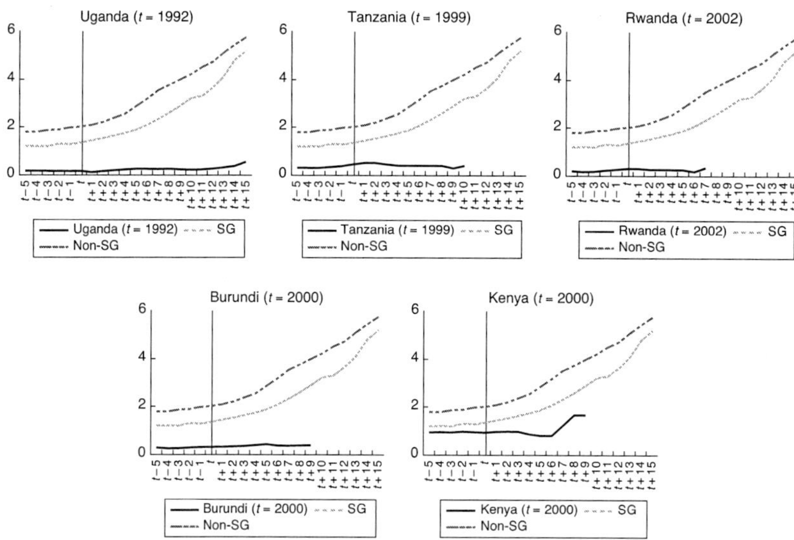

Figure 2.19 Telephone Lines (per 100 people)

Sources: World Bank, World Development Indicators database; and authors' calculations.

Note: Observations are linearly interpolated because source data are available only in increments of every five years. Non-SG = country with nonsustained growth; SG = country with sustained growth.

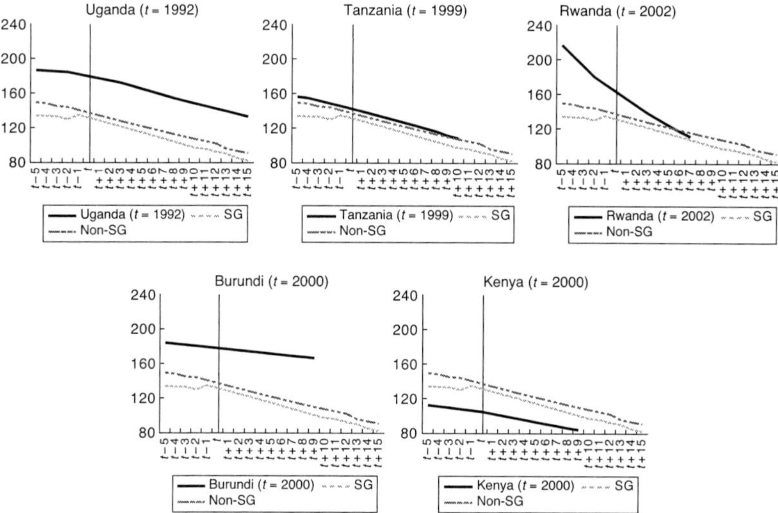

Figure 2.20 Under-Five Mortality Rate (per 1,000)

Sources: World Bank, World Development Indicators database; and authors' calculations.

Note: Observations are linearly interpolated because source data are available only in increments of every five years. Non-SG = country with nonsustained growth; SG = country with sustained growth.

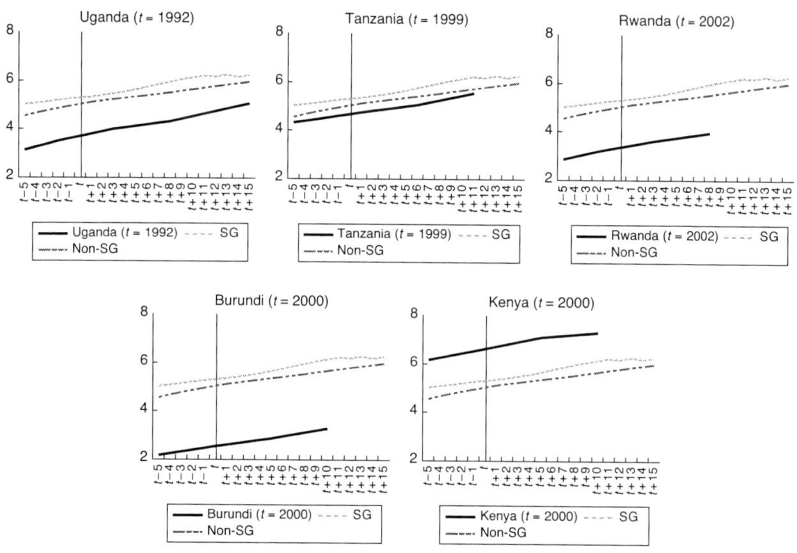

Figure 2.21 Average Years of Schooling

Sources: Barro and Lee (2010); and authors' calculations.
Note: Observations are linearly interpolated because source data are available only in increments of every five years. For SG and Non-SG, only observations whose *t* are after 1980 are included. Non-SG = country with nonsustained growth; SG = country with sustained growth.

SGs, both for health conditions and education, giving the country a comparative advantage in human capital. On the other hand, Burundi lags behind the other EAC countries in health and education, which has likely contributed to the country's steady decline in productivity and lower growth.[13]

The EAC falls short of SGs in two important areas for sustained growth: domestic financial depth generally associated with high domestic savings and external competitiveness.

Limited Financial Depth and Low Domestic Savings

For the EAC, financial deepening is occurring very slowly and remains well below SGs. Credit to the private sector as a percent of GDP is one-fourth the levels in SGs. Kenya—which has the most developed financial markets in the region—had a higher level of credit to the private sector around the year 2000 compared with SGs at the start of their growth episode. But the level has since declined (Figure 2.22). This development coincides with the deterioration of the fiscal balance, indicating the possibility of crowding out by the public sector. Burundi, where commercial banks play a dominant role in the economy, experienced rapid credit growth since the end of the civil war in 2005, although it has slowed in recent years.

[13] Isaksson (2007) and others have tried to identify channels to enhance total factor productivity, including education, health, openness, competitiveness, institutions, infrastructure, and financial development.

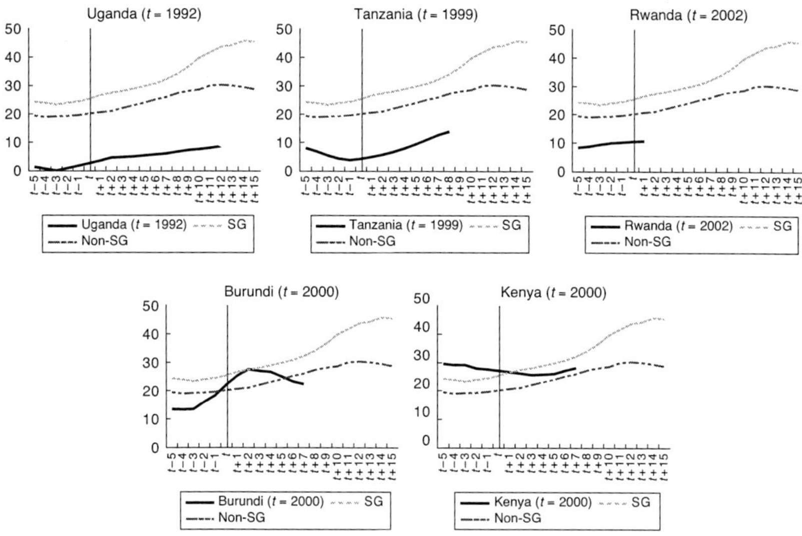

Figure 2.22 Ratio of Credit to Private Sector to GDP (Five-year moving average)

Sources: World Bank, World Development Indicators database; and authors' calculations.
Note: Non-SG = country with nonsustained growth; SG = country with sustained growth.

Unlike SGs, EAC growth has been financed in part by external savings. While domestic savings picked up rapidly in SGs after their take-off, quickly narrowing the gap between savings and investment, the growth in savings has been weaker in the EAC (Figure 2.23). EAC countries have relied on external resources—mainly donor aid—to finance the bulk of investment. Official development assistance (excluding debt relief) has averaged more than 15 percent of GDP since the growth take-off in Rwanda, Tanzania, and Uganda, well above the average for SGs (Figure 2.24). The data from SGs and non-SGs, however, provide little evidence that donor aid supports higher productivity and growth.[14]

Financial sector liberalization has been quicker in the EAC compared with SGs (Figure 2.25). Structural reforms since the mid-1990s rendered the banking sector more market based, with more competition and privatization. Capital account restrictions have also been reduced. However, since financial sector liberalization alone did not distinguish SGs from non-SGs, a greater focus on maintaining macroeconomic stability—especially avoiding large fiscal deficits that tend to crowd out resources available for private sector credit—may be more important to enhancing financial deepening in the EAC.

Notwithstanding the extensive liberalization, the region's financial markets remain small, segmented, and illiquid. A recent study by FinScope (2009) shows that less than a third of the population in Rwanda, Tanzania, and Uganda has

[14] A recent study on the impact of scaling up aid to meet the Gleneagles commitments, however, suggests that aid can have a substantial positive influence on growth as long as projects financed by aid are well designed and implemented.

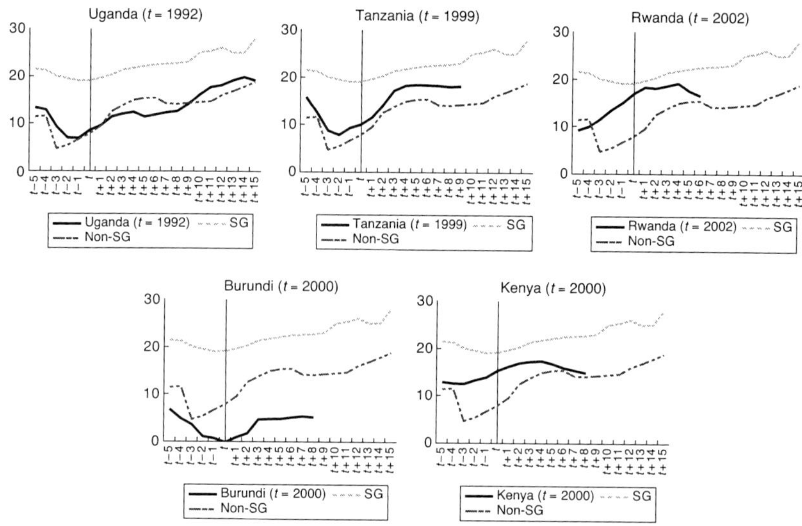

Figure 2.23 Ratio of Domestic Savings to GDP (Five-year moving average)

Sources: IMF, World Economic Outlook database; and authors' calculations.
Note: Non-SG = country with nonsustained growth; SG = country with sustained growth.

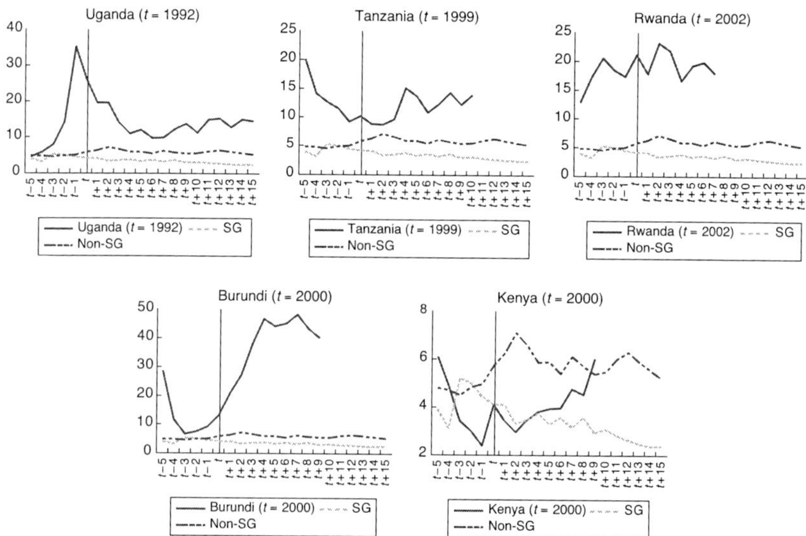

Figure 2.24 Ratio of Official Development Assistance, Excluding Debt Relief, to GDP (Five-year moving average)

Sources: IMF, World Economic Outlook database; Organization for Economic Cooperation and Development, OECD.Stat; and authors' calculations.
Note: Non-SG = country with nonsustained growth; SG = country with sustained growth.

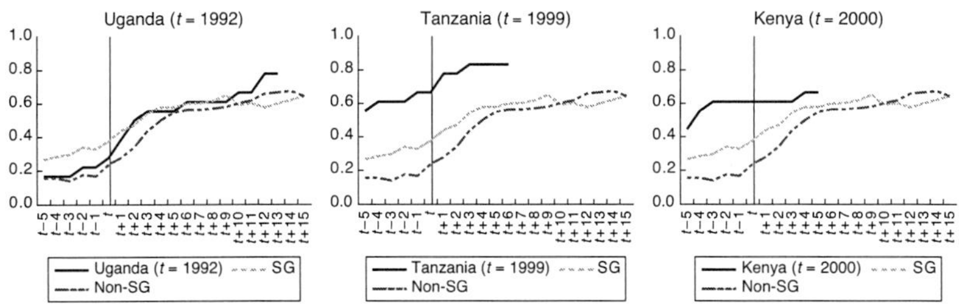

Figure 2.25 Financial Liberalization: 0 (fully repressed)–1 (fully liberalized)

Sources: Abiad, Detragiache, and Tressel (2008); and authors' calculations.
Note: Non-SG = country with nonsustained growth; SG = country with sustained growth.

access to formal financial services, compared with nearly two-thirds in other developed financial markets, such as South Africa. Nonbank financial institutions, such as pension funds or insurance companies, are in most cases only embryonic. Recently, however, greater efforts are being made to increase financial inclusion by opening more bank branches, promoting microfinance institutions and saving and credit cooperatives, and locating these institutions where the poor and the disadvantaged live and work. To sustain these efforts, financial literacy campaigns are being stepped up in a number of EAC countries. These efforts are further complemented with building a sound regulatory framework for nonbank financial institutions and increasing supervisory capacity. Other innovations, such as mobile banking—including the innovative M-Pesa mobile banking platform in Kenya—have emerged as a promising vehicle to broaden access to financial services and savings instruments (Kimenyi and Ndungu, 2009; Jack and Suri, 2010).

Domestic financing costs also hamper financial market deepening in the EAC. Uncertain property rights (in part related to weaknesses in land titling) hamper the assessment and enforcement of collateral, credit information on borrowers is patchy, and the legal and regulatory framework insufficient to facilitate the swift resolution of commercial disputes. All these factors continue to pose risks to credit delivery and increase financial costs. Although private sector credit growth has increased, it has largely focused on consumer financing, particularly mortgages. Access to finance for budding small- and medium-size enterprises has been limited to the largely unregulated informal financial sector. With the exception of Kenya, domestic capital markets are shallow and stock exchanges are well below the size required to support the economies' financing needs. Continued efforts are needed to tackle these deeply rooted obstacles to financial deepening. Here again, regionally coordinated approaches can bring larger and faster benefits. Recent examples of regional approaches to financing that attracted regional and international investors are encouraging developments. These include Kenyan authorities' partial financing of their infrastructure investment through a series of local currency infrastructure bonds with long maturities, and several initial public offerings and cross-listings in the region.

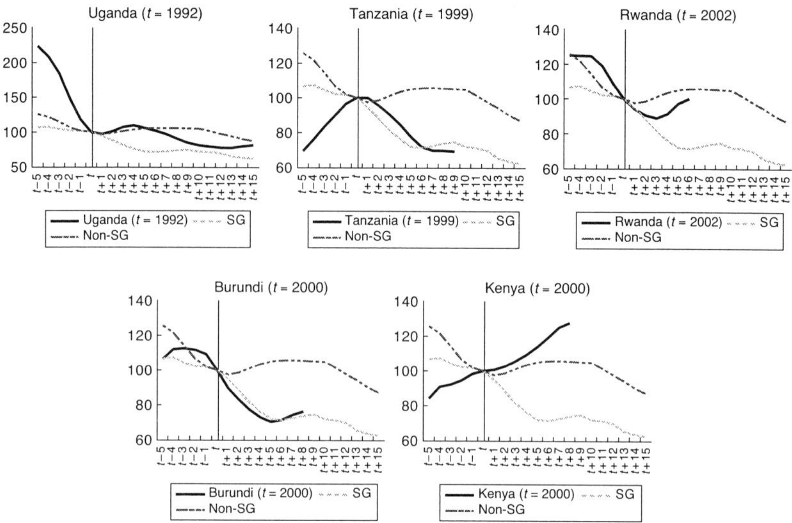

Figure 2.26 Real Effective Exchange Rate ($t = 100$, five-year moving average)

Sources: IMF, World Economic Outlook database; and authors' calculations.
Note: Non-SG = country with nonsustained growth; SG = country with sustained growth.

External Competitiveness

Unlike SGs, real exchange rate behavior in the EAC has not necessarily translated into external competitiveness. When real exchange rates depreciated in Burundi and Tanzania, similar to SGs, there was a corresponding deterioration in current account deficits (Figures 2.26 and 2.27). In Rwanda and Kenya, current account deficits also deteriorated in the face of real exchange rate appreciation. Only Uganda, where the real exchange rate remained broadly unchanged, has seen a slight improvement in its current account. Structural factors including diversification and regulatory costs of doing business better explain the external competitiveness of EAC countries, as discussed below.

Unlike the export-led growth of SGs, exports have played a relatively small—albeit growing—role in the growth take-off of EAC countries. While the SGs rapidly increased the share of exports in their GDP to 30–40 percent soon after their take-offs, the increase has been more protracted and subdued in the EAC (Figure 2.28). The share of exports in GDP remains at less than 15 percent of GDP in Burundi, Rwanda, and Uganda some seven to eight years into their growth episodes. Kenya and Tanzania have export shares of about 25 percent of GDP, inching up to SGs.

Underlying more subdued export growth in the EAC, regulatory bottlenecks hamper the region's competitiveness. Although a common market is in place, nontariff barriers are still high in the region and common standards and harmonized regulations have yet to be agreed upon. While EAC members have

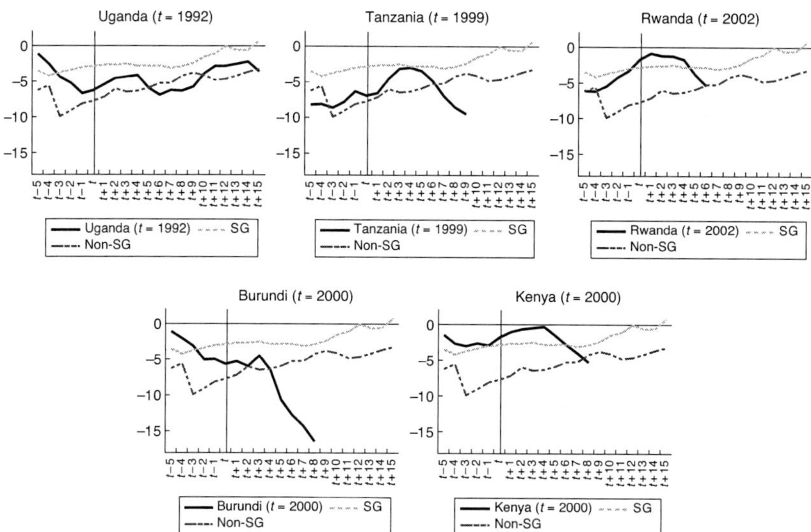

Figure 2.27 Ratio of Current Account Balance to GDP (Five-year moving average)

Sources: IMF, World Economic Outlook database; and authors' calculations.
Note: Non-SG = country with nonsustained growth; SG = country with sustained growth.

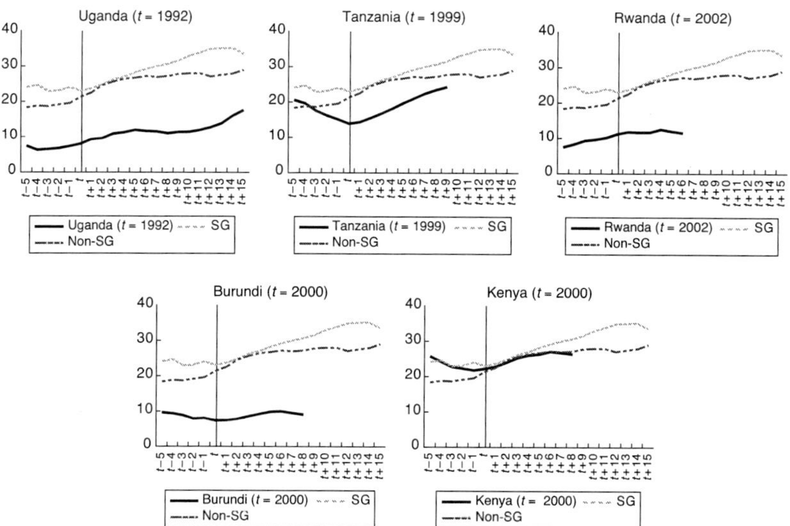

Figure 2.28 Ratio of Exports to GDP (Five-year moving average)

Sources: IMF, World Economic Outlook database; and authors' calculations.
Note: Non-SG = country with nonsustained growth; SG = country with sustained growth.

embraced market-supportive policies at the broader level and often put in place legal frameworks amicable to investors, business surveys show that enforcement is problematic (World Economic Forum, 2010). Investment incentives are uncoordinated and often enterprise-specific. Such obstacles not only constrain investment and export levels, but also hamper private investment in infrastructure, further increasing costs. In addition, they deter innovation and, thus, output and export diversification. Although most EAC country authorities have plans to improve the investment climate, progress to date has been uneven across the region, with only Rwanda implementing ambitious and comprehensive reforms. In addition, reform efforts have not been closely coordinated at the regional level, thereby reducing their impact. Removing these remaining obstacles could facilitate faster export growth for the region.

Opportunities exist to expand exports, particularly in mining and oil, but these sectors need to be cautiously developed for these gains to be translated into sustained growth. In Tanzania, gold exports already account for more than a third of total exports of goods and services, while in Uganda oil production is expected to account for close to 10 percent of GDP and up to one-third of government revenues. Considerable exploration findings in nickel, uranium, and oil and natural gas across the region are believed to have significant potential. Export expansion in this area can quickly lift output and government revenues, but harnessing such activities into longer-term growth raises the significant policy challenge of avoiding the "natural resource trap."[15] Early, determined policy action is needed to preserve competitiveness and ensure that revenue from commodity exports is successfully intermediated into productive spending and investment in other sectors of the economy.

CONCLUSIONS AND POLICY PRIORITIES FOR SUSTAINED GROWTH

Prudent macroeconomic policies, productivity gains, financial sector depth, and a competitive external sector are important to sustaining growth. Comparing the growth performance of countries that have achieved sustained growth against those that accelerated but failed to achieve this, we find that SGs tend to maintain (1) low inflationary environments and low fiscal deficits; (2) steady improvements in productivity encouraging higher investment, especially FDI; (3) high domestic savings and private sector credit underpinned by liberalized financial markets; and (4) competitive external sectors fostering export growth with better current account balances. These findings concur with various growth determinants found in recent literature.

[15]Collier (2007) and others. Commodity exporters have fallen into a detrimental long-term growth because of the adverse impact of commodity exports on productivity, the real exchange rate, and institutional development and governance.

Within the EAC, Rwanda, Tanzania, and Uganda have grown at rates comparable to SGs and share many of the key characteristics of sustaining growth. Similar to SGs, the growth upturn in Rwanda, Tanzania, and Uganda has coincided with a period of low inflation and low budget deficits, while improved business environments and government stability have contributed to strong productivity gains and increasing FDI, in some cases exceeding SGs.

A number of challenges remain for Rwanda, Tanzania, and Uganda to stay on the path of SGs. Unlike SGs, external savings, mainly donor grants, has primarily financed growth in these countries. Domestic savings and financial deepening in Rwanda, Tanzania, and Uganda are much lower compared with the SGs. Similarly, the contribution of exports to growth has been fairly limited in the three countries, with widening current account deficits, compared with the SGs. This is attributable to weak competiveness, including the high costs of doing business in the region. Physical and human capital are also lagging in EAC countries, which could impede further productivity gains, especially over the longer term.

Elsewhere in the EAC, Burundi and Kenya have only recently started to grow after many years of stagnant growth or contractions. Burundi has suffered from unstable macroeconomic performance and poor quality of institutions and physical and human capital. Although levels of investment, savings, and exports are all lower in Burundi compared with Rwanda, Tanzania, and Uganda, the benchmarking exercise suggests that the more fundamental constraint for Burundi is poor quality of institutions, infrastructure, and human capital. Doing business in Burundi is seen to be the most difficult in the region, its child mortality rate remains stubbornly high, and the level of education is by far the lowest in the EAC.

Macroeconomic and government instability may be dampening growth in Kenya. Real GDP growth rates have been trending upward since 2000 in Kenya, but not high enough to be considered accelerated. Kenya, unlike the other EAC countries, has a deep financial sector and a large export sector, even compared with SGs. Kenya's health conditions and education perform better than SGs. Nevertheless, productivity of Kenya has been declining until recently. This may reflect rising fiscal deficits and inflation since 2000 and a less stable government at least in recent years.

The EAC is at a critical juncture at which policy decisions will determine whether they follow the path of SGs—thereby accelerating the move to middle-income status—or non-SGs. With the growth rates of Rwanda, Tanzania, and Uganda generally closely tracking those in SGs, it is now critical for them to ensure that accelerated growth is translated into sustained growth—and for Burundi and Kenya to boost their current growth momentum into full-fledged growth acceleration. For this, the following policy recommendations will be important, albeit with different priorities for each EAC country:

- Maintain macroeconomic stability, namely low inflation and low budget deficits.
- Deepen financial sectors to mobilize domestic savings.

- Develop stable institutions and a conducive business climate.
- Improve competiveness and diversify exports.
- Overcome the bottlenecks of infrastructure and human capital.

Maintaining macroeconomic stability—low inflation and fiscal deficits—is important for all EAC countries. Fiscal deficits in the EAC have risen in recent years in line with planned fiscal stimulus policies amid the global recession. Recent increases in fiscal deficits may have been important to sustain growth over the short term, but they could be an impediment for sustaining growth over the longer term if they are not appropriately unwound. Also, inflation rose sharply in 2011, reflecting rising global food and fuel prices as well as drought-induced food shortages in the region. This will have to be carefully managed to avoid second-round effects that could have more lasting effects on longer-term inflation. Maintaining macroeconomic stability also requires that natural resource export proceeds are managed carefully to avoid real exchange rate appreciation.

Intensified efforts are needed to deepen regional integration and help the EAC to cooperatively achieve its key policy priorities. The mechanism of regional surveillance backed up by appropriate convergence criteria could be used to mutually ensure prudent macroeconomic management by the members. Financial integration would allow the pooling and mobilization of scarce domestic savings and efficient allocation of such savings. Well-designed regional infrastructure projects could help overcome bottlenecks of physical infrastructure and encourage efficient use of invested resources. Free movement of goods, services, and capital would enhance competition across the region, thereby boosting productivity and output growth.

In the external sector, raising the EAC's export potential requires continued focus on improving productivity across the region. In particular, a better educated and skilled labor force as well as a better business environment and improved infrastructure—including regional transportation, energy, and information technologies—will reduce production costs and facilitate higher-value exports. Stepped-up efforts to increase agricultural productivity, for example, could both raise the EAC's export potential and lift incomes in areas where the poorest segments of populations are concentrated. In the near term, the region could broaden its export markets to neighboring Democratic Republic of Congo and South Sudan, especially food crops and light manufactured goods, while efforts are put in place to penetrate broader international markets over the longer term. This would require investments in upgrading rural road networks and simplification of customs and border procedures.

Expanding exports may also demand, at least in the initial years, targeted catalytic interventions in natural niche sectors in which EAC countries could build up or strengthen their comparative advantage, overcome latecomer handicaps, and establish a market presence. Coordinated interventions should cover complementary areas (skills, transportation, technology, market access). These interventions should be carefully targeted, both sectorally and geographically.

Resources are insufficient to enhance skills, roads, and power in the entire region at the same time. An equal distribution of these limited resources will not give any area sufficient traction to become competitive. Regional coordination—with a common focus, for example, on a few trade corridors—could help mobilize financing and increase returns. To prevent "state capture," export push policies should be time bound with clear exit strategies. More broadly, the fiscal cost of regional coordination should be strictly constrained, given the many other demands faced by governments, particularly in the social area.

The private sector should be closely involved in the design of such interventions, helping identify concrete needs and efficient delivery modes. Targeted areas should be selected transparently, with a focus on their impact on the sustainability of both exports and productivity. Given its potential for expanding exports and reducing poverty, agriculture would likely offer the greatest payoff from targeted support.

REFERENCES

Abiad, A., E. Detragiache, and T. Tressel, 2008, "A New Database of Financial Reforms," IMF Working Paper 08/266 (Washington: International Monetary Fund).

Barro, R. J., 2003, "Determinants of Economic Growth in a Panel of Countries," *Annals of Economics and Finance*, Vol. 4, No. 2, pp. 231–274.

Barro, R., and J. W. Lee, 2010, "A New Data Set of Educational Attainment in the World, 1950–2010," NBER Working Paper No. 15902 (Cambridge, Massachusetts: National Bureau of Economic Research).

Barro, R. J., and X. Sala-i-Martin, 2004, *Economic Growth,* 2nd ed. (New York: McGraw Hill).

Berg, A., J. D. Ostry, and J. Zettelmeyer, 2012, "What Makes Growth Sustained?" *Journal of Development Economics*, Vol. 98, No. 2, pp. 149–166.

Bosworth, B. P., and S. M. Collins, 2010, "The Empirics of Growth: An Update," *Brookings Papers on Economic Activity* (Washington: Brookings Institution).

Collier, P., 2007, *The Bottom Billion: Why the Poorest Countries Are Failing and What Can Be Done About It* (New York: Oxford University Press).

Commission on Growth and Development, 2008, "The Growth Report: Strategies for Sustained Growth and Inclusive Development" (Washington: World Bank).

FinScope, 2009, "Demand, Access and Use of Financial Services in Rwanda, Tanzania, and Uganda." Available via the Internet: http://www.finscope.co.za/finscope/pages/Initiatives/Countries/Tanzania.aspx?randomID=9c464c57-2ff9-4d50-8086-0a7f496075a3&linkPath=3_1&lID=3_1_13.

Hausmann, R., L. Pritchett, and D. Rodrik, 2004, "Growth Accelerations," NBER Working Paper No. 10566 (Cambridge, Massachusetts: National Bureau of Economic Research).

International Monetary Fund, 2008, *Regional Economic Outlook: Sub-Saharan Africa* (Washington: International Monetary Fund).

Isaksson, A., 2007, "Determinants of Total Factor Productivity: A Literature Review," Research and Statistics Staff Working Paper 2/2007 (Vienna: United National Industrial Development Organization).

Jack, W., and T. Suri, 2011, "Mobile Money: The Economics of MPESA," NBER Working Paper No. 16721 (Cambridge, Massachusetts: National Bureau of Economic Research).

Javorcik, B. S., 2004, "Does Foreign Direct Investment Increase the Productivity of Domestic Firms? In Search of Spillovers through Backward Linkages," *American Economic Review*, Vol. 94, No. 3, pp. 605–627.

Johnson, S., J. D. Ostry, and A. Subramanian, 2007, "The Prospects for Sustained Growth in Africa: Benchmarking the Constraints," IMF Working Paper 07/52 (Washington: International Monetary Fund).

Kimenyi, M. S., and N. S. Ndungu, 2009, "M-PESA Mobile Banking Statistics, Central Bank of Kenya" (Washington: Brookings Institution).

McAuliffe, C., S. C. Saxena, and M. Yabara, 2012, "The East African Community: Prospects for Sustained Growth," IMF Working Paper 12/272 (Washington: International Monetary Fund).

Radelet, S., 2010, "Emerging Africa: How 17 Countries Are Leading the Way" (Washington: Centre for Global Development).

Ranganathan, R., and V. Foster, 2011, "East Africa's Infrastructure: A Continental Perspective," Policy Research Working Paper 5844 (Washington: World Bank).

Rodrik, D., 1999, "Where Did All the Growth Go? External Shocks, Social Conflict, and Growth Collapses," *Journal of Economic Growth*, Vol. 4, No. 4, pp. 385–412.

World Economic Forum, 2010, *The Global Competitiveness Report 2010–2011* (Geneva: World Economic Forum).

Xu, G., 2011, "Growth Accelerations Revisited," *Econ Journal Watch*, Vol. 8, No. 1, pp. 39–56.

CHAPTER 3

Economic Convergence to Support the East African Monetary Union

NABIL BEN LTAIFA, MASAFUMI YABARA, AND ORAL WILLIAMS

Since 2000, the East African Community (EAC) has had a customs union and common market, and is now implementing a comprehensive regional infrastructure program to support the development of a single market for free trade among partner countries. To deepen integration, the EAC has set the goal of establishing an East African Monetary Union (EAMU) through macroeconomic convergence and the harmonization of monetary and exchange rate policies, payment and settlement systems, financial sector supervision, as well as harmonized statistics.

To benefit from a monetary union, convergence is needed to facilitate closer economic integration through trade, investment, and factor mobility. Convergence is also critical to foster strong economic performance to support the eventual adoption of a single currency. To support a shift to fixed bilateral exchange rates and a common monetary policy, the preparatory stages for monetary union typically involve steps to ensure a convergence of inflation rates and progressively greater bilateral exchange rate stability. Compliance with the convergence criteria would help establish a track record of maintaining sound macroeconomic policies for EAC member countries in a "nominal convergence." This chapter briefly surveys convergence criteria in other monetary unions and reviews the degree of compliance by EAC member countries with nominal convergence criteria. While "real convergence" is not an explicit objective for monetary union, this chapter examines the degree of comparability in real per capita income.

PROMOTING NOMINAL CONVERGENCE

As in the Maastricht Treaty criteria establishing the European Union, the EAC criteria focus on nominal rather than real convergence. The EAC Council in 2007 revised and adopted the original macroeconomic convergence criteria (Box 3.1), but revised again in 2013 to encompass criteria outlined in Box 3.2. The original convergence criteria were set for three different stages spanning consecutive periods: 2007–10 (Stage I), 2011–14 (Stage II), and 2015 (Stage III).

BOX 3.1 East African Community: Original Macroeconomic Convergence Criteria

Stage I (2007–10)

Primary Criteria

1. Overall budget deficit excluding grants of not more than 6 percent of GDP, and including grants of not more than 3 percent of GDP.
2. Annual average inflation not exceeding 5 percent.
3. External reserves of more than 4 months of imports of goods and nonfactor services.

Secondary Criteria

4. Achievement and maintenance of stable real exchange rates.
5. Achievement and maintenance of market-based interest rates.
6. Achievement of sustainable real GDP growth of not less than 7 percent.
7. Sustained pursuit of debt reduction initiative on domestic and foreign debt (i.e., reduction of total debt as a ratio of GDP to a sustainable level).
8. National savings of not less than 20 percent of GDP.
9. Reduction of current account deficit excluding grants as a percentage of GDP to a level consistent with debt sustainability.
10. Implement the 25 Core Principles of Bank Supervision and Regulation based on the agreed Action Plan for Harmonization of Bank Supervision.
11. Adherence to the Core Principles for Systematically Important Payment Systems by modernizing payment and settlement systems.

Stage II (2011–14)

Primary Criteria

- Reduced ceilings on overall budget deficit excluding grants (no more than 5 percent of GDP), and including grants (no more than 2 percent of GDP).
- Target for annual average inflation as in Stage I.
- External reserves target increased to 6 months of imports of goods and nonfactor services.

Secondary Criteria

- Maintenance of market-based interest rates, real GDP growth target, pursuit of debt sustainability, domestic savings target, and sustainable current account deficit (as in Stage I).

Stage III (2015)

- Introduction and circulation of a single East African Currency.

Source: EAC (2009).

BOX 3.2 Macroeconomic Convergence Criteria Under the East African Community Monetary Protocol

The agreed criteria to help pave the way for a common currency and to ensure consistency of policies under monetary union consist of four primary convergence criteria, complemented by three nonbinding, indicative convergence criteria to serve as early warning indicators.

Primary Convergence Criteria

1. Ceiling on headline inflation of 8 percent.
2. Fiscal deficit (including grants) ceiling of 3 percent of GDP.
3. Ceiling on gross public debt of 50 percent of GDP in net present value terms.
4. Reserve cover of 4.5 months of imports.

Indicative Criteria

1. Core inflation ceiling of 5 percent.
2. Fiscal deficit (excluding grants) ceiling 6 percent of GDP.
3. Tax-to-GDP ratio of 25 percent.

Source: EAC Monetary Union Protocol, Kampala, Uganda, November 30, 2013.

The macroeconomic convergence criteria represent only one pillar of a sustainable monetary union. Although important, they are not sufficient (Figure 3.1). A country may perform well by the standards of convergence criteria, but still be implementing policies that pose risks to monetary union. Two more pillars are needed to support the framework of sustainable monetary union. One supports a periodic comprehensive review of macroeconomic conditions and policies. For the EAC, country performances would be assessed according to individual circumstances. The other needed pillar for monetary union in the EAC supports a set of region-wide policies to ensure that national policies are corrected, in which the convergence criteria or broader surveillance activities identify risks to monetary union. In addition, highly harmonized statistics are needed to support the entire framework.

OTHER MONETARY UNIONS

The convergence criteria adopted by other prospective monetary unions share features with the EAC and euro area. Annex Table A3.1 summarizes the criteria adopted prior to monetary union by the Caribbean Monetary Union, the European Monetary Union (EMU) in its preaccession phase prior to the adoption of the euro, the Gulf Cooperation Council, and the West African Monetary Zone, as well as three existing monetary unions—the West African Economic and Monetary Union, the Central African Economic and Monetary Community, and the Eastern Caribbean Currency Union. Probably reflecting the influence of the EMU, all the preaccession criteria of these monetary unions, whether prospective

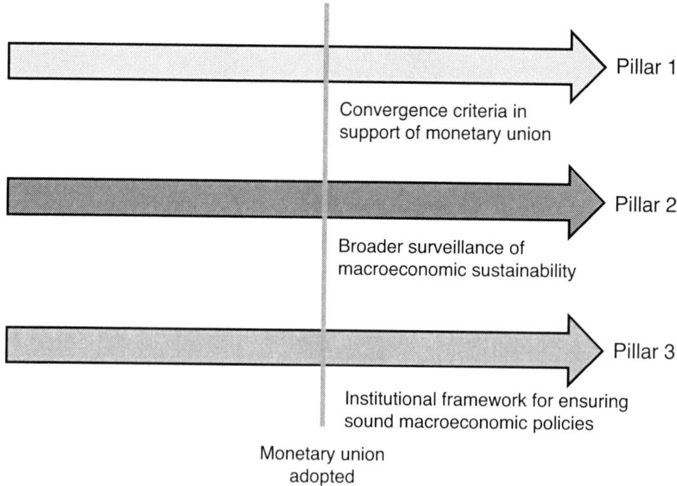

Figure 3.1 Elements of a Macroeconomic Convergence Framework

Source: Authors.

or existing, include limits on inflation and fiscal deficits. All except the West African Monetary Zone have limits on public debt, and four of seven regimes have criteria for interest rates. Convergence criteria on inflation and exchange rates also reflect the influence of the EMU, which strongly emphasized the importance of nominal convergence prior to the adoption of the euro.

The limits for these core nominal convergence criteria vary across regions:

- **Inflation** is subject to ceilings varying from 3 percent in the Communauté Financière Africaine (CFA), 8 percent in the EAC, and 10 percent in the West African Monetary Zone, or requirements not to exceed the zone inflation average by more than 1.5 percentage points (Caribbean Monetary Union and EMU) or 2 percentage points (Gulf Cooperation Council).
- The limit on the overall **fiscal deficits** ranges from 3 percent of GDP in the Caribbean Monetary Union, EAC, EMU, and Gulf Cooperation Council to 4 to 5 percent in the West African Monetary Zone, with the CFA adopting a limit on the basic budget balance.[1]
- **Public debt** is required to remain below 60 percent of GDP for the EMU and Eastern Caribbean Currency Union, and 70 percent of GDP for the CFA and Gulf Cooperation Council. For the Caribbean Monetary Union, limits are imposed only on external debt service obligations (15 percent of exports), while the EAC has established a limit of 50 percent of GDP in net present value terms.

[1] Tax and nontax revenues plus budget grants, minus current expenditures and domestically financed capital expenditures.

- **Interest rate** criteria vary from a requirement that rates not exceed the zone average by more than 2 percentage points (defined for the EMU in terms of long rates and the Gulf Cooperation Council as short rates), and that real interest rates be positive (the West African Monetary Zone).

The EAC differs in not explicitly constraining currency flexibility in the pre-accession period. Gulf Cooperation Council and Eastern Caribbean Currency Union members peg to the U.S. dollar, thereby enforcing bilateral currency stability. For the CFA franc zone, the equivalent peg is to the euro.[2] For the EMU and the West African Monetary Zone, an exchange rate mechanism is established prior to accession, with limits on deviations from the mechanism.[3] For the Caribbean Monetary Union, a similar regime restricts bilateral exchange rate movements to no more than 1.5 percent over a three-year period. By contrast, the EAC has agreed to allow the exchange rate to float prior to the adoption of a single currency. With divergent inflation across EAC countries in the pre-accession period, stable real exchange rates could be consistent with differing rates of nominal depreciation. Equally, to the extent that the trade weights used in calculating real exchange rates vary across the EAC, real exchange rate stability may be consistent with widely varying movements against a third currency, such as the euro or U.S. dollar.[4]

Despite some common features, regional convergence criteria also have unique elements. For the CFA franc zone and the West African Monetary Zone, fiscal targets are unusually detailed, with goals for revenues (17 percent of GDP in the West African Economic and Monetary Union, and non-oil fiscal revenue greater than or equal to 17 percent of non-oil GDP for Central African Economic and Monetary Community), domestically financed public investment (at least 20 percent of revenues for the West African Monetary Zone), and public sector wages (less than 35 percent of revenues for both the West African Monetary Zone and CFA). The West African Monetary Zone and CFA rules also prohibit the accumulation of domestic expenditure arrears.

All monetary unions set limits on central bank financing of fiscal deficits. Some have a zero limit on such financing, while the West African Monetary Zone

---

[2] For the CFA and Eastern Caribbean Currency Union, the choice of an external nominal anchor reflected a pattern of trade inherited from a colonial past. For the Gulf Cooperation Council, the choice of a U.S. dollar peg reflects the fact that trade is predominantly denominated in dollars.

[3] The exchange rate mechanism for EMU countries specified a grid of bilateral central exchange rates between the potential partners and a set of country-specific bands within which exchange rates were allowed to fluctuate. The central rates could be adjusted by mutual agreement, but for the two years leading to entry countries were not to devalue their central rates, and had to manage their economies so as to remain within a ±2.5 percent band of the parities (Adam and others, 2012).

[4] In a rather extreme case, if one EAC member traded entirely with U.S. dollar–based economies and another with euro-based economies, they could achieve stable real exchange rates by pegging to the U.S. dollar and euro, respectively. However, if they did so, bilateral exchange rates within the EAC would not converge, and would vary in line with U.S. dollar–euro movements.

requires that such financing not exceed 10 percent of the previous year's tax revenues. In the Central African Economic and Monetary Community, central bank financing is limited to 20 percent of the previous year's fiscal revenue, but this provision is expected to be phased out. In the EAC, central banks finance only temporary shortfalls in government revenue, governed by their respective national rules: (1) in Burundi up to a maximum of 12.5 percent of previous years' revenue, but to be phased out by 2016; (2) in Kenya, up to a maximum of 5 percent of the latest audited revenue; (3) in Rwanda, 11 percent of the previous year's revenue; (4) in Tanzania, 12.5 percent of the three-year average revenue collected; and (5) in Uganda, 18 percent of the previous year's revenue.

Outside the EMU, requirements for reserve cover are relatively common. More than 3 months of import cover are required for the Caribbean Monetary Union and the West African Monetary Zone, and 4.5 months cover by the EAC and Gulf Cooperation Council. Under the Eastern Caribbean Currency Union currency board regime, international reserves should be sufficient to cover at least 60 percent of currency in circulation, but in practice coverage is in excess of 90 percent.

EAST AFRICAN COMMUNITY COMPLIANCE WITH PRIMARY CONVERGENCE CRITERIA

The EAC convergence criteria are not precisely defined in statistical methodology or breadth of coverage. To ensure effective and even-handed monitoring of compliance, there is a need to harmonize data based on common statistical definitions. To underpin the collection of harmonized data, oversight over compilation of data for verification of the convergence criteria should be assigned to a qualified body. The EAC Secretariat currently lacks a well-resourced regional statistics department, and this might be one priority for institutional development to underpin the EAMU process.

Fiscal Deficit

The EAC has embraced the principle that member countries should demonstrate strong public debt and fiscal deficit positions ahead of monetary union. Large fiscal deficits could hamper the ability of new monetary authorities to deliver low inflation if deficits are monetized. Equally, a country with a high debt-to-GDP ratio has an incentive to press for high "surprise" inflation to erode the real value of their debt stock. Recognizing these risks, low-debt countries will seek a reduction in debt ratios for the most highly indebted countries prior to entry into a monetary union.

The EAC ceiling on country fiscal deficits is a core convergence criterion and is key to anchoring fiscal policy. The primary convergence criteria have established an overall deficit of 3 percent of GDP, including grants. Most monetary unions (Annex Table A3.1) feature a convergence criterion of this type. In principle, fiscal deficits and debt should be monitored on a common, broad basis to

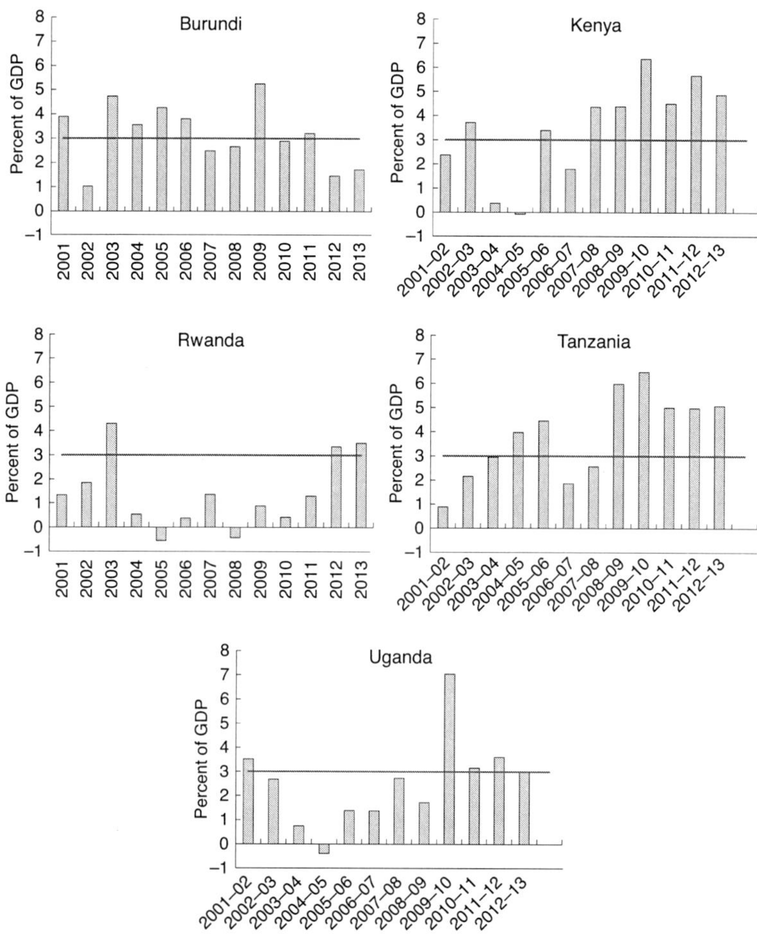

Figure 3.2 Primary Criterion: Overall Fiscal Deficit-to-GDP Ratio (Including grants) *(Not more than 3 percent)*

Source: IMF, African Department database.

best capture the full breadth of public activities that have a macroeconomic impact. EAC member-country compliance with the overall deficit including grants has been uneven for several reasons, including the need to scale up investments to address infrastructure gaps and responses to the global financial crisis.

On average, EAC countries met the fiscal deficit criterion including grants prior to the start of the crisis in 2008, but not subsequently when the fiscal performance of EAC countries was mixed (Figure 3.2). Rwanda and Uganda met the 3 percent deficit ceiling on balance for a few years compared with other member countries. Since 2009, however, fiscal deficits have increased across the region, partly in the context of the global financial crisis.

At the same time, the fiscal deficit measure excluding temporary incomes is an important gauge of fiscal sustainability. Where grant incomes are volatile, a surge in funding tends to strengthen the deficit measured including grants, even if underlying fiscal performance is deteriorating. This will only become evident when grant inflows return to more normal levels. For this reason, there are strong grounds for monitoring deficits excluding grants, even if they are at very different levels across EAC countries, reflecting underlying differences in grant inflows.

The ceiling for the deficit excluding grants still has a role in fiscal surveillance. Any ceiling on the deficit excluding grants has the potential to constrain the use of donor funding, which continues to play a significant role in the majority of EAC countries (Figure 3.3). Since the narrow deficit criterion including grants is the critical measure for purposes of gauging financing needs and debt sustainability, the criterion on the deficit excluding grants would still be useful for fiscal surveillance as it provides a measure of the degree of domestic revenue mobilization over time. This would align member countries, efforts to raise domestic revenues with donors' objectives of gradually unwinding grants over the medium to long term.

EAC countries were less successful in meeting the fiscal deficit criteria excluding grants (Figure 3.3). On average, these were substantially above the 6 percent of GDP ceiling, and by a steadily increasing margin. Only Kenya, which receives limited grant receipts,[5] met the deficit ceiling excluding grants on a sustained basis. Burundi's deficit excluding grants is more than 15 percent of GDP, reflecting massive aid inflows in recent years following substantial postconflict development needs.

Deficits measured excluding natural resource revenues also need be monitored carefully. The recent discovery of nonrenewable resources in several EAC countries will have implications for assessing the fiscal stance as these resources are exploited. Typically, natural resource incomes have a finite lifetime, based on the size of the oil or mineral deposits. In the Central African Economic and Monetary Community, for example, national inflation is closely linked to the size of non-oil fiscal deficits rather than the overall deficit. Exploiting these resources produces a period of high incomes associated with license fees, royalties, and other taxes. While this can support a temporary period of higher expenditure, countries often save part of their income stream to extend the period over which higher expenditures can be sustained, and to avoid the sort of sharp rise and subsequent reversal of spending that poses the strongest risk of Dutch disease. Natural resource revenues are also subject to volatility, linked to changes in global commodity prices. Periods of high prices can strengthen fiscal performance, even when there is an underlying deterioration in the nonresource accounts. Given these considerations, the deficit measured excluding resource incomes provides a more reliable guide to longer-term fiscal sustainability as well as to the short-term "fiscal impulse" in aggregate demand terms. That said, as

[5] Kenya received grants equivalent to 0.7 percent of GDP in 2010–11.

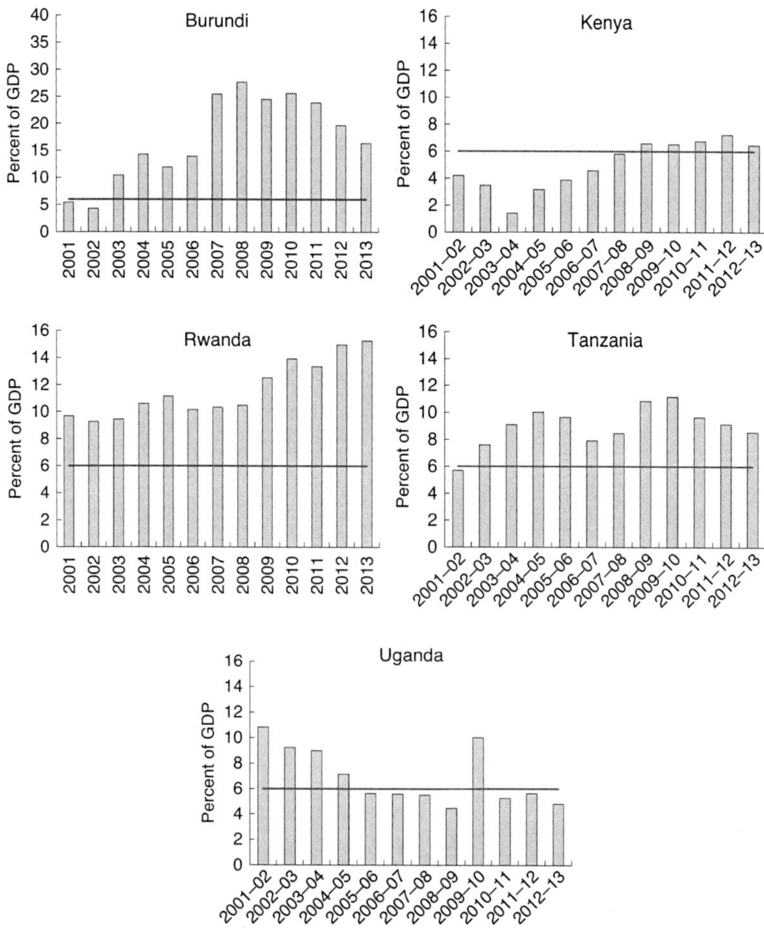

Figure 3.3 Secondary Criterion: Overall Fiscal Deficit-to-GDP Ratio (Excluding grants) *(Not more than 6 percent)*

Source: IMF, African Department database.

with donor grants, the appropriate deficit measured excluding resource incomes will vary across EAC countries depending on the projected lifetime value of incomes from the resource base.

Public Debt

A broad debt sustainability framework will help underpin the criterion on fiscal deficits. The EAC convergence criteria define a limit on public debt of 50 percent of GDP in net present value terms. Explicit gross public debt limits under the EMU, Eastern Caribbean Currency Union, CFA franc zones, and Gulf Cooperation Council are in the range of 60–70 percent of GDP. A more explicit

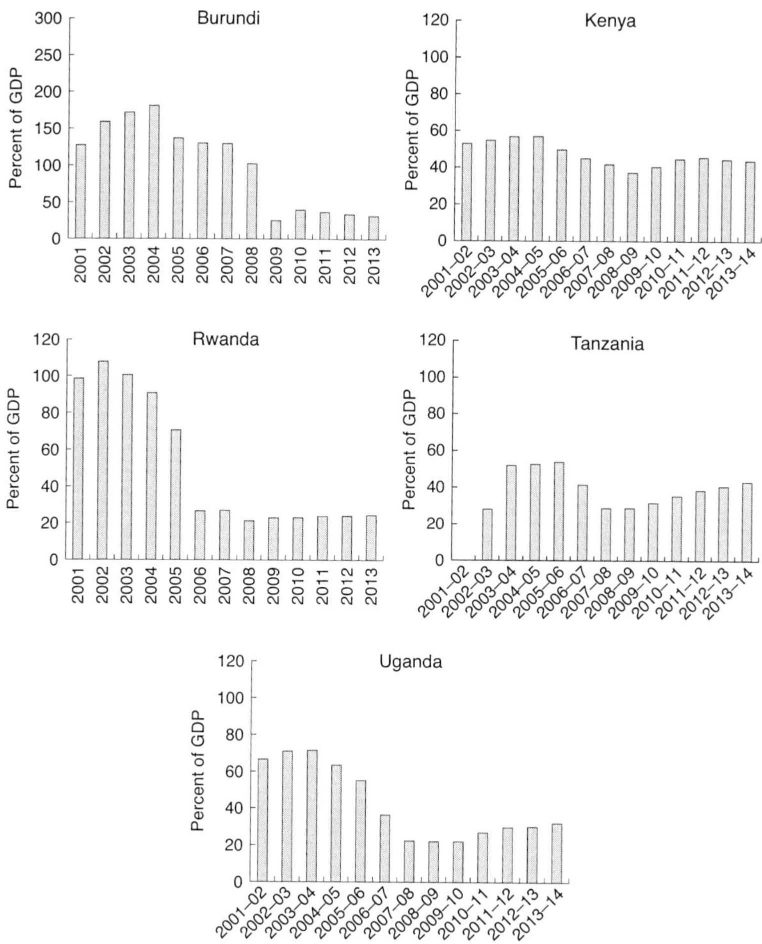

Figure 3.4 Gross Public Debt *(Percent of GDP)*

Source: IMF, African Department database.

debt framework rooted in debt sustainability analyses for the member countries would establish the EAC's capacity to accumulate debt given the cost of debt, growth prospects, and the existing debt levels.

In 2011, most EAC countries had debt-to-GDP ratios in the range of 23–50 percent of GDP, although the composition of this debt is highly concessional (Figure 3.4). A debt criterion of 50 percent of GDP in net present value terms would provide more fiscal space because of the current concessional nature of the debt, but this will change over time as some EAC countries scale up public investments through increased recourse to nonconcessional borrowings. During the 2000s, EAC countries benefited from a cumulative $4.2 billion in debt relief in net present value terms, which reduced the stock of debt considerably. The associated reduction in debt service costs permitted a corresponding increase in priority spending. The challenge will be to maintain debt on a sustainable path over the medium-term while permitting the scaling up of investments to address the EAC's infrastructure gap and other developmental needs. A prudent deficit and how it is financed is key to avoiding unsustainable debt levels that could have significant negative effects on economic activity. High debt requires high taxes to finance it and puts upward pressure on real interest rates, thereby "crowding out" private investment. Countries that have defaulted on their debt have, on average, a higher ratio of public debt to GDP, a higher debt-to-revenue ratio, a higher proportion of external debt in total public debt, and a lower ratio of broad money to GDP (IMF, 2003). Ideally, a broad definition of public sector debt would incorporate the borrowing activities of not only the central government but also local governments, the central bank, public enterprises, and other public agencies.

Inflation

Establishing the inflation convergence criterion is relatively demanding because the region is subject to large external shocks. As shown in Figure 3.5, EAC countries have missed the inflation criterion of 8 percent in recent years primarily because of large food and fuel shocks. In theory, the transition to monetary union could be managed at any inflation level, provided that cross-country differences in inflation are not large and sustained enough to distort internal competitiveness over time. In practice, however, it is difficult to stabilize national inflation at moderate or high, rather than low rates. Thus, aiming for the EAMU based on common inflation of close to 15 percent, for example, would not be practical. At the same time, however, the EAC has little experience of sustained low inflation in the 2–3 percent range achieved in many advanced economies. This is because food and fuel purchases represent a larger part of the consumer-price-index basket for EAC households than for advanced economies, so that shocks to global energy prices or imported food prices have a larger impact on headline inflation. Since these shocks are external to the EAC region and do not significantly impact on internal competitiveness, it is not clear that they should be an impediment to monetary union, provided that other convergence indicators are favorable.

By contrast, in some regional arrangements the inflation ceiling is defined in terms of regional trends. Thus, in several convergence frameworks (such as the Caribbean Monetary Union, Gulf Cooperation Council, EMU), inflation ceilings are not set in absolute terms, but rather in relation to the zone average, or relative to an average for the best-performing members. In the EMU, for example, inflation should not be more than 1.5 percentage points above the three best-performing EMU countries. To the extent that headline inflation rises for all EAC members during food or fuel price shocks, this would allow a region-wide increase in inflation while preventing exceptional increases for individual members. However, in practice, the weight of food and fuel products in the overall price index varies across EAC countries, and some countries see much larger headline inflation effects from a given food or fuel price shock. This would

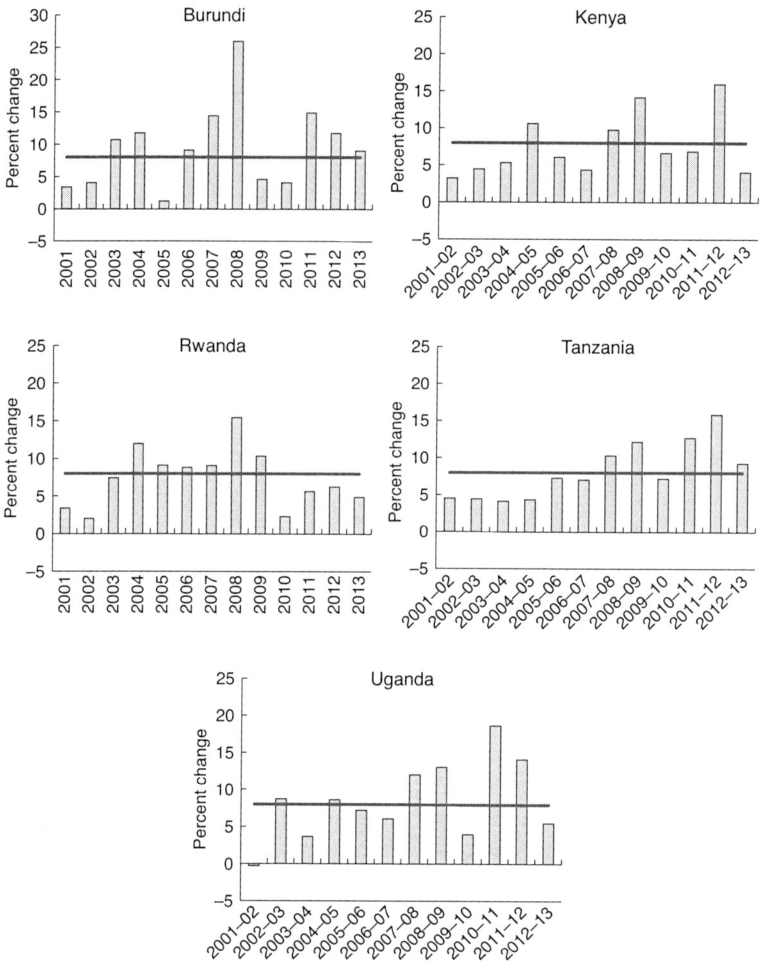

Figure 3.5 Primary Criterion: Annual Average Inflation Rate *(Not exceeding 8 percent)*

Source: IMF, African Department database.

require a relatively large margin to accommodate differential price movements, which would undermine the effectiveness of the convergence criterion in more normal inflationary environments.

Reserve Coverage

Strong international reserve cover provides the resources to support the currency in the event of balance of payments shocks. This could be in the context of an exchange rate mechanism ahead of monetary union, or for smoothing intervention in support of the new currency after accession. The EMU is unusual among current and prospective monetary unions in not setting a target for reserve cover

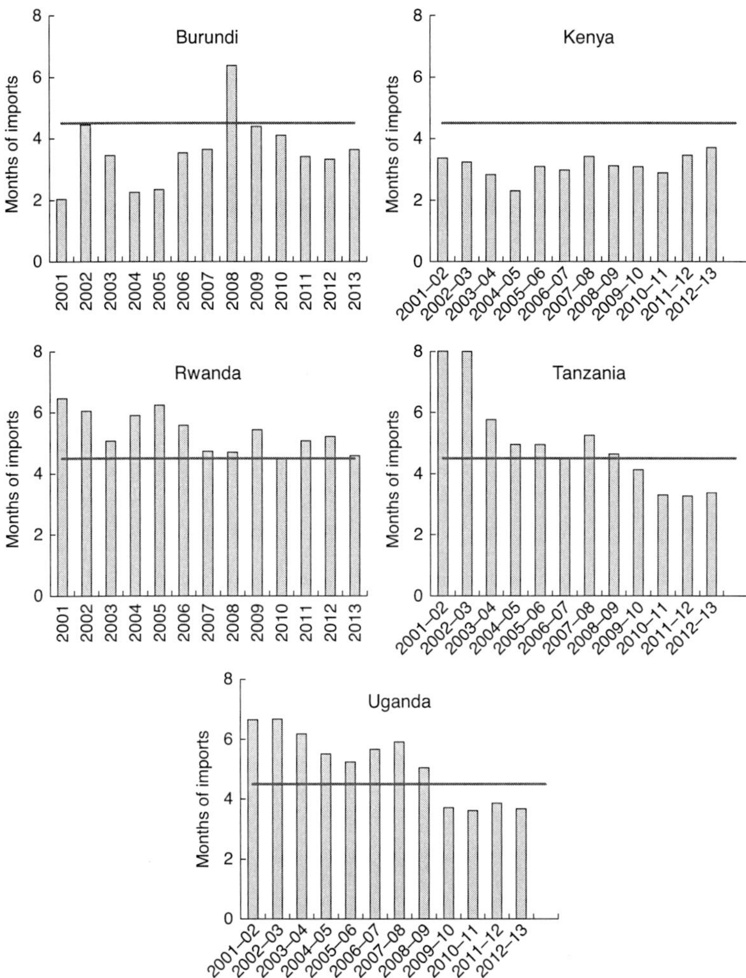

Figure 3.6 Primary Criterion: Foreign Exchange Reserves (*At least 4.5 month's imports of goods and nonfactor services*)

Source: IMF, African Department database.

(Annex Table A3.1). For the EMU, the ability to support national currencies during the preaccession period was gauged in terms of European rate mechanism compliance, while reserve cover after accession was less critical given the float of the euro against other currencies. For the smaller, more open African economies, the exchange rate is a more important determinant of inflation than for the euro area, and this tends to foster interest in a degree of currency stability. Given that the EAC will adopt a managed float regime for its new currency, this will require an adequate reserve base, and members acceding to the currency union will be expected to contribute to this reserve stock (Figure 3.6).

Achieving higher reserve targets may be quite demanding and difficult to justify given the role of exchange rates as a shock absorber. For example, if EAC countries were to target 6 months of imports as initially envisaged to achieve this, countries would need to tighten their balance of payments significantly (Box 3.1). This would require the adoption of restrictive domestic demand policies with repercussions for economic growth. For example, governments could increase spending by widening the deficit but not absorb the aid (i.e., no corresponding widening of the current account so that a portion of donor inflows is saved in international reserves rather than spent). This response would be problematic as the aid dollars stay in reserves, so the increase in government spending must be financed by government borrowing from the domestic private sector or by printing money. Alternatively, the central bank could purchase foreign currency from the banking system, while sterilizing the associated liquidity creation through bond sales. The latter would tend to raise interest rates and slow private sector credit growth. On the assumption that the future single currency would float with only light intervention, the criterion of 4.5 months of import cover broadly matches current EAC practices.[6]

A recent study on reserve adequacy in the EAC countries found that reserve levels toward end-2009 provided adequate safety buffers (Drummond and others, 2009). At that time, reserve coverage ranged from about 3.5 months of imports in Kenya to about 6 months in Burundi, with Rwanda, Tanzania, and Uganda in the range of 4 to 5 months of cover. While the authors noted that their findings were sensitive to model specification and assumptions, they concluded that the appropriate level of pooled reserves for the EAC region under a common currency would decline with the flexibility of the exchange regime to be adopted (i.e., the more flexible the exchange rate, the less reserves would be needed). The degree of integration between the countries would also likely decline, as higher integration makes the region less vulnerable to external shocks. These conclusions are consistent with recommendations in other studies, which also argue that reserves only provide a temporary and partial solution to vulnerabilities that stem from a lack of economic diversification and weak policy and institutional frameworks in low-income countries (Dabla-Norris, Kim, and Shirono, 2012).

PROMOTING REAL CONVERGENCE

For countries to benefit from a regional monetary union, optimal currency theory suggests that their economies should be highly integrated, with ideally somewhat similar economic structures. This could be referred to as real convergence. Since the member countries share a common monetary and exchange rate policy, they should be subject to the same sort of shocks, so that corrective monetary and

[6] In the context of IMF programs, 3–4 months of reserve cover of imports is usually considered as a minimum for a low-income country. A slightly higher target might be advisable to provide a buffer against a very volatile environment.

exchange rate adjustments are mutually beneficial. Where shocks are asymmetric, a high degree of structural flexibility, such as real-wage flexibility and mobility of labor, can help avoid lasting shifts in intraunion competitiveness.

Real convergence can be measured in several ways. The literature tends to focus on whether cross-country differences in per capita incomes and productivity are narrowing over time (see the "sigma" and "beta" convergence approaches in Barro and Sala-i-Martin, 1995).[7] Consideration is also given to whether differences in labor markets and economic structures are narrowing. Moves to more synchronous business cycles and closer trade integration are also two aspects of real convergence.

Progress toward real convergence is commonly treated as implicit by prospective monetary unions. The regional country groups considering currency union in Africa (Annex Table A3.1) are based, to some degree, on a view by members that they have achieved, or are achieving, sufficient real convergence to represent optimal currency areas. However, the degree of real convergence between members, and whether it is adequate to support monetary union, is rarely assessed explicitly.[8]

Some argue that real convergence is not critical ex ante, and that monetary union will foster real converge ex post. There is support in the economic literature for the idea that nominal convergence leads to real convergence. With the benefits of currency union (price stability, fiscal discipline, reduction of uncertainty, and so on), investment and trade will respond favorably, leading to stronger economic growth. The growth impact is expected to be larger for countries that were formerly more unstable and at lower levels of income relative to their peers, resulting in real convergence through catch-up growth. Real convergence can also benefit from structural reforms within a currency union. For example, the adoption of the euro was associated with an accelerated pace of deregulation and other structural reforms in product markets.

Real convergence within currency unions is not guaranteed, however. Although the poorest members of the euro area experienced rapid catch-up growth, a legacy of inflexible labor markets, excessive and inefficient state intervention, and restrictions on product market competition remained. This has cautionary implications for prospective currency unions that anticipate that issues of real convergence can be assumed away on the grounds that they will be resolved by the currency union process itself.

---

[7] Sigma (σ)-convergence occurs if the cross-sectional distribution of income per capita decreases over time. Beta (β)-convergence evaluates whether growth rates have a tendency to converge toward the baseline rate.

[8] Although real convergence was not a formal test for membership of the euro area, this was effectively the approach adopted by the United Kingdom in 2003 when it established "five economic tests" for its adoption of the euro. These were as follows: (1) Are economic structures and business cycles sufficiently compatible for the permanent adoption of the euro? (2) If problems emerge, is there sufficient flexibility to deal with them? (3) Would adopting the euro promote investment in the United Kingdom? (4) Would euro membership benefit the United Kingdom's financial services industry? and (5) Will the euro boost growth, stability, and employment creation in the United Kingdom?

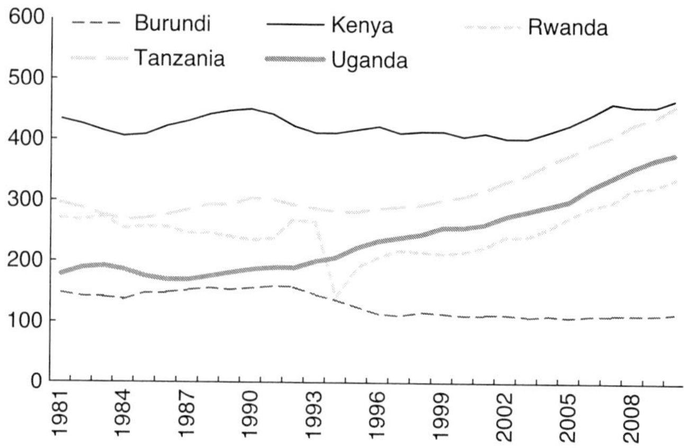

Figure 3.7 East African Community: GDP per Capita (Constant 2000 U.S. dollars)

Sources: World Bank, World Development Indicators; and authors' calculations.

East African Community Convergence in Income per Capita

There is evidence that the EAC has achieved a degree of real convergence in recent years. One proxy for this is provided by real income per capita. Although similar levels of income per capita are not strict criteria for an optimal currency area, similar income levels may help align countries' institutional capacities and policy priorities. From this perspective, Rwanda, Tanzania, and Uganda have closed their income gaps relative to Kenya through rapid per capita growth in the 1.5–2.5 percent annual range over the past 30 years (Figure 3.7). By contrast, the income gap between Kenya and Burundi has widened over the same period, reflecting average declines in Burundi's income per capita of about 0.5 percent per annum after years of conflict.

Empirical tests confirm progress in income convergence in the EAC. The standard deviation of real income per capita across countries (sigma) has significantly declined in the last 15 years, with the exception of Burundi (Figure 3.8). That said, the data show income divergence when Burundi is included. When Burundi is excluded, countries with lower income levels grew more in the period from 1996–2010 (Table 3.1).

Trade Integration

EAC countries have taken significant steps to promote trade integration. A customs union was established in 2005, followed by the launch of a common market in 2010. Internal tariffs on goods from other EAC countries were eliminated over a five-year period to end-2009. A common external tariff was established for imports from outside the region. These efforts resulted in a reduction of tariff

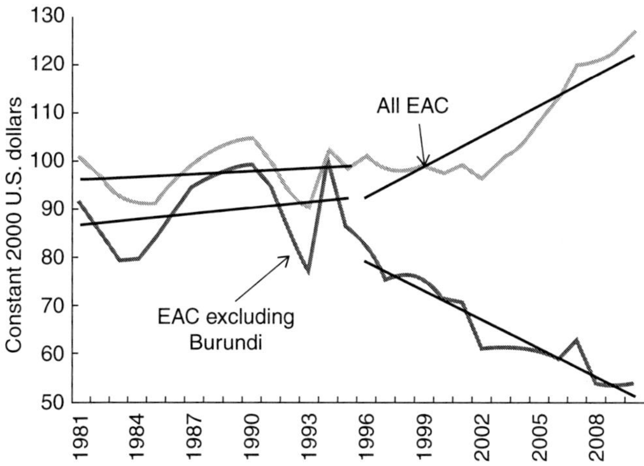

Figure 3.8 EAC Sigma Convergence of Income per Capita

Sources: World Bank, World Development Indicators; and authors' calculations.
Note: EAC = East African Community.

TABLE 3.1

Estimated Beta Convergence

All EAC			EAC excluding Burundi		
1981–2010	**1981–95**	**1996–2010**	**1981–2010**	**1981–95**	**1996–2010**
0.001	–0.030 **	0.018 ***	–0.028	–0.053	–0.029 **
[0.007]	[0.012]	[0.005]	[0.025]	[0.036]	[0.014]

Source: Authors' calculations.
Note: *** denotes significant at the 1 percent and ** at the 5 percent levels. EAC = East African Community.

rates in the EAC. While nontariff barriers are found to be remaining in wide-ranging fields, such as lengthy customs administrative procedures and lack of harmonized standards, member countries are committed to further reducing these barriers, including through time-bound programs for eliminating identified nontariff barriers (Okumu and Nyankori, 2010).

There is only limited progress to date toward greater trade integration among EAC countries. The U.S. dollar value of intra-EAC exports has broadly trebled from $0.6 billion in 2000 (the start of the customs union) to $2.3 billion in 2012 (Figure 3.9). At the same time, exports beyond the EAC have also risen quite rapidly, and the share of intra-EAC exports in total exports rose only modestly from 18 percent in 2005 to 20 percent in 2012. Moreover, intra-EAC trade represented a larger share of total exports in 2000, at a time when commodity export prices were lower, than they are today. With EAC countries continuing to develop new resource exports (oil in Uganda, gold and natural gas in Tanzania), it appears likely that intra-EAC trade will remain only a small fraction of total exports for the foreseeable future, especially if global commodity prices remain strong.

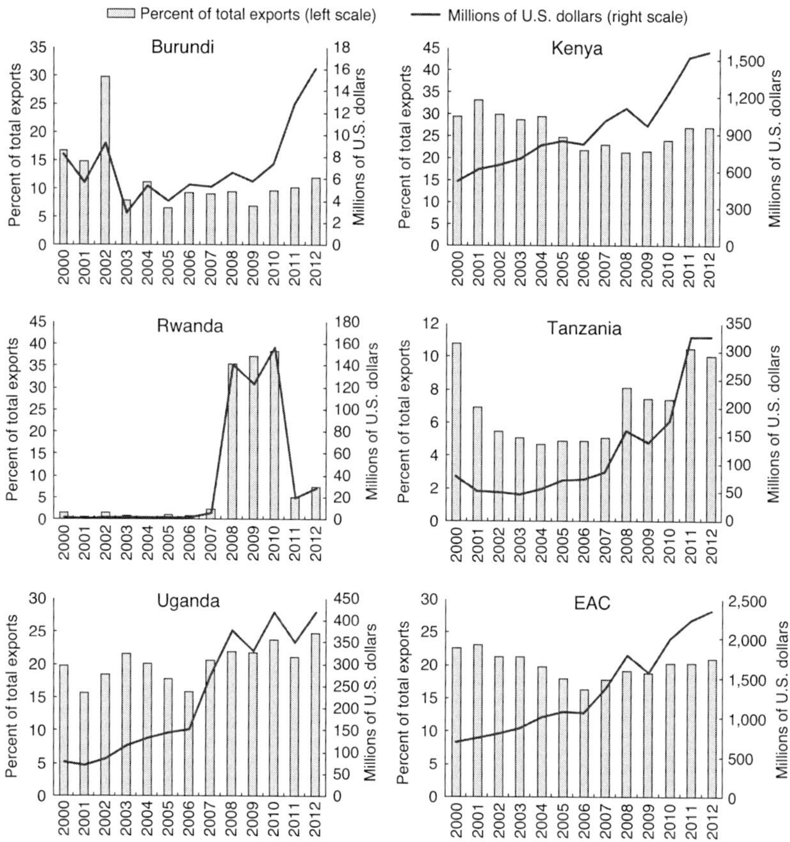

Figure 3.9 Intraregional Exports, 2000–12

Source: IMF, Direction of Trade Statistics database.
Note: EAC = East African Community.

CONCLUSIONS

EAC countries are adopting common convergence criteria that share similar features with those of other monetary unions. Compliance with these criteria is mixed and will need to be revisited and supported by common statistical definitions. Agreement among EAC countries on nominal convergence criteria represents the first pillar toward establishing a monetary union. The criteria are designed to provide simple, easy-to-interpret rules for macroeconomic management. They will need to be accompanied by a period of surveillance to ensure compliance to underpin macroeconomic stability and to safeguard the convergence process. A successful EAMU will require an institutional apparatus to enforce sound macroeconomic policies at the national level. Consideration will need to be given to designing a workable institutional setup under which EAC regional authorities have the necessary capacity to constrain policymaking at the national level, when the latter poses risks to monetary union.

ANNEX 3.1

TABLE A3.1

Comparison of Convergence Criteria Across Monetary Unions

Objectives	East African Community	Caribbean Monetary Union	West African Monetary Union (the West African Monetary Zone)	CFA Franc Zone (WAEMU)	CFA Franc Zone (Central African Economic and Monetary Community)	Gulf Cooperation Council	European Monetary Union	Eastern Caribbean Monetary Union (Eastern Caribbean Currency Union)
Exchange rate convergence	Achievement and maintenance of stable real exchange rates.	Maintain a stable exchange rate for at least three years before monetary union (with bilateral exchange rates not fluctuating more than 1.5 percent).	± 15 percent against the West African Monetary Zone, Exchange Rate Mechanism (ERM) II, under the European Monetary System.	Peg to the euro.	Peg to the euro.	Peg to the U.S. dollar.	Applicant countries should have joined ERM II under the European Monetary System for two consecutive years and should not have devalued their currencies during the period.	Peg to the U.S. dollar.
International reserves	Four months of imports.	Three months of imports for at least one year.	Three months of imports.	n/a	n/a	Four months of imports.	n/a	International reserves should back at least 60 percent of currency in circulation.
Public debt	public-debt-to-GDP ratio of 50 percent in net present value terms.	External debt service of no more than 15 percent of exports.	n/a	Less than 70 percent of GDP.	Less than 70 percent of GDP.	Total public debt less than 70 percent of GDP; central government debt less than 60 percent of GDP.	Gross government debt not above 60 percent of GDP. If this ceiling cannot be met, the ratio should be approaching the reference value at a satisfactory pace.	Gross public and publicly guaranteed debt not to exceed 60 percent of GDP.

(continued)

TABLE A3.1

Comparison of Convergence Criteria Across Monetary Unions (*continued*)

Objectives	East African Community	Caribbean Monetary Union	West African Monetary Union (the West African Monetary Zone)	CFA Franc Zone (WAEMU)	CFA Franc Zone (Central African Economic and Monetary Community)	Gulf Cooperation Council	European Monetary Union	Eastern Caribbean Monetary Union (Eastern Caribbean Currency Union)
Fiscal deficit	Overall budget deficit (including grants) not more than 3 percent of GDP; deficit excluding grants not more than 6 percent of GDP (secondary criterion).	Below 3 percent of GDP.	4 to 5 percent of GDP.	Basic budgetary balance to be zero or positive.	Adjustable criterion on non-oil basic budget balance.	Not above 3 percent of GDP.	Not to exceed 3 percent of GDP. Exceptional and temporary breaches of the ceiling may be granted.	Primary balance of the public sector to be consistent with achieving and maintaining an agreed public debt target by 2020.
Inflation	Annual average inflation not to exceed 8 percent.	In the year prior to monetary union, inflation not to be more than 1.5 percentage points higher than the three countries with the lowest (positive) inflation.	Less than 10 percent.	Less than 3 percent.		Not more than 2 percentage points above the average for Gulf Cooperation Council members.	Not more than 1.5 percentage points higher than the average for the three best-performing European Union member states.	n/a

Interest rates	Maintain market-based interest rates.	n/a	Positive real interest rates.	n/a	n/a	Short-term interest rates should not be more than 2 percentage points higher than the average for the lowest three members.	Long-term interest rates should not be more than 2 percentage points higher than in the three member states with lowest inflation.	n/a
Taxation	Secondary criterion of tax-to-GDP ratio of 25 percent.	n/a	Taxes should be greater than 20 percent of GDP.	Taxes should be greater than 17 percent of GDP.	Non-oil fiscal revenue should be no less than 17 percent of non-oil GDP.	n/a	n/a	n/a
Public expenditure arrears	n/a	n/a	Zero	No accumulation of domestic or external arrears.	No arrears of more than 120 days maturity.	n/a	n/a	n/a
Savings and investment		n/a		n/a	n/a	n/a	n/a	n/a
Public sector wages	n/a	n/a	No higher than 35 percent of revenues.	No higher than 35 percent of revenues.		n/a	n/a	n/a
Central bank credit to the government	n/a	n/a	Less than 10 percent of the previous year's tax revenues.	Less than 20 percent of the previous year's tax revenues.	Less than 20 percent of previous year's revenues (criterion to be phased out by 2012).	n/a	Zero ceiling.	Up to 40 percent of reserves.

Source: Authors.
Note: n/a = not applicable; WAEMU = West African Economic and Monetary Union.

REFERENCES

Adam, C., P. Kessy, K. Combe, and S. O'Connell, 2012, "Exchange Rate Arrangements in the Transition to the East African Monetary Union," unpublished (London: International Growth Center).

Barro, R. J., and X. Sala-i-Martin, 1995, *Economic Growth* (New York: McGraw Hill).

Dabla-Norris, E., J. Kim, and K. Shirono, 2012, "Optimal Precautionary Reserves for Low-Income Countries: A Cost-Benefit Analysis," IMF Working Paper 11/249 (Washington: International Monetary Fund).

Drummond P. F. N., A. Mrema, S. Roudet, and M. Saito, 2009, "Foreign Exchange Reserve Adequacy in East African Community Countries," IMF African Department Paper 09/1 (Washington: International Monetary Fund).

East African Community (EAC) Monetary Affairs Committee, 2009, *Achievements, Challenges, and Way Forward (1998–2008).* Kampala: EAC.

International Monetary Fund, 2003, "Is Public Debt in Emerging Markets too High?" *World Economic Outlook* (Washington, September).

Okumu, L., and J. C. O. Nyankori, 2010, "Non-tariff Barriers in EAC Customs Union: Implications for Trade between Uganda and Other EAC countries," Research Series 113621 (Kampala: Economic Policy Research Centre).

CHAPTER 4

The Fiscal Policy Challenges of Monetary Union in East Africa

SANJEEV GUPTA AND JIMMY MCHUGH

The establishment of a single East African currency is taking on an increased sense of urgency.[1] The East African Community (EAC) has established a high-level task force, and work is already under way to prepare a draft protocol for monetary union.[2] The task force, which began its work in early 2011, will revisit a wide range of issues, including the convergence criteria for East African Monetary Union (EAMU). It is also discussing the establishment of an East African Monetary Institute, as well as legislation outlining the funding and operation of a future East African central bank.

The EAC has already created a monetary affairs committee with a remit to harmonize monetary and exchange rate policies. EAC countries have also set up a ministerial committee on fiscal affairs to complement the work of the Monetary Affairs Committee. In this regard, tentative steps have been taken toward greater regional fiscal coordination. Finance ministers now hold regular regional pre-budget and post-budget consultative meetings. Considerable progress has been made toward harmonizing excise taxes and value-added tax rates, including a regional double-taxation agreement.[3]

EAMU will pose challenges for the design of fiscal policy. It will require a single, centralized East African monetary authority operating within the context of at least five national fiscal authorities.[4] Each EAC member country faces unique development challenges, with each country often confronted by large country-specific economic shocks. Once the single East African currency is established, uncoordinated fiscal policies—in particular, large deficits and rapid debt accumulation—could weaken monetary and price stability unless enforcing mechanisms are put in place to prevent this from happening.

This chapter is a revised version of *The East African Community after Ten Years: Deepening Integration*, edited by Hamid Davoodi (2012).

[1] Article 5 of the East African Community Treaty, signed in 2000, commits participating states to establish a customs union, a common market, and, ultimately, a monetary union.

[2] The task comprises technical working groups covering areas such as macroeconomic policies, statistics, financial markets, and payments and settlements infrastructure.

[3] On November 30, 2010, EAC member countries signed the Agreement for the Avoidance of Double Taxation and the Prevention of Fiscal Evasion with Respect to Taxes and Income.

[4] Pending the inclusion of South Sudan.

This chapter examines the fiscal policy challenges inherent in the EAMU project. To set the stage, it reviews the recent fiscal performances of EAC countries, especially in the wake of the global financial crisis. The crisis and the concomitant disruption to global economic activity provides an informative backdrop to considering the design of fiscal policy, both in the preparatory stages for monetary union and the long-term arrangements that need to be in place once a single currency is introduced.

This chapter examines the design of the fiscal convergence criteria for EAMU. Since 2007, EAC countries have been obliged to meet a comprehensive list of macroeconomic targets, including explicit objectives for fiscal deficits. Nevertheless, a number of areas are highlighted where the current EAMU criteria could be fine-tuned in the context of the new EAMU protocol currently under consideration.

We believe that the EAC will have to implement complementary reforms, in three areas in particular. The first pertains to the coverage, timeliness, and quality of fiscal data. The second covers the strengthening of public financial management systems in member countries and ensuring that these systems are harmonized across all countries. And third, there is considerable scope for harmonizing tax and customs procedures to strengthen regional trade.

EAC countries need to consider some unresolved issues that are prerequisites to the long-term success of the proposed single currency. For example, they will need to establish permanent fiscal rules and a multilateral fiscal surveillance regime to oversee their implementation and enforcement. In addition, limitations on central bank credit to national governments will need to be set and natural resource revenues properly managed. Given the size and frequency of recent economic shocks, effective risk sharing will also have to be an essential pillar of EAMU. Important considerations will also arise with the overlapping membership of EAC countries with other regional integration initiatives in Africa.

OVERVIEW OF REGIONAL FISCAL DEVELOPMENTS

Macroeconomic policy management has strengthened within the EAC in recent years. Fiscal performance was particularly strong just prior to the global financial crisis. Between 2003 and 2008, all countries kept their overall deficits including grants below 5 percent of GDP (Figure 4.1 and Table 4.1). In contrast, deficits excluding grants were large in some cases, exceeding 26 percent of GDP, reflecting diversity among EAC countries and the high dependence of some countries on external grants (Figure 4.2 and Table 4.1). Prudent fiscal policies and relatively high growth rates, along with sizable debt relief operations,[5] reduced public debt ratios across the region (Figure 4.3 and Table 4.2). In 2003, debt ratios in all EAC countries were in excess of 60 percent of GDP.

---

[5]Burundi reached the completion point for Highly Indebted Poor Countries and Multilateral Debt Relief Initiative in January 2009, when it received $1,495 million of debt relief in nominal terms. Rwanda reached a completion point in May 2005, receiving $620 million in debt relief.

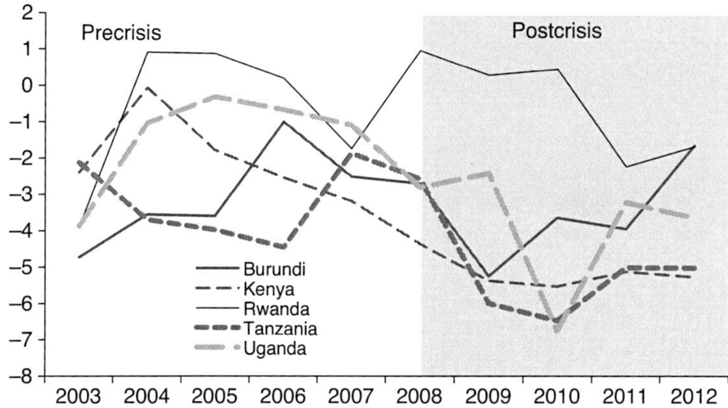

Figure 4.1 East African Community: General Government Deficits Including Grants, 2003–12 *(Percent of GDP)*

Source: IMF, World Economic Outlook database.

TABLE 4.1

East African Community, Deficit Indicators 2003–12 *(Percent of GDP)*

	2003	2005	2007	2009	2012
Overall deficit, including grants					
Burundi	−4.7	−3.6	−2.5	−5.3	−1.7
Kenya	−2.4	−1.8	−3.2	−5.4	−5.3
Rwanda	−3.9	0.9	−1.7	0.3	−1.7
Tanzania	−2.1	−4.0	−1.9	−6.0	−5.0
Uganda	−3.9	−0.3	−1.1	−2.4	−3.6
Overall deficit, excluding grants					
Burundi	−10.4	−11.9	−25.5	−24.5	−19.8
Kenya	−4.3	−3.0	−4.3	−6.2	−6.6
Rwanda	−9.0	−10.8	−10.7	−11.4	−12.5
Tanzania	−7.0	−10.0	−7.9	−10.9	−9.1
Uganda	−10.3	−8.4	−5.9	−5.2	−5.7

Source: IMF, World Economic Outlook database.

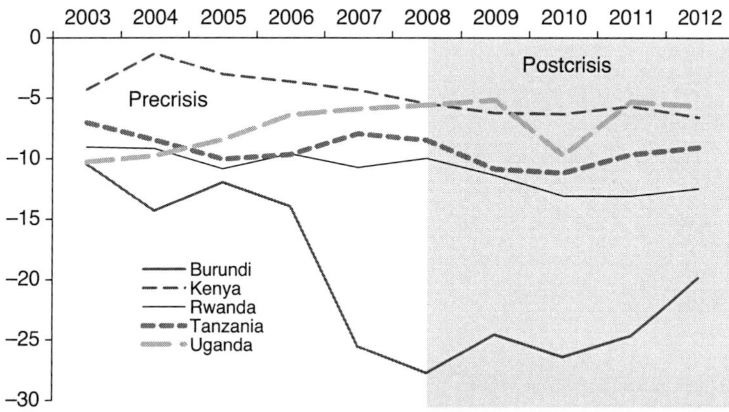

Figure 4.2 East African Community: General Government Deficits Excluding Grants, 2003–12 *(Percent of GDP)*

Source: IMF, World Economic Outlook database.

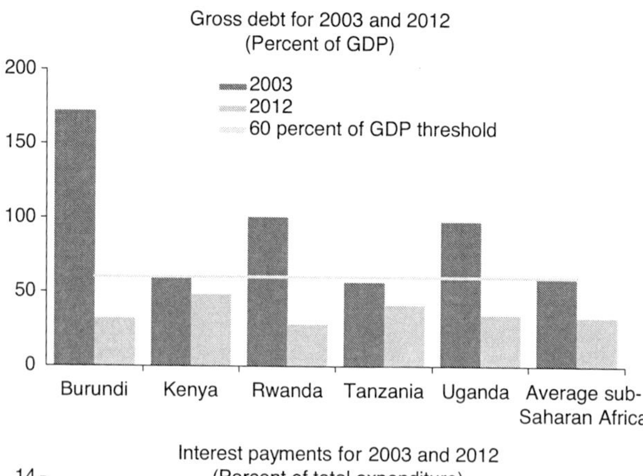

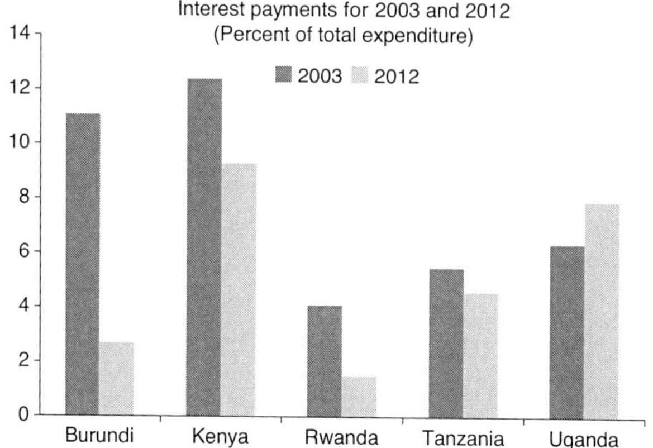

Figure 4.3 East African Community: Gross Debt and Interest Payments, 2003 and 2012 *(Percent of GDP)*

Source: IMF, World Economic Outlook database.

TABLE 4.2

East African Community, Debt Indicators 2003–12
(Percent of GDP)

	2003	2005	2007	2009	2012
Gross debt					
Burundi	172.0	137.0	128.5	40.0	32.0
Kenya	60.6	50.8	46.0	47.5	48.2
Rwanda	100.6	70.7	26.9	22.9	28.0
Tanzania	56.6	56.0	28.4	32.6	41.4
Uganda	97.6	77.2	23.6	22.2	34.5
External debt					
Burundi	170.3	131.1	108.3	21.6	19.7
Kenya	38.7	31.7	23.9	25.3	29.2
Rwanda	85.2	58.3	23.6	14.0	18.4
Tanzania	62.3	48.7	23.6	28.1	35.0
Uganda	57.1	44.9	11.4	22.2	26.0

Source: IMF, World Economic Outlook database.

In Burundi, Rwanda, and Uganda, the ratios were 100 percent or higher. By 2008, headline debt ratios had fallen to 50 percent or less for all EAC countries, while the unweighted regional average was 36 percent. This improvement in overall debt ratios is mirrored in lower external indebtedness.

Debt relief operations created fiscal space in four out of five EAC countries through lower interest costs (Figure 4.3).[6] The fall in debt-servicing costs was greatest in Burundi, where interest payments fell from 11 percent of total expenditures in 2003 to around 2 percent in 2012.

Revenue performance has improved across the region, despite the absence of significant resource revenues. In four out of five countries, total revenues as a percent of GDP have increased during the last decade (Figure 4.4). Revenue mobilization was particularly impressive in Kenya and Tanzania. Between 2003 and 2012, both countries increased their total revenues by over 5 percentage points of GDP (Figure 4.4, lower left panel). Tanzania enjoyed the strongest improvement in tax revenues, from slightly less than 10 percent of GDP in 2004 to over 15 percent in 2012. Over the same period, Kenya improved tax collection by 3.6 percentage points. The improvements were less dramatic in Rwanda and Uganda, where the revenue increase was in the range of 1–2 percentage points of GDP. The exception is Burundi, where tax revenues did not show any increase (Figure 4.4).

The composition of tax revenues changed, shifting from taxation of international trade toward domestic sources (Figure 4.3 and Table 4.3). In 2004, international taxes on average accounted for 15 percent of total revenues. By 2012, this had fallen to 9 percent. The biggest changes were in Rwanda and Burundi, where previously international taxes accounted for over 20 percent and 24 percent of revenues, respectively. In 2012, those ratios had fallen to 10 percent and 8 percent, respectively. The relative contribution of taxes on goods and services has fallen slightly, by 4 percentage points, whereas taxes on income, profits, and capital gains have increased by 7 percentage points in the EAC.

The region has experienced substantial volatility in grant flows—an issue that complicates the design of macroeconomic objectives for EAMU (Figure 4.4, upper left panel). In general, some EAC countries are heavily dependent on external assistance. In Burundi, external assistance accounts for over 50 percent of total revenues, but in Rwanda the ratio is 45 percent. Uganda's dependence on external assistance has fallen since 2006, when grants amounted to almost 9 percent of GDP and 38 percent of total government revenues. By 2011, these had fallen to 2.3 percent and 17 percent, respectively. This decline was accompanied by an increase in nontax revenue, rising from 11 percent of GDP in 2004 to 13 percent in 2011. Tanzania has received a broadly constant volume of grants as a percent of GDP. In contrast, grants have not figured prominently in Kenya. External assistance fell from just under 2 percent of GDP in 2002 to less than 1 percent

[6]Kenya did not receive debt relief and was not part of the Highly Indebted Poor Country initiative.

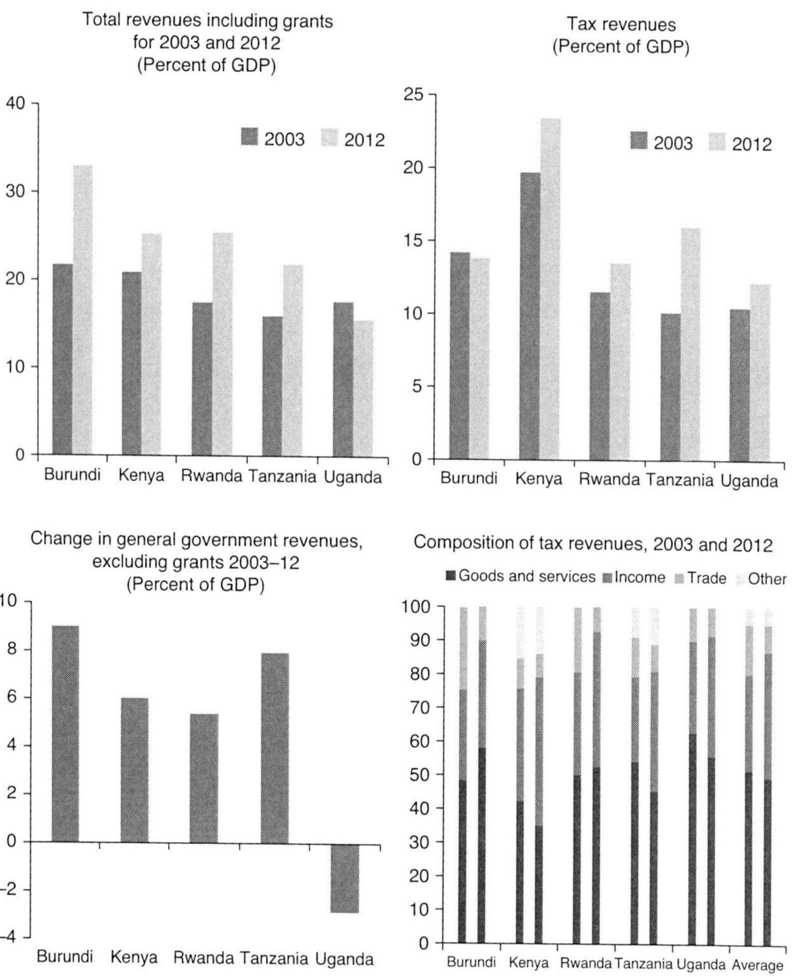

Figure 4.4 East African Revenue, Revenue Performance, 2003 and 2012

Source: IMF, World Economic Outlook database.

just before the crisis. In terms of revenue composition, grants have typically remained below 5 percent of Kenya's total revenues.

Strong revenue performance is reflected in higher public expenditure, particularly in social sectors (Figure 4.4). By 2012, average EAC public expenditure exceeded 20 percent of GDP. The increase was greatest in Burundi, partly reflecting higher external assistance. Across the region, expenditure on health and education as a percent of GDP increased, with particularly large positive changes recorded in Burundi and Tanzania (Figure 4.5).

TABLE 4.3

EAC Composition of Tax Revenues
(Percent of total revenues)

	2003	2012
Taxes on goods and services		
Burundi	48	58
Kenya	42	35
Rwanda	50	53
Tanzania	54	45
Uganda	63	56
Average	52	49
Taxes on income, profits, and capital gains		
Burundi	27	32
Kenya	34	44
Rwanda	30	40
Tanzania	25	35
Uganda	27	36
Average	29	37
Taxes on international trade		
Burundi	24	10
Kenya	9	7
Rwanda	19	7
Tanzania	12	8
Uganda	10	8
Average	15	8
Other revenues		
Burundi	0	0
Kenya	0	14
Rwanda	0	0
Tanzania	9	11
Uganda	0	0
Average	2	5

Source: IMF, World Economic Outlook database.
Note: EAC = East African Community.

The East African Community and the Global Financial Crisis

Overall, EAC countries were less affected by the global financial crisis than advanced and emerging market economies. Financial market linkages between advanced and low-income countries are generally weak, and this limited the scope for contagion. Furthermore, prior to the crisis, EAC countries had strengthened their policy frameworks, increased trade openness, and, as noted, successfully reduced debt levels (IMF, 2009).

The global financial crisis generated only a modest slowdown in EAC growth rates, which declined from a precrisis average of 6.8 percent to 5.7 percent (Table 4.4).[7] The slowdown was more muted than for all sub-Saharan Africa, where average growth rates declined from 6.5 percent to 4.4 percent. The

[7]The precrisis period refers to unweighed average growth rate from 2003–07; the postcrisis period refers to 2008–11.

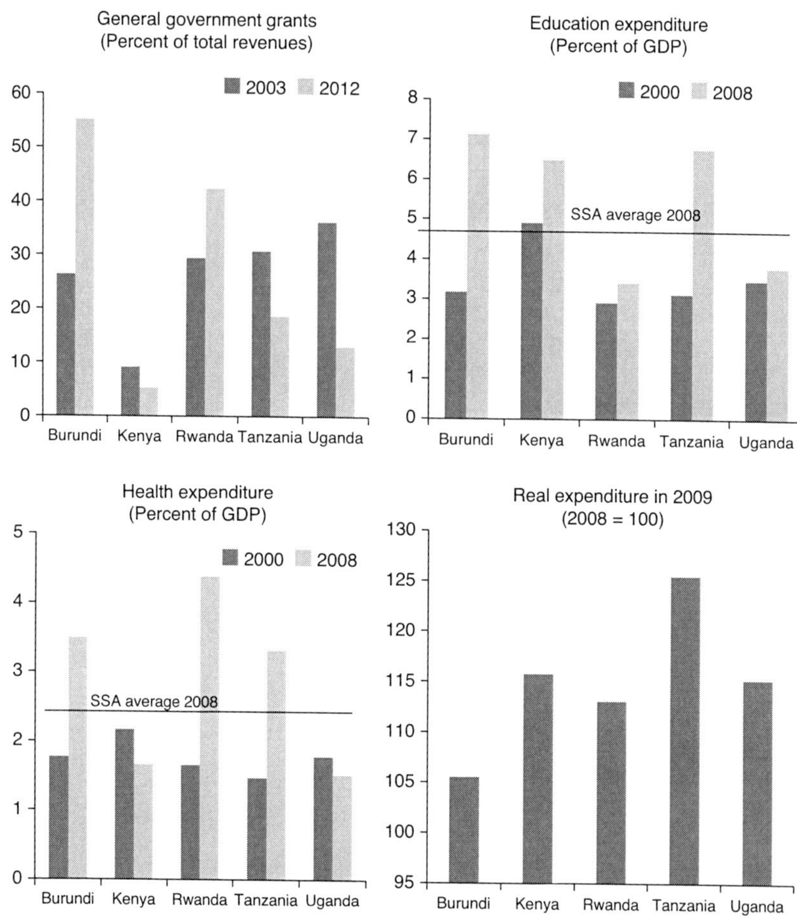

Figure 4.5 East African Community: Expenditures and Grants

Source: IMF, World Economic Outlook database.
Note: SSA = sub-Saharan Africa.

TABLE 4.4

GDP Growth Rates in Africa
(Average annual percent change)

	2003–07	2008–12
East African Community	6.9	5.5
Sub-Saharan Africa, all countries	6.4	4.5
Sub-Saharan Africa, middle-income	4.7	2.9

Source: IMF, World Economic Outlook database.

slowdown was even more marked for sub-Saharan middle-income countries, where average growth decelerated from 4.7 percent to just 2.5 percent.

Nevertheless, the crisis emphasized the ongoing vulnerability of EAC countries to large adverse shocks. While growth rates held up well during the crisis, EAC countries were affected through other channels, notably higher food and fuel prices and deteriorating external balances. In Burundi, headline inflation rose from 4.1 percent in December 2010 to 13.3 percent by October 2011. In Kenya and Tanzania, a severe drought reduced agricultural and hydropower generation, pushing the inflation rate above 15 percent in both countries. In Uganda, the current account deficit deteriorated due to weaker external demand, reaching 12.5 percent of GDP during fiscal year 2012.[8] This vulnerability and the need to respond to shocks will influence both the design of the EAC's fiscal objectives as well as the fiscal infrastructure following the adoption of the single currency.

Within the region, fiscal policy played a key role in supporting growth during the crisis. Increased fiscal space offered EAC countries some room to adopt countercyclical fiscal policies in 2009. In real terms, government expenditures increased in all EAC countries (Figure 4.5, lower right panel). Fiscal policy became more expansionary in 2009 when Burundi, Kenya, and Tanzania recorded deficits including grants of 5 percent or greater. The exception is Rwanda. During the crisis, Rwanda maintained a tight fiscal stance, accumulating surpluses in 2008–10 and allowing only modest real increases in expenditures in 2011–12. As the crisis unfolded, the composition of expenditures within the EAC shifted toward public investment. Between 2008 and 2011 in all EAC countries, capital expenditures as a percent of total expenditures increased (Figure 4.5, lower left panel). This partly reflects a longer term trend in which capital expenditures increased as a percent of GDP (Figure 4.5, lower right panel).

THE RATIONALE FOR EAST AFRICAN MONETARY UNION FISCAL CONVERGENCE CRITERIA

To fully benefit from monetary union, the EAC should meet the conditions for an optimal currency area (Mundell, 1961). In principle, countries should have a broadly similar economic structure. In the event of economic shocks, participating countries are affected in broadly similar ways and so a single harmonized policy response is appropriate. In practice, a complete harmonization of economic structure is not possible. Even within countries, there are large regional differences and shocks will always have a considerable asymmetric component. Therefore, a high degree of labor and capital mobility, coupled with price and wage flexibility, can therefore provide a crucial supporting mechanism absorbing unfavorable asymmetric shocks. Furthermore, once a single currency is established, it should be bolstered by a risk-sharing system, such as an automatic fiscal transfer mechanism to redistribute resources to member states that have been negatively affected by economic shocks.

Countries embarking on monetary union must ensure that they have achieved sufficient real and nominal convergence to ensure the long-term stability of the single currency. Greater convergence is, to some extent, an endogenous process

[8]The fiscal year corresponds to June through June.

(Buti and Sapir, 1998). Monetary union encourages economic and financial integration. Capital flows to less-developed regions promote economic growth, leading to a harmonization of per capita incomes. Nevertheless, the creation of a central bank and the elimination of national currencies are not sufficient. Countries must ensure they are sufficiently prepared for dealing with the greater macroeconomic discipline demanded by monetary union.

Given their vulnerability to large shocks, EAC countries have recognized the importance of real and nominal convergence as a prerequisite for moving toward a single currency. In 2007, EAC states adopted a comprehensive set of macroeconomic targets, defining objectives for inflation, reserve accumulation, exchange rates, growth, current account balances, national savings, bank supervision, and fiscal objectives such as debt and deficits.

Fiscal policy raises a number of challenges in the context for monetary union:

- Uncoordinated national fiscal policies can conflict with the objectives of price stability. Fiscal policies, pursued with only national objectives in mind, can create a negative externality on the other members of a monetary union. Each member can in principle pursue policies that can affect price levels through changes in aggregate demand. The central bank could counteract these unilateral actions by raising interest rates for the monetary union as a whole—and this could tighten monetary conditions in other member states, leading to lower investment and output and higher unemployment. In extreme cases, unilateral fiscal policies can lead to fiscal crises that threaten the monetary union's very credibility. In the event of a crisis, the central bank could come under overwhelming pressure to bail out spendthrift governments, thus fueling inflation and harming the stability of the union. Ultimately, these bailouts could threaten its existence.
- A related issue is the opportunity for fiscal "free riding." For various reasons, a member state may pursue policies leading to large budget deficits and an unsustainable issuance of public debt. This flow of new debt could raise interest rates for the monetary union as a whole, leading to detrimental consequences for investment and growth.

This means that a high degree of fiscal policy coordination is essential in a monetary union. The fiscal policy discipline demanded by a successful monetary union is onerous and difficult to achieve. Therefore, an extended period of preparation is therefore inevitable. Here, the policies of individual member states are gradually melded together to form a coherent fiscal policy for the whole monetary union.

In practical terms, fiscal policy coordination is achieved through the adoption of numerical fiscal targets and a regional institutional infrastructure that oversees compliance toward achieving these goals. Fiscal targets should provide dependable indicators of the stability and sustainability of public finances as well as their resilience to economic shocks. Normally, these targets comprise a stock objective that measures public sector indebtedness and a flow objective that assesses the state of current fiscal policies.

The rationale for a debt criterion is uncontroversial. Excessive debt levels and the inability to rollover debt at reasonable interest rates will ultimately be the fulcrum of any crisis leading to the destabilization of a monetary union. Furthermore, high levels of debt are an impediment to growth (Cecchetti, Madhusudan, and Zampolli, 2011; Kumar and Woo, 2010; Reinhart and Rogoff, 2010). Debt servicing costs crowd out other expenditures. The debt objective can be defined in terms of gross or net debt. Coverage could just comprise the general government or the whole public sector. The deficit or flow objective measures the current fiscal stance. As such, it measures how current policies will likely affect the future stability of the monetary union. The deficit objective also raises definitional issues. Should the target be the overall balance of the general government or should it exclude external grants? Should the flow objective reflect underlying economic developments, which would suggest a structural balance rather than the headline overall balance objective? All these issues are taken up in the following sections.

To achieve macroeconomic harmonization, countries must accurately communicate their policy intentions to other member states. For this, a regional institutional framework is needed that can observe and report harmonized fiscal targets. This requirement opens up issues of data comparability, coverage, and quality. Furthermore, member states must understand the future fiscal objectives of their regional partners, which should be communicated within a medium-term policy framework.

EAST AFRICAN MONETARY UNION FISCAL CONVERGENCE CRITERIA—CURRENT ISSUES

In 2007, the East African Community Council adopted the EAMU macroeconomic convergence criteria, coupled with an ambitious timetable that envisaged the introduction of a single currency by 2015 (Figure 4.6). These criteria established a three-stage process. The initial preparatory stage was tentatively scheduled to last from 2007 to 2010, followed by an intermediate stage from 2011 to 2015, followed by the adoption of a single currency in 2015.

During the initial preparatory phase countries embarked on a process of economic harmonization. EAC countries were obligated to achieve three primary objectives on fiscal policy, inflation, and reserve accumulation. In turn, the primary fiscal objective comprises of two parts: the overall deficits excluding grants should be no greater than 6 percent of GDP and the overall deficit including grants should be no greater than 3 percentage points of GDP. The preparatory phase also had an extensive list of secondary criteria, including a debt objective. The EAMU's debt objective is qualitative rather than quantitative. While there is no explicit debt target on debt, countries should have sustained reductions of domestic and external debt as a ratio of GDP.

During the second intermediate stage, fiscal targets will be tightened. The fiscal deficit objective excluding grants is reduced to 5 percent of GDP, while the objective including grants is reduced to 2 percentage points of GDP. The debt

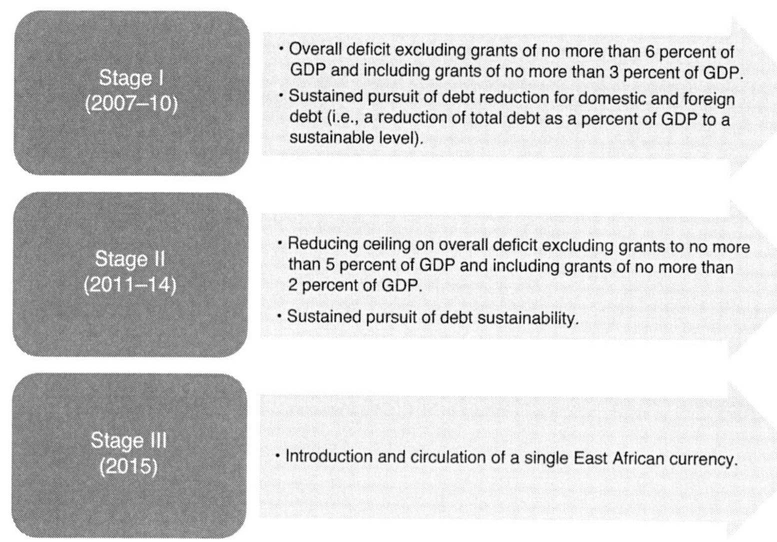

Figure 4.6 East African Community: Convergence Road Map

Source: Authors.

objective remains qualitative as before. There is no expectation of a reduction in the debt-to-GDP ratio, implying that EAC countries should have reached debt levels consistent with debt sustainability by the time they reach stage two of the monetary union process.

During the third and final stage, the new single East African currency will begin to circulate among participating states. The EAMU had not yet adopted any formal fiscal objectives for the period after the new currency has been adopted. This leaves open the question on what the institutional framework for fiscal policy will be once the new currency has been introduced.

EAST AFRICAN MONETARY UNION FISCAL CRITERIA—THE ISSUES

The global financial crisis has highlighted a number of issues related to the EAMU fiscal objective. Should, for example, the fiscal criteria be amended to allow some flexibility in the event of large shocks? Following the global financial crisis, fiscal deficits increased to support demand, but at the cost of moving away from the convergence benchmarks. This also raises a question over the timetable for monetary union, since recent EAC deficits are now higher than the benchmarks specified in the initial stage of the criteria for EAMU. So should the EAC adopt a more flexible timetable monetary union?

The EAC has the opportunity to adjust the criteria as part of the redrafting of the EAMU protocol, which is currently under way. The most immediate issue concerns the headline fiscal objective—the deficit target. The original criteria, defined in 2007, specifies two deficit targets: one including grants and the other excluding them. As explained in the following, there is a good case for simplifying the objective, focusing on the overall deficit including grants, while monitoring the other target for surveillance purposes. Furthermore, the convergence criteria should be supported by a series of indicative fiscal benchmarks; for example, indicators that look at the composition and growth of expenditures and, in the case of countries with considerable resource wealth, fiscal indicators adjusted for resource revenues. There are also important issues on the access that individual countries have to central bank credit. To ensure the credibility and independence of central banks, EAC countries will have to impose restrictions on these credit facilities.

There is also a strong case for revising the criteria covering debt sustainability. The current criterion lacks specificity and could be strengthened by introducing numerical targets. If this revision is introduced, the criterion would then need a precise definition. And the question in this respect is whether it should be defined in terms of gross or net public debt.

Beyond the questions relating to the design of debt and deficit convergence criteria, there are other important supplementary issues that should be included in the new draft protocol. The EAC should develop a series of indicative fiscal benchmarks that monitor the quality of public expenditure, take account of the growing importance of natural resource revenues within the region, and devise targets for limiting the dependence on central bank credit by national governments.

EAC countries must also look beyond numerical macroeconomic objectives and examine institutional readiness for monetary union. In this regard, they need to improve data reporting, public financial management, and the harmonization of customs procedures and tax rates.

Providing Credible Escape Clauses in the Event of Large Shocks

Currently, the EAMU road map has no explicit provisions for an escape clause in the event that an individual country is confronted with a large economic shock. Ideally, the criteria should not be excessively restrictive so that a countercyclical policy response aimed at stabilizing output is prohibited. Part of the reason lies in the inherent difficulty in designing escape clauses in developing and emerging market economies, where business cycles and output gaps are difficult to identify empirically.

In principle, any relaxation of fiscal objectives should only occur in exceptional circumstances. Excessive use of escape clauses could undermine policy credibility and weaken fiscal discipline. Therefore, it is essential that EAC countries establish comprehensive rules for exceptions to the EAMU criteria as well as procedures for assessing whether these are valid. In turn, this emphasizes the importance of strengthening regional multilateral surveillance to provide an objective basis for identifying the magnitude of shocks and when it is appropriate for EAMU countries to deviate from the fiscal criteria.

TABLE 4.5

General Government Grants
(Percent of GDP)

	2003	2008	2012
Burundi	5.7	25.0	18.2
Kenya	1.9	1.1	1.3
Rwanda	5.1	10.9	10.8
Tanzania	4.9	5.9	4.1
Uganda	6.4	2.8	2.0

Source: IMF, World Economic Outlook database.

Should the East African Monetary Union Deficit Target Be Revised?

What is the best fiscal deficit objective for the EAMU? For most EAC countries, external grants are a large source of total revenues. But grant flows have been extremely volatile. In Burundi, external assistance has ranged from around 6 percent of GDP in 2003 to almost 25 percent in 2008. Grant flows to Rwanda have varied between 5 and 12 percent of GDP (Table 4.5). As a practical matter, the majority of EAC countries would find it impossible to meet both deficit objectives simultaneously unless there is a hefty reduction in external grants. Therefore, under the current EAMU criteria for the initial stage, if grants are larger than 3 percent of GDP, a country would need to save the surplus resources with potential effects for domestic resource mobilization.

A plausible option would be to streamline the deficit criteria by focusing on a single target: the overall deficit including grants. This definition has the merit that it provides a direct link between current policies and aggregate demand, as well as debt accumulation, and therefore gauges the impact of fiscal policy on medium-term sustainability.

At the same time, the overall deficit excluding grants also imparts critical information about the fiscal stance. In particular, it illustrates the extent of an economy's dependence on aid flows and the extent to which external grants may crowd out domestic resource mobilization (Benedek and others, 2012). The overall deficit excluding grants should therefore be monitored during surveillance, but it should not be part of EAMU convergence criteria

Should the East African Monetary Union Convergence Criteria Include a Numerical Debt Target?

The definition of the EAC debt objective is problematic. As noted earlier, this target is open to misinterpretation and is unlikely to provide the transparency needed to ensure a sustainable reduction of debt levels. It is also anomalous given that other monetary unions such as the European Monetary Union, Eastern Caribbean Currency Union, West African Economic and Monetary Union, and Central African Economic and Monetary Community, as well as proposed monetary unions such as the South African Development Community and Gulf Cooperation Countries have explicit debt objectives that all participating states are expected to pursue.

A numerically defined fiscal objective would resolve this difficulty. Indeed, explicit debt limits are a common feature of other monetary unions, which tend to range between 60–70 percent of GDP. The EAC member countries would need to collectively determine an appropriate numerical target. Debt sustainability needs to be assessed on the basis of current debt levels, the growth potential within the EAC, and an assessment of projected debt-servicing costs.

A debt objective in the range of 60 percent of GDP may be high for EAC countries. They are likely to face limited access to international financial markets in the short term, but greater vulnerability to external shocks as well as greater growth volatility. Furthermore, relatively low government revenue-to-GDP ratios in some countries limit the capacity to service large public sector debt stocks, despite substantial progress toward strengthening domestic tax base in most countries. In addition, external grant flows have tended to be highly volatile. Therefore, a lower debt objective would be more prudent.

Should the Debt Target Be Expressed in Terms of Gross or Net Debt?

The distinction between net and gross debt is significant. Changes in gross and net debt have differed during the economic crisis. Both definitions have their merits. Gross debt is the most common reference for assessing fiscal sustainability. Gross debt is a relatively straightforward measure of fiscal vulnerability. Coverage issues are comparatively easy to resolve, with gross debt capturing all liabilities except those from equity, financial derivatives, and so on. In general, data for gross debt are easily available.

Conceptually, net debt is a preferable concept. Net debt adjusts for financial assets held by governments (e.g., those acquired from natural resource revenues or government equity holdings in large domestic corporations). Net debt also resolves the inconsistency arising from the fact that governments receive a flow of income from their assets, something that is acknowledged in annual government accounts, but implicitly ignored in gross debt calculations. However, the data reporting requirements for net debt are more stringent since governments must make assessments of the stock of available assets. Measuring financial assets is relatively straightforward. However, nonfinancial assets raise difficult issues of valuation. There is also the further complication that net debt should be consolidated across government entities.

There are alternative benchmarks. The EAC could, for example, adopt a target defined either in terms of the present value of debt as a ratio of GDP. Alternatively, a debt service objective could be defined either in terms of revenues, exports, or GDP. Unfortunately, these lack the simplicity and transparency of gross or net debt, expressed as a ratio of GDP.

Supporting the Debt Target with Indicative Benchmarks

The streamlined fiscal objective should be complemented with a wider set of monitoring benchmarks for national budgets. The underlying rationale for monitoring the overall balance excluding grants is a sound one. It also imparts critical information about the sustainability of the fiscal stance. In particular, it illustrates the extent of an economy's dependence on aid flows and the extent to which external grants may crowd out domestic resource mobilization. Therefore, it would be appropriate to retain this objective for surveillance purposes.

EAC countries should also monitor deficits excluding national resource flows. In a number of member countries, significant natural resources have been discovered. In the future, resource-related taxes will become an increasingly important component of public sector revenues. While natural resource discoveries will strengthen revenue bases, they also bring their own fiscal management problems.

Resource revenues tend to be volatile and can encourage temporary and unsustainable increases in public expenditures. To reduce expenditure volatility, EAC countries should develop a common framework for measuring prudent levels of expenditure from natural resource revenues. Furthermore, resource revenues are exhaustible, giving rise to difficult decisions about what proportion of revenues should be consumed today and how much should be saved and invested.

One potentially important fiscal benchmark could be the nonresource primary balance. This indicator excludes both resource-related revenues as well as interest expenditures. This measure provides a more reliable measure of the impact of government policies on domestic demand. Using this as part of the policy framework would help decouple expenditures from the inevitable volatility from resource revenues.[9]

Limiting Central Bank Overdraft Facilities

To guarantee the independence of the regional central bank, EAC countries will have to limit government overdraft facilities at their respective central banks. Currently, EAC member states depend heavily on these facilities to fund temporary cash flow difficulties. However, these facilities complicate monetary policy operations and reduce central bank control over monetary aggregates.

The region, meanwhile, has not yet established a deep and liquid market for domestic government debt securities. This limits the options for public sector cash management. EAC member states should first harmonize these overdraft facilities, defining a single ceiling for all countries in the region. Once this has been achieved, the EAC should develop a timetable for gradually reducing these overdrafts by the time the single currency is adopted. EAC countries should establish an absolute limit on central government credit and an end-of-year "clearance" objective in which overdraft balances are zero. Given the importance of this issue to the independence of the regional central bank, this timetable should have the status of a mandatory convergence criterion.

---

[9]A further rationale for using the nonresource primary balance can be found in IMF, 2012.

Providing a Realistic Timetable for East African Monetary Union

In principle, EAC countries by now should have met the convergence criteria set out in stage one. Despite substantial progress, the EAC still has some way to go to meet the fiscal deficit criteria (including or excluding grants). Therefore, the schedule set out in the road map should therefore be considered to be indicative as member countries are still working toward meeting the initial stage of EAMU.

In recent years, EAC member countries have not met the stage one fiscal deficit objective on a consistent basis. In 2012, only one country—Rwanda—had met the 3 percent of GDP overall deficit including grants target. Tanzania recorded a deficit of 6 percent of GDP. In Uganda, the deficit reached 7.3 percent of GDP. Between 2009 and 2011, Burundi, Kenya, Tanzania, and Uganda all recorded overall deficits including grants in excess of 5 percent at least for one year in that period. In terms of the deficit target excluding grants, EAC countries are much further away from meeting the EAMU criteria. Only Kenya has managed to maintain an overall balance excluding grants below 5 percent of GDP on a consistent basis. In Burundi and Tanzania, the ratio has been in excess of 10 percentage points of GDP since 2009.

Therefore, EAC countries may wish to adopt a less rigid timetable for completing the fiscal criteria. In particular, the overriding objective should be that they develop the necessary degree of fiscal harmonization to ensure the ultimate success of monetary union.

Improving Fiscal Data Collection and Reporting

Timely and comparable fiscal data is a prerequisite for an effective macroeconomic harmonization process. This ensures that reported data accurately reflects the full coverage of government accounts. A broad coverage of fiscal data permits the identification of any emerging fiscal difficulties in a timely manner. It also ensures comparability of fiscal positions across countries.

There are appreciable divergences in the coverage and timeliness of fiscal data across EAC countries. Burundi, Kenya, and Tanzania report central government data. Only Uganda reports general government data. Two of five members—Rwanda and Uganda—report fiscal data on a quarterly basis, which is not adequate for fiscal surveillance. The other EAC countries report this monthly. There are also large stock-flow discrepancies between deficit and debt. In Kenya, these can be as high as 5 percentage points of GDP.[10]

Improvements in the quality of fiscal data will help prevent the use of accounting stratagems to achieve the fiscal coverage criteria. Typically, these stratagems

[10] Dippelsman, Dziobek, and Gutiérrez Mangas (2012) reported that debt coverage can have a large effect on assessments of debt sustainability. Depending on the definition of the government, the debt-to-GDP ratios for a country at any given time can range from 40 percent to over 100 percent. Debt statistics, for example, may include or exclude state and local governments and may cover all debt instruments or just a subset. The authors suggest that gross debt of the general government should be globally adopted as the headline indicator.

will inflate revenue performance or fail to report higher spending, for example, through public–private partnerships, treating privatization receipts as revenues, securitization, or the sale of future revenues.[11] Over the long term, such efforts tend to weaken fiscal performance and store up difficulties for the future.

EAC countries have begun preparatory work to harmonize statistics. They have established a Committee on Statistics that is working with institutions such as central banks and ministries of finance. The committee has identified six priority areas: monetary statistics, financial soundness indicators, the consumer price index, government financial statistics, balance of payments, and national accounts.

Strengthening Public Financial Management

Aligning and strengthening public financial management systems in the EAC will be a prerequisite for fiscal convergence and an integral bulwark for ensuring good governance, promoting transparency and accountability, and increasing fiscal discipline.

Within the EAC there are substantial weaknesses in public financial management systems, requiring a substantial reform agenda. This includes the need to strengthen legal frameworks and systems, reform budget preparation processes, and improve budgeting and accounting classification. Treasury systems remain weak and, more generally, there is a need to upgrade cash-and debt-management procedures to modernize financial accounting and reporting systems and improve expenditure control monitoring.

In addition to strengthening the public financial management infrastructure at the national level, EAC countries need to ensure that their structures are aligned with partner countries. Inevitably, this will require appropriately revising organic budget laws to accommodate the requirements of the monetary union. Here, the EAC will need to establish a common legal and regulatory framework as well as adopt international standards for accounting reporting and auditing.

Harmonizing Customs and Tax Rates and Procedures

The EAC Customs Union, which was created in 2005, is a vital building block of monetary union. Nevertheless, there remains much to be done to ensure that it becomes fully operational. In principle, a customs union requires the establishment of common external tariffs, a disputes resolution mechanism, the elimination of internal tariffs, effective rules of origin, nondiscrimination, and the harmonization of customs and noncustoms procedures. A particularly difficult issue will be the elimination of national exemptions from customs duties. To achieve these objectives, each country will have to amend national legislation to align it with the requirements of the customs union. This process is often time-consuming as each member has its own legislative agenda, which can sometimes be regarded as a less important legislative priority.

---

[11] For further details, see Irwin (2012).

The EAC will have to develop mechanisms for revenue sharing and transparent accounting. Each country will need to properly record and account for payments made at customs houses and border points. The customs union will also demand the timely exchange of data whereby each state has an information technology system compliant with other member states. Furthermore, intelligence and tax information need to be easily shared to ensure that enforcement activity is properly supported.

A harmonized tax system will facilitate the free movement of goods and capital and thus lay the basis for greater real convergence. Indeed, tax harmonization is an explicit objective of the protocol creating the EAC Common Market.[12] Within the EAC, there are different value-added tax rates, exemptions, and zero ratings. There are also divergent value-added tax registration thresholds, varying definitions of tax bases, different tax exemptions, rules on depreciation, and capital allowances.

LOOKING BEYOND EAST AFRICAN MONETARY UNION

Although the EAC has articulated a detailed road map for monetary union, thought needs to be given to the postadoption period once the new currency is in circulation. In particular, there are three key issues that deserve consideration:

- **The nature of the postadoption institutional and policymaking structure.** The EAC will have to construct permanent fiscal rules to ensure fiscal discipline as well as establish an effective mechanism for multilateral fiscal surveillance.
- **The mechanism to deal with asymmetric shocks.** The EAC will need to consider an appropriate response in the event that one or more member countries are confronted with a large unfavorable shock.
- **The relationship between EAMU and other regional monetary initiatives.** There is the unresolved question concerning the role of EAMU in the context of the wider move toward economic integration in Africa.

Postadoption Policy Coordination Structures

To ensure the sustainability of the new currency, the EAC will need to develop effective macroeconomic policy coordination structures. Strong fiscal discipline will be essential if the future single currency is to succeed. This will require three components: establishing fiscal rules, undertaking fiscal surveillance to ensure that countries are adhering to those rules, and introducing mechanisms for enforcing fiscal discipline.

---

[12]Article 32 of the Protocol on the Establishment of the East African Community Common Market states: "The Partner States undertake to progressively harmonize their tax policies and laws to remove tax distortions in order to facilitate the free movement of goods, services and capital and to promote investment within the Community." Article 83 2 (e) of EAC Treaty also requires EAC countries to harmonize their tax policies.

A successful and sustainable monetary union requires a high degree of coordination between the supranational central bank and national-level fiscal authorities. Effective fiscal and monetary policy coordination, in particular for dealing with constraints on debt and deficits, are prerequisites for successful monetary union. Therefore, binding and credible fiscal rules are essential.

Effective fiscal surveillance will be critical to achieving macroeconomic policy coordination. EAC countries need to identify imbalances early on and ensure that corrective actions are promptly taken. To do this, the EAC will need to delegate responsibility for surveillance to a body charged with monitoring fiscal developments and reporting findings to national authorities. The EAC recently created a fiscal affairs committee that over time could be transformed into an independent body responsible for EAC multilateral surveillance.

Enforcing fiscal discipline will be imperative. The EAC will have to develop mechanisms for countries to take corrective actions in the event member states fail to maintain fiscal discipline. In political terms, enforcing multilateral fiscal rules could be difficult. Countries infringing fiscal rules can apply pressure on partner countries to relax them. To counter this, the EAC will have to establish strong institutional capacity.

Fiscal Risk-Sharing Mechanisms

The EAC has not yet spelled out how the EAMU will deal with country-specific shocks once monetary union has been established. In other words, what fiscal risk mechanisms will be in place to confront potentially destabilizing shocks? The issue has become more acute given recent developments within the euro area. Mechanisms to share risks and absorb the negative consequences of shocks need to be developed. Since labor mobility is limited within the EAC, and structural rigidities hamper rapid price adjustment, the impact of country-specific shocks is likely to be protracted and painful.

There is a wide range of potential fiscal risk-sharing mechanisms that could be established when a single currency is introduced. These include (1) a system of intergovernmental transfers, (2) the issuance of supranational EAC bonds, and (3) the creation of an EAC fiscal stabilization fund. Regardless of the chosen mechanism, the EAC would also need to establish transparent governance structures.

The EAC could in principle develop a system of intragovernmental transfers, which could be made effective to address shocks faced by individual member states. Intragovernmental transfers have two broad objectives. First, transfers can help meet a redistributive objective, partially equalizing incomes across member states. Second, they can play a macroeconomic stabilization role, counteracting the negative effects of shocks. In the context of monetary union, the stabilization objective is paramount, since it will discourage individual member states from undertaking fiscal policy measures that conflict with the price stability objectives of the EAC central bank.

Supranational EAC bonds offer an alternative risk-sharing mechanism. If the EAC borrows collectively, market access could be secured at sustainable interest rates when individual member states come under stress. The issuance of a unified EAC bond raises issues about legacy debt issued by individual member states. For example, in the event of a debt crisis, which instrument would have seniority? This issue could, in theory, be resolved by the complete mutualization of the existing debt stock. But currently, EAC countries have different levels of indebtedness, and this would raise a further complex subject of how the responsibility for servicing legacy debt would be allocated.

EAC countries could also create a regional stabilization fund. In the event of a country-specific shock, EAMU members could access the fund for resources to meet any fiscal shortfalls. The fund could then be replenished when output returns to the long-run trend. It would need to be financed through initial contributions from member states, and it would require strong governance structures to ensure that it was run according to the objective of responding to shocks independent of political influence.

Monetary Union in the Context of African Economic Integration

Over the last decade, African countries have entered into a number of ambitious regional integration initiatives. The EAC's drive toward monetary union coincides with other initiatives to strengthen regional economic cooperation, including monetary integration. The Common Market for Eastern and Southern Africa has also expressed a desire to create a monetary union. Its membership and that of the South African Development Community partly overlap with the EAC, creating conflicting obligations for those who are members of the two regional organizations. At some point, these countries will have to decide which organization they want to belong to.

CONCLUSIONS

The global financial crisis highlighted many of the recent policy achievements of the EAC region. Fiscal policy management has improved over the last decade. Public debt ratios have fallen, revenue performance has improved, and the composition of tax revenues has shifted from international taxes to domestic sources. Despite the widespread disruption to the global economy, East African growth rates have remained broadly in line with those prior to the crisis.

The improved fiscal performance laid the basis for a robust response to the global crisis. Before the crisis, EAC countries had built up fiscal space that provided the opportunity for countries to implement countercyclical fiscal policies. Public investment has increased, both as a share of total spending and as a percent of GDP. Important social sector expenditures have also increased as a percent of GDP.

At the same time, the crisis has emphasized the region's ongoing vulnerability to large economic shocks. Over the last two years, EAC countries have experienced large supply-side shocks from higher global fuel prices, as well as a regional drought. Balance-of-payments difficulties have emerged and headline inflation rates have picked up across the region.

East Africa's vulnerability to shocks underscores the need to reexamine the design of EAMU convergence criteria. The current criteria have no formal flexibility in the face of large external shocks. As a consequence of the crisis, deficit levels in EAC countries are now some distance from meeting the objectives outlined in the initial phase of the EAMU road map. In this context, the EAC should consider formulating credible procedures for countries to relax the fiscal criteria in the event of large economic shocks. Furthermore, the current EAMU timetable has also been overtaken by events, pointing to the need to develop a more flexible approach to the timing for introducing the new currency with an emphasis on credible and sustainable convergence.

Although the overall framework is broadly appropriate, the decision to redraft the EAMU protocol provides an opportunity for EAC countries to revise and strengthen the criteria. The criterion on the fiscal deficit excluding grants should be eliminated as a mandatory objective, but retained for fiscal surveillance purposes, particularly to evaluate revenue mobilization efforts. The protocol could also establish a wider set of indicative fiscal benchmarks. These supplementary indicators should assess the quality of public expenditures. Furthermore, EAC countries should also begin to track the nonresource primary balances to provide a more reliable measure of the impact of government policies on domestic demand. EAC countries should also establish explicit ceilings on gross public debt as part of a broader regional debt sustainability framework. There is also a need to improve the institutional framework underpinning fiscal policy, in particular, data reporting and coverage, as well as public financial management.

The EAC should look beyond the preadoption phase and consider the institutional framework once the single currency is finally adopted. EAC countries will need to give more attention to the institutional architecture needed to ensure the long-term sustainability of the new currency. They will have to establish credible fiscal rules and multilateral surveillance structures and enforcement mechanisms. There are a number of unresolved issues, including the development of regional risk-sharing mechanisms. Overlapping membership of regional organizations could also pose difficult questions in achieving convergence.

REFERENCES

Benedek, D., E. Crivelli, S. Gupta, and P. Muthoora, 2012, "Foreign Aid and Revenue: Still a Crowding Out Effect?" IMF Working Paper 12/186 (Washington: International Monetary Fund).

Buti, M., and A. Sapir (eds.), 1998, *Economic Policy in EMU* (Oxford: Clarendon Press).

Cecchetti, S., M. Madhusudan, and F. Zampolli, 2011, "The Real Effects of Debt," BIS Working Papers No. 352 (Basel: Bank for International Settlements).

Davoodi, H., 2012, *The East African Community after Ten Years: Deepening Integration*, Conference Proceedings (Washington: International Monetary Fund).

Dippelsman, R., C. Dziobek, and C. A. Gutiérrez Mangas, 2012, "What Lies Beneath: The Statistical Definition of Public Sector Debt," IMF Staff Discussion Note (Washington: International Monetary Fund).

International Monetary Fund, 2009, *The Implications of the Global Financial Crisis for Low-Income Countries* (Washington).

———, 2012, "Macroeconomic Policy Frameworks for Resource-Rich Developing Countries," IMF Staff Discussion Note (Washington, August).

Irwin, T., 2012, "Accounting Devices and Fiscal Illusions," IMF Staff Discussion Note SDN/12/02 (Washington: International Monetary Fund).

Kumar, M. S., and J. Woo, 2010, "Public Debt and Growth," IMF Working Papers No. 10/174 (Washington: International Monetary Fund).

Mundell, R. A., 1961, "A Theory of Optimum Currency Areas," *American Economic Review*, Vol. 51, No. 4, pp. 657–665.

Reinhart, C. M., and K. S. Rogoff, 2010, "Growth in a Time of Debt," *American Economic Review*, Vol. 100, No. 2, pp. 573–578.

CHAPTER 5

Implications of Monetary Union for National Fiscal Institutions in East Africa

RICHARD HUGHES

As discussed in the previous chapter, regional monetary integration requires enhanced fiscal coordination among member countries of the East African Community (EAC). Enhanced fiscal cooperation is needed in monetary unions in general for three main reasons. Over the long term, member states need to be prevented from running unsustainable fiscal policies that could undermine the long-term credibility of the common currency. In addition, member states need to ensure that the national fiscal stance is consistent with the region-wide monetary policy being pursued by the regional monetary authority. In the near term, member states need to rely on fiscal policy as the principle tool for managing domestic aggregate demand in the face of country-specific macroeconomic shocks.

Recognition of the need for enhanced fiscal coordination in monetary unions has prompted most common currency areas to adopt some form of fiscal convergence criteria applicable to all member states. To ensure national fiscal policies are sustainable over the long term, these convergence criteria typically take the form of upper limits on government fiscal deficit and debt. For example, the European Union's (EU's) 1997 Stability and Growth Pact required all member states to keep their fiscal deficits lower than 3 percent of GDP and debt below 60 percent of GDP.[1] To ensure that national fiscal policies also support macroeconomic stability over the medium term, these convergence criteria often also require member states to target a fiscal balance over the next three to five years. For example, the West African Economic and Monetary Union's (WAEMU's) 1999 Stability, Growth, and Solidarity Pact requires all member states to target a zero or positive fiscal balance (excluding grant-financed expenditure) over the medium term.[2] To allow national fiscal policy to support domestic demand in the face of country-specific macroeconomic shocks, these fiscal convergence

[1] Resolution of the European Council on the Stability and Growth Pact, Amsterdam, June 17, 1997 (97/C 236/01).

[2] Pacte de Convergence, de Stabilité, de croissance, et de solidarité, December 1999 (Règlement N° 11/99/CM/UEMOA).

criteria sometimes make explicit allowance for countercyclical fiscal policy. For example, in the 2005 revisions to its Stability and Growth Pact, the EU called for member state's medium-term fiscal policy objectives to be expressed in cyclically adjusted terms.

The effective monitoring and enforcement of these fiscal convergence criteria typically requires the harmonization of member states' institutional arrangements for fiscal reporting and budgetary management. Fiscal convergence criteria need to be applied consistently and fairly across member states. This requires, among other things, common definitions of "government," common bases for measuring their fiscal deficits and debts, common methodologies for measuring and adjusting for cyclical effects, and common time frames and formats for reporting fiscal data. If they are to be respected, fiscal convergence criteria also need to shape all aspects of national fiscal policymaking from budget preparation through to end-of-year financial reporting. This requires national budget frameworks that can meet the demands of rule-based fiscal policymaking. The need to harmonize institutional arrangements for national fiscal policymaking in common currency areas has prompted several monetary unions to adopt directives on the budget frameworks of member states. Beginning in 1997, the WAEMU has introduced six directives that set minimum standards for member states' annual budget laws, public accounting, budget classification, chart of accounts, summary fiscal reporting, and fiscal transparency.[3] The Central African Economic and Monetary Community (CEMAC) introduced a similar set of public financial management directives in 2008.[4] As part of its efforts to strengthen fiscal oversight and governance in Europe, the EU adopted in 2011 a new fiscal compact that included eight new regulations and directives regarding member states' budget frameworks and fiscal reporting arrangements.[5]

This chapter considers the implications of East African Monetary Union (EAMU) for national fiscal institutions in the EAC. In doing so it:

- discusses the implications of monetary integration for national fiscal institutions;
- reviews recent efforts to harmonize national fiscal institutions in monetary unions in the EU and in Africa (specifically CEMAC and the WAEMU);
- assesses the degree of harmonization between national fiscal institutions of the five EAC member states relative to the 27 member states of the EU; and
- recommends a series of actions to help EAC member states to prepare for enhanced fiscal cooperation in the context of eventual monetary union.

---

[3] WAEMU Directives 01,06,07,08,09,10/2009/CM/UEMOA, 2009.
[4] CEMAC Directives 01-06/11-UEAC-190-CM-17, 2011.
[5] EU Regulations No. 1173-7/2011, 2011, and Directives 2011/85/EU, 2011.

IMPLICATIONS OF MONETARY UNION FOR NATIONAL FISCAL INSTITUTIONS

As discussed in the previous section, monetary unions typically rely on a set of fiscal convergence criteria to promote fiscal policy coordination among member states. These often take the form of numerical limits and/or targets for fiscal deficits or government debt, and are typically set out in regional treaties, such as the EU's 1997 Maastricht Treaty or the WAEMU's 1994 Dakar Treaty. However, as long as fiscal policy remains the preserve of national governments, the surveillance and enforcement of regional fiscal rules depends on the quality and consistency of the institutional arrangements that govern fiscal policymaking in individual member states.

Translating regional fiscal rules into national fiscal outcomes requires strong legal, institutional, and procedural arrangements at each phase of the national fiscal policymaking cycle. As shown in Figure 5.1, one can identify six key fiscal institutions that need to be in place in all member states to ensure effective regional fiscal coordination across:

- fiscal responsibility legislation which translates regional fiscal convergence criteria into legally-binding *national fiscal rules*,
- *fiscal risk management* arrangements which ensure that national fiscal rules are met on a range of macroeconomic scenarios,
- *medium-term budget frameworks* which translate national fiscal rules into a multiyear plan for government revenue and expenditure,
- a *top-down sequence to budget preparation and approval* which ensures that annual budgets are consistent with government's medium-term budget plans,
- *expenditure controls* which ensure that annual budget limits are respected during execution, and
- *fiscal accounting, reporting, and audit arrangements* which ensure that fiscal convergence criteria are accurately monitored and consistently applied.

The rest of this section discusses how these national fiscal institutions support fiscal coordination in a monetary union.

National Fiscal Rules

Given that fiscal policy typically remains the competence of member states in monetary unions, regional fiscal convergence criteria need to be given legal effect in each member state. This is often done through the passage of some form of fiscal responsibility legislation that requires the government to state and adhere to one or more numerical fiscal targets or rules in preparing and executing its annual budget. These national fiscal rules are sometimes directly transposed from the regional fiscal convergence criteria themselves and are sometimes more stringent than those criteria.

The need for regional fiscal convergence criteria to be translated into national fiscal rules is reflected in the public financial management directives introduced by monetary unions in Europe and Africa. For example, Article 5 of the EU's

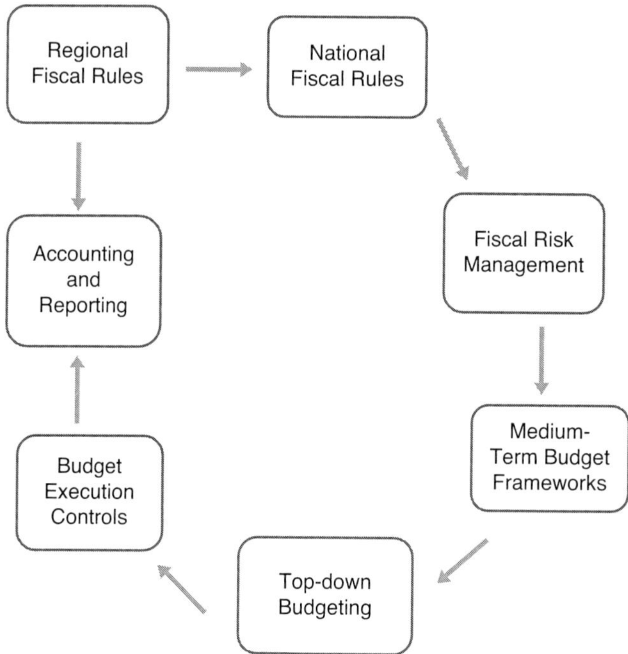

Figure 5.1 Implications of Monetary Union for National Fiscal Institutions

Source: Author.

2011 Budgetary Frameworks Directive requires each member state to "have in place numerical fiscal rules which are specific to it and which effectively promote compliance with its obligations deriving from the Treaty on the Functioning of the European Union."[6] In Central Africa, Article 7 of the WAEMU's Budget Directive required each member state to "define a medium-term fiscal objective which is consistent with the Central African Economic and Monetary Community convergence criteria."[7]

Experience with fiscal rules over the past decade has highlighted a number of desirable characteristics. Recent surveys of the performance of fiscal rules across different countries suggest that the most successful fiscal rules tend to be:

- enshrined in national legislation either in constitutions, through a free-standing fiscal responsibility law or via a clause in the national public finance or organic budget law;
- comprehensive in coverage so that they apply not only to the central government budget but to a broader definition of the public realm, such as the general government or public sector;

[6] European Council Directive 2011/85/EU, November 8, 2011.
[7] CEMAC Directive 01/11-UEAC-190-CM-22.

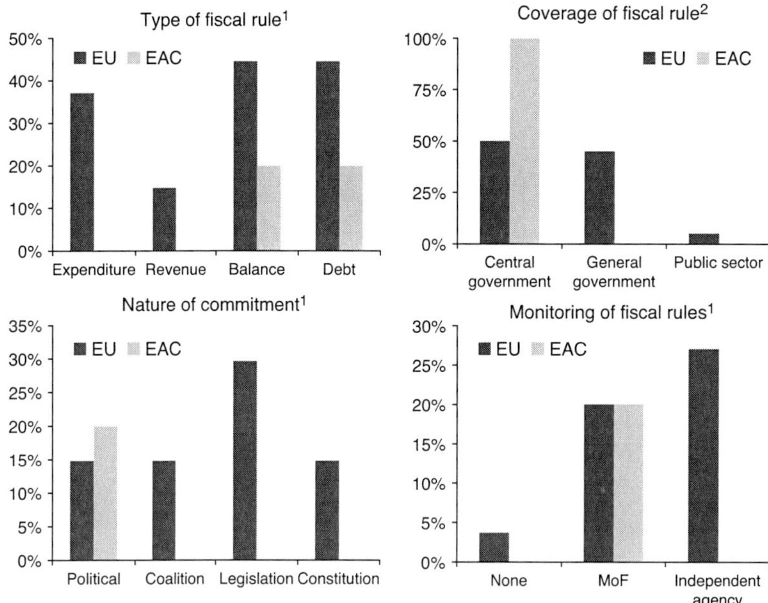

Figure 5.2 National Fiscal Rules in the European Union and East African Community

Sources: IMF, Fiscal Rules Database; and author's estimates.
Note: EAC = East African Community; EU = European Union; MoF = Ministry of Finance.
[1] Percent of all member countries.
[2] Percent of member countries with at least one fiscal rule.

- expressed over the medium-term (i.e., a period of 3–10 years); and
- monitored by independent fiscal institutions such as a fiscal council or parliamentary budget office.

By comparison with the EU, national fiscal rules are relatively rare and weakly specified in the EAC. As shown in Figure 5.2, around half of the EU members had at least one national fiscal rule in place compared with only one of the EAC's members (Kenya). The EU's fiscal rules tend to be broader in coverage, with around half applying to the general government or public sector. By contrast, Kenya's fiscal rules apply only to the central government. The EU's fiscal rules are also increasingly enshrined in national laws or constitutions, whereas Kenya's fiscal rule is merely a political commitment of the government. Independent fiscal agencies are playing an increasingly important role in monitoring government's compliance with their fiscal rules, although one EAC country, Uganda, has such an institution in place (the Parliamentary Budget Office).

Fiscal Risk Management

If member states are to adhere to regional and national fiscal rules, they need to ensure their fiscal settings are consistent with meeting those rules on a range of scenarios. This requires member state governments to have in place

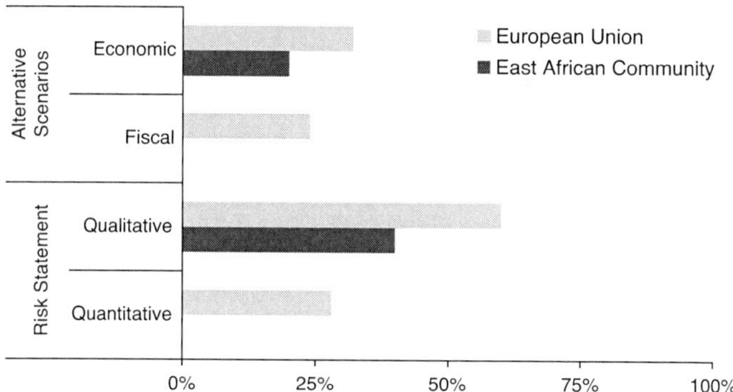

Figure 5.3 Fiscal Risk Reporting in the European Union and the East African Community (*Percent of member countries*)

Sources: Organization for Economic Cooperation and Development, Budget Practices and Procedures Database; and author's estimates.

mechanisms for evaluating the fiscal risks that can threaten the achievement of those rules. These mechanisms typically include the preparation of comprehensive fiscal risk statements, which evaluate both (1) the sensitivity of the government's fiscal forecast to changes in underlying macroeconomic assumptions; and (2) the estimate and disclosure of discrete risks to the public finances such as guarantees, public–private partnerships, and natural disasters.

The public finance directives of both CEMAC and the EU include obligations on their member states to report on fiscal risks. Section IV.1 of the 2011 CEMAC Directive on Fiscal Transparency and Good Governance includes a requirement that member governments' "annual budget documents presented to Parliament be accompanied by a report which identifies and evaluates the principal fiscal risks."[8] Article 4 for the 2011 EU Budget Frameworks Directive requires all member states to provide macrofiscal sensitivity analysis showing the "paths of the main fiscal variables under different assumptions as to growth and interest rates."

The disclosure of fiscal risks remains relatively underdeveloped in both the EU and the EAC. As shown in Figure 5.3, just under one-third of EU member states include alternative macroeconomic scenarios in their budget documentation, and one-quarter present the fiscal implications of these alternative macroeconomic assumptions. Among the five EAC member countries, only one routinely provides alternative economic scenarios in their budget documentation and none routinely provides alternative fiscal scenarios. Disclosure of discrete fiscal risks is more advanced in both regions with 60 percent of EU members states and 40 percent of EAC member states including some qualitative discussion of specific fiscal risks in their budget documentation. However, less than 30 percent of EU member states and no EAC ones routinely publish quantified fiscal risk statements as part of budget documentation.

[8] CEMAC Directive 06/11-UEAC-190-CM-22.

Medium-Term Budget Frameworks

Medium-term budget frameworks are a set of institutional and procedural arrangements through which governments commit to a particular path or plan for expenditure over a period beyond the annual budget horizon. In the context of monetary unions, such frameworks provide an institutional mechanism for member states to demonstrate that their current fiscal policy settings are consistent with respecting both regional and national fiscal rules not only in the budget year but also in the years beyond. The frameworks vary in time horizon, institutional coverage, degree of commitment, and level of detail. However, experience suggests that the simplest and most effective medium-term budget framework models cover a three- to five-year horizon, focus on controlling expenditure at either the aggregate or ministerial level, and set binding multiyear limits on expenditure which are only revised every two, three, or four years. By contrast, more indicative medium-term budget framework models that provide detailed multiyear projections of expenditures at the program or line item level and which are revised on an annual or infra-annual basis seem to contribute little to the establishment of multiyear fiscal discipline. The public finance directives of the CEMAC, the WAEMU, and the EU oblige their members to produce indicative medium-term budget frameworks. Article 53 of the 1997 the WAEMU directive on annual budgets requires each members' annual budget document be accompanied by "multi-year expenditure planning documents which forecast, for a period of a least three years, the indicative evolution of expenditure and outcomes expected under each program."[9] Article 9 of the EU's 2011 budget frameworks directive stipulates that all member states "shall establish a credible, effective medium-term budget framework providing for the adoption of a fiscal planning horizon of at least 3 years."[10]

While medium-term budget frameworks are more prevalent in the EAC than the EU, they tend to be the less binding in the EAC than the EU. As shown in Figure 5.4, all five EAC countries have in place medium-term budget frameworks that cover the next three years as opposed to only 64 percent of EU countries. At the same time, the frameworks in the EAC tend to focus on detailed planning of expenditure at the program or line item level rather than maintaining overall expenditure discipline at the aggregate or ministerial level as in the EU. This is partly a function of the influence of external donors on the design of the medium-term budget frameworks in East Africa who regard these frameworks as a means to coordinate externally and domestically financed activity in particular sectors or for specific projects. The emphasis on detailed, bottom-up planning over broad, top-down discipline in the design of medium-term budget frameworks in the EAC can also be seen from the prevalence of rolling or indicative frameworks among EAC countries. In fact, all revise their medium-term budget framework ceilings every year compared with the EU, where 28 percent of countries'

[9] WAEMU Directive 06/2009/CM/UEMOA, 2009.

[10] EU Directive 2011/85/EU, 2011.

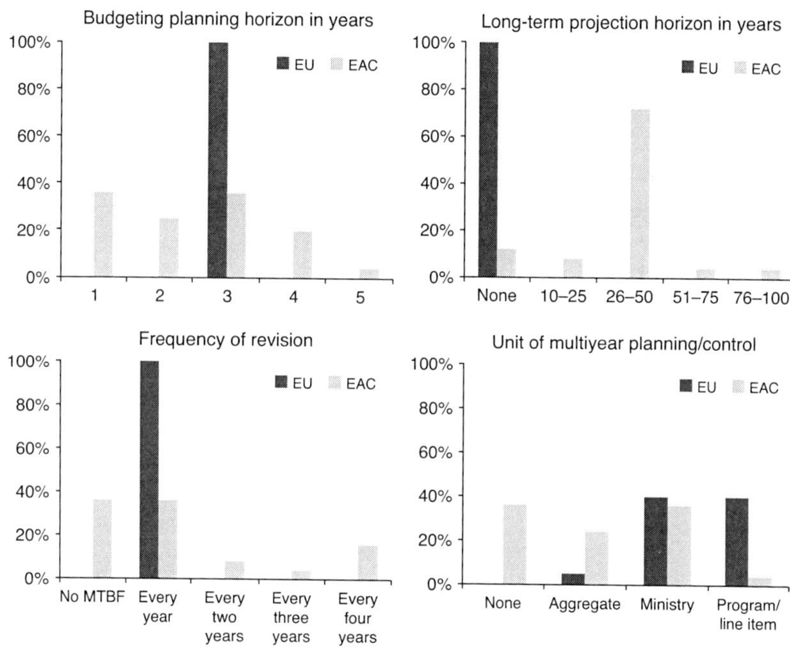

Figure 5.4 Medium-Term Budget Frameworks in the EU and EAC *(Percent of member countries)*

Sources: Organization for Economic Cooperation and Development, Budget Practices and Procedures Database; and author's estimates.
Note: EAC = East African Community; EU = European Union; MTBF = medium-term budget framework.

frameworks fix multiyear expenditure ceilings that are not revised for two, three, or even four years.

Top-Down Budgeting

If the multiyear expenditure limits set out in a member state's medium-term budget framework are to be respected, the preparation and approval of annual budgets need to follow a top-down approach. This implies that the government makes a binding decision on expenditure at the aggregate level before deciding on the allocation of expenditure between individual ministries or programs. Where a country also has a medium-term budget framework in place, the expenditure limits set out in the previous year's framework usually provide the initial limit for the following year's budget. Comparisons between bottom-up and top-down approaches to annual budget preparation suggest the latter are more effective in ensuring that the approved budget is consistent with the government's medium-term budgetary and fiscal objectives.

A top-down approach to budgeting is a requirement under the CEMAC, the WAEMU, and EU public finance directives. Article 57 of the 2009 the WAEMU directive on the annual budget requires member states to submit a medium-term economic and budgetary strategy to parliament for a budget orientation debate

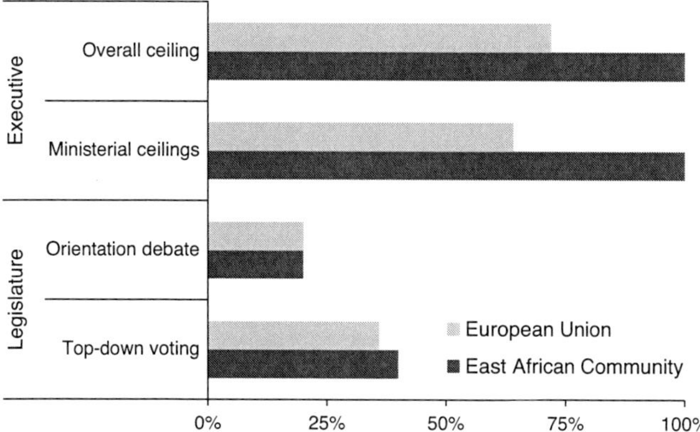

Figure 5.5 Top-Down Budgeting in the East African Community and the European Union (*Percent of member countries*)

Sources: Organization of Economic Cooperation and Development, Budget Practices and Procedures Database; and author's estimates.

before the end of the second trimester of a year. The EU's 2011 directives on strengthening economic and fiscal surveillance applies a top-down approach at the regional level by introducing the so-called European semester in which member states submit their medium-term budget frameworks to the European Council and European Commission for their approval in April prior to preparing their annual budgets.[11] Article 10 of the budget frameworks directive then requires that member states' "annual" budget legislation shall be consistent with the provisions of the medium-term budget framework. Specifically, revenue and expenditure projections and priorities resulting from the medium-term budgetary framework shall constitute the basis for the preparation of the annual budget.[12] Finally, to ensure that the final budget approved by the national legislatures of member states remains consistent with the medium-term budget framework limits approved at the start of the budget process, both CEMAC (Article 54) and the WAEMU (Article 59), and directives on the annual budget prohibit legislatures from proposing amendments to the annual budget law that increase expenditure or reduce revenues.

Top-down budgeting is more prevalent among EAC countries than in the EU, though in both regions the budget process in the legislature continues to follow a largely bottom-up process. As shown in Figure 5.5, all EAC member state governments set overall and ministerial ceilings at the start of the budget process. This compares with only 72 percent of EU countries setting overall ceilings and 64 percent setting ministerial ceilings. At the same time, only 20 percent of EU and EAC countries' legislatures hold formal budget orientation debates. And in

[11] EU Regulations No 1175/2011, 2011.

[12] EU Directive 2011/85/EU, 2011.

only 36 percent of EU countries and 40 percent of EAC countries do legislatures first approve the overall expenditure level before voting on the allocation of expenditure between ministries, programs, and line items.

Budget Execution

Once the annual budget has been approved by parliament, hopefully in line with regional and national fiscal rules, member-state governments need to have in place the expenditure controls that ensure budgetary limits are not exceeded during execution. Robust expenditure controls regimes comprise a range of preventative, compensatory, and punitive measures for dealing with overspending. Among the most important are systems of commitment control that prohibit line ministries from making expenditure commitments that exceed their appropriations. Where these controls fail to contain emergent expenditure pressures, most governments set aside a small, unallocated contingency reserve within their budget to fund these unforeseen expenditures. In cases where this contingency reserve is exhausted and it becomes necessary to exceed one or more appropriations approved by parliament, governments should be obliged to seek prior legislative approval via a supplementary budget. If ministries are found to have exceeded their appropriations without prior approval of parliament, then administrative, financial, or criminal penalties should be imposed on the parties responsible.

Provisions concerning expenditure control feature more prominently in the public finance directives of the CEMAC and the WAEMU than those of the EU. Both the CEMAC and the WAEMU directives on their annual budgets devote an entire chapter to budget execution. The CEMAC directive has the most elaborate set of requirements in this area which, among other things, obliges member states to (1) grant the minister of finance the power to nullify appropriations in cases where the government's fiscal objectives are threatened, (2) identify the officers in each ministry responsible for the enforcement of expenditure controls in each ministry and public entity, (3) ensure that systems are in place to prevent expenditure commitments from exceeding appropriations released to each ministry or entity, (4) require governments to seek legislative approval via a supplementary budget for any breach of the limits approved by parliament, and (5) have in place an escalating set of sanctions to be levied against those officers responsible for financial mismanagement. By contrast, the EU 2011 budget frameworks directive concerns itself primarily with budget preparation and fiscal reporting with no specific provisions relating to budget execution.

Controls over budget execution are another area where EAC countries lag behind those in the EU, despite the latter's lack of any specific regional obligations in this area. The organic budget laws of 40 percent of EAC member countries permit the government to overspend their original budget up to a certain amount before they are obliged to seek parliamentary approval of a supplementary budget. By contrast, only 8 percent of EU countries include such a loophole in their organic budget laws. Central contingency reserves tend to be less common in the EAC than in the EU with only two of the five EAC members including some

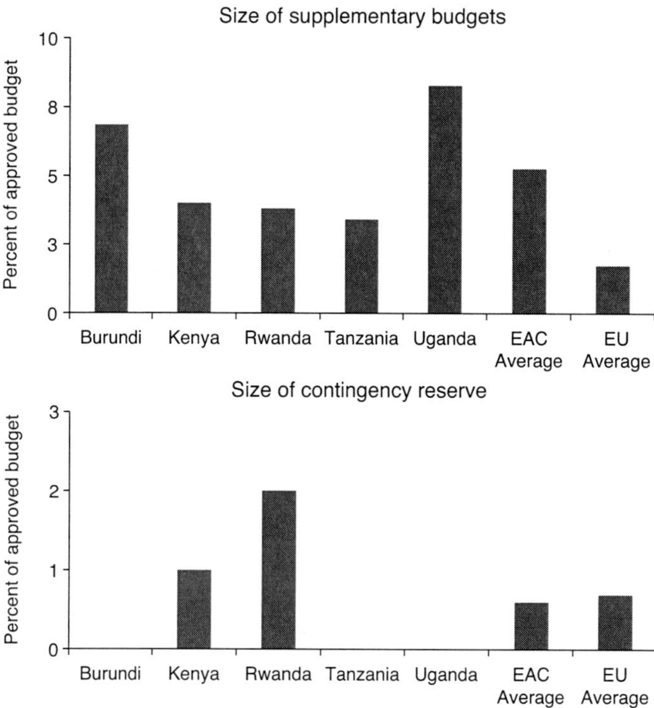

Figure 5.6 Budget Execution in the East African Community (EAC) and the European Union (EU)

Sources: Organization of Economic Cooperation and Development, budget practices and procedures database; and public expenditure and financial accountability reports.

central reserve provision in their budgets compared with 80 percent among EU countries. As a result, supplementary budgets tend to be more common and larger among EAC countries than in the EU, with the average overspending among EAC countries at over 5 percent per year, compared with an average of less than 2 percent among EU countries (Figure 5.6).

Fiscal Reporting

The effectiveness of the surveillance of member states' compliance with regional fiscal convergence criteria depends on the quality of national fiscal reporting practices. The consistent application of regional fiscal rules requires standardized institutional coverage, accounting basis, and formats for fiscal reporting. The proactive surveillance of member states' compliance with those rules requires common standards for the frequency and timelines of reporting. To ensure the integrity of reported data, fiscal data should be prepared in line with international statistical and accounting standards, disseminated by an independent statistics agency (in the case of fiscal statistics), and audited by an independent audit body (in the case of financial accounts).

The CEMAC, the WAEMU, and EU public finance directives all place considerable emphasis on the harmonization of fiscal reporting standards and practices across their members. Five of the six CEMAC and the WAEMU public finances directives relate to various aspects of fiscal reporting including member states' transparency, accounting standards, budget classifications, charts of accounts, and summary fiscal statements.[13] The EU budget frameworks directive requires all member states to report in line with the EU's own statistical standards, the 1995 European System of Accounts. The directive also instructed the European Commission to assess the suitability of requiring all member states to adopt International Public Sector Accounting Standards as the basis for the production and complication of public accounting data.

Fiscal reporting practices are considerably more comprehensive and harmonized across EU member states than among EAC countries. As shown in Table 5.1, the coverage of fiscal statistics among EAC countries is limited to either budgetary central government or central government in four of the five EAC countries. Only Rwanda publishes fiscal data covering the whole of general government (consolidating central government, local government, and social security funds). By contrast, in the EU all member states are required to report fiscal data for the general government. Fiscal reports among EAC countries typically include only cash transactions, though Burundi and Uganda report some accrual-based flows. Coverage of stocks is even more limited with only two countries providing some balance sheet information. In the EU, member states are obliged to report stocks of financial assets and liabilities. Reporting of fiscal data is relatively frequent among EAC countries with three of five countries publishing data on a monthly basis, though sometimes with a lag of two months or more. In the EU, member states are required to report data only on a quarterly basis, although many report more frequently. Finally, assurances of data integrity are general weaker among EAC countries than in the EU. Only two of five EAC countries undertake the full set of consistency checks (between flow measures, between stock measures, and between flows and changes in stocks), which are required among EU member states. In none of the five EAC countries is responsibility for compilation and dissemination of fiscal data vested in an independent agency, whereas this is a requirement of all EU member states.

CONCLUSIONS

A concerted effort to enhance and harmonize national fiscal institutions among EAC countries is required if the fiscal convergence criteria underpinning any monetary union are to be respected. The effort will require reforms in all member

[13] CEMAC Directives 02,03,04,05,06/11-UEAC-190-CM-17, 2011. WAEMU Directives 01,07,08,09, 10/2009/CM/UEMOA, 2009.

TABLE 5.1

Fiscal Reporting in the East African Community (EAC) and European Union

	EAC Member Countries					
	Burundi	**Kenya**	**Rwanda**	**Tanzania**	**Uganda**	**European Union**
Coverage of institutions	Central government	Budgetary central government	General govern-ment	Budgetary central govern-ment	Central government	General government
Coverage of flows	Commitment	Cash	Payment orders	Cash	Modified cash	Modified accrual
Coverage of stocks	None	None	None	Financial liabilities	Financial assets and liabilities	Financial assets and liabilities
Frequency of reporting	Monthly	Monthly	Quarterly	Quarterly	Monthly	Quarterly
Consistency checks	Flows	Stocks, flows, and stock flow	Stocks	Stocks	Stocks, flows, and stock flow	Stocks, flows, and stock flow
Statistics agency	Ministry of Finance	Semiauto-nomous agency	Ministry of Finance	Ministry of Finance	Semiauto-nomous agency	Independent agency

Source: Authors.

states and at all stages of the budget cycle. The foregoing analysis identifies the need for action to:

- require all EAC countries to legislate for comprehensive, medium-term, and independently monitored fiscal rules that are consistent with meeting EAC-wide convergence criteria and can be temporarily exceeded only in exceptional circumstances;
- routinely analyze, disclose, and manage fiscal risks arising from both macroeconomic shocks and discrete sources;
- adopt more binding medium-term budget frameworks that ensure national fiscal rules are supported by credible, multiyear budget plans;
- adopt a more top-down approach to the discussions and voting on the annual budget in national legislatures to ensure that budgets approved by parliaments are consistent with government fiscal rules and medium-term budget plans;
- require all EAC countries to make adequate provision for contingencies during budget preparation and tighten the rules around the use of supplementary budgets; and
- improve the comprehensiveness, timeliness, and reliability of fiscal reporting.

Based on the experiences of other monetary unions, bringing about the harmonization of national fiscal practices will require the development of a national budget frameworks directive. Such a directive, modeled on those of the EU, the CEMAC, and the WAEMU, would need to specify the minimum requirements of the budget frameworks of those EAC member states wishing to join the monetary union. This directive needs to be supported by a program of technical and mutual assistance to help countries bring their fiscal institutions and practices into line with the requirements of the directive. The implementation of the budget frameworks directive also needs to be monitored and enforced through a process of peer review by EAC member countries and/or central monitoring by the EAC secretariat.

REFERENCES

Harris, J., R. Hughes, G. Ljungman, and C. Sateriale, "Medium-Term Budget Frameworks in Advanced Economies: Objectives, Design, and Performance," in *Public Financial Management and It's Emerging Architecture,* edited by Marco Cangiano, Teresa Curristine, and Michel Lazare (Washington: International Monetary Fund), chapter 4.

International Monetary Fund, 2009, "Fiscal Rules: Anchoring Expectations for Sustainable Finances," IMF Policy Paper (Washington, December).

Radev, A., and P. Khemani, 2009, "Commitment Controls," IMF Technical Notes and Manuals 09/04 (Washington: International Monetary Fund).

CHAPTER 6

Building a Framework to Harmonize Monetary Policy

ARMANDO MORALES

This chapter discusses a strategy and a timetable for harmonizing national monetary policy frameworks across the East African Community (EAC). The priority for harmonization is to cement credibility in the introduction of a monetary union, especially by ensuring low and stable inflation. Harmonization therefore needs to be gradual, given still-significant differences across EAC partner states in the degree of exchange rate flexibility, the use monetary instruments, the weight given to monetary aggregates, and the role of policy interest rates in monetary operations.

EAC interest in monetary union has historical precedent. The East Africa shilling was adopted in 1922 by countries ruled by the British (Kenya, Uganda, Tanganyika, and, in 1936, Zanzibar). After independence, local currencies were introduced, but they continued being fully and freely convertible into sterling in Kenya, Uganda, and Tanzania to continue benefiting from explicit and implicit subsidies. Sterling depreciation in the late 1960s and early 1970s and slow progress in economic integration across EAC countries led to the disintegration of the sterling area in 1972. Following a period of divergence of inflation targets and interest rates, the East African Currency Area was formally ended in 1977 (Graboyes, 1990).

Plans to relaunch the EAC initiative in the 2000s, including the adoption of a currency union in 2012, proved ambitious. The focus has moved to develop a protocol for monetary union, with a 10-year preparation period before moving to a currency union starting on the date of approval of the protocol. Although the extent and pace of harmonization will be a joint decision by countries in the monetary union, a comprehensive effort should ensure the proper allocation of technical skills, the establishment of a track record to build credibility well ahead of union, and clear progress in integrating financial markets and infrastructure.

Differences in national monetary policy regimes present a wide selection of practices that need to be harmonized. This comprises the legal frameworks governing national central bank activities and the range of tools used for monetary policy control. In principle, the East African Monetary Union (EAMU) protocol envisions that participating national central banks would be subordinate to a new East African Central Bank and that national central banks would implement monetary operations on behalf of the regional monetary authority in support of the monetary union. In anticipation of that, the central banks would benefit from conducting monetary policy using the same set of monetary tools.

The next section looks at the role of harmonization of monetary policy frameworks in the move to a currency union in the EAC, the relevant priorities, achievable outcomes, and sequencing issues. The following sections look at experiences in other currency unions and regional blocks, discuss legal and institutional frameworks in the EAC, analyze monetary policy frameworks and compare monetary operations and instruments, and identify critical areas in the preparation of a common currency area.

HARMONIZING MONETARY POLICY FRAMEWORKS

Harmonization Role and Priorities

What is the role of harmonization of monetary policy frameworks in the move to a currency union? In planning for this, participant countries must acknowledge the preexistence of national central banks with a given track record on monetary policy effectiveness. This is a significant difference with most existing currency unions, which are in practice a continuation of arrangements established before their member countries became independent. Therefore, a relevant question for EAC countries is whether some degree of harmonization of existing monetary policy frameworks would support the transition to a currency union. In principle, harmonizing some features of monetary policy frameworks should help the transition to a currency union for the following reasons:

- Harmonizing the framework for monetary operations requires commitments that in turn would provide an opportunity to establish a track record of coordination and give credibility to the eventual currency union.
- Harmonizing policy frameworks will facilitate the coordination of policies in the face of common shocks, helping to minimize the differences between individual countries' business cycles and contributing to a smoother transition over the medium term.
- Working together toward achieving low and sustainable inflation would provide immediate benefits to EAC countries by minimizing the risks of instability as monetary union approaches.

But harmonizing monetary policy regimes can, in itself, be a complex undertaking requiring careful planning and an assessment of the costs and benefits at every stage of the process. Its complexity depends in part on the successor exchange rate regime for the new common currency. If maintaining exchange rate flexibility under the new currency is the preferred option, a gradual, multiyear process of harmonization will be required. But if an exchange rate peg is preferred, harmonization requirements may be less pressing. Furthermore, the higher the envisioned degree of decentralization across national central banks, the more harmonization will be needed to minimize the risk of coordination failures.

The priority for harmonization should be to achieve low and stable inflation. Recent experience with rapid acceleration of inflation in several EAC countries shows that challenges remain in achieving this goal. Mechanisms to ensure strict fiscal discipline will be important to this effort, by enhancing monetary policy effectiveness and minimizing the possibility of disruptions. However, harmonizing national monetary policy frameworks at the outset does not seem advisable until significant progress is made on keeping inflation low. Differences across EAC countries in the degree of exchange rate flexibility, the way monetary instruments are used, the weight given to monetary aggregates, and the role of policy interest rates in monetary operations are still significant.

Scope for Harmonization

Current monetary policy regimes and practices differ across EAC countries. The exchange rate regime is classified as floating in only three—Kenya, Tanzania, and Uganda. Policy interest rates are binding for monetary operations Kenya, Rwanda, and Uganda. And both Kenya and Uganda are moving away from hard targets on reserve money. These differences reflect a range of underlying factors:

- *Legislative history.* Legal frameworks for central bank operations reflect historical national priorities. Recent changes in national central bank laws have been driven by institutional initiatives for reform (in Rwanda) and by broader political reforms, such as Kenya's new constitution.
- *Extent of donor funding.* For Rwanda and Burundi, foreign aid inflows are a significant source of fiscal revenue and foreign exchange. Here, monetary policy is dominated by issues related to the management of the monetary and foreign exchange repercussions of these inflows into these economies.
- *Financial depth and development.* In Kenya and Uganda, which are the most financially developed in the region, the behavior of economic agents appears to have become more sensitive to changes in interest rates. Therefore, these countries give more weight to interest rate changes in their policy decisions.
- *Instances of fiscal dominance.* Although central bank financing of national budgets is generally subject to defined limits in EAC countries, instances of exceptional financing can arise, usually when efforts to fund budgets using market-based instruments result in excessive interest costs. Where central banks are required to provide ad hoc funding in excess of defined limits, monetary policy autonomy and effectiveness can be undermined.

Transition: Starting and End Points

The extent of the harmonization challenge depends, in part, on the effectiveness of monetary policy regimes. As discussed later, central bank approaches to monetary policy design and implementation are evolving within the EAC. Although the inflation record in member countries has improved over the last decade, inflation reached double digits again in 2012.[1] Improving the internal consistency of countries' monetary policy frameworks will require fully market-determined interest rates, clear government financing arrangements, and transparent communication of policies, even if national monetary frameworks are not fully aligned.

The extent of the harmonization challenge also depends on the successor exchange rate regime for the new single currency.[2] Under a currency peg, the institutional challenges are greatly reduced, because of the elimination of monetary independence. Under this regime, the operating responsibilities of national central banks would be limited, and the need for harmonized or coordinated activities reduced. By contrast, if the EAC maintains exchange rate flexibility under the new currency, the East African Central Bank and national central banks will face the challenge of operating an independent monetary policy. This will require the use of a range of monetary policy instruments and operations to achieve the inflation objective—activities that would need to be harmonized across national central banks to prepare for operating in a decentralized system.

Sequencing Harmonization

The timeline for the move to a monetary union will have implications for harmonization. The timetable for strengthening the effectiveness of monetary policy, harmonizing legal frameworks, and developing common monetary policy practices and instruments will need to be consistent with the decision on the starting date for monetary union. In Europe's Economic Monetary Union (EMU), institutions to guide monetary integration were established at an early stage, and a program of reforms was adopted on a multiyear basis. This chapter implies that sufficient time is available in advance of monetary union to allow a sequencing of the preparatory reforms to monetary frameworks, probably right after the enactment of the protocol.

The following considerations are important for the design of the timetable for harmonization, and will be the reference for the recommendations:

- *Costs and benefits of reforms*. Reforms are, by their nature, costly to implement. Agreement at a national and regional level takes time, experts may need to be hired, new institutional structures will need to be launched, and new skills will need to be learned, among other things. At the same time, poorly designed reforms can be counterproductive and may lead to undesired outcomes. Given these considerations, monetary policy reforms should prioritize areas where benefits are high, risks of inaction are great, or where an early start is needed to allow for the fine-tuning of outcomes.

---

[1]The EAC 2012 average inflation was 15 percent against a median of 6.5 percent for sub-Saharan Africa.

[2]Options for the new currency regime are considered in Chapter 8 by C. Adam and others.

- *"Variable geometries" alternatives should be considered.* Because of the disparity of practices across EAC countries, there may be a case for focusing on harmonization in some areas across a smaller group of countries at the outset, and bringing in remaining countries once workable practices have been developed. This two-speed convergence approach could be adopted either in the run-up to monetary union or as part of the monetary union process itself, with some countries joining ahead of others; for example, by setting a set of preconditions based on agreed convergence criteria.
- *Flexibility in the introduction of reforms* should strike a balance between trying to make fast progress in harmonization and keeping commitments realistic, taking into account disparities across countries. A "do-no-harm" approach will help gain acceptance of agreements during harmonization.

Complementary efforts will support progress in the harmonization of the conduct of monetary policy:

- Fiscal arrangements should be given priority to facilitate a steady reduction of the extent of fiscal dominance. The possible use of fiscal rules should be assessed, including enforcement mechanisms, taking into account institutional capacity constraints and individual reform plans (e.g., fiscal decentralization in Kenya).
- Statistics should be upgraded under common definitions. This is especially important for measures of inflation, chiefly on headline and core inflation. Other important areas include the classification of monetary, financial, and fiscal accounts.
- The regulatory framework should be gradually adapted to internationally recognized and agreed practices. This includes capital account regimes, capital market regulations, and prudential frameworks for financial activities that take into account the evolving nature of the work in this area.

LESSONS FROM OTHER CURRENCY UNIONS

International experience shows that harmonization should be consistent with the choice of exchange rate regime and the desired level of autonomy of the central bank under monetary union. Experience suggests that aligning the policy environment in EAC countries before the implementation of monetary union with its envisaged arrangements should minimize the probability of disruptions. Experience also shows that harmonization can be supportive of macro policies prior to adopting a common currency. Harmonization can help "discover" the parity between currencies in the absence of an external anchor and ensure consistency between centralized policies and decentralized operations. Harmonization can also facilitate capacity improvement to ensure effective coordination between national central banks.

Choice of Exchange Rate Regime

The exchange rate regimes of existing monetary unions are a variety of free floats, pegs, and anchor currencies. The euro and the South African rand both float. The franc in the CFA franc zone comprising the West African Economic and Monetary Union and the Central African Economic and Monetary Community is pegged to the euro, and the Eastern Caribbean Currency Union is pegged to the U.S. dollar. Current plans for an EAMU are consistent with exchange rate float experiences; the historical experience of the failed East Africa shilling is consistent with the exchange rate peg experiences.

In floating regimes, the currency of the largest economy has served or still serves as an anchor for a common monetary policy:

- The South African rand remains the anchor for the Common Monetary Area formed by some members (South Africa, Lesotho, Swaziland) of the Southern Africa Customs Union. The arrangement functions as an effective currency board.
- The deutschmark served as the effective anchor for the European Union's exchange rate mechanism for several years in the lead up to the euro. Tensions from diverging macroeconomic developments (growth, inflation, fiscal policies) and the Bundesbank's understandable focus on German economic developments led some countries to reconsider their commitment to the exchange rate mechanism until a common currency was adopted. The euro operates as a floating global reserve currency, with minimal intervention in support of the currency.

The period between the adoption of a common exchange rate arrangement and monetary union exceeded 10 years in both cases. The Common Monetary Area was formed in 1986, 14 years after the formation of the Rand Monetary Area. In the case of the European Union, the period between the adoption of an exchange rate mechanism and full monetary union was 20 years (1979–1999).

Centralized versus Decentralized Monetary Operations

Decentralized monetary policy operations require upfront harmonization and integration. In such an arrangement, monetary and exchange rate policies are decided centrally in existing currency unions, but they differ substantially in the degree of centralization of monetary policy and foreign exchange operations. The European System of Central Banks and European Central Bank statute explicitly stipulates that operations should be delegated to national central banks "to the extent deemed possible and appropriate." At the other end of the spectrum is the Eastern Caribbean Currency Union, which has no national central banks but a "resident representative" in each country. It is worth noting that in currency peg regimes there were no national central banks in place at the outset.

The degree of centralization has important implications for resource requirements and prior harmonization and regional integration efforts in the lead up to a monetary union. The less centralized are monetary policy operations, the more important is the role of harmonization of monetary policy frameworks before the implementation of a common monetary policy. Progress with harmonization will help reduce the scope for inconsistency between centralized policy and decentralized operations that could undermine the efficacy of monetary policy.

Central Bank Autonomy

Effective fiscal rules for monetary financing of member governments are a critical foundation for a currency union and the credibility of a common monetary policy. The stance of fiscal policy remains a sovereign decision for member countries in a monetary union. All monetary unions have strict limits in place on the use of central bank advances and direct financing to governments. Such restrictions have been binding and in general have been observed, although the CFA franc zones found it necessary to tighten the rules and gradually phase out the use of central bank advances entirely.

Limited financing options may also help enforce fiscal discipline. The smaller Common Monetary Area countries do not have access to financing from the South African Reserve Board and are not able to issue rand-denominated debt. Also, bilateral agreements with the South African Reserve Bank require 100 percent foreign exchange coverage for their domestic currency base. Spending has therefore been limited to domestic revenue and proceeds from the revenue-sharing arrangement of the South African Customs Union.

Harmonization Experience

Harmonization requirements are more relevant for floating union-wide currencies. The EMU experience shows that harmonization in a floating currency regime is more demanding because, without an external anchor, macroeconomic stability relies on the effectiveness of instruments and operations. An established track record in the use of common instruments and operations would help minimize uncertainty and reinforce credibility ahead of the adoption of a common currency.

EMU harmonization involved intensive multiyear coordination. As noted, 20 years elapsed between the adoption of an exchange rate mechanism and full monetary union, with a strong regional institution to lead integration launched 5 years ahead of monetary union. The European Monetary System, with its exchange rate mechanism (a system of intervention corridors around bilateral exchange rates) was in place until 1979. In 1989, the broad design of monetary union was approved by the European Council, and the European Monetary Institute was created in 1994, with the convergence criteria agreed upon three years later and the common currency born in 1999.

Monetary policy effectiveness was important to the EMU transition. Reflecting the strong anti-inflation discipline of the Bundesbank, the deutschmark quickly became a de facto anchor of the exchange rate system, even though the nominal anchor was the European Currency Unit, a weighted basket of the participating currencies. In fact, to stay in the exchange rate mechanism "snake," participating central banks ceded a good deal of monetary policy sovereignty to the Bundesbank.

The creation of the European Monetary Institute played a key role in facilitating the harmonization efforts for EMU. The institute led the bulk of the detailed, technical preparatory work between 1995 and 1997.[3] Technical staff provided reports on strategic and implementation issues to be approved by policymakers. Work on a policy framework and the convergence criteria took place separately from monetary policy operational issues, with the latter broken into five substantive themes: monetary policy instruments and their preunion harmonization, decentralized execution of liquidity management, integration of money markets, structural demand for money and central bank balance sheets, and integration of interbank markets and payment systems.

LEGAL AND INSTITUTIONAL FRAMEWORKS GOVERNING THE CONDUCT OF MONETARY POLICY

Decentralized versus Centralized Arrangements

A decentralized model for EAC member states has a number of advantages (European Central Bank, 2010). National expertise located in national central banks will continue to be available both to the governors, as participants in the governing council, and to the working of the system of central banks as a whole. At an early stage, a decentralized model helps minimize disruption in the transition. To function properly, national central banks will have to be legally subordinate to the East African Central Bank in areas where the monetary authority has competence. Specific advantages of this model are:

- National central banks would contribute to the preparation of briefing material reflecting a national perspective, and comments from that perspective on material prepared in the East African Central Bank.
- The governors, directors, and senior officials of national central banks would represent the EAMU to a domestic audience, and they would need support from staff in their national central bank to carry out this role.
- National central bank researchers would contribute analysis and statistics in close contact with reporting institutions, including ensuring compliance with requirements, timely delivery, and data quality control.
- Monetary and foreign exchange market operations also require close contact with national financial institutions, and knowledge of national financial markets and instruments (including acceptable collateral).
- In case of dispersion of country risk premiums across EAC countries once monetary union is in place, it would help to keep open market operations conducted by national central banks, at least until macroeconomic convergence progresses significantly.

---

[3]Before the European Monetary Institute, a committee of central bank governors met at the Bank for International Settlements in Basel, supported by a small group of economic analysts.

Key Differences in National Legal Frameworks

Harmonization of institutional arrangements across EAC partner states would benefit from a common understanding on legal mandates and central bank autonomy. Ultimately, the design of legal and institutional frameworks depends on the desired relationship between the East African Central Bank and treasuries. Two important elements of central bank autonomy concern policy coordination with treasuries and central bank lending to the government. The draft EAMU Protocol in principle aims at regulating coordination between monetary and fiscal policies and envisages the gradual phasing out of national central bank lending to governments.

Central Bank–Treasury Relations

The legal frameworks of central banks in the EAC show certain distinctive features regarding central bank autonomy relative to the treasury. While some jurisdictions have strong legal safeguards in place to protect their national central bank against political influence while facilitating policy coordination with the treasury, other jurisdictions explicitly authorize the treasury to give central banks binding policy instructions. Although in the area of monetary financing the legal frameworks of central banks are less divergent, terms of temporary financing including the maximum amount to be lent to the government and the repayment modalities differ. Moreover, in practice, central bank financing to the government has at times been accommodated by resorting to a flexible application of legal restrictions (Annex Table A6.1).

Legal Mandates

EAC central banks mandates diverge mainly in their legal powers, in particular for monetary policy instruments. In the EAC, legal frameworks differ in the way they govern the use of indirect monetary policy instruments (i.e., open market operations, credit operations, and minimum reserve requirements):

- For open market operations, the differences relate to the type of instruments (government versus corporate securities) and type of legal operations (buying and selling versus repurchase agreements).
- Although all EAC central banks may enter into credit operations, the legal framework diverges for counterparties, maturity, collateral requirements, and their creditor positions.
- The legal framework for minimum reserve requirements needs further harmonization for the group of financial institutions subject to such requirements, discretion regarding certain types of institutions or liabilities, remuneration of minimum reserves, and whether the law sets a maximum reserve ratio.

The statutory objectives of EAC central banks are similar but not synchronized. All EAC jurisdictions expect their central banks to ensure price stability and all have financial stability responsibilities and promote government economic policies. However, central bank acts have different objectives and/or priorities, such as for financial supervision.

The institutional allocation of powers over foreign exchange is different in EAC jurisdictions. Not all the legal frameworks specify who is responsible for determining the foreign exchange regime. Legal frameworks assign different roles for treasuries in policy formulation. And in most jurisdictions the law does not ensure that the foreign exchange regime and policy should be consistent with the objective of price stability.

Legal Safeguards

Legal safeguards for central bank autonomy should be strengthened in all the central bank acts of EAC member states. With a view to establishing a strong autonomy framework in the East African Central Bank, the legal frameworks of national central banks should explicitly confirm their autonomy and include safeguards to protect their operational and financial autonomy and the autonomy of their decision makers. A number of key areas that need to be addressed are as follows:

- Statutory autonomy is not always ensured in EAC jurisdictions. In most countries, there is no explicit prohibition on instructions, and in only three is there an explicit statement that the central bank has operational and financial autonomy.
- Financial autonomy should be strengthened. Although all EAC central banks appear to have budgetary autonomy, rules on profit determination and the treatment of unrealized revaluation gains, profit distribution gains, and recapitalization requirements and modalities lack clarity, compromising the financial autonomy of EAC central banks.
- The personal autonomy of EAC central bank officials should be improved. Legal frameworks in EAC jurisdictions diverge on qualification requirements, grounds for dismissal, appointment and dismissal procedures, due process requirements, and length of mandates.

MONETARY POLICY FRAMEWORKS AND THEIR EFFECTIVENESS

Key Differences in National Monetary Policy Frameworks

The path toward monetary union must take into account differences in existing national monetary policy frameworks and their effectiveness. As discussed in the following, EAC countries currently give different emphasis to the monetary aggregates, exchange rates, and interest rates at the heart of their monetary policy frameworks, and these approaches need to be harmonized under a single currency. The success of this regime change will, in turn, likely reflect the effectiveness of the preexisting monetary frameworks in delivering low and stable inflation.

The evolution of inflation and monetary aggregates show some commonalities across EAC countries. In particular, inflation has remained below 10 percent for all countries except during external shocks. By the same token, inflation across the EAC has accelerated faster than other regions hit by shocks, including sub-Saharan

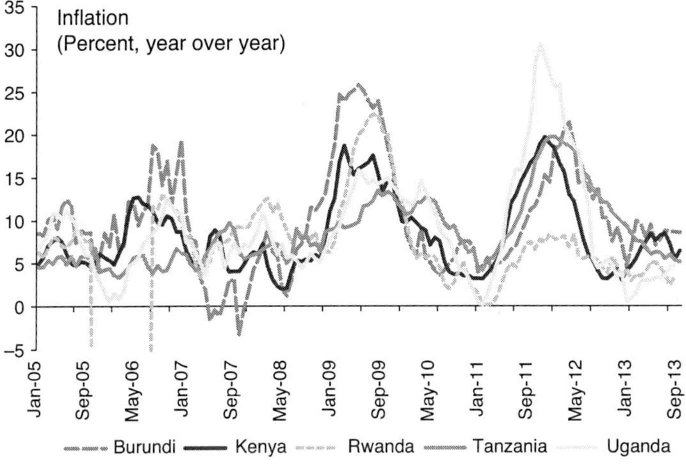

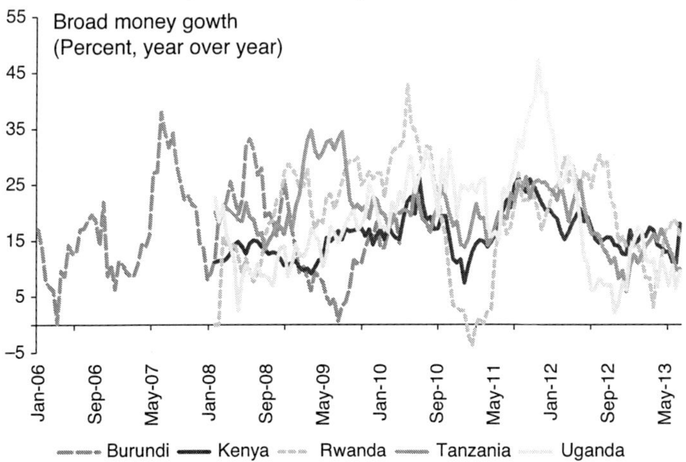

Figure 6.1 Inflation and Broad Money Growth in East African Community Countries

Source: National central banks.

Africa, suggesting delays in the appropriate monetary policy response. Broad money growth also shows some correlation explained by an increase in financial intermediation in the region that is somehow reversed when inflation shocks hit their economies (Figure 6.1).

By contrast, policies across EAC countries have only shown some degree of convergence in recent years. The lack of correlation among policy rates also reflects differences in design and implementation. Changes in base money appear volatile and heterogeneous across countries, to a large extent explained by differences in

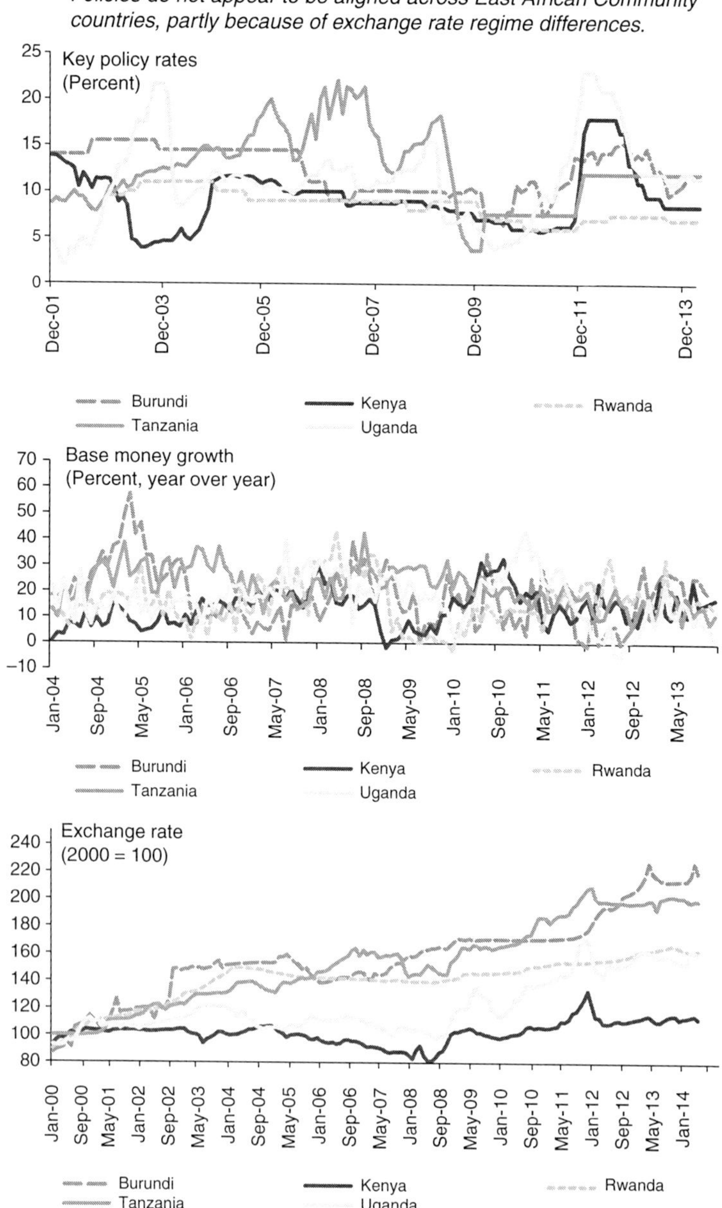

Figure 6.2 Policy Rates, Base Money, and Exchange Rates in East African Community Countries

their de facto exchange rate regimes. In turn, these explain different trends in the evolution of international reserves, despite a joined commitment to increase their level. In short, despite progress in recent years, some differences across the monetary policy frameworks of EAC countries are significant (Figure 6.2).

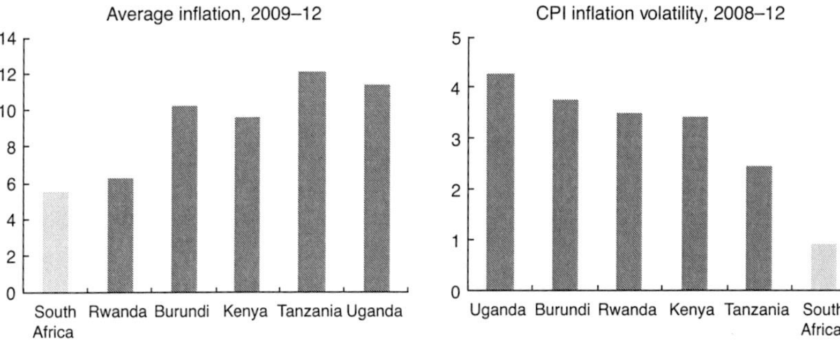

Figure 6.3 Inflation and Inflation Volatility in South Africa and the East African Community

Source: National central banks.
Note: CPI = consumer price index.

More progress is needed in all monetary frameworks in EAC countries to achieve low and stable inflation. Before the 2010–11 episode of food price inflation, all countries showed average inflation of around 10 percent, higher than their country targets. Differences in policy frameworks do not seem to affect the level of inflation, although higher inflation volatility in Burundi and Rwanda may be associated with their larger exposure to external price shocks. Assessing the implementation of policy frameworks and the transmission of policy decisions across EAC countries will help understand the challenges to improve monetary policy effectiveness (Figure 6.3).

Differences in Exchange Rate and Interest Rate Policies

No country in the region uses exchange rates as a de jure nominal anchor; however, the degree of exchange rate flexibility is different across countries. Exchange rate regimes in Kenya, Tanzania, and Uganda have been classified as floating for the last four years in the IMF's Annual Report on Exchange Arrangements and Exchange Restrictions. Burundi and Rwanda are currently classified as managed floating and stabilized, respectively. Kenya allows its exchange rate to respond to market pressures to a much larger extent than other EAC countries, about 25 percent compared to 10 percent of Uganda in recent times, and 8 percent in Tanzania (Figure 6.4) (Slavov, 2011).

Use of monetary aggregates and policy interest rates is evolving. The Central Bank of Kenya adopted in 2011 a new monetary policy framework that gives more prominence to the policy interest rate. Under the new monetary policy framework, the Central Bank of Kenya uses the policy interest rate to guide interbank rates to achieve its net domestic assets operational target. The Bank of Uganda is moving to a form of inflation targeting "lite." Under this framework, the operating target will be a publicly announced central bank interest rate centered on the seven-day interbank rate. The central bank will refrain from

	Degree of EMPs translated into exchange rate moves (EMP coefficient)[1]	
	1999–2010	2005–10
Burundi	0.07	0.02
Rwanda	0.00	0.00
Tanzania	0.08	0.08
Kenya	0.25	0.24
Uganda	0.07	0.10

Figure 6.4 Measuring Exchange Rate Flexibility in East African Community Countries

Source: Slavov (2011).
Note: EMP = exchange market pressures.
[1] EMP coefficient between zero and 1.

99 percent significant.
90 percent significant.
Not significant.

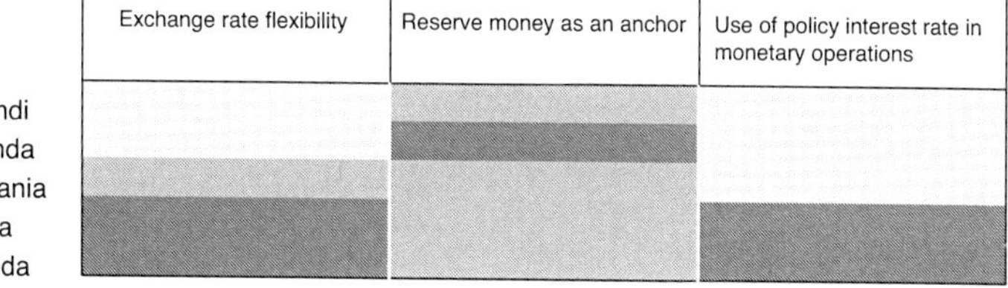

Figure 6.5 Features of Monetary Policy Frameworks in East African Community Countries

Source: Author.
Note: Dark gray denotes full flexibility.

direct central bank financing of the deficit. The Banque de la République du Burundi, the National Bank of Rwanda, and the Bank of Tanzania operate under a money targeting framework (Figure 6.5).[4]

Generally, EAC countries are increasingly relying on interest rates as financial markets develop and dependence on foreign exchange inflows decline. In 2012, Rwanda and Burundi committed to allowing greater exchange rate flexibility and promoting the development of their foreign exchange markets. And Kenya and Uganda are moving toward a greater role for the policy interest rate, initially introduced as a signaling device.

[4] Central banks operating under a reserve money program use M3 as a nominal anchor or intermediate target (except Burundi, which uses M2).

Differences in Monetary Policy Transmission and the Macroeconomic Environment

A two-way interaction between increasing financial intermediation and monetary policy transmission can be seen across EAC countries. Money multipliers and velocity become unstable with financial development and less relevant for transmission, which is generally confirmed by studies conducted by EAC central banks and the International Growth Center.[5] In Kenya and Uganda, increasing focus on interest rates in policy decisions has resulted in lower interest rate volatility (before, that is, the recent surge in inflation), which in turn favors financial intermediation.

The choice of monetary policy frameworks in EAC countries is conditioned by the nature of central bank–treasury relations, the financial environment, and the structure of the balance of payments (Figure 6.6). The higher the government's use of monetary financing, the lower its reliance on market securities for monetary operations. Also, the higher the excess reserves, the lower the elasticity of market interest rates to changes in money market rates. And the higher the share of foreign exchange flows channeled out of interbank markets, the lower exchange rate flexibility. A number of challenges in the coordination between monetary and fiscal policy remain. Government monetary financing is a concern. It appears much larger in Burundi than in the other EAC countries. Significant central bank financing for the government limits the scope for relying on market instruments to conduct monetary policy. At times, EAC governments are reluctant to borrow on market terms due to concerns over collusion, preferring instead to use central bank financing, sometimes under ad hoc arrangements that undermine central bank room to maneuver in conducting monetary policy.

- Burundi and Rwanda absorb large foreign inflows relative to foreign exchange receipts and fiscal revenue. The size of these inflows relative to the size of the economy explains some reluctance to allow for exchange rate flexibility. Not surprisingly, Kenya shows higher exchange rate flexibility, consistent with the insignificant share of foreign aid inflows in total foreign exchange receipts.
- Kenya also shows the highest degree of financial deepening, coupled with the lowest structural liquidity surplus across EAC countries. Liquidity injection operations through foreign exchange purchases, open market operations, and/or the overnight lending facility are more relevant in Kenya relative to countries with low financial deepening and high structural liquidity surpluses. Here, the challenges are more related to mopping up liquidity effectively to minimize commercial banks' excess reserves.

---

[5]Velocity and multiplier are unstable in Kenya (Sichei and Kamau, 2010), and the money multiplier is unstable in Rwanda and Uganda in the short term. For Tanzania, the multiplier is stable in the long term, but not in the short term (Adam and Kessy, 2010), while velocity is generally stable (Adam and others, 2010).

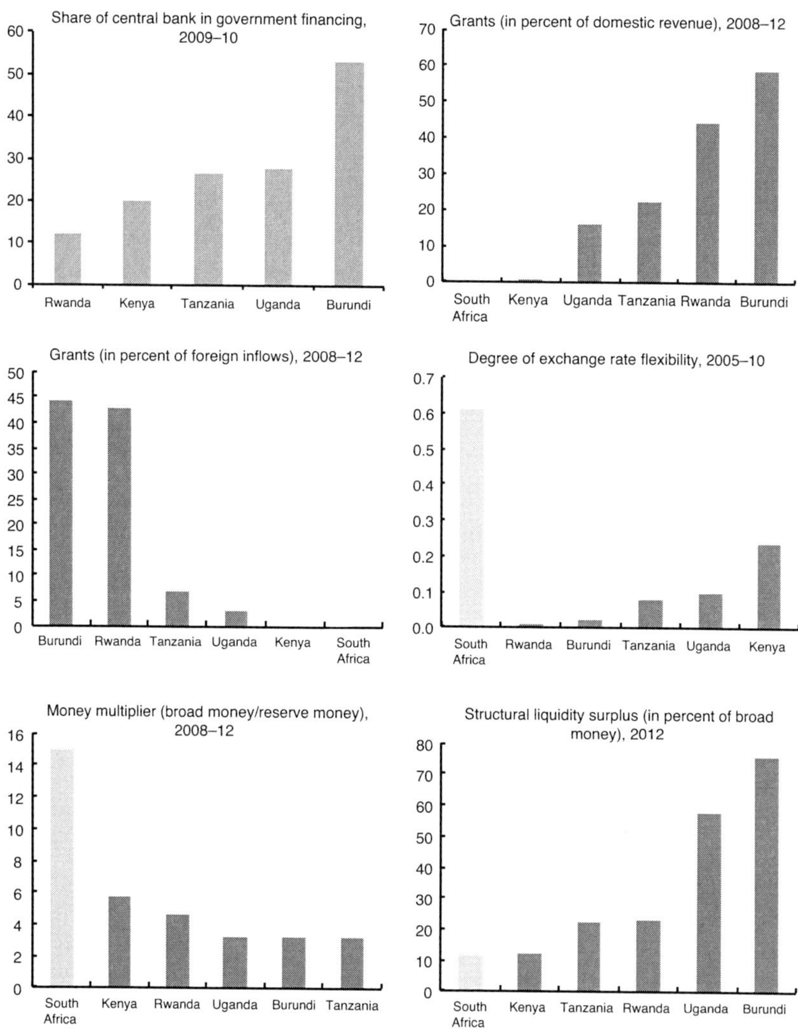

Figure 6.6 Macroeconomic Factors Conditioning the Choice of Monetary Policy Frameworks in East African Community Countries

Source: Author.

Apparent weakness in monetary transmission channels in EAC countries is partly explained by an accommodating policy bias that is inconsistent at times with the inflation objective. An accommodating policy bias may have hampered the impact of policies on market behavior. For example, Davoodi, Dixit, and Pinter (2013) find that reserve money and the policy rate often move in conflicting directions. In the presence of shocks, countries tend to maintain an accommodating bias long after evidence of demand pressures emerges. Andrle and others (2013) find that monetary policy in Kenya during the 2011 food inflation episode remained accommodating despite significantly low interest rates and diminishing global demand weakness.[6] Stepanyan (2012) finds a similar pattern in EAC countries as a whole, relative to other sub-Saharan African countries.[7]

Anecdotal evidence points to the pursuit of multiple objectives as a factor explaining lack of consistency of monetary policy in EAC countries at times. In particular, central banks often use policy rates to try to persuade commercial banks to keep lending interest rates low to help accelerate credit growth. Also, the impact of high credit growth on inflation is often understated on the grounds that fast credit growth is required to enhance financial deepening and, as such, should not threaten stability.[8] Furthermore, government financing needs occasionally lead central banks to make decisions not always consistent with stabilization targets.

Preliminary evidence suggests that, despite overall weak transmission, interest rates, credit, and the exchange rate are effective channels from policy decisions to prices and economic activity. By adapting methodologies to low-income countries, the evidence suggest that the specific features of EAC economies enable monetary transmission in a manner that is different from the standard literature.[9] Incorporating high volatility of output, flexible wages, and an accommodating bias to a monetary policy model for Kenya still leads to features of monetary policy transmission common to emerging markets (Andrle and others, 2012). Combining different specifications of vector autoregression models, Davoodi, Dixit, and Pinter (2013) find that the exchange rate and the credit channels from policies to inflation are active for Kenya.

---

[6]Andrle and others (2013) model transmission of monetary policy in Kenya using a small dynamic-linear monetary model with calibrated parameters adapted to the specific features of Kenya, incorporating food and nonfood price dynamics via two separate Phillips Curves and a Taylor-type monetary policy rule.

[7]Using a panel structural vector autoregression model that allows for dynamic heterogeneity among countries, Stepanyan (2012) finds that EAC countries (as well as Ethiopia) show food inflation shocks have a more lingering impact on consumer prices, with more prolonged second round effects and higher inflation inertia.

[8]Actually low financial intermediation was found irrelevant for monetary policy transmission for a sample of emerging market countries. The willingness to allow exchange rate flexibility was found to be a more important determining factor (Saizar and Chalk, 2008).

[9]As in other low-income countries, the way monetary policy transmission channels in EAC countries function is likely different from that in the standard literature. In particular, the interest rate channel may drive credit and consumption decisions rather than investment, and the exchange rate channel transmission may take place through inflation pressures expectations and portfolio decisions rather than through exports, given the low export base of low-income countries and their low sensitivity to exchange rate changes.

MONETARY POLICY INSTRUMENTS AND PRACTICES

Key Differences in the Use of Monetary Instruments

Major differences exist among EAC countries in the role of the policy rate, the design of liquidity absorption tools, and reserve requirement systems (Figure 6.7). EAC countries have similar arrangements for injecting liquidity, but no standing deposit facilities are in place in any EAC country. This is partly explained by chronic large excess reserves held by commercial banks. Policy decisions are generally made by a monetary policy committee.

Liquidity Forecasting

Liquidity forecasting capabilities need to be strengthened in all EAC countries. High-frequency information on government transactions remains deficient and complicated by the absence of a single treasury account (except in Rwanda and Burundi). The use of market indicators is still evolving. However, in Kenya and Uganda, selective market information is incorporated into their short-term projections.

Policy Decision Making

All EAC central banks have a monetary policy committee responsible for formulating and implementing monetary policy, but their composition and mandates differ. Monetary policy committee provisions are established in legislation in Kenya and Tanzania, with the ministry of finance having a larger role in Kenya, where it appoints four external members (two external members are appointed in Tanzania). In Uganda, all members come from the central bank (in Tanzania, they all have voting power), and in Rwanda, the monetary policy committee is composed of members from the central bank except for one representative from the university. However, in Tanzania the permanent secretaries from the ministries of finance of Tanzania Mainland and Zanzibar and the accountant general attend as invitees. Frequency of meetings ranges from weekly (Uganda) to bimonthly (Kenya, Tanzania). All EAC central banks would benefit from improved analytical support, communication mechanisms, and, in some cases, information flows to facilitate a more informed decision making.

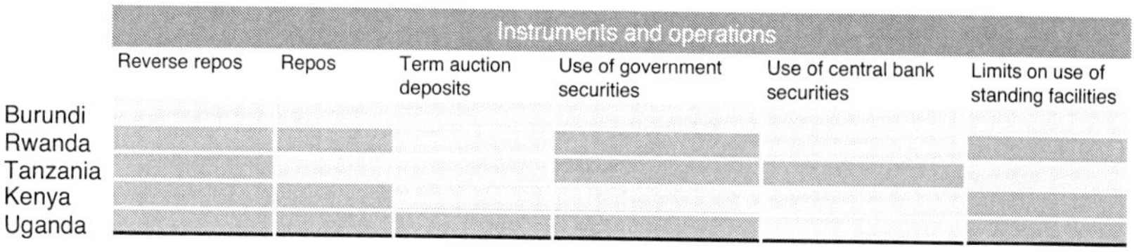

	Instruments and operations					
	Reverse repos	Repos	Term auction deposits	Use of government securities	Use of central bank securities	Limits on use of standing facilities
Burundi						
Rwanda						
Tanzania						
Kenya						
Uganda						

Figure 6.7 Features of Monetary Instruments and Operations in East African Community Countries

Source: Author.
Note: Dark grey = yes.

CENTRAL BANK CREDIT TO THE GOVERNMENT

Central banks in the region provide direct advances to governments, in most cases with a ceiling set as a percent of government revenues. Interest is charged on credits except in the case of the Bank of Uganda. Governments use this facility intensively, exceeding legal ceilings occasionally.

Policy Interest Rates

The role of the policy rate differs across countries reflecting differences in their monetary policy frameworks. The Central Bank of Kenya, National Bank of Rwanda, and Bank of Uganda set their policy rates independent of market rates. The Bank of Uganda defines the policy rate as the target around which the bank guides interbank rates. The Central Bank of Kenya is moving in the same direction, but still emphasizes the policy rate's role as a signaling device. All EAC central banks link their policy rate to their corresponding standing lending facility rates. Under the Central Bank of Kenya's monetary policy framework, interest rates on repo/reverse repo operations use the policy rate as a ceiling/floor. In Rwanda, an interbank interest rate corridor guides interest rate developments, with the National Bank of Rwanda policy rate playing a signaling role.

Reserve Requirements

Key features of reserve requirements differ significantly across EAC countries. Differences include the following (Figure 6.8):

- Required reserve ratios range from 3 percent in Burundi to 10 percent in Tanzania, applied uniformly to their deposit base (except in Tanzania where the reserve ratio for government deposits is 30 percent).
- The reserve base includes domestic and foreign currency deposits in all countries, including government deposits. But in Rwanda, the base also includes payable accounts.
- Eligible reserve assets consist of deposits at the central bank in all five EAC countries, plus 10 percent of vault cash in Uganda for banks with more than 10 branches (5 percent for the rest). In Tanzania, required reserves are deposited in a designated account.
- Reserves on foreign currency deposits are denominated in the domestic currency in Kenya, Tanzania, and Uganda, and in foreign currency in Rwanda. In Burundi, both domestic and foreign currency can be used.
- Average deposits are used for the computation of requirements in all countries except Tanzania. The maintenance period ranges from 7 days in Rwanda to 30 days in Burundi and Kenya. In Burundi and Tanzania, the reserve base are not lagged, which complicates the liquidity management of banks.
- Required reserves are not remunerated in any EAC country. Penalties on reserve deficiencies vary across EAC central banks.

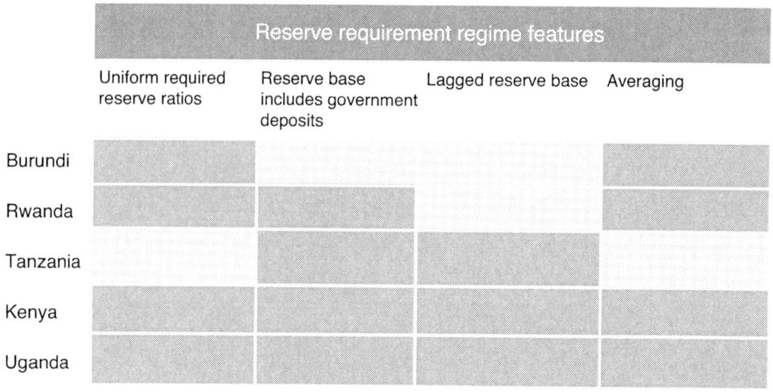

Reserve requirement regime features

Uniform required reserve ratios
Reserve base includes government deposits
Lagged reserve base
Averaging

Burundi
Rwanda
Tanzania
Kenya
Uganda

Figure 6.8 Reserve Requirements in East African Community Countries

Source: Author.
Note: Dark grey = yes.

Banks in all five EAC countries maintain considerable excess reserves; indeed, more than required. However, differences in design and the lack of development of interbank markets explain differences in precautionary reserves and, therefore, the magnitude of "free" reserves other than for precautionary motives is difficult to gauge. Moreover, the distribution of excess reserves is uneven, with a few small banks often tapping central bank resources.

Liquidity Injection and Mop-up Tools

Liquidity injections are conducted mainly through reverse repos of government securities and foreign exchange purchases across EAC countries.[10] Foreign exchange purchases are used for the provision of liquidity by all countries. Burundi uses collateralized seven-day loans instead of reverse repos. For other countries, the tenor of reverse repo operations ranges from 7 days in Kenya and Rwanda, to overnight to 62 days in Uganda.

Mop-up instruments show more differences across countries than instruments for liquidity injection. All central banks use foreign exchange sales explicitly or implicitly to mop up liquidity, extensively in Burundi and Rwanda, less frequently in Kenya. The Central Bank of Kenya, Bank of Uganda, and National Bank of Rwanda are also equipped with repo operations, and the Bank of Uganda also uses term auction deposits. No government securities are issued for liquidity management purposes. The Bank of Tanzania uses government securities,

[10] Regardless of the terminology used by each central bank in the region, in this report "repos" are transactions to absorb liquidity and "reverse repos" are transactions to inject liquidity. For example, Tanzania denominates repo to transactions where exchange of government securities actually does not take place.

Treasury bills for debt and liquidity management, and Treasury bonds for debt management. The government bears the sterilization costs in Rwanda and Uganda, unlike the Banque de la République du Burundi, and the Central Bank of Kenya. In Tanzania, the central bank and treasury share sterilization costs based on a memorandum of understanding.

Standing Facilities

All EAC central banks have lending standing facilities in place, but no deposit facilities. Maturities range from overnight in Kenya to up to three months in Uganda. Access to overnight lending is unlimited in principle, but subject to collateral. Most central banks require government securities as eligible collateral, but the National Bank of Rwanda and Banque de la République du Burundi also accept promissory notes and commercial paper. In Kenya, Rwanda, and Uganda, interest rates charged for use of these facilities are set relative to the policy rate (policy rate plus 6 percent in Kenya and plus 4 percent in Rwanda and Uganda). Typically, the interest rate charged on these facilities constitutes a ceiling for interbank interest rates. In Burundi and Tanzania, standing facility interest rates are linked to market rates.

Recently, access to lending facilities has been limited in some cases out of concerns over significant demand for liquidity in times of high inflation. In Uganda, the central bank exercises discretion in the provision of liquidity through its standing facility beyond the equivalent of 25 percent of the borrower bank's reserve requirement. In Kenya, the use of this facility more than twice in a week is subject to further scrutiny by the central bank. In Rwanda, access to this facility is entirely subject to the central bank's discretion.

LOOKING AHEAD

Harmonizing Monetary Policy Frameworks

Harmonizing monetary policy frameworks before the adoption of the common currency would enhance credibility in the process. Achieving and maintaining low inflation before a monetary union is established would increase the credibility of the new central bank and thus reduce the cost of moving to a new framework. In turn, a successful transition will provide an effective anchor to consolidate gains in achieving price stability. The move to a common policy framework will benefit from clear progress in aligning financial development across EAC countries. Thus, complementary measures to remove obstacles for financial development and integration across EAC countries should be a key component of the strategy to harmonize monetary policy frameworks.

Significant progress in other elements of the convergence strategy needs to be reached to support the move to a common monetary policy framework. In particular, government monetary financing should decline significantly to buttress the effectiveness of existing monetary policy frameworks. Likewise, the external position should be strengthened to help contain excessive exchange rate volatility.

Moving to a common monetary policy framework will require low and stable inflation to be achieved for a sufficiently long period to make it credible.

A hybrid arrangement with increasing reliance on policy interest rates and flexible exchange rates may be more appropriate. A hybrid framework should ensure that all countries will be in a position to accumulate international reserves in line with regional commitments. Common full-fledged inflation targeting does not appear feasible in the immediate term, as this would require some track record of using interest rates to guide monetary policy. And this is still a work in progress in Kenya and Uganda,

Any arrangement should give priority to the accumulation of foreign exchange by EAC central banks as an important source of permanent liquidity. The operations framework and the exchange regime should be consistent with the planned accumulation of international reserves by the central banks. These alternative arrangements could use monetary aggregates as an intermediate step while international reserves increase to a sufficiently high level. In Kenya, a ceiling on net domestic assets and a floor on net international reserves have proved useful to guide monetary policy decisions.

A two-speed approach to convergence of monetary policy frameworks would facilitate moving ahead with harmonization plans. Countries where economic agents have revealed sensitivity to central bank interest rate decisions—Kenya, Uganda, and perhaps Tanzania—may coordinate the adaptation of their frameworks to the new realities of the market, while countries in transition to a more flexible exchange rate (Burundi, Rwanda) may not need to change their operational targets until progress with harmonization in other areas is well advanced.

Harmonizing the Conduct of Monetary Policy

Several steps can be taken while improvements in macroeconomic convergence take hold (Figure 6.9). Although further progress in macroeconomic convergence will help consolidate stability, especially by reducing government monetary financing, some critical steps could be taken at the outset, namely the implementation of the East African Monetary Institute, the harmonization of features of some existing instruments, and the harmonization of rules for central bank financing of the government. This should be accompanied by decisive action to reduce inflation.

A concerted effort to pay increasing attention to market signals as markets develop is advisable. A strategy to harmonize monetary policy frameworks in the long term focusing on achieving low and stable inflation with available tools would be of benefit, as would assessing the evolving role of interest rates with the view of gradually allowing for more exchange rate flexibility.

The strategy to harmonize the conduct of monetary policy will be influenced by the choice of the transitional exchange rate arrangement in the path to monetary union. If the two-speed approach option is agreed upon, implementation of a transitional exchange rate arrangement would need to be delayed until the

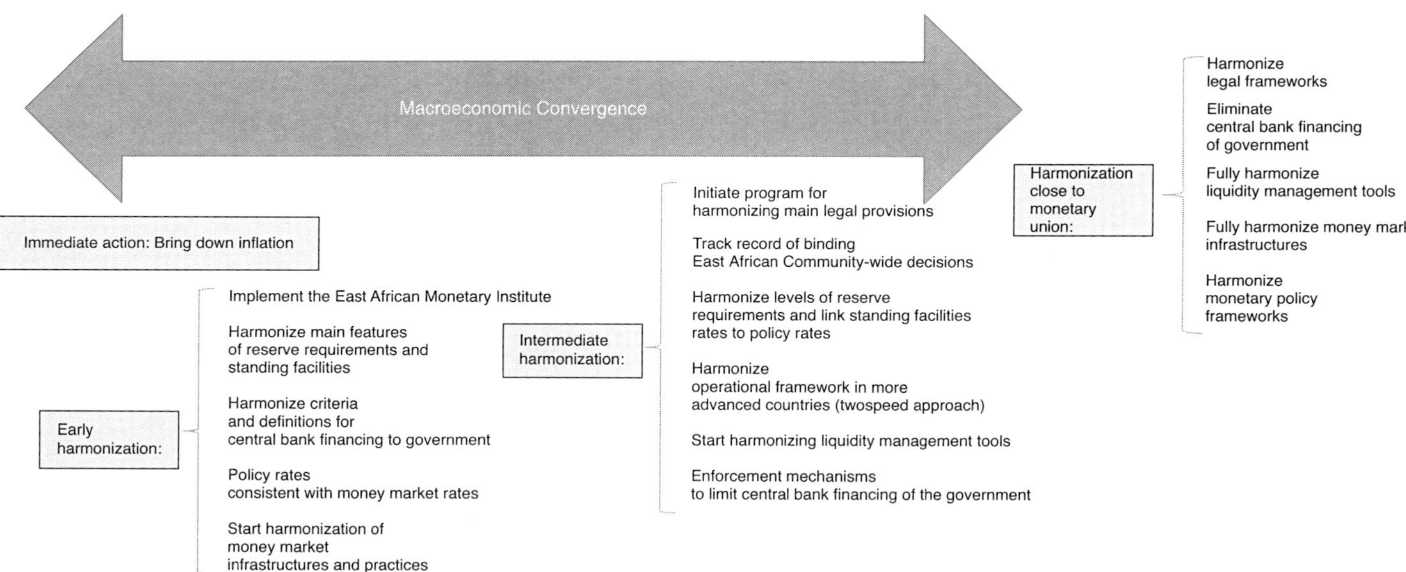

Figure 6.9 Strategy to Implement a Framework for Harmonizing the Conduct of Monetary Policy in the East African Community

countries using a de facto exchange rate anchor felt comfortable in allowing the exchange rate to float.

Harmonizing practices for temporary central bank financing of government operations should be adopted at an early stage, and followed by a more comprehensive agreement on limiting central bank financing to EAC governments that may or may not be validated by changes in national legislation. However, following agreement among EAC members, the EAMU protocol should be explicit in limiting financing to the government under all possible modalities and clear in the definitions to be used (national governments, public entities, and so on) to avoid loopholes that may weaken the perception of the degree of commitment to minimize fiscal dominance under a currency union. Eventually, an agreement on a schedule to set binding limits to central bank financing to the government, restricted to the provision of overdraft facilities based on uniform criteria, would help to introduce discipline in the implementation of monetary policy.

Harmonizing Central Bank Instruments and Operations

As a general approach, the harmonization of existing instruments should be undertaken, and this should start in areas that facilitate a smooth transition, ensuring that harmonization does not interfere with the current national monetary policy frameworks in place. A plan to gradually harmonize the main features of reserve requirements should be introduced at this stage. Harmonizing key features of standing lending facilities would also be feasible and desirable. Harmonizing these features is not incompatible with differences in financial development. EAC central banks should conduct an assessment of pros and cons of the choice of liquidity absorption tools.

Initiatives to harmonize and integrate market infrastructures should start early; specifically:

- Goals on upgrading and harmonizing money market infrastructures and practices will be needed. Improving money market infrastructures (payment and settlement systems, frameworks for repurchase agreements, and so on) will ensure that the capacity to inject/absorb liquidity is comparable across countries before taking more significant steps toward a currency union.
- Decisive steps toward integrating regional money markets would be supportive of harmonization efforts. This would require the harmonization of capital account regimes, market infrastructures and practices, capital markets, and financial prudential frameworks. Structural and regulatory impediments to interbank and money market integration could usefully be eliminated in a gradual manner to allow intraregional financial flows without causing disruption in local markets.

EAC countries should exchange views regularly on their experiences with liquidity forecasting and on the preparations for monetary policy committee meetings. In particular, a common approach to improve analytical support of the monetary policy committee should help countries to acquire a better understanding of market reaction to policy decisions and will also be valuable in informing harmonization plans. The analytical support should include full use of market indicators and a continuous effort to upgrade communication mechanisms and information flows based on the regional experience.

In the medium term, harmonization efforts should build up from plans initiated at the early stage:

- Levels of reserve requirements can be harmonized after a period accumulating experience under harmonized regimes.
- A unique set of liquidity absorption tools can be identified (e.g., repo operations), keeping in mind the impact on central banks' balance sheets for each EAC member.
- Interest rates of standing facilities should ideally be aligned with policy rates and harmonize tenors, amount, and room for discretion for central banks. The feasibility of using standing deposit facilities with the same features across the EAC should be assessed once harmonization is well under way.
- Ideally, too, central bank financing of the government needs to be eliminated in a regional arrangement, with some transitional provisions that allow the regional central bank some prorated allocation until market-based mechanisms for government financing are fully developed in each country.

Harmonizing Legal Frameworks

Harmonization of legal frameworks could be lengthy, involving political commitments. As it requires careful consideration and prior agreements involving legislative bodies in individual countries, it does not seem advisable to initiate this process at an early stage. Even so, this does not preclude the introduction of an institutional framework that could help enforce agreements across EAC countries in the process of harmonization.

The EAC is considering establishing an East Africa Monetary Institute, inspired by the European Monetary Institute, which was set up in the euro area four years before monetary union. The introduction of an East Africa Monetary Institute would help the move from intercountry coordination to the discussion of supranational considerations. The dedication of full-time staff to prepare the relevant analytical and technical work to support informed decisions by designated authorities would be a major step to raise awareness in public and private sector economic agents in the region of the implications of moving toward a monetary union.

A strong track record of implementing binding decisions through the East African Monetary Institute will enhance the credibility of the eventual East African Central Bank when monetary union is in place. Visible progress in pre-union harmonization will highlight the efficacy of the eventual decentralized execution of monetary policy and liquidity management. While a harmonized legal framework is designed, EAC central banks could operate under the principles of autonomy and establishing clear common objectives, which in itself would contribute to institutional strengthening as agreements are enforced.[11] This will reinforce credibility in monetary policy across the region and contribute to positive expectations about the eventual move to a monetary union.

Harmonization of the legal frameworks should take place only at a later stage in line with prior agreements within EAC member countries. The new legal frameworks should prioritize objectives in such a fashion that both the East African Central Bank and national central banks are able to use their legal powers for monetary policy and other policy areas to pursue distinct primary policy objectives. Also, legal powers and policy instruments should be aligned with one or more functions, which in turn support one or more objectives, to help manage expectations of economic agents and to strengthen central bank accountability.

[11] In fact, EAC central banks in many cases already operate with more autonomy than granted in the law.

ANNEX 6.1

TABLE A6.1

Main Features of Legal Frameworks Affecting the Conduct of Monetary Policy Across East African Community Countries

	Burundi	Kenya	Rwanda	Tanzania	Uganda
Legal Status					
1. Statute	Charter of the Bank of the Republic of Burundi (Law 1/34 of 2008)	The Central Bank of Kenya Act (Chapter 491)	Law 55/2007 on governing the National Bank of Rwanda	The Bank of Tanzania Act, 2006	The Bank of Uganda Act (Chapter 51)
2. Legal personality	Yes	Yes	Yes	Yes	Yes
3. Public/private entity	Public entity	Public entity	Public entity	Not specified	Not specified
4. Shareholders	Fully owned by government	Fully owned by government	Fully owned by government	Fully owned by government	Fully owned by government
5. Application of companies act	No provision	No	No provision	No provision	No provision
Statutory Autonomy					
1. Explicit statement	Yes	No	Yes	Yes	No
2. Governmental interference					
Giving instructions	No	Yes	No	No	Yes
Deferring/suspending decisions	No	No	No	No	No
Censoring decisions	No	No	No	No	No
Mandatory consultation regarding central bank decisions	No	Yes	No	No	No
3. Financial autonomy					
Governmental interference in budget	No	No	No	No	No
Governmental interference in disposition of profit/loss	No	Consultation with minister	No	No	No
Distribution of unrealized profits	Prohibited	Unclear	Prohibited	Prohibited	Unclear
Recapitalization by government	Yes	No provision	Yes	Yes	Yes

(continued)

TABLE A6.1

Main Features of Legal Frameworks Affecting the Conduct of Monetary Policy Across East African Community Countries *(continued)*

	Burundi	Kenya	Rwanda	Tanzania	Uganda
Threshold of recapitalization	10% of total assets	–	General reserves become negative	Holding negative net assets	No specification
4. Lending to government	Yes	Yes	Yes	Yes	Yes
Maturity	– Intraday credit – Purchasing treasury bills of less than 13 weeks	No limitation	No limitation	– 180-day advances – 12-month government bonds	No limitation
Ceiling of total lending	No limitation	5% of government recurrent revenue	11% of current state revenue	12.5% of government revenue	18% of government recurrent revenue
Requirement of clearing outstanding at the end of year	No	No	No	No	No
Legal Mandate					
1. Objectives					
Primary	Domestic price stability	Stability in general level of prices	Price stability. Stable and competitive financial system	Domestic price stability	Economic stability
Others	Stability of the financial system. Contribution to implementation of economic policies	Stable market-based financial system. Support the economic policy	Support general economic policies	Integrity of the financial system. Sound monetary, credit, and banking conditions. Support general economic policy	–
2. Statutory responsibilities					
Formulating monetary policies	Yes	No (minister of finance)	Yes	Yes	Yes
Implementing monetary policy	Yes	Yes	Yes	Yes	Yes
Determining exchange rate regime	No provision	No provision	No (president on a request of the central bank)	No provision	No provision

Determining exchange rate policy	Yes	Yes	Yes	Yes, under consultation with minister of finance	Yes, under consultation with minister of finance
Implementing exchange rate policy	Yes	Yes	Yes	Yes	Yes
Managing reserves	Yes	Yes	Yes	Yes	Yes
Issuing banknotes	Yes	Yes	Yes	Yes	Yes
Fiscal agent	Yes	Yes	Yes	Yes	Yes
Payment system services	Yes	Yes	Yes	Yes	Yes
Supervising financial institutions	Yes	Yes	Yes	Yes	Yes
Emergency liquidity assistance	Yes	No provision	No provision	Yes	No provision
3. Monetary policy instruments					
Open market operations	Yes	Yes	Yes	Yes	Yes
Credit operations with banks	Yes	Yes	Yes	Yes	Yes
Minimum reserve requirement	Yes	Yes	Yes	Yes	Yes
Instruments for direct control	No	No	No	No	Yes, amount and period of investments and loans. Interest rate on deposits
Governance Structure					
1. One-/two-tier governance structure	Two-tier	Two-tier	One-tier	One-tier	One-tier
2. Governing bodies for policy setting	General council	Monetary policy committee, only for monetary policy	Board of directors	Board of directors	Board of directors
Executive members	Governor, two deputy governors	Governor, deputy governor, two executives	Governor, deputy governor	Governor, three deputy governors	Governor, deputy governor
Nonexecutive members	Five members	Four members	Four administrators	Four members	Four to six members
Ex officio members	No	Secretary to the treasury	No	Two secretaries to the treasury	Secretary to the treasury
Voting rights	–	No	–	Yes	Yes

(continued)

TABLE A6.1

Main Features of Legal Frameworks Affecting the Conduct of Monetary Policy Across East African Community Countries *(continued)*

	Burundi	Kenya	Rwanda	Tanzania	Uganda
Policy implementation	Management committee	Board of directors	Same as a policy-setting body	Same as a policy-setting body	Same as a policy-setting body
Members	Governor, two deputy governors	Governor, deputy governor, secretary of treasury, five nonexecutive members	–	–	–
3. Appointment					
Governor: By	President on the proposal of minister for finance	President	President	President	President on the advice of the cabinet
Term	Five years	Four years	Six years	Five years	Four years
Renewal	Renewable	Renewable	Renewable	Renewable	Renewable
Deputy governor: By	Same as governor	Same as governor	Prime minister	Same as governor	President on the advice of the cabinet
Term	Same as governor	Same as governor	Same as governor	Same as governor	Same as governor
Renewal	Same as governor	Same as governor	Same as governor	Same as governor	Same as governor
Nonexecutives: By	Same as governor	Minister (monetary policy committee). Same as governor (board)	Prime minister	Minister of finance	Minister of finance
Term	Same as governor	Three years (monetary policy committee). Same as governor (board)	Four years	Three years	Same as governor
Renewal	Same as governor	Same as governor (monetary policy committee, board)	Same as governor	Same as governor	Same as governor
4. Dismissal					
Governor: By	President on the proposal of minister for finance	President on the consultation with a special tribunal	President	No specification	President[1]

Grounds	Bankruptcy, breach of law, unjustified absences, serious misconduct	Bankruptcy, conviction of felony, unsound mind, unjustified absences, incompetent	No provision	Bankruptcy, conviction of felony, unsound mind, unjustified absences	Inability to perform the functions of his or her office arising from infirmity of body or mind; misbehavior or misconduct; or incompetence
Deputy governor: by	Same as governor	President	Prime minister	No specification	President
Grounds	Same as governor	Same as governor	No provision	Same as governor	Same as governor
Nonexecutives: by	Same as governor	President	No provision	No specification	President
Grounds	Same as governor	Same as governor	No provision	Same as governor	Same as governor
Appeal procedures for dismissal	No provision	A tribunal may be appointed by the president	No provision	No provision	No provision
5. Internal oversight					
Audit committee	Yes	No provision	No provision	Yes	No provision
Members	Three nonexecutive members of general council	–	–	Not specified	–
Appointed by	General council	–	–	Not specified	–
Internal audit function	Yes, chief internal auditor	No provision	No provision	Yes (head of internal audit)	No provision
Appointment of chief internal auditor/members of auditors' board	General council on the proposal of management committee	–	–	Board of directors	–
Term	Three years	–	–	Three years	–
Reporting to	General council	–	–	Governor, audit committee	–
Policy-setting body powers					
Oversight of management	No	Yes	No	No	No
Establishing/monitoring risk management procedures	No	No	No	No	No
Establishing/monitoring financial reporting procedures	Yes	Unclear (oversight for financial management)	Yes	Unclear (approval of budget)	No

(continued)

TABLE A6.1

Main Features of Legal Frameworks Affecting the Conduct of Monetary Policy Across East African Community Countries *(continued)*

	Burundi	Kenya	Rwanda	Tanzania	Uganda
6. External accountability					
Independent external audit	Yes	Yes	Yes	Yes	No
Accounting standards	International Financial Reporting Standards	No provision	"Commercial"	"International"	No provision
Reporting to government	Yes	Yes	Yes	Yes	Yes
Reporting to parliament	Yes	Yes	No	Yes	Yes
Financial statements published	Yes	Yes	Yes	Yes	No provision
Deadline for publication	Three months after the end of year	No provision	Six months after the end of year	Three months after the end of year	–

Source: Author.
Note: – = not applicable.
[1] Based on the 1995 constitution.

REFERENCES

Adam, C., and P. J. Kessy, 2010, "Assessing the Stability and Predictability of the Money Multiplier in the EAC: The Case of Tanzania" (London: International Growth Center).

Adam, C., P. J. Kessy, J. J. Nyella, and S. A. O'Connnel, 2010, "The Demand for Money in Tanzania" (London: International Growth Center).

Andrle, M., A. Berg, R. Armando Morales, R. Portillo, and J. Vlcek, 2013, "Forecasting and Monetary Policy Analysis in Low-Income Countries: Food and non-Food Inflation in Kenya," IMF Working Papers 13/61 (Washington: International Monetary Fund).

Davoodi, H. R., S. Dixit, and G. Pinter, 2013, "Monetary Transmission Mechanism in the East African Community: An Empirical Investigation," IMF Working Paper 13/39 (Washington: International Monetary Fund).

European Central Bank, 2010, "Study on the Establishment of a Monetary Union among the Partner States of the East African Community."

Graboyes, R., 1990, "The EMU: Forerunners and Durability," Federal Reserve Bank of Richmond, *Economic Review*, Vol. 76 (July/August), pp. 8–17.

Saizar, C., and N. Chalk, 2008, "Is Monetary Policy Effective When Credit is Low?" IMF Working Paper No. 08/288 (Washington: International Monetary Fund).

Sichei, M., and A. Kamau, 2010, "Demand for Broad Money in Kenya: 1996-2009," unpublished (Nairobi: Central Bank of Kenya).

Slavov, S., 2011, "De Jure versus De Facto Exchange Rate Regimes in Sub-Saharan Africa," IMF Working Paper 11/198 (Washington: International Monetary Fund).

Stepanyan, A., 2012, "Second round effects of common and idiosyncratic shocks in SSA," unpublished (Washington: International Monetary Fund).

CHAPTER 7

How Strong Is the Monetary Transmission Mechanism in the East African Community?

HAMID R. DAVOODI, SHIV DIXIT, AND GABOR PINTER

The leaders of the five partner states of the East African Community (EAC) decided in 2007 to fast track agreements on key protocols of the East African Monetary Union (EAMU) by 2012. A successful EAMU depends, among other things, on effective harmonization of existing monetary policies and operations across the EAC in transition to a future common monetary policy. The EAMU is expected to enhance the benefits of the EAC Customs Union and the EAC Common Market and deepen integration. It is also expected to reduce the costs and risks of conducting business transactions across national boundaries, as well as make way for a single currency, remove the costs of transactions in different currencies, and reduce the risk of adverse exchange rate movements in intra-EAC trade.

An important issue for each country is the effectiveness of their monetary transmission mechanisms (MTM)—the policy instruments used in each country and the channels through which changes in these instruments are transmitted into changes in real GDP and inflation, and the relative importance of each channel.[1] In particular, we need to understand the extent to which the MTM differs across EAC countries and reasons for such differences.

A potential finding of significant heterogeneity would pose challenges for the harmonization of monetary policies and for the design and conduct of a common monetary policy for monetary union. A common monetary policy would dictate the use of the same instrument across all countries and then an expansionary

We wish to thank Peter Allum, Michael Atingi-Ego, Andy Berg, Jorge Canales Kriljenko, David Dunn, EAC central banks, Etibar Jafarov, Nils Maehle, Catherine McAuliffe, Peter Montiel, Rafael Portillo, Rogelio Morales, Steve O'Connell, Catherine Pattillo, Oral Williams, Mary Zephirin, and seminar participants in the IMF's African Department Monetary Policy Network for helpful discussions and comments. Shiv Dixit and Gabor Pinter were at the IMF when this research was initiated.

[1]The focus of MTM is on how it affects output and inflation (Taylor, 1995), though monetary policy also affects other macroeconomic indicators and is influenced by them (Bernanke and Gertler, 1995; Ireland, 2008).

monetary policy—an exogenous positive shock to reserve money, for example—that should not be expansionary in one country and contractionary in another.

Studying the MTM is not only important for the design and effectiveness of monetary policy in countries in transition to a monetary union, but continues to be relevant in countries already in monetary unions, such as the euro area, the Eastern Caribbean Monetary Union, and two monetary unions in sub-Saharan Africa: the West African Economic and Monetary Union and the Central African Economic and Monetary Community.[2]

The vast empirical literature on monetary transmission has primarily focused on developed economies. The most distinguishing characteristic of the MTM in developed countries is the focus on prices (interest rates, exchange rates, and other asset prices) rather than quantities (money, credit, base money, bonds, foreign assets, and so on).[3] In contrast, the prevailing orthodoxy of the MTM in low-income countries has been its focus on quantities rather than prices. This difference is often attributed to weak institutional frameworks, oligopolistic banking structures, shallow financial markets, and extensive central bank intervention in foreign exchange markets in low-income countries.

Mishra, Montiel, and Spilimbergo (2010) revisited the prevailing orthodoxy of the MTM in low-income countries. They provide theoretical arguments about why bank lending channels might be more effective in low-income countries than other channels and find this channel to be either weak or unreliable. Specifically, they provide cross-country evidence of a weak interest rate pass-through[4]—from central bank lending rates to money market rates and from money market rates to commercial banks' lending rates—though they do not empirically investigate the impact of changes in the interest rate or other monetary policy instruments on prices and real output in low-income countries.

On the other hand, a recent study of sub-Saharan Africa finds that monetary policy is perhaps more effective in this region than commonly believed (IMF, 2010). The study, based on a panel vector autoregression of sub-Saharan African countries in the past decade, finds that a contractionary monetary policy—defined either by lower reserve money growth or a higher central bank discount rate—decreases output growth significantly, but the impact on inflation and its statistical significance depends on the measure of the monetary policy instrument. A decline in reserve money (the operating target for many sub-Saharan African countries) reduces inflation as expected, though the decline is not statistically different from zero. However, an increase in the central bank discount

[2] See Peersman and Smets (2001) and European Central Bank (2010) for the European Monetary Union, Laurens (2005) for the Eastern Caribbean Currency Union, van den Boogaerde and Tsangarides (2005) for the West African Economic and Monetary Union, and Iossifov and others (2009) for the Central African Economic and Monetary Community.

[3] This view is evolving, however. For example, the global financial crisis of 2007–08 led some to argue for a credit-focused monetary policy in advanced economies and output and inflation goals for monetary policy (Christiano, Illut, Motto, and Rostagno, 2010) and for supplementing monetary policy with an active role for macroprudential policies (Bean and others, 2010; Issing, 2011).

[4] See also IMF (2010) for evidence of weak interest rate pass-through in Africa.

rate or policy rate (the operating target for a small number of sub-Saharan African countries) has a statistically significant impact on inflation, but, surprisingly, it increases inflation—the so-called price puzzle.

These disparate findings on the effects of monetary policy may show the presence of different operating targets across countries and the need to conduct country-specific studies of MTMs that control for heterogeneities. In contrast to these cross-country studies, little is known about the MTM in EAC countries; studies have so far used a narrow set of methodologies and data sets. Moreover, no literature review has been conducted covering all EAC countries. On the latter, Davoodi, Dixit, and Pinter (2013) conduct an extensive review of the literature that shows the MTM is strong in Kenya, though only compared to prices, but that it is generally weak in the rest of the EAC for output or prices.

This chapter makes two contributions to a study of the MTM in the EAC:

- We apply the latest methodologies from time-series analysis to each EAC country, including Bayesian vector autoregression and factor-augmented vector autoregression, two techniques that have not been used in studies of the MTM in the EAC.
- We use a methodology that quantifies the relative importance of various channels of the MTM in each EAC country.

The outline of this chapter is as follows: The next section describes the conduct of monetary policy and the existing institutional framework, which is the starting point for harmonizing the conduct of monetary policy. This section shows how reserve money targeting, the dominant monetary policy framework in the EAC, is implemented in the vector autoregression. After that, we describe six channels of the MTM. Then, we describe the various vector autoregression methodologies. The next section describes the data. The penultimate section presents the empirical results, including an evaluation of the relative strengths and weaknesses of various channels of the MTM in each EAC country. Finally, we offer some conclusions.

CONDUCT OF MONETARY POLICY IN THE EAST AFRICAN COMMUNITY

Instruments, Targets, and Goals

EAC central banks use open market operations as the main instrument of monetary policy implementation, but also rely on standing facilities, changes in reserve requirements, required reserve averaging, and foreign exchange operations. But differences exist in the application of these instruments among member countries' central banks, most notably in the computation of the cash reserve requirement. Reserve money is the operating target for monetary policy and broad money is the intermediate target. Price stability is the overriding goal for monetary policy, but central banks also support economic growth and financial stability (Figure 7.1).

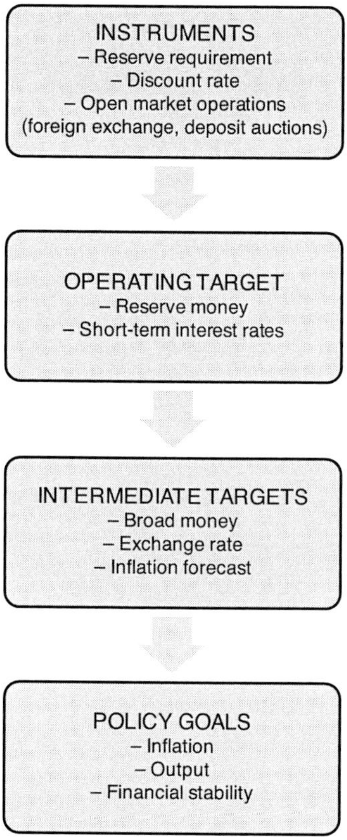

INSTRUMENTS
– Reserve requirement
– Discount rate
– Open market operations
(foreign exchange, deposit auctions)

OPERATING TARGET
– Reserve money
– Short-term interest rates

INTERMEDIATE TARGETS
– Broad money
– Exchange rate
– Inflation forecast

POLICY GOALS
– Inflation
– Output
– Financial stability

Figure 7.1 Monetary Policy: Instruments, Targets, and Goals

Source: Authors.

In July 2011, the Central Bank of Uganda declared inflation-targeting lite as its monetary policy framework. Under an inflation-targeting framework, inflation forecasts are often the intermediate target by which a central bank attempts to anchor inflation expectations. In November 2011, the Central Bank of Kenya adopted a new monetary policy framework that gives more prominence to its policy interest rate though, unlike Uganda, it did not declare a shift to inflation-targeting lite. Practices can differ, though, as countries gain experience in the conduct of a new monetary policy framework. The empirical work in this chapter excludes these periods of marked shift in the monetary policy framework.

Monetary Policy Framework

For the sample period used in this chapter, all central banks use reserve money targeting—widely known as the reserve money program (RMP) for countries with an IMF program—as their monetary policy framework. There are two building blocks of monetary policy formulation in an RMP. The first involves setting an

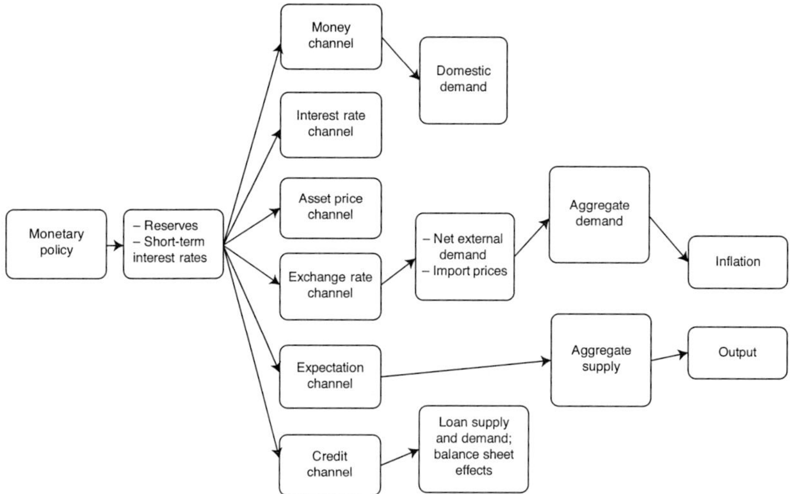

Figure 7.2 Inside the Monetary Transmission Mechanism

Source: Authors.

intermediate target for broad money. This is not under the direct control of the central bank, but provides a useful signal about current or prospective movements in inflation and output, and the final monetary policy goals. The second relates the intermediate target to an operating target, which is reserve money. It is under the effective control of the central bank but further from policy goals; in other words, it has a longer policy lag than broad money. The target for broad money is set to be consistent with macroeconomic policy goals regarding economic growth and inflation; hence, income velocity. The target for reserve money is set taking into account assumptions about the money multiplier (i.e., relating broad money to reserve money) and seasonality.

In practice, the implementation of the RMP has departed from the standard textbook quantity theory of money and become more flexible during the implementation of monetary policy. This is sometimes referred to as flexible RMP. This can be done by accommodating shifts in money multipliers and velocity (e.g., money demand shocks, financial deepening), two factors in part determined by portfolio decisions of individuals, and by incorporating unanticipated shocks to output and inflation (e.g., better-than-projected agriculture activities, large shifts in global food and fuel prices). This may cause monetary aggregates to deviate substantially from ex ante monetary targets. Uganda conducted a flexible RMP from September 2009 to June 2011. The increasing use of a small set of high frequency data and regular and sometimes more frequent meetings of monetary policy committees also enable central banks in the region to help fine-tune the monetary policy stance.

What is often called the MTM is depicted in Figure 7.2. The figure is a stylized look at the main channels of an MTM. Some are present in the EAC and some not. Some indicators may also not apply at this stage, such as a market-determined or timely survey-based measure of inflation expectations, but some channels may require the availability of high-frequency data, such as monthly indexes of real economic activities. Figure 7.2 also shows the feedback rules from output and inflation to monetary policy, thus enabling systemic responses of monetary policy to developments in inflation and output. The empirical challenge is to disentangle this endogenous monetary policy response from an exogenous monetary policy. Different models of MTMs essentially use different identification criteria to address this challenge. How each channel in the MTM could work is shown in the next section.

CHANNELS OF THE MONETARY TRANSMISSION MECHANISM

Regardless of the monetary policy framework used in practice, central bankers want to know how changes in monetary policy instruments affect inflation and output, and the timing and size of such effects.

Traditionally, the effects of monetary policy actions are thought to be transmitted via money or credit channels—the so-called money versus credit view of monetary policy. In the former, changes in the nominal quantity of money affect spending directly, whereas in the latter open market operations induce changes in interest rates that affect spending. In some models, credit rationing and financial accelerators can have additional effects on output and prices. Most models rely on some form of nominal price or wage rigidity to draw the hypothesized links between money, interest rates, and output. We now cover in more detail how each channel works.

Money Channel

This channel is perhaps the oldest one that effectively assumes changes in reserve money are transmitted to broad money via the money multiplier (i.e., that banks are in the business of creating inside money). This argument also assumes a role for individuals holding components of broad money, currency in circulation, and various forms of deposits. The money view of monetary policy assumes aggregate demand moves in line with money balances used to finance transactions and affect the split of nominal GDP between real GDP and the price level. It is this idea that forms the basis for broad money representing the intermediate target in many central bankers' money-focused monetary policies (Mishkin, 1998).

Interest Rate Channel

The interest rate channel has been the traditional channel of monetary policy since the first developments in macroeconomic theory. This channel can be summarized in the standard Keynesian Investment/Saving-Liquidity Preference Money Supply framework, whereby an expansionary monetary policy leads to a fall in the real interest rate, thus decreasing the cost of capital and stimulating investment. This then results in an increase in aggregate demand and output. It is important to note that real spending decisions are only affected by changes in real interest rates and that monetary policy authorities only have direct control over short-term nominal interest rates. The crucial factor linking the monetary base with real interest rates—and ultimately determining the effectiveness of the interest rate channel—is the slow adjustment of the price level. "Price stickiness" causes movements in the monetary policy rate, which has a significant effect on short-term real interest rates. In addition, the rational expectations hypothesis of the term structure suggests that long-run real interest rates are determined by expectations about future short-term real interest rates. Monetary policy authorities are therefore able to use short-term policy rates to influence long-run real interest rates through price stickiness and the term structure, which then affect the real economy.

Exchange Rate Channel

In small, open economies, one of the most important monetary policy channels is the exchange rate channel. The extent to which monetary policy can affect movements in the exchange rate is largely influenced by the theory of uncovered interest rate parity. This simple theoretical relationship suggests that the expected future changes in nominal exchange rates are related to the difference between the domestic and foreign interest rates. In theory, the uncovered interest rate parity enables the monetary policy authority to influence the exchange rate, which in turn affects the relative prices of domestic and foreign goods, thus affecting net exports and output. For example, a cut in the monetary policy rate would make domestic deposits less attractive compared to foreign deposits, leading to a fall in the demand for domestic currency. As a result, the domestic currency would depreciate, making domestic goods cheaper compared to foreign goods and leading to an increase in net exports and total output. The effectiveness of the exchange rate channel is determined by the uncovered interest rate parity condition, but its empirical validity has often been criticized. As a result, many experts suggest that this should be augmented with a risk-premium term, implying that foreign investors, upon buying domestic financial assets, require compensation not only for expected depreciation but also for holding domestic assets.

Credit Channel

Asymmetric information in financial markets provides the basis for the credit channel of monetary transmission. Bernanke and Gertler (1995) offer a detailed description of how imperfections in credit markets may cause a monetary contraction to lead to an increase in the external finance premium faced by borrowers and to a decrease in the loan supply. It is important to note that the credit channel is often referred to as an amplifier of traditional monetary channels rather than a stand-alone mechanism. Economists usually distinguish between two types of credit channels stemming from imperfections in financial markets: the bank-lending channel and the balance-sheet channel. The bank-lending channel is based on the assumption that a monetary contraction, which decreases bank reserves and bank deposits, lowers the quality of bank loans available. The balance-sheet channel is related to the effects monetary policy can exert on the net worth of businesses and households. A monetary contraction decreases the net worth of firms through its cash flows and the value of collateral, thus leading to a higher external finance premium associated with more severe moral hazard problems. This in turn would reduce the level of lending, investment, and output.

Asset Price Channel

Traditional monetary theory suggests that monetary contraction, through an increase in the discount rate of financial assets, may lead to a fall in asset prices, which will then further affect the real economy. Mishkin (1995) singles out two main mechanisms through which monetary policy shocks are propagated by changes in equity prices. First, the theory of Tobin's q suggests that when equities are cheap relative to the replacement cost of capital, firms do not want to issue new equities to purchase investment goods, leading to a decline in investment. Second, equity prices may have substantial wealth effects on consumption because of the permanent income hypothesis. A rise in stock prices increases the value of financial wealth, thus increasing the lifetime resources of households as well as the demand for consumption and output. A similar mechanism is applied to prices of other assets such as housing, which is a substantial component of wealth. Therefore, the MTM also operates through land and housing price channels.

Expectation Channel

Because modern monetary policy analysis is based on forward-looking and rational economic agents, the expectation channel is in effect fundamental to the working of all channels of the MTM. In practice, this channel is mainly operational in developed economies with well-functioning and deep financial markets. For example, expectations of future changes in the policy rate can immediately affect medium- and long-term interest rates. Monetary policy can also guide economic agents' expectations of future inflation and thus influence price developments. Inflation expectations matter in two important areas. First, they influence the level of the real interest rate and thus determine the impact of any specific nominal interest rate. Second, they influence price and money wage-setting behavior and feed through into actual inflation in subsequent periods. Similarly, changes in monetary policy stances can influence expectations about the future course of real economic activities by affecting inflation pressures expectations and the ex ante real rate and guiding the future course of economic activities.

EMPIRICAL METHODOLOGY

Vector autoregression models are the most widely used methodology to analyze the MTM. Their use for monetary policy analysis started with the seminal work of Sims (1980) and his recursive methodology has been used widely. In fact, most studies of the MTM in low-income countries, as reviewed by Mishra, Montiel, and Spilimbergo (2010), have used vector autoregressions with the majority of studies using recursive vector autoregressions. Studies of the MTM in developed economies also continue to use vector autoregressions and their variants, as reviewed by Christiano and others (1999) for the United States; Weber, Gerke, and Worms (2009) for the euro area; and more recently by Boivin, Kiley, and Mishkin (2011) for the United States and other Group of Seven economies.[5]

We use three variants of structural vector autoregression to study the MTM in the EAC: standard recursive structural vector autoregressions, Bayesian vector autoregressions, and factor-augmented vector autoregressions. Recursive structural vector autoregressions assume a recursive relationship between errors of a reduced-form vector autoregression and remain the most widely used methodology in the literature on the MTM. However, this method may suffer from problems of overparameterization and misspecification, which undermine the robustness of the empirical results. To tackle these problems, two additional methods are applied. First, the standard ordinary least squares estimation of the recursive structural vector autoregression is replaced by Bayesian estimation techniques (Litterman, 1986). Bayesian methods provide an effective treatment for problems of overparameterization by the use of prior information.[6]

Second, factor methods are used that allow for the use of information contained in other variables while simultaneously reducing the number of parameters in the vector autoregression. Each variant is estimated for each country separately, allowing for country-specific dynamics in the evolution of the MTM. Factor-augmented vector autoregressions are estimated following Bernanke, Boivin, and Eliasz (2005). These methods assume a larger information set is being used by central bankers and different estimation methods that provide useful checks on the robustness of the results from the recursive structural vector autoregression models. We refer readers to Davoodi, Dixit, and Pinter (2013) for a detailed discussion of these vector autoregression methodologies.

DATA

Estimation of a monthly vector autoregression model requires the compilation of measures of money, price level, asset prices, and GDP at monthly frequencies. Data on the first three indicators were obtained from IMF databases, national authorities, and staff estimates. However, GDP data are available only at quarterly frequencies for all EAC countries except Burundi.

[5]There are nevertheless alternative methods for monetary policy analysis such as dynamic stochastic general equilibrium models that impose a more theoretically motivated structure on the data; see Christiano, Trabandt, and Walentin (2010) for a recent review. Owing to increasing computational capacity, these models have become widely used among central bankers and have produced some promising results for low-income countries as well (Berg and others, 2010; O'Connell, 2011).

[6]See Chapter 10 of Canova (2007) for a detailed review of Bayesian vector autroregressions and how these methods may be useful for shrinking the parameter space of the model

At best, there may be 10 years of quarterly data for each country except Burundi. The starting date for each country's quarterly national accounts is as follows: Kenya (2000 first quarter), Rwanda (2006 first quarter), Uganda (1999 fourth quarter), and Tanzania (2001 first quarter). This data set amounts to 40 observations at the maximum, which may not offer sufficient degrees of freedom for statistical inference given the nature of time lags and the number of variables needed even for a small, low-order vector autoregression.[7]

We need to generate proxies for real GDP at quarterly frequency for Rwanda before 2006 first quarter and for Burundi for all periods. Our strategy is as follows: For Rwanda, in the years before 2006 for which quarterly GDP data are not available, seasonality factors of quarterly data post-2006 are applied to annual real GDP to interpolate to quarterly frequency. For Burundi, because its production structure is similar to Rwanda's, we generate a quarterly series of real GDP by applying Rwanda's quarterly seasonality factors to Burundi's annual GDP data. Monthly estimates of GDP are then derived for all EAC countries by interpolating quarterly GDP data using a cubic spline, a widely used technique.[8] Finally, the monthly estimates are seasonally adjusted using the X-12 ARIMA method.

The benchmark model is estimated from January 2000 to December 2010 on log levels, except for interest rate series, which are in percent. This is a widely used specification in the literature. Use of levels rather than first differences preserves any long-run relationship, if present, and does not affect statistical inference (Sims, Stock, and Watson, 1990).[9]

A structural vector autoregression model consisting of six endogenous and four exogenous variables is estimated for each country. The endogenous variables are real GDP, the consumer price index (CPI), reserve money, short-term interest rate, credit to private sector, and the nominal effective exchange rate. The four exogenous variables that affect endogenous variables are a global oil price index, a global food price index, U.S. federal funds rate, and U.S. industrial production. The latter two are proxies for global demand conditions, whereas global food and fuel prices are expected to affect, among other things, inflation and output beyond external demand factors.

To check for the robustness of our results, the Bayesian vector autoregression model is applied to the dataset explained previously. In addition, factor-augmented vector autoregression methods are used by adopting principal component methods as follows: The first principal component of the four exogenous variables is used as an exogenous variable. The first principal component of two endogenous variables (credit and nominal effective exchange rates) and additional variables,

[7] As suggested earlier, a six-variable vector autrogression with a constant, a time trend, two lags of each variable, plus contemporaneous values of our four exogenous variables results in estimation of 18 parameters, leaving only 22 degrees of freedom at maximum.

[8] Many studies of MTM in advanced countries also use interpolated monthly GDP data. See Bernanke, Boivin, and Eliasz (2005).

[9] Results of Johansen's cointegration tests were inconclusive. Moreover, the cointegration vectors are hard to interpret given the number of variables involved.

M1, M2, M3,[10] are constructed. This essentially leads to the estimation of a vector autoregression with five endogenous variables and one exogenous variable, hence reducing the parameter space and mitigating problems of over-parameterization. Finally, the benchmark structural vector autoregression model specification will be estimated on a longer sample for each country going back to the mid-1990s.

EMPIRICAL RESULTS

The benchmark results for each EAC country are obtained by estimating country-specific structural vector autoregression models from January 2000 to December 2010, using recursive identification methods. For all countries, we chose the vector autoregression lag length using the standard lag length selection criteria (Akaike, Shwarz, Hannan-Quinn), final prediction error, and so on. We found a maximum lag length of three, which was also sufficient to generate serially uncorrelated vector autoregression errors. In contrast, most empirical work on MTM in advanced countries uses 6 to 12 lags for monthly data, or two to four quarters for quarterly data. While some may expect monetary policy to take time to have an effect in the EAC, this view seems to be based entirely on the experience of advanced economies and the conventional wisdom, driven in part from Milton Friedman's early work that "lags in monetary policy are long and variable." Adding more lags beyond three months, which we also did, results in increasing problems of overparameterization, associated with larger confidence bounds for impulse responses, reflecting the increase in noise and imprecision.

That said, we should also point out that the effects of monetary policy in some EAC countries do last beyond three months because cumulative effects are only built up over time and show up in cumulative impulse responses. However, the main difference with impulse responses in advanced countries is that effects of monetary policy in the EAC are short lived. If a confidence interval for impulse responses includes zero, then monetary policy has no statistically significant effect on either prices or output. In other words, the MTM is weak. As the horizon is expanded beyond six months, impulse responses become wider, rendering either economically insignificant results, statistically insignificant results, or both. We could choose to have a weaker inference standard than the conventional confidence intervals of plus and minus two standard errors (a 95 percent confidence interval).

If we opt, for example, for a 90 percent confidence interval, it could increase the Type II error (probability of accepting a false hypothesis that MTM is strong when it is in fact weak). Davoodi, Dixit, and Pinter (2013) report the 95 percent confidence interval, showing that the MTM is weak in the EAC. The results reported subsequently use a 90 percent confidence interval, showing a somewhat stronger MTM.

---

[10] M3 is not used in the factor-augmented vector autoregression for Burundi because the data are not available.

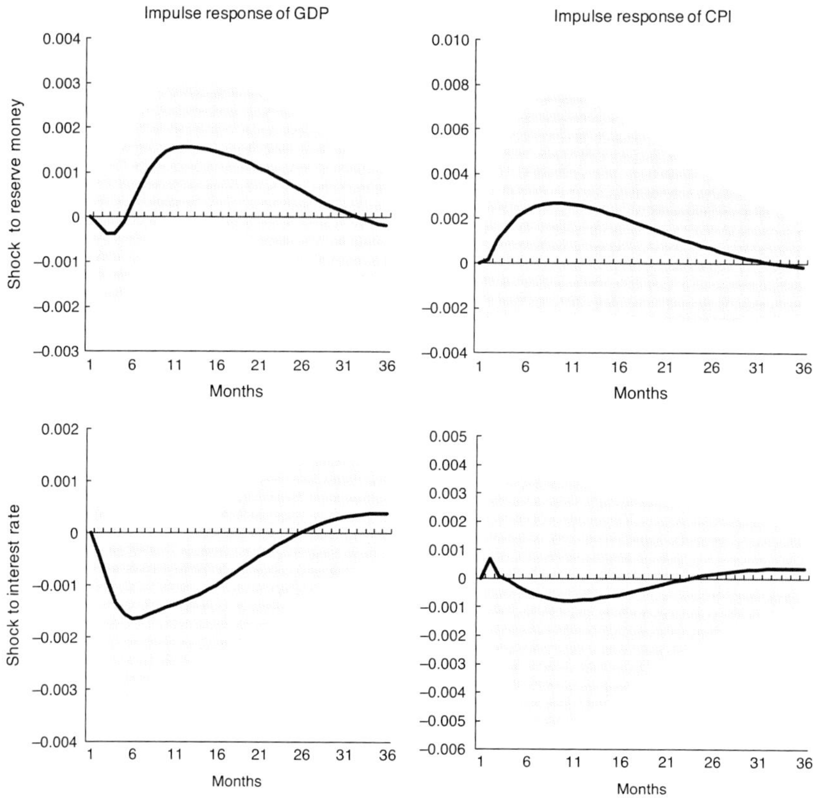

Figure 7.3 Structural Vector Autoregression Impulse Responses for Burundi

Source: Authors' calculations.

Note: Shocks are one standard deviation; vertical axes are percentages, horizontal axes are months, and the shaded areas denote the 90 percent confidence bands. CPI = consumer price index.

Burundi

The first row of Figure 7.3 shows the impulse responses of output and prices to a one standard deviation positive shock in reserve money (monetary loosening) in our baseline recursive model, whereas the second row depicts those to a positive shock in the policy rate (monetary tightening). Because of the lack of a structured interbank market, we use the Treasury bill rate as the policy interest rate in the baseline vector autoregression for Burundi. One lag was selected by the Akaike, Schwarz, and Hannan-Quinn information criteria. However, we proceeded with two lags to avoid serial correlation of residuals at the first lag order.

We find that output responds positively and significantly to a shock in reserve money, albeit with a considerable lag that spans almost a year. Its response to a shock in the Treasury bill rate is prompt (peaking in six months) and sustained over a longer period though not statistically significant. Nesting our recursive vector autoregression into a factor-augmented vector autoregression model, however,

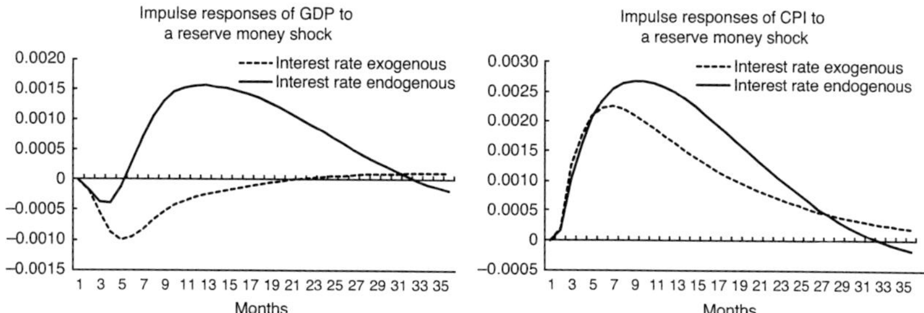

Figure 7.4 Testing the Interest Rate Channel in Burundi

Source: Authors' calculations.

Note: The solid lines show the impulse responses from the benchmark structural vector autoregression with six endogenous variables; the dashed lines show the impulse responses from the structural vector autoregression with five endogenous variables. CPI = consumer price index.

generates relatively muted impulse responses of output to shocks in both reserve money and the Treasury bill rate and a more pronounced response of prices to an interest rate shock. This perhaps illustrates the instability of the MTM in Burundi.

To ascertain the relative strength of the interest rate channel, we re-run the vector autoregression with the Treasury bill rate exogenized (i.e., lagged values of the Treasury bill rate are treated as exogenous variables in a smaller vector autoregression involving GDP, CPI, reserve money, credit, and the nominal effective exchange rate [Figure 7.4]). Such a procedure generates a vector autoregression identical to the original, except that it prevents any responses within it that pass through the interest rate.[11] Activating the interest rate channel in this fashion morphs a negative impulse response of output to innovations in reserve money to a positive (and statistically significant) response. The channel also has a positive impact on prices. We note that this considerable swing is only captured when using the Treasury bill rate as opposed to the indicative discount rate. Similar dynamics can be observed even when the credit and exchange rate channels are inactivated, demonstrating the robustness of the interest rate channel in Burundi. We conclude that movements in interest rates amplify the impact of reserve money on output and the price level. Interest rates therefore appear to be a transmission channel, but the effect is not statistically significant, given the direct impact of interest rates on either output or the price level.

Kenya

The results of the benchmark model with recursive identification are shown in Figure 7.5, which displays the impulse responses of GDP and CPI to a one standard deviation shock to reserve money and the repo rate.[12] Similar to Cheng (2006), the results suggest that a positive shock to the policy rate has a significant

---

[11] See Morsink and Bayoumi (2001) for this approach.

[12] The time series switches to reverse the repo rate from June 2009 onward. Re-running the vector autroregression that ends in May 2009 does not change the results.

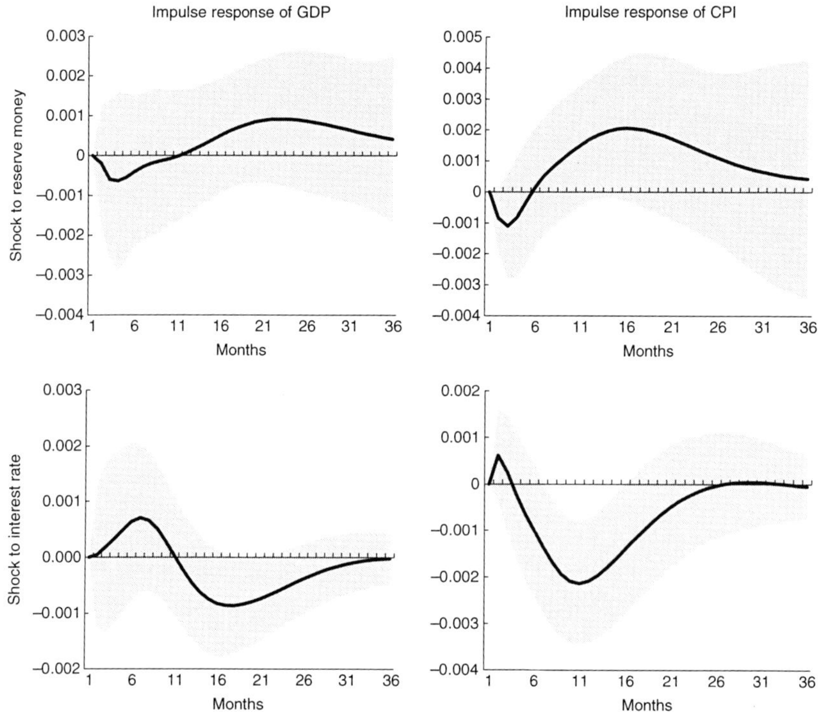

Figure 7.5 Structural Vector Autoregression Impulse Response for Kenya

Source: Authors' calculations.

Note: Shocks are one standard deviation; vertical axes are percentages, horizontal axes are months, and the shaded areas denote the 90 percent confidence bands. CPI = consumer price index.

and persistent effect on CPI, which peaks 9 to 11 months after the shock. A positive shock to reserve money has a positive impact on CPI that is in line with economic theory and peaks later at 15 months, later than an interest rate shock. Both types of shocks have no statistically significant effect on GDP.

Davoodi, Dixit, and Pinter (2013) show that a shock to both reserve money and the policy rate has a significant impact on the nominal effective exchange rate and credit, whereas a shock to the nominal effective exchange rate corresponding to an unexpected nominal exchange rate appreciation and a shock to credit corresponding to an unexpected credit expansion both have a significant impact on CPI. Since the two shocks are by construction orthogonal, these results can be interpreted as indirect evidence on the existence of an exchange rate and credit channel of monetary policy.

To undertake a direct assessment of the nominal effective exchange rate and credit channels, we analyze the effects of a monetary policy shock in a vector autoregression in which the target variable associated with the given channel is endogenous, and then compare these results to those from running a vector autoregression in which

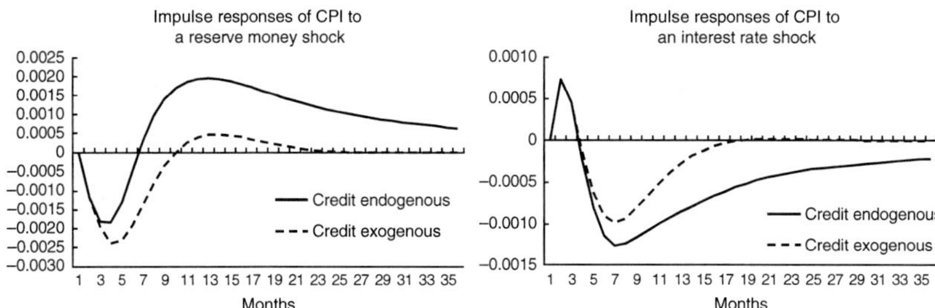

Figure 7.6 Testing the Credit Channel in Kenya

Source: Authors' calculations.

Note: The solid lines show the impulse responses from the benchmark structural vector autoregression with six endogenous variables; the dashed lines show the impulse responses from the structural vector autoregression with five endogenous variables. CPI = consumer price index.

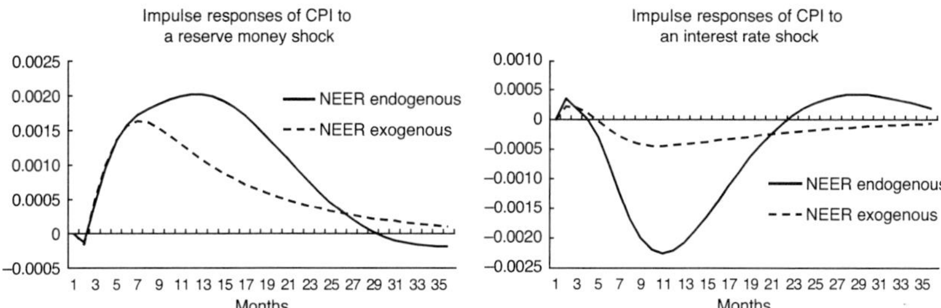

Figure 7.7 Testing the Exchange Rate Channel in Kenya

Source: Authors' calculations.

Note: The solid lines show the impulse responses from the benchmark structural vector autoregression with six endogenous variables; the dashed lines show the impulse responses from the structural vector autoregression with five endogenous variables. CPI = consumer price index; NEER = nominal effective exchange rate.

the same target variable is exogenous. This exercise essentially involves comparing the effects of monetary policy shocks in a five-variable vector autoregression including GDP, CPI, reserve money, interest rate, and credit with the those obtained by a four-variable vector autoregression whereby credit is made exogenous. Figure 7.6 shows these results and confirms that allowing for the endogenous presence of the credit variable increases the impact of a monetary policy shock on CPI.

The results associated with the exchange rate channel are shown in Figure 7.7. The endogenous presence of the nominal effective exchange rate magnifies the impact of both types of monetary policy shock, though the presence of the exchange rate channel seems more pronounced in a policy shock. Studies (Cheng, 2006) have shown that Kenya's nominal exchange rate is highly sensitive to changes in the short-term interest rate, which then affects the overall price level through import prices. The right panel of Figure 7.7 can be seen as direct evidence for this.

This exogeneity–endogeneity exercise has been used to test for other channels of monetary policy transmission as well, but none of them had any significant impact on the way monetary policy shocks affect the CPI.

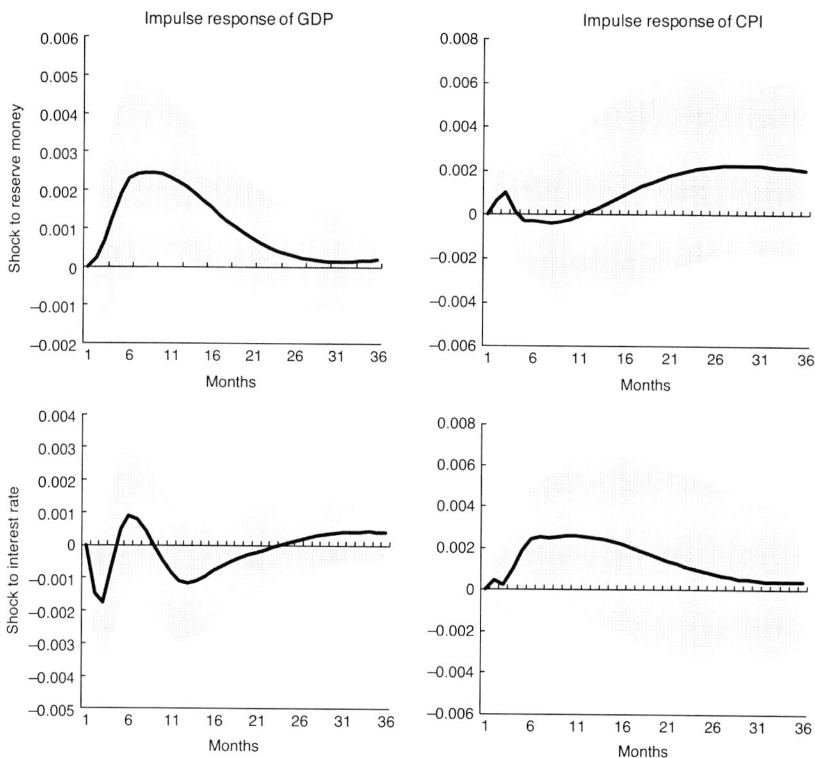

Figure 7.8 Structural Vector Autoregression Impulse Response for Rwanda

Source: Authors' calculations.

Note: Shocks are one standard deviation; vertical axes are percentages, horizontal axes are months, and the shaded areas denote the 90 percent confidence bands. CPI = consumer price index.

Rwanda[13]

A reserve money shock induces a positive and statistically significant output effect, but no price effect. A positive response of prices to a shock in the key repurchase rate[14] is counterintuitive, providing a price puzzle that lasts for quite some time (Figure 7.8). The factor-augmented vector autoregression approach not only confirms the positive response of output to a shock in the monetary base, but also reduces the extent of the price puzzle in our recursive specification. This alludes to the success of the factor-augmented model in extracting pertinent information from the expanded dataset of macroeconomic variables.

A shock to private sector credit has a significant effect on output for the first 5 months and on the price level for the first 15 months, both of which are statistically

[13] Sensitivity tests employed to check for robustness include accounting for historical periods, including lags of exogenous variables, excluding exogenous variables, replacing policy rate with the lending rate. See Davoodi, Dixit, and Pinter (2013).

[14] Time-series spliced with discount rate prior to January 2007.

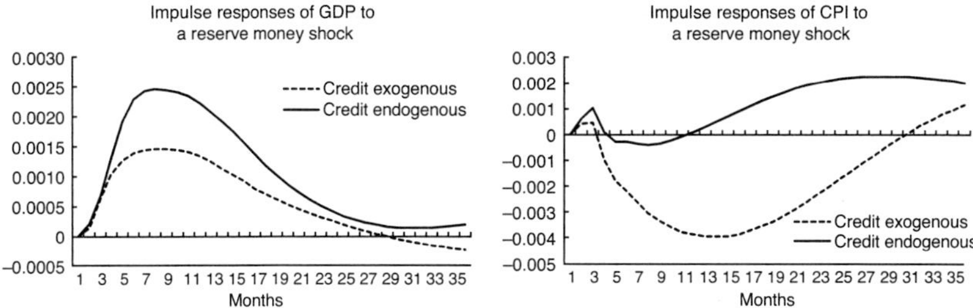

Figure 7.9 Testing the Credit Channel in Rwanda

Source: Authors' calculations.
Note: The solid lines show the impulse responses from the benchmark structural vector autoregression with six endogenous variables; the dashed lines show the impulse responses from the structural vector autoregression with five endogenous variables. CPI = consumer price index.

significant. The significant influence of reserve money on the private sector credit sector also suggests that it may be an important channel in monetary transmission (Davoodi, Dixit, and Pinter, 2013). To examine this further, we re-ran the vector autoregression with lags of private sector credit exogenized, and compared it to our baseline results (Figure 7.9). This exercise confirms the credit channel in Rwanda is indeed strong. The credit channel seems to be stronger statistically for the response of GDP to a reserve money shock than the response of CPI to a reserve money shock.

Tanzania

In a recursive vector autoregression model estimated for 2000–10, a positive shock to reserve money increases the CPI in the first year and half, though the effect is not statistically significant (Figure 7.10). However, this impact becomes highly significant when the vector autoregression is estimated over the longer period (January 1993 to December 2010) in our baseline recursive structure. We reach similar conclusions using Bayesian vector autoregression and factor-augmented vector autoregression. Under the latter, a shock to reserve money has statistically significant positive output effects consistent with the Bank of Tanzania, the central bank, using a much larger information set, including credit and broad money aggregates, commodity prices, than that in the baseline vector autoregression for the conduct of monetary policy.

Using either sample period, a positive shock to the interest rate increases the CPI, the price puzzle that was also evident in Rwanda and partly in Kenya, but the impact is not statistically significant. In fact, the confidence interval for all impulse responses for output and price level include zero, which indicates weak monetary transmission.

These findings are similar to those of Montiel and others (2012) for Tanzania, who employ recursive and nonrecursive vector autoregressions. These authors attribute the weak MTM to the shallowness of financial markets and the oligopolistic structure of the banking system. Although these factors may play a role, the weak MTM can also result despite a stable velocity (Adam and others, 2012) if the money multiplier is unstable in the short run, a result found by Adam and Kessy (2010).

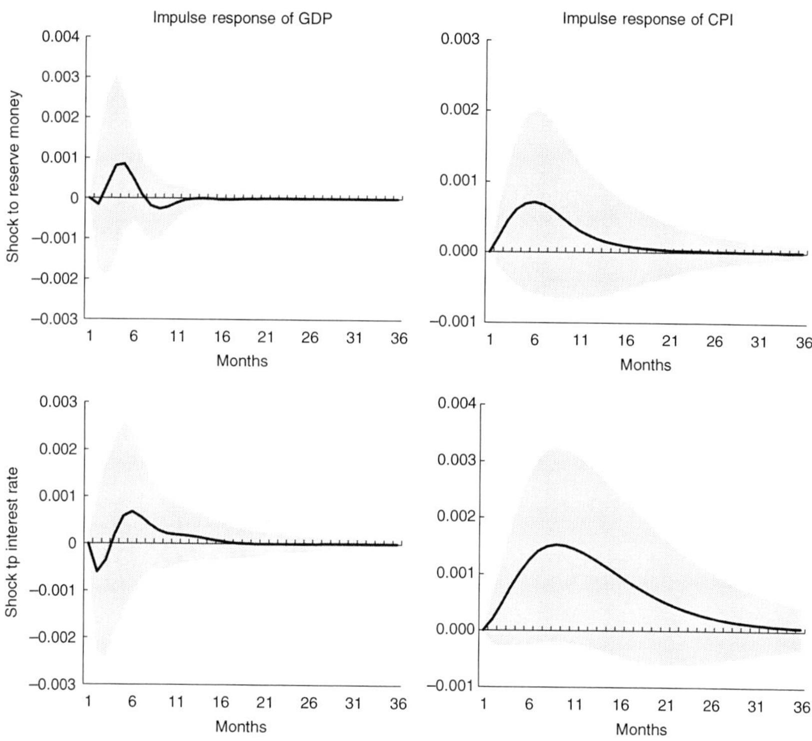

Figure 7.10 Structural Vector Autoregression Impulse Responses for Tanzania

Source: Authors' calculations.

Note: Shocks are one standard deviation; vertical axes are percentages, horizontal axes are months, and the shaded areas denote the 90 percent confidence bands. CPI = consumer price index.

However, other possibilities should not be ruled out. For example, stability of the money multiplier and velocity as reported in Davoodi, Dixit, and Pinter (2013) showed that the money multiplier is relatively stable but velocity is relatively unstable, the opposite of that found by Adam and Kessy (2010). Our findings are consistent with the interpretation that shocks to reserve money are transmitted to money. But transmission from money to prices or output is weak because shifts in velocity, caused perhaps by financial innovations, may attenuate any aggregate demand effects. The finding of a strong effect of money on prices in the short and long run, as reported by Adam and others (2012), could be due to the addition of error correction terms or disequilibrium in various markets to an otherwise standard money demand that may have corrected shifts in velocity, thus restoring the role of reserve money as an inflation anchor in Tanzania's RMP.[15]

[15]This result is not unique to Tanzania. For example, covering a group of 17 sub-Saharan African countries, Barnichon and Peiris (2008) show that the real money gap has a statistically significant contemporaneous impact on inflation.

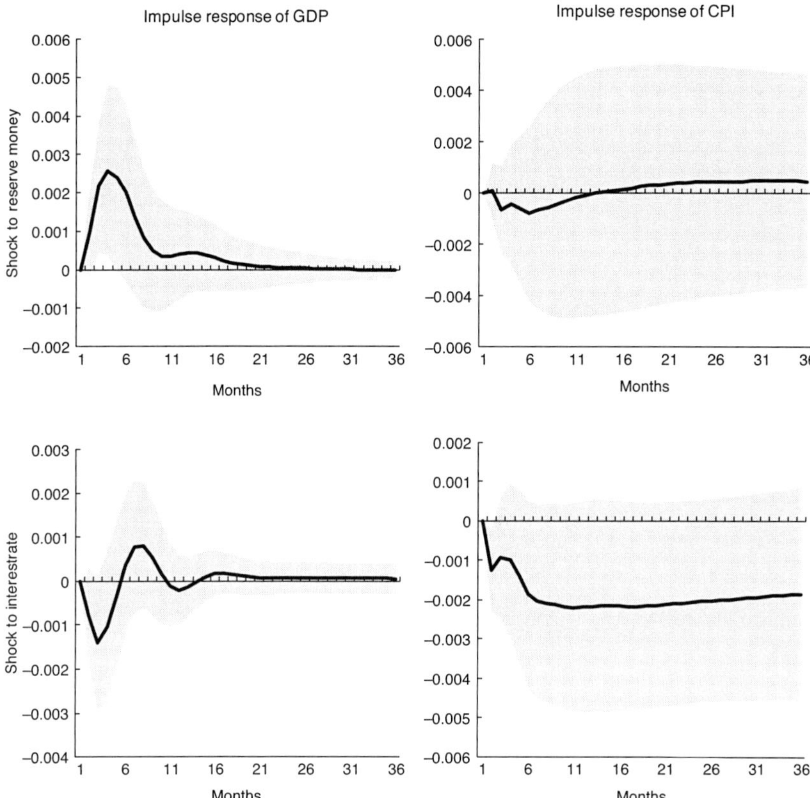

Figure 7.11 Structural Vector Autoregression Impulse Responses for Uganda

Source: Authors' calculations.
Note: Shocks are one standard deviation; vertical axes are percentages, horizontal axes are months, and the shaded areas denote the 90 percent confidence bands. CPI = consumer price index.

Other reasons exist for the weak MTM in Tanzania, given our vector autoregression results and those of Montiel and others (2012). For example, the exchange rate channel could play a role in Tanzania, as in Kenya, but the presence of capital controls may be limiting its usefulness. Removal of capital controls by 2015, an objective of the Tanzanian authorities, should strengthen the role of the exchange rate and the interest rate channels.

Uganda

As in Rwanda, Uganda's output responds significantly to positive shocks to reserve money over the short term, while leaving prices unfettered (Figure 7.11). This mechanism is sustained even when exogenous variables are dropped from the model. Conversely, a positive shock to the policy rate has an ambiguous effect on output, but a persistent deflationary impact on prices. Estimating the vector autoregression with five lags, as opposed to three in the baseline specification, generates a more pronounced impulse response of CPI to innovations in the policy

TABLE 7.1

Variance Decomposition

	GDP		CPI	
	Reserve Money	Interest Rate	Reserve Money	Interest Rate
Burundi	8.3	7.6	4.5	0.3
Kenya	5.4	3.8	19.3	12.8
Rwanda	12.7	3.1	3.9	4.4
Tanzania	0.7	0.7	1.4	11.1
Uganda	11.8	2.7	0.3	7.2

Source: Authors.
Note: CPI = consumer price index.

rate. The results of the factor-augmented vector autoregression specification generally mimic the dynamics of the baseline specification, with one important difference: the interest rate increases reduce inflation under a factor-augmented vector autoregression more than a simple structural vector autoregression or Bayesian vector autoregression. This perhaps shows that the Central Bank of Uganda uses a much larger information set in deciding interest rate changes.[16] Our findings are in marked contrast to those of Mugume (2011), who finds that all monetary transmission channels are inactive in Uganda.

Results from Variance Decomposition

It is important to quantify the relative importance of shocks in variability of inflation and output and not just the mean dynamics, which is what the impulse responses suggest. Results from variance decomposition of the estimated vector autoregressions show (Table 7.1):

- Changes in output are more due to shocks to reserve money than to the interest rate. This is largest in Uganda and Rwanda, a finding that is consistent with our impulse response analysis.
- Inflation is more due to shocks to the interest rate than shocks to reserve money. This is more pronounced in Tanzania and Uganda. The result is surprising for Tanzania because it runs counter to the findings from impulse response analysis, but it is consistent with the impulse response analysis for Uganda.

Summary of Main Results

Using a 90 percent confidence interval in evaluating statistical inference of impulse responses, we summarize and interpret our results as follows:

- An expansionary monetary policy (i.e., a positive shock to reserve money) increases output significantly in Burundi, Rwanda, and Uganda, but has no statistically significant effect on prices in any EAC country. This result is

[16]It is also worth noting that fitting our baseline recursive vector autoregression on a longer time frame (September 1995 to December 2010) increases the magnitude and life of the shocks drastically, suggesting that transmission channels have withered over time.

consistent with the presence of a flat, short-run, aggregate supply curve in the EAC. An unstable money multiplier or unstable income velocity of money does not seem to have affected the MTM in Burundi, Rwanda, and Uganda, at least compared to output. Even if velocity is unstable, the finding of strong output effects from shocks to reserve money shows that shifts in velocity have not been large enough and/or in the wrong direction to offset the expansionary effects of reserve money on output.

- Monetary policy, as measured by shocks to reserve money, has short lags in Uganda (statistically significant output effects for the first 6 months only), but long lags in Burundi and Rwanda (statistically significant output effects from 6 to 15 months).
- An expansionary monetary policy (a negative shock to the policy rate) increases prices significantly in Kenya and Uganda and output in Burundi, Kenya, and Rwanda.
- Monetary policy, as measured by shocks to the policy rate, has long lags for prices and output for all EAC countries (varying from 5 months in Burundi to 36 months in Uganda). Rwanda has the shortest lag (three to five months).
- Channels of the MTM differ across the EAC, with exchange rate and credit channels being important in Kenya, credit in Rwanda, and interest rate in Burundi.
- The policy rate seems to matter more to the evolution of prices in countries with deeper financial markets and more competitive banking systems, such as Kenya and Uganda.
- Interest rates typically decline in response to a positive shock to reserve money, an effect that is statistically significant at a 90 percent confidence interval in three countries (Burundi, Kenya, Uganda). So movements in money and interest rates are consistent with each other.

What explains the lack of significance in the other EAC countries (Tanzania and Rwanda)? The negative response of interest rates to a positive shock in reserve money should strengthen the contractionary (expansionary) effect of a negative (positive) shock to reserve money. But we find that a shock to reserve money and the policy rate sometimes move in directions that exert expansionary and contractionary impulses, resulting in a statistically insignificant impact of either reserve money or policy rate on prices. This interpretation seems to explain our findings for Tanzania and Rwanda. This may also indicate that attempts to choose simultaneously prices (interest rates) and quantities (reserve money) that are inconsistent with each other can weaken the MTM, the role of interest rates, and the development of market-determined interest rates and exchange rates.

CONCLUSIONS

As in emerging or frontier market economies, some EAC countries have begun conducting monetary policy through prices (interest rates) rather than quantities (monetary aggregates), although adherence to any stated targeting rule varies across countries. As in developed countries, the shift away from a money-focused monetary policy seems to be taking place as a result of, among other things, possible structural shifts in money demand and money multipliers, as well as a deepening of the financial sector and openness of the economy to international flows.

Some EAC countries have found it operationally relevant to work with a flexible RMP, which takes into account shifts in velocity and multipliers and other exogenous shocks that affect monetary targets. Uganda, for example, implemented a flexible RMP from September 2009 through June 2011 that delinked short-term liquidity from structural liquidity management. Uganda has formally shifted to an inflation-targeting lite monetary policy framework with a direct focus on prices (short-term interest rate as the operating target) rather than on quantities (reserve money) while continuing to monitor developments in monetary and credit aggregates, external environment, output gap, and inflationary expectations.

In some EAC countries and during particular episodes, monetary policy may have been conducted by simultaneously choosing both prices and quantities. Such an approach, common in countries with shallow financial markets and limited experience with competitive auctions of central bank liquidity papers, tends to undermine development in the interbank markets and reduces the role of interest rates and exchange rates in the MTM.

Kenya and, to some extent, Tanzania and Rwanda have also started relying more on changes in the policy rate to guide monetary policy while continuing to use direct instruments (e.g., changes in reserve requirement ratio) to alter monetary policy conditions. Complicating the problem has been the role of commercial banks, as their lending rates tend to be sticky and not responsive to changes in the policy rate. The credit channel will take time as banks learn to work within a new monetary policy framework.

Strengthening the MTM in the EAC requires, among other things, addressing the following factors and policies, some of which are developmental in nature and would take time to implement:

- Ensure that monetary targets and interest rate policies are consistent with each other. Interest rates play a supporting role in a money-focused monetary policy if reserve money continues to be the operating target. In theory, interest rates are endogenous when money is being targeted and should be allowed to play such a role.
- A high share of currency in circulation in reserve money reduces the role a central bank can play in affecting cost conditions in the economy. As a result, regulating a small part of reserve money, namely, bank reserves, will not be as effective. An interest rate–focused monetary policy may not suffer from the same fate.
- A large informal economy reduces the role monetary policy can play in influencing cost conditions in financing economic activities, a factor that could go hand in hand with a higher share of currency in circulation. The size of an informal economy and share of currency in circulation could become less of a binding constraint if interest rates fully reflect liquidity

conditions and monetary policy and the public becomes aware of the cost of holding idle money balances.

- A low financial depth or low access to finance reduces the scope and reach of monetary policy.
- A shallow and limited integration of interbank foreign exchange and money markets reduces the effectiveness of the exchange rate and interbank interest rates in transmitting changes in monetary policy.
- Limited competition in the banking sector can reduce interest rate pass-through because actions by monetary authorities may not be fully transmitted to changes in credit availability, loan rates, or deposit rates.
- High commercial bank excess reserves reduce the role a central bank can play in regulating the market for bank reserves, and, hence, liquidity in the economy. Banks can simply draw on these balances to lend, which may undo central bank actions.
- Capital controls can weaken the MTM. The presence of significant capital controls can make the exchange rate channel or interest rate channel ineffective because exchange rates and interest rates may not respond to changes in market fundamentals, and capital flows may cease to operate effectively in both directions.
- High-quality and high-frequency data can help. The noise in the data-generating process for the EAC and low-income countries may be responsible for a weak MTM. This may make it harder to isolate the effects of monetary policy and lack of timely data may lead to policy errors. Clearly, improvements in data availability, particularly at high frequency, can give meaningful signals to central bankers and the public; hence, allowing timely responses to developments in economic activities.

REFERENCES

Adam, C. S., D. Kwimbere, W. Mbowe, and S. O'Connell, 2012, "Food Prices and Inflation in Tanzania," International Growth Center WP/12/0459 (London: International Growth Center).

Adam, C., and P. J. Kessy, 2010, "Assessing the Stability and Predictability of the Money Multiplier in the EAC: The Case of Tanzania" (London: International Growth Center).

Barnichon, R., and S. J. Peiris, 2008, "Sources of Inflation in Sub-Saharan Africa," *Journal of African Economies*, Vol. 17, No. 5, pp. 729–746.

Bean, C., M. Paustian, A. Penalver, and T. Taylor, 2010, "Monetary Policy after the Fall," paper presented at Jackson Hole, Wyoming, Conference.

Bernanke, B. S., and M. Gertler, 1995, "Inside the Black Box: The Credit Channel of Monetary Policy Transmission," *Journal of Economic Perspectives*, Vol. 9, No. 4, pp. 27–48.

Bernanke, B., J. Boivin, and P. S. Eliasz, 2005, "Measuring the Effects of Monetary Policy: A Factor-Augmented Vector Autoregressive (FAVAR) Approach," *The Quarterly Journal of Economics*, Vol. 120, No. 1, pp. 387–422.

Boivin, J., M. T. Kiley, and F. S. Mishkin, 2011, "How Has the Monetary Transmission Mechanism Evolved Over Time?" in *Handbook of Monetary Economics*, ed. by M. Friedman and M. Woodford, Vol. 3, pp. 369–422 (Amsterdam: North Holland).

Canova, F., 2007, *Methods for Applied Macroeconomic Research* (New Jersey: Princeton University Press).

Cheng, K. C., 2006, "A VAR Analysis of Kenya's Monetary Policy Transmission Mechanism: How Does the Central Bank's Repo Rate Affect the Economy?" IMF Working Paper 06/300 (Washington: International Monetary Fund).

Christiano, L., J. Eichenbaum, M. Evans, and C. Evans, 1999, "Monetary Policy Shocks: What Have We Learned and to What End?" in *Handbook of Macroeconomics*, ed. by M. Woodword and J. Taylor (Amsterdam: North Holland).

Christiano, L. J., M. Trabandt, and K. Walentin, 2010, "DSGE Models for Monetary Policy," NBER Working Paper No. 16074 (Cambridge, Massachusetts: National Bureau of Economic Research).

Christiano, L. J., C. Ilut, R. Motto, and M. Rostagno, 2010, "Monetary Policy and Stock Market Booms," paper presented at Jackson Hole, Wyoming, Conference.

Davoodi, H. R., S. Dixit, and G. Pinter, 2013, "Monetary Transmission Mechanism in the East African Community: An Empirical Investigation," IMF Working Paper No. 13/39 (Washington: International Monetary Fund).

European Central Bank, 2010, "Monetary Policy Transmission in the Euro Area, a Decade after the Introduction of the Euro," *Monthly Economic Bulletin*. http://www.ecb.int/pub/mb/html/index.en.html.

International Monetary Fund, 2010, "Monetary Policy Effectiveness in Sub-Saharan Africa," Ch. 2 in *Regional Economic Outlook: Sub-Saharan Africa* (Washington, October). http://www.imf.org/external/pubs/ft/reo/2010/AFR/eng/sreo1010.htm.

Iossifov, P. N. K., M. Takebe, R. York, and Z. Zhan, 2009, "Improving Surveillance Across the CEMAC Region," IMF Working Paper No. 260 (Washington: International Monetary Fund).

Ireland, P., 2008, "Monetary Transmission Mechanism," in *The New Palgrave Dictionary of Economics*, ed. by L. Blume and S. Durlauf (Hampshire: Palgrave Macmillan, 2nd ed.).

Issing, O., 2011, "Lessons for Monetary Policy: What Should the Consensus Be?" IMF Working Paper No. 11/97 (Washington: International Monetary Fund).

Laurens, B. J., 2005, "Monetary Policy Implementation at Different Stages of Market Developments," IMF Occasional Paper No. 255 (Washington: International Monetary Fund).

Litterman, R. B., 1986, "Forecasting with Bayesian Vector Autoregressions–Five Years of Experience," *Journal of Business & Economic Statistics*, Vol. 4, No. 1, pp. 25–38.

Mishkin, F. S., 1995, "Symposium on the Monetary Transmission Mechanism," *Journal of Economic Perspectives*, Vol. 9, No. 4, pp. 3–10.

Mishkin, F. S., 1998, "International Experiences with Different Monetary Policy Regimes," *Journal of Monetary Economics*, Vol. 43, No. 3, pp. 579–605.

Montiel, P., C. Adam, W. Mbowe, and S. O'Connell, 2012, "Financial Architecture and the Monetary Transmission Mechanism in Tanzania," Working Paper 12/0343 (Oxford: International Growth Center).

Morsink, J., and T. Bayoumi, 2001, "A Peek Inside the Black Box: The Monetary Transmission Mechanism in Japan," *IMF Staff Papers*, Vol. 48, No. 1, pp. 22–57.

Mugume, A., 2011, "Monetary Transmission Mechanisms in Uganda," Bank of Uganda Working Paper, Vol. 4, No. 1 (Kampala: Bank of Uganda).

O'Connell, S. A., 2011, "Towards a Rule-Based Approach to Monetary Policy Evaluation in Sub-Saharan Africa," *Journal of African Economies*, Vol. 20 (African Economic Research Consortium Supplement 2), pp. 36–66.

Peersman, G., and F. Smets, 2001, "The Monetary Transmission Mechanism in the Euro Area: More Evidence from VAR Analysis," European Central Bank Working Paper No. 91 (Frankfurt: European Central Bank).

Sims, C. A., 1980, "Macroeconomics and Reality," *Econometrica*, Vol. 48, No. 1, pp. 1–48.

———, J. H. Stock, and M. W. Watson, 1990, "Inference in Linear Time Series Models with Some Unit Roots," *Econometrica*, Vol. 58, No. 1, pp. 113–144.

Taylor, J. B., 1995, "The Monetary Transmission Mechanism: An Empirical Framework," *Journal of Economic Perspectives*, Vol. 9, No. 4, pp. 11–26.

van den Boogaerde, P., and C. Tsangarides, 2005, "Ten Years After the CFA Franc Devaluation: Progress Toward Regional Integration in the WAEMU," IMF Working Paper No. 05/145 (Washington: International Monetary Fund).

Weber, A. A., R. Gerke, and A. Worms, 2009, "Has the Monetary Transmission Process in the Euro Area Changed? Evidence Based on VAR Estimates," BIS Working Paper No. 276 (Basel: Bank for International Settlements).

CHAPTER 8

Exchange Rate Arrangements in the Transition to East African Monetary Union

CHRISTOPHER S. ADAM, PANTALEO KESSY, CAMILLUS KOMBE, AND STEPHEN A. O'CONNELL

This chapter considers alternative exchange rate arrangements for the countries of the East African Community (EAC) in the transition to monetary union. Three main considerations shape our analysis. First, while existing exchange rate policies differ in some important ways across the EAC, the partner states wish to achieve a common exchange rate policy during the transition to union. Second, since the transition may well occupy several years or more, the arrangements adopted during this period should be consistent with macroeconomic stability and financial development on a country-by-country basis. Third, transition should be designed to avoid real exchange rate misalignment in the first few years of union.

In focusing on how to move to union, we are intentionally leaving aside the deeper question of whether monetary union is in fact desirable for these countries. Growing empirical literature takes a largely skeptical view, based on the lack of an asymmetry in the impact of economic shocks across the community and the limitations of cross-border labor mobility and other substitutes for intra-community adjustments in monetary policy and exchange rates (European Central Bank [ECB], 2010; Kigabo, Masson, and Masson, 2012).

Debrun, Masson, and Pattillo (2010) add that although a reduction in inflation bias is one of the potential benefits of monetary union, central banks in the EAC may be able to accomplish this unilaterally, through institutional measures that build on their relatively strong inflation performance over the past decade, without ceding control to a supranational institution. But these reservations are not decisive. Global evidence suggests, for example, that entering a monetary union tends endogenously to reduce some forms of macroeconomic asymmetry across members (De Grauwe, 2009). And while asymmetries will surely persist, the transition process itself represents an opportunity to reduce the union's exposure to asymmetric shocks—including financial and fiscal spillover that may be exacerbated rather than reduced by union—and to strengthen alternative mechanisms for macroeconomic adjustment. The issue of how to move to union therefore remains of considerable interest, both for the EAC and for other regions where political or economic considerations may favor deeper economic integration.

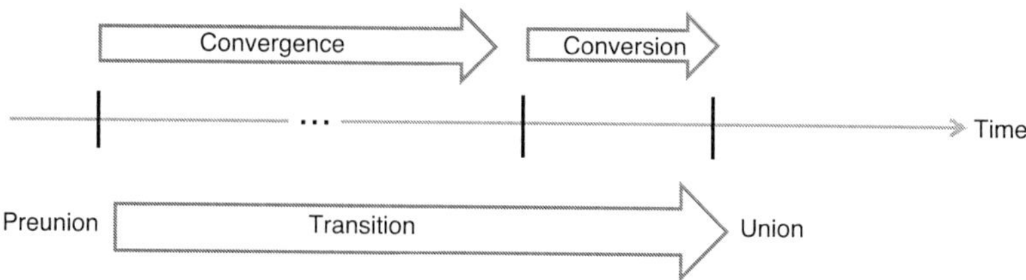

Figure 8.1 The Transition to Monetary Union

Exchange rate commitments played a central role in Europe's transition to monetary union, and the main question we address in this chapter is whether the EAC countries should follow suit by adopting a grid-plus-band system in the run up to union. Our answer, on balance, is no. There is a straightforward trade-off in the EAC case between the costs of tight exchange rate commitments during the convergence period and their potential value in acclimatizing the partner states to the loss of intraunion exchange rate flexibility once union is accomplished. The ECB, in its comprehensive report on the transition to union in the EAC, resolves this trade-off in favor of an exchange rate grid (ECB, 2010). We resolve it in favor of managed floats with country-level inflation targets. More specifically, we distinguish two broad phases of the transition, as Figure 8.1 illustrates: a convergence phase of uncertain duration, during which the partner states work to achieve a set of preconditions that may or may not include exchange rate criteria, followed by a brief conversion phase that should be of fixed duration and that follows an irrevocable decision to move to union. Our view is that tight exchange rate commitments are appropriate only in the final stage, a stage we view as some way off and that we argue should probably be no more than a year in duration.

We begin the chapter by setting out the initial conditions we consider important for guiding the choice of exchange rate arrangements during the transition. Then, we review the evolution of exchange rate policy in the EAC, emphasizing the increasingly uniform commitment of member states to an open capital account. Next, we assess the degree to which international capital mobility constrains monetary policy in the EAC. While direct measures suggest a limited degree of financial integration with global markets, an indirect, regression-based approach delivers a distinctly different impression. Particularly in Kenya and Uganda, we find that foreign exchange market pressures generated by discretionary changes in monetary policy are consistent with a substantial degree of short-term capital mobility. These findings suggest that tight, but adjustable exchange rate commitments could be subject to speculative attack, particularly if made over any considerable period.

Following that, we address the appropriate exchange rate regime for the transition. We characterize alternative regimes according to the approach they adopt to anchoring inflation at the community-wide level and the scope they leave, if any, for monetary autonomy at the country level. We defend our preference for a managed float in terms of the structure and history of the EAC and with reference to our earlier evidence on capital mobility.

Then, we focus on the conversion phase. We discuss the introduction of an East African Currency Unit (EACU) and the choice of conversion parities. We argue that the method for choosing conversion parities should be subject to advance agreement by the partner states, both to avoid damaging misalignments at the outset of union and to discourage competitive depreciations during the convergence phase. The costs of initial misalignment will of course be relatively minor if nominal wages and prices can adjust rapidly to real exchange rate disequilibrium. A straightforward econometric approach suggests, however, that wage and price adjustment is not markedly more rapid in the EAC countries than in emerging market or advanced economies with flexible exchange rates. This finding underscores the relevance of adequate exchange rate assessments at the outset of the convergence phase.

We conclude our analysis by briefly considering the postunion impact of monetary union on real exchange rates and competitiveness. Using evidence from the CFA franc zone, we argue that one of the main impacts of union is likely to be a convergence of equilibrium real exchange rates across partner countries. Thus, for example, equilibrium real exchange rates will depreciate in resource-abundant members of the monetary union, moderating some portion of their Dutch disease, whereas resource-poor partners will experience a real appreciation and a shift in the composition of their exports toward the region and away from the rest of the world.[1] Finally, we close the chapter with a summary of our contributions and a pointer to areas for further research.

CURRENT EXCHANGE RATE POLICIES

The three large countries of the EAC currently operate managed floats, with fully open capital accounts in Kenya and Uganda and a liberalization under way that will remove most of the remaining capital account restrictions in Tanzania. The context for these choices predates the reconstitution of the three-member community in 2001 and the accession of Burundi and Rwanda in 2007. Operating independently in the first half of the 1990s, each of the big three (Kenya, Tanzania, Uganda) implemented a set of reforms designed to eliminate a distorting system of foreign exchange rationing, develop an interbank market for foreign exchange, and establish a unified and market-determined exchange rate. Uganda and Kenya liberalized their exchange controls very substantially in the mid-1990s, dismantling

[1] Dutch disease is the apparent relationship between the increase in exploitation of *natural resources* and a decline in competitiveness. The mechanism is that an increase in revenues from natural resources (or inflows of foreign aid) will make a given nation's currency stronger compared to that of other nations (appreciation), resulting in the nation's other exports becoming more expensive for other countries to buy, making the manufacturing sector less *competitive*.

controls on the capital account as well as the current account. Tanzania liberalized the current account fully, but has only recently begun to liberalize its capital controls as part of harmonization efforts within the EAC. It is highly likely that the exchange rate policy framework the union-wide central bank adopts will be close in outline to the framework currently operated in the big three countries, with a flexible, market-determined exchange rate and a largely open capital account. Burundi and Rwanda appear to be on a gradual path to such a regime, and would be likely to continue on this path even in the absence of monetary union.

In Adam and others (2012) we provide a summary of current foreign exchange market arrangements and operating procedures in the EAC. Four of the five countries are formally committed to exchange rate convertibility for current account purposes.[2] There are differences across countries, however, in de facto exchange rate flexibility, stringency of capital controls, and sophistication of interbank foreign exchange markets. In its classification of de facto exchange rate regimes, the IMF characterizes the regime in Kenya, Tanzania, and Uganda as managed floating, Rwanda as a crawl-like regime, and Burundi as a stabilized regime (as of 2011). These differences in exchange rate flexibility are apparent, particularly over the past few years, in Figure 8.2, which tracks EAC exchange rates against the U.S. dollar over the past decade.

In terms of operating procedures for exchange rate management, Kenya, Uganda, and Tanzania deploy comparable frameworks in which the authorities commit to a floating exchange rate whose value is determined in the interbank foreign exchange market, and structure their foreign exchange operations around reserve coverage and liquidity management objectives established in their reserve money programs. The reserve money programs in these countries are anchored, in turn, on explicit targets for inflation. Similar arrangements are not yet fully in place in Rwanda and Burundi, but both countries are working to develop interbank foreign exchange markets and are moving in the direction of greater exchange rate flexibility.

These differences in exchange rate management within the EAC are reflected in the structural characteristics of the foreign exchange markets. In Kenya, Uganda, and Tanzania, the markets are perceived to be broadly competitive, and the central banks are an important but not decisive player in the market. Central banks may seek to trim short-run volatility in the market, but would not normally expect to be able to decisively influence the underlying rate. In Rwanda and Burundi, where foreign aid flows to government account for around half of all foreign exchange inflows, and where the private financial sector is less developed, the central banks are the decisive players and, to a large degree, still the market makers. Residual controls on the capital account in Tanzania and the lower levels of financial sector and capital market development in Rwanda and Burundi would suggest that these countries continue to experience significant insulation from portfolio capital flows and the associated risk of speculative pressures on the

[2] Dates of accession to Article VIII status in the IMF are as follows: Kenya and Uganda 1994, Tanzania 1996, and Rwanda 1998. Burundi has not yet ratified Article VIII.

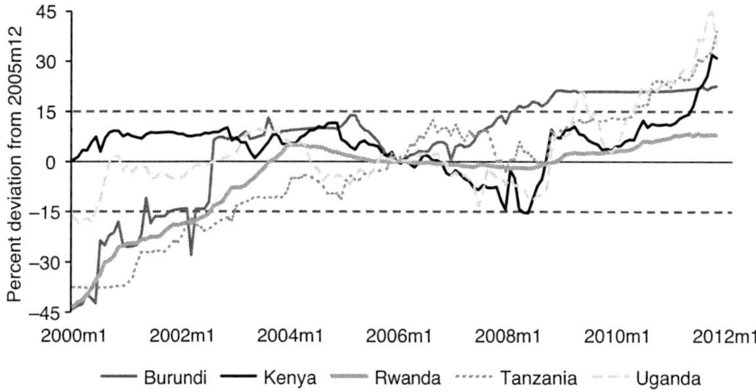

Figure 8.2 East African Community Exchange Rates

Source: IMF, International Financial Statistics database.
Note: The figure shows log differences relative to 2005m12, multiplied by 100 to convert into approximate percentage differences.

currency. As we will see in the next section, these differences are apparent in indirect measures of capital mobility, although they do not show up strongly in direct comparisons of the volume of private capital flows.

ASSESSING SHORT-TERM CAPITAL MOBILITY

Portfolio behavior is a potentially powerful source not only of day-to-day pressures in foreign exchange markets, but also of speculative attacks that can test a central bank's commitment to a fixed exchange rate. These attacks can be costly for the economy whether they succeed or fail. A successful attack produces a large devaluation, with its impact on inflation, external debt burden, and central bank credibility, and a failed attack may require an aggressive monetary policy response that damages the domestic economy through very high interest rates. The celebrated *trilemma* proposition in international macroeconomics states that in the presence of high capital mobility, a central bank must choose between exchange rate targets and domestic targets for monetary policy: it cannot sustain strong exchange rate commitments unless it is prepared to abandon domestic objectives when this is required to defend the exchange rate. This reasoning is one of the influences behind the move in Kenya and Uganda to exchange rate flexibility in the 1990s, when they were also choosing to open their capital accounts. Regardless of the other merits of flexible exchange rates (such as in supporting exchange rate unification, and allowing rapid adjustment of the real exchange rate to terms of trade shocks), a flexible rate was thought necessary to support each country's commitment to an open capital account.

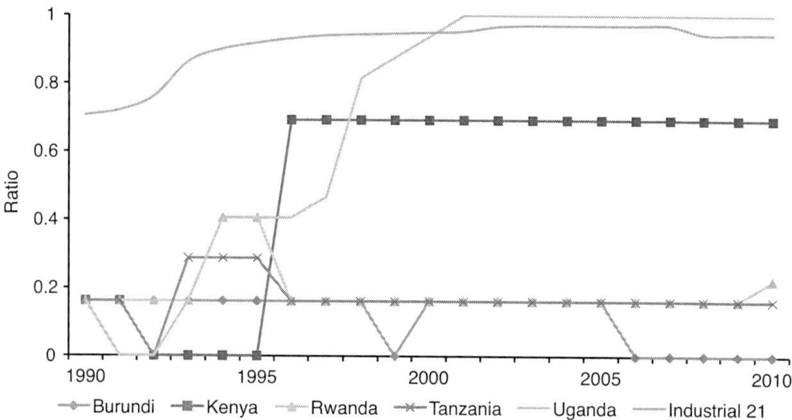

Figure 8.3 De Jure Capital Account Openness, 1990–2010

Source: Chinn and Ito (2008).

Concerns about the trilemma also apply, of course, to exchange rate commitments during the transition to monetary union. Once union is consummated, intraunion exchange rates are eliminated as potential sources of speculative capital flows. But during the transition, the advisability of tight exchange rate commitments depends on the degree to which these commitments may be exposed to speculative attack. This in turn depends on the degree of de facto capital mobility on a country-by-country basis, particularly in short-maturity claims, which are thought to be more responsive to transitory changes in market sentiment.

Capital mobility can be assessed either directly, by looking at the stringency of legal restrictions on capital movements (de jure openness) or the volume of cross-border flows (de facto openness), or indirectly, by assessing the impact of portfolio behavior on domestic interest rates and exchange rates. We employ both approaches in this section.

Figure 8.3 shows the Chinn and Ito (2008) measure of de jure financial openness, which is based on the prevalence of legal restrictions on capital account transactions as reported in the IMF's *Annual Report on Exchange Arrangements and Exchange Restrictions*. This measure varies quite substantially across the EAC. Even excluding the industrial countries, Burundi was at the bottom of the global distribution of de jure financial openness in 2010 (7th percentile), and Tanzania was in the 44th percentile along with South Africa. Rwanda was in the 45th, and Kenya the 68th. Uganda was in the most financially open group in the world in 2009, whether including industrial countries or not.[3]

[3] Capital account liberalization is ongoing in Rwanda and Tanzania, so the Chinn-Ito indexes may show increases for 2011 and 2012.

TABLE 8.1

Stock Measures of De Facto Capital Account Openness
(Financial assets + liabilities/gross domestic product [%], group and period medians)

Country or Region	Lane and Milesi-Ferretti Measure 2005–08	Adjusted Lane and Milesi-Ferretti Measure 2005–08
Burundi	217	64
Kenya	74	41
Rwanda	62	33
Tanzania	87	53
Uganda	88	55
East African Community	**87**	**47**
South Africa	157	148
Africa	122	71
Latin America and Caribbean	155	127
South and East Asia	144	95
OECD	415	409

Sources: Lane and Milesi-Ferretti (2007); IMF, World Development Indicators database and Global Development Finance database.
Note: OECD = Organization for Economic Cooperation and Development.

These differences in legal openness are not strongly reflected, however, in measures based on observed private capital flows. Table 8.1 reports a measure of de facto financial openness based on gross transactions in the capital account. The Lane and Milesi-Ferretti measure (2007) is the sum of total external financial assets and liabilities as a share of GDP; this is the stock analog, for the capital account, of a widely used measure of de facto openness to trade in goods and services.[4] The table also reports an adjusted Lane and Milesi-Ferretti measure that corrects for the prevalence of what might best be characterized as nonmarket financial claims in low-income countries. Following Dhungana (2008), this measure deletes official reserves (excluding gold) on the asset side and concessional debt owed to official creditors on the liability side. We show medians rather than means because of the presence of extreme values in the sample.[5]

As noted by Dhungana (2008), sub-Saharan Africa appears to be significantly less integrated into global capital markets once the nonmarket flows are excluded. The EAC is comparable to the rest of Africa in this respect, including Kenya, which is surprisingly low given its relatively advanced degree of

[4]The trade measure is the sum of imports and exports divided by GDP. Financial assets and liabilities include foreign direct investment, portfolio equity, debt, financial derivatives, and, on the asset side, foreign exchange reserves (including gold).

[5]These tend to be associated with small economies and economies in which GDP at official exchange rates may be significantly undermeasured. In sub-Saharan Africa, these include Liberia (adjusted openness measure = 863 percent), Seychelles (240 percent), Guinea-Bissau (220 percent), Lesotho (200 percent), the Gambia (140 percent), and São Tomé and Príncipe (140 percent).

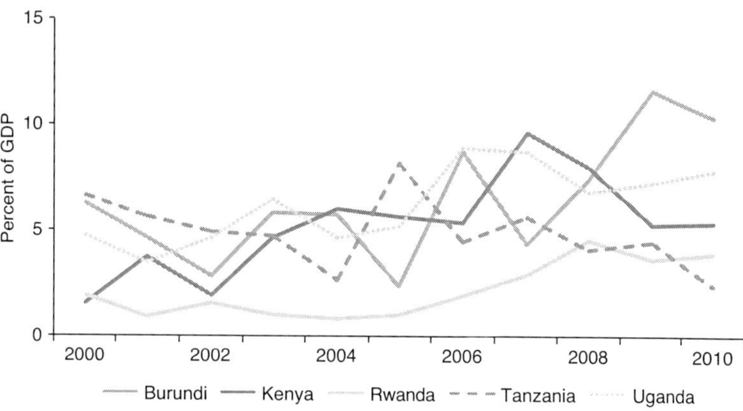

Figure 8.4 Gross Financial Account Flows

Source: IMF, International Financial Statistics database.
Note: Gross financial flows consist of foreign direct investment, portfolio flows, financial derivatives, and long-term debt flows (denoted "other investment" in the International Financial Statistics database). Our measure of long-term debt flows omits flows attributed to "general government" or "monetary authority."

financial development (see also O'Connell and others, 2010).[6] Figure 8.4 tracks recent developments by showing a flow version of the unadjusted Lane and Milesi-Ferretti measure—the ratio of gross financial flows to GDP for the past decade. While all EAC countries except Tanzania have experienced at least a modest trend increase in gross flows in recent years, these flows remain small by comparison with GDP, both in absolute terms and by the standards of other countries in sub-Saharan Africa. They also differ by less across the countries of the EAC than might be expected given their sharp differences in de jure openness.

The direct measures therefore suggest that a substantial gap exists between the degree of legal openness in the EAC and the actual volume of international capital flows. What matters for monetary policy, however, is capital mobility at the margin. If this is increasing rapidly, or if short-term capital movements are poorly captured in the capital account, then these direct measures may underestimate the degree to which capital mobility constrains monetary policy in the EAC.

The remainder of this section assesses de facto short-term capital mobility in the three large countries of the EAC indirectly by adapting a time-honored methodology that dates from Porter (1972) and is widely used in the industrial country and emerging markets literature. The central idea is that an unanticipated

[6]The unadjusted Lane and Milesi-Ferretti data suggest that Burundi's capital account is much more open than that in the EAC's larger and more developed economies. This anomaly is consistent with the evidence for small economies with doubtful-quality GDP data, and, in the case of Burundi, is driven in part by very high external official indebtedness. Much of the anomaly is eliminated when we adjust for nonmarket transactions.

monetary expansion, such as an increase in domestic credit to the government, reduces domestic interest rates and thereby encourages portfolio substitution in favor of foreign assets. If the monetary authority is committed to a fixed exchange rate, the induced capital outflow drains international reserves, producing a contraction in the monetary base that partially or fully offsets the original expansion. The offset coefficient is the share of the original monetary expansion that is offset through capital outflows. This can be measured in principle at each horizon (such as a month or a quarter), with the size of the offset coefficient indicating the degree to which de facto short-term capital mobility imposes a constraint on monetary policy. In Kenya, Tanzania, and Uganda, where the monetary policy framework and exchange rate regime have been reasonably stable for over a decade, we have sufficient data to apply a modified version of the offset coefficient approach to measure the degree to which portfolio behavior imposes a constraint on monetary policy.

Two adaptations are required, however, before this approach can be applied to countries on managed floats, rather than fixed exchange rates, and in which the central bank routinely engages in foreign exchange transactions with other parts of the public sector. To accommodate flexible exchange rates, we broaden the focus from reserve losses to exchange market pressure, defined as the sum of reserve losses and exchange rate depreciation.[7] An unanticipated monetary expansion now creates a combination of reserve losses and exchange rate depreciation, with the size of the overall impact dependent on the degree of capital mobility and the mix between reserve losses and depreciation dependent on the central bank's behavior.

The second adaptation arises from the prevalence of intragovernmental transactions in foreign exchange on the balance sheets of central banks in low-income countries. An aid inflow, for example, initially produces a simultaneous increase in central bank reserves and reduction in domestic credit, as the domestic-currency value of the inflow is credited to the relevant government ministry. The induced change in domestic credit, however, has nothing to do with monetary policy, and the directly offsetting change in international reserves has nothing to do with private capital flows. The reverse pattern occurs when a government ministry spends a portion of previously received budget support on imports. We control for these intra–public-sector transactions by allowing for an unobserved "aid" shock that is unrelated to monetary policy and that moves the current values of net domestic and net foreign assets in equal and opposite directions on the central bank's balance sheet.

To identify the dynamic impact of monetary policy changes on exchange rates and reserves, we estimate monthly structural vector autoregressions in logs of net domestic assets (*NDA*), net foreign assets (*NFA*), and the nominal exchange rate (*S*) for January 2002 to May 2011.[8] We proceed separately, country by country,

---

[7]This variable was introduced by Eichengreen, Rose, and Wyplosz (1994); variants have been used extensively in the literature on balance of payments crises.

[8]Data limitations preclude extending the sample to earlier years. The vector autoregressions include seven lags and a full set of centered monthly seasonal dummies.

measuring all three variables in first differences in order to guarantee stationarity of the residuals.[9] Our interest is in the impulse responses of the exchange rate and reserves to changes in monetary policy. To estimate these responses, we need to identify a set of unanticipated changes in monetary policy in the sample. We do this by assuming that the reduced form shocks to net domestic assets, net foreign assets, and the exchange rate, all of which we can observe directly from the reduced form vector autoregression, are linearly related to a set of unobservable structural shocks to monetary policy (*M*), aid (*A*), and the private sector's desired balance of payments (*B*). Denoting the latter shocks by ε_t, our identifying assumptions can be summarized by

$$\begin{pmatrix} u_t^{NDA} \\ u_t^{NFA} \\ u_t^{s} \end{pmatrix} = \begin{bmatrix} 1 & -1 & 0 \\ -\alpha & 1 & \beta-1 \\ \gamma & 0 & \beta \end{bmatrix} \begin{pmatrix} \sigma_M \varepsilon_t^M \\ \sigma_A \varepsilon_t^A \\ \sigma_B \varepsilon_t^B \end{pmatrix} = \begin{bmatrix} c_{11} & -c_{22} & 0 \\ c_{22} & c_{22} & c_{23} \\ c_{31} & 0 & c_{33} \end{bmatrix} \begin{pmatrix} \varepsilon_t^M \\ \varepsilon_t^A \\ \varepsilon_t^B \end{pmatrix} \quad (8.1)$$

along with the requirement that the structural shocks are mutually uncorrelated, with zero means and unit variances.

At the heart of this identification scheme is the relationship $u_t = C\,\varepsilon_t$ where C is an invertible matrix with positive terms on the diagonal.[10] We need three restrictions to identify C, which we obtain in equation (8.1) by assuming (1) that the private sector's structural balance-of-payments shock ε_t^B does not contemporaneously affect the change in domestic credit; (2) that the aid shock ε_t^A does not contemporaneously affect the exchange rate, and (3) that all contemporaneous and mutually offsetting movements in domestic credit and international reserves reflect internal transactions in foreign exchange between the central bank and the rest of the public sector.[11]

The expected signs of the elements of C follow those of the first matrix in equation (8.1). The diagonals and C_{31} are therefore expected to be positive, while c_{21} and c_{23} are expected to be negative. The variances of the structural shocks can be inferred from C using $c_{11} = \sigma_M$, $c_{22} = \sigma_A$, and $c_{33} - {}_{23} = \sigma_B$. Table 8.2 shows our estimates of the elements of C. These estimates have the correct signs in all cases and are generally highly statistically significant.

---

[9]We adjust net foreign and domestic assets for exchange rate valuation effects and measure both variables as shares of the lagged monetary base.

[10]Following the standard structural vector autoregression approach, $u_t = C\,\varepsilon_t$ implies $\Omega = CC'$, where the covariance matrix of ε_t is a 3×3 identity matrix and where $\Omega = E[uu']$ is the covariance matrix of reduced-form shocks. Ω can be estimated from the reduced-form vector autoregression, but because Ω is symmetric, this estimate only delivers six restrictions on the elements of C. Equation (8.1) shows the three additional restrictions we are imposing in order to identify the C matrix and recover the structural shocks.

[11]A final bit of structure in equation (8.1) comes from interpreting σ_B as the impact of the balance-of-payments shock on exchange-market pressure, defining the latter as the sum $u_t^s - u_t^F$, of exchange-rate-depreciation and reserve losses. This restricts the difference between the (3,3) element and the (2,3) element of the first matrix to be 1. In the absence of an independent estimate of the standard deviation σ_B, however, this property does not impose an additional restriction on the elements of C.

TABLE 8.2

Coefficient Estimates for the *C* Matrix

Coefficient	Kenya	Tanzania	Uganda
c_{11}	2.15 (5.16***)	4.37 (5.9***)	5.54 (6.05***)
c_{21}	−0.13 (−0.29)	−0.96 (−1.4)	−2.41 (−2.50***)
c_{22}	4.14 (14.90***)	6.74 (14.4***)	8.53 (14.42***)
c_{23}	−1.14 (−2.89***)	−0.39 (−0.8)	−2.08 (−4.18***)
c_{31}	0.92 (2.72***)	0.08 (0.31)	1.45 (5.22***)
c_{33}	1.53 (7.49***)	1.70 (14.40***)	1.43 (5.78***)

Source: Authors' calculations.

Note: *t*-statistics are in parentheses; * denotes significance at the 10 percent level, ** at the 5 percent level, and *** at the 1 percent level. All vector autoregressions are estimated from January 2002 to May 2011 (excluding lags) and include seven lags and monthly seasonal dummies.

In Figure 8.5, we show the cumulative impulse responses of net foreign assets and the exchange rate to a one-time shock to domestic credit. These results should be treated with caution; the standard error bounds around our vector autoregression coefficients are large, and generally only the first month of impulse responses is statistically significant. The results nonetheless suggest that there is greater exposure to short-term capital mobility in the EAC than is indicated by the de facto direct approaches. In all three countries, an unanticipated monetary expansion produces a decline in reserves and a depreciation of the nominal exchange rate, consistent with a managed float in which the authorities "lean against the wind" to limit the short-run volatility of the exchange rate. These impacts are small in Tanzania, consistent with its relatively closed capital account as indicated by the de facto measures. Kenya and Uganda, by contrast, show substantial impacts, with roughly half of the monetary impulse offset through a drain in reserves within a six-month horizon, despite the willingness of their central banks to tolerate a weakening exchange rate.

The cumulative impact of a monetary expansion on exchange market pressure, defined as the sum of reserve losses and exchange rate depreciation,[12] is roughly equal to the size of the initial monetary impulse in Kenya and Uganda, and is easily twice the impact observed in Tanzania. Kenya's impacts emerge more gradually than Uganda's, consistent with the greater openness of Uganda's capital account; but in both countries, the results suggest that portfolio behavior exerts a substantial constraint on monetary policy. In Kenya's case, in particular, the size of the cumulative impacts suggest that the de facto measures considered previously may seriously underestimate that country's integration with global financial markets.

In interpreting these varied results, we place weight on the increasing sophistication of interbank markets in the EAC countries, and also on the recent liberalization of capital controls within the EAC itself. While the EAC countries are well short of the trilemma, their scope for maintaining tight exchange rate

[12] Eichengreen, Rose, and Wyplosz (1994) introduced this variable; variants have been used extensively in the literature on balance-of-payments crises.

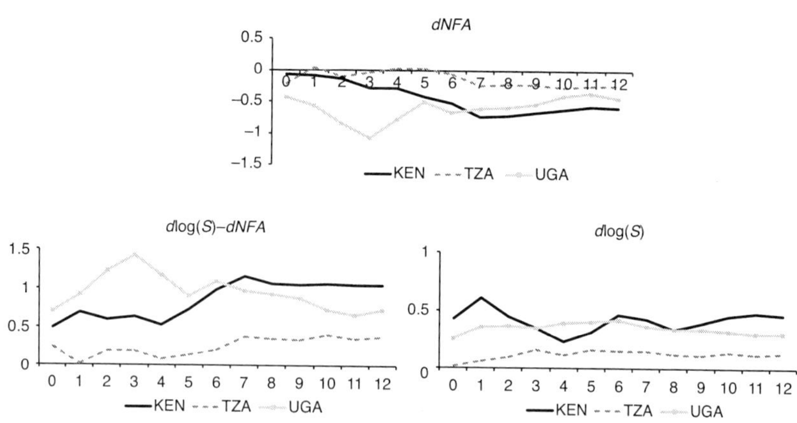

Figure 8.5 Cumulative Impulse Responses to a One-Unit Shock to Net Domestic Assets

Source: Authors' calculations.

Note: Three-variable structural vector autoregression in the change in adjusted net domestic assets, the change in adjusted net foreign assets (*dNFA*) and the change in the log of the nominal exchange rate in local currency per U.S. dollar [*dlog(S)*]. See Annex 8.1 for a definition of the variables. KEN = Kenya; TZA = Tanzania; UGA = Uganda.

commitments while simultaneously pursuing domestic monetary policy objectives is limited. This is particularly true for Kenya and Uganda. But as capital movements become freer within the EAC, portfolio capital will be able to move between each member and global markets indirectly, via transit through partners whose capital accounts are more open to the rest of the world. As in a free trade area without a common external tariff, the de facto exposure of each participant to external markets will tend to converge to that of the most open partner.

EXCHANGE RATE OPTIONS FOR THE CONVERGENCE PHASE

The convergence phase is of uncertain duration because it depends on political developments and on the pace at which the partner states can put convergence criteria in place. Exchange rate policies for this phase should therefore be consistent with the successful conduct of monetary policy for a potentially extended period. In analyzing the options, we place a particular emphasis on the transparency of alternative arrangements, their suitability for the EAC countries, and how they anchor inflation. We assume that, regardless of the option chosen, countries will work during the convergence phase to deepen market integration and harmonize financial market regulations.

Europe's Experience

Should nominal exchange rate commitments, in particular, convergence criteria for intraunion nominal exchange rates play a central role in the lead-up to monetary union? The complete elimination of intraunion exchange rates is of course the single most obvious consequence of adopting a common currency, and the appropriateness of this commitment plays a central role in the theory of optimal currency areas. In Europe, moreover, where the convergence phase spanned nearly three decades, nominal exchange rate commitments played a prominent role throughout transition. The exchange rate mechanism specified a grid of bilateral central exchange rates between the potential partners and a set of country-specific bands within which exchange rates were allowed to fluctuate. The central rates could be adjusted by mutual agreement, but for the two years leading to entry, countries were not to devalue their central rates and were to manage their economies so as to remain within a ±2.5 percent band of the parities without experiencing severe pressure. The central rates ultimately served as conversion rates: in May 1998, the entering members announced that they would convert to the euro on January 1, 1999, at the prevailing central rates. At the time of the announcement, no member was more than ½ percent from its central parity. Subsequent movements gradually closed the gaps to zero in the weeks and days before conversion (De Grauwe, 2009).

Not surprisingly, an agreement to limit cross-country exchange rate movements during the transition period features prominently in the ECB study of the prospective East African monetary union (ECB, 2010). A mutual grid is also a feature of the transitional arrangement among the countries of the Gulf Cooperation Council. But the advisability of such a scheme for the EAC countries is not obvious. Unlike either the European countries or the Gulf Cooperation Council members, who were on pegged arrangements before entering the transition period, the three large countries of the EAC operate de facto flexible exchange rate regimes and have done so for some time. The European grid, moreover, was subject to multiple speculative attacks during the transition, and while the Gulf states have been largely free of such concerns, their success in maintaining fixed pegs to the dollar predates the transition period and may be due in large part to an unusual combination of labor market flexibility and fiscal flexibility. These conditions are not prevalent in the EAC.[13] For these reasons, we consider a range of options for the convergence phase, including one in which exchange rate commitments are absent altogether.

Key Trade-Offs

Independently of their exchange rate histories, any set of countries planning to enter a monetary union faces the looming elimination of intraunion exchange rates as a macroeconomic adjustment mechanism. Here, we briefly review three potentially important arguments in favor of convergence criteria for nominal exchange rates during the transition, and two arguments against.

---

[13] Willett, Al-Barwani, and El Hag (2009) point out that more than half of the labor force is composed of guest workers in a number of Gulf Cooperation Council countries. This affords an unusual degree of labor market flexibility. Oil wealth, in turn, affords an unusual degree of fiscal flexibility and obviates the need for active exchange rate management to maintain external balance.

The first argument in favor of limiting the flexibility of intraunion exchange rates during the transition is that this may endogenously increase the flexibility of other national economic variables—wages and prices, labor mobility, fiscal policy—that will necessarily bear the brunt of addressing real exchange rate misalignments in the postunion period. The partners will therefore enter the union on a stronger footing for handling asymmetric shocks. This argument, however, accepts a set of well-known costs of limited flexibility, articulated in the following, for benefits that are highly uncertain and that may be secured, at least in part, through policy initiatives that directly target enhanced flexibility.

The second argument is that members may seek to depreciate their exchange rates during the transition in order to enter the union on a highly competitive footing. By preventing this behavior, nominal exchange rate criteria would avoid the erosion of national inflation anchors during the transition, while also limiting the extent of real exchange rate misalignment at the outset of union. We will argue here that the second of these concerns is best handled by setting conversion rates based on an empirical assessment of real exchange rate misalignment. We therefore focus here on the first.

The concept of local exchange rate competition plays a central role in the work of Debrun, Masson, and Pattillo (2005, 2010) on monetary unions in Africa. These authors argue that the formation of a union reduces the average degree of inflation bias across partners, by eliminating the ability of each partner to depreciate relative to the others. The empirical relevance of this argument, however, depends crucially on the strength of the intragroup externality from exchange rate depreciation. In Europe, this externality was widely thought to be important because the union itself was each member's largest trading partner. At least currently, however, the EAC countries trade much less with each other than the European countries did. It is doubtful, therefore, that intraunion exchange rates, as opposed to exchange rates vis-à-vis global markets, are an important focus of national concerns about competitiveness.

If the intraunion externality is relevant for the EAC, therefore, it must operate either via large anticipated *increases* in local trade or via linkages to global markets. One such channel may be competition for foreign direct investment (FDI). If the partner states view themselves as competing for labor-using FDI that would serve either a growing EAC single market or global export markets, then intraunion depreciation may be viewed as a way of attracting such FDI by reducing national wage costs, measured in global currencies, relative to the wage costs of partners. Our view is that although some such motivation may be present,[14] it can be adequately contained through a combination of convergence criteria on inflation and the option of adjusting conversion parities for severe misalignment.

The final argument in favor of exchange rate criteria is that a successful union requires a full understanding and acceptance by the partner states of their impending loss of monetary sovereignty. Exchange-rate commitments involve a reduction

[14] Concerns about the location of FDI were cited as among the acute strains within the three-member EAC in the early postindependence period.

in monetary autonomy and may also involve explicit cooperation across partners. As convergence criteria, therefore, they may help to ensure that partner states confront the implications of a decision that may be costly to maintain as well as to reverse (Beetsma and Giuliodori, 2010). Europe's experience suggests that this concern may be the strongest of the three we have mentioned. The current challenges of the euro area have emerged despite a process of political legitimization that spanned nearly 35 years and that allowed partners with serious reservations about monetary integration to remain outside the euro area, for an initial period for all European Union members, and indefinitely in at least one case (the United Kingdom). Our view, however, is that explicit discussions and ex ante agreements on fiscal union are the appropriate locus for handling this concern in the EAC case.

Any considerations in favor of exchange rate criteria have to be balanced against two potentially substantial costs associated with limited nominal exchange rate flexibility during the transition. The first is exposure to speculative attacks. We argued in the previous section that this cannot be ignored in the EAC, in the context of open capital accounts and an ongoing increase in de facto capital mobility.

The second is the loss of nominal exchange rate flexibility as a mechanism for avoiding intraunion real exchange rate misalignments during a potentially extended transition. The countries of the EAC will remain subject to asymmetric shocks during the transition period, including transitory changes in the terms of trade, aid, or financial flows and more permanent shocks associated with natural resource discoveries and, possibly, catch-up growth in Burundi and Rwanda.[15] If domestic wages and prices are relatively inflexible, nominal exchange rate adjustments will have an important role to play in securing the requisite real exchange rate adjustments. The next section provides indirect and perhaps surprising evidence of the limited degree of short-run wage/price flexibility in the EAC. While we view this evidence as provisional, it suggests a potentially important ongoing role for intraunion flexibility in nominal exchange rates.

A Taxonomy of Alternatives

Table 8.3 summarizes the five leading options for exchange rate management during the convergence phase. The options differ on two main and related dimensions. The first is the strength of exchange rate commitments on a country-by-country basis and therefore the degree to which exchange rate commitments provide an anchor for inflation. The options here range from a

[15]The last point refers to the Harrod-Balassa-Samuelson effect, whereby the poorer of two partners tends to experience a bilateral real appreciation as it converges to global productivity norms at a faster rate than its richer partner. With a purchasing power parity–adjusted real income that is easily two-thirds below that of the remainder of the EAC, Burundi in particular would be expected to experience a gradual equilibrium real appreciation within the EAC, regardless of the progress to monetary union. Many economists would expect monetary union to accelerate this process, for example, by enhancing Burundi's access to international capital markets (as occurred in the euro area), or accelerating price convergence in regionally produced goods and services, or both.

TABLE 8.3

Options for Exchange Rate Management During the Convergence Phase

Option	Nominal anchor	Locus of monetary policy autonomy
1—***Managed float*** with inflation targets	National money growth or inflation targets	National
2—***External grid***	National exchange rate pegs	National (limited by peg)
3—***Delegated anchor*** and internal grid	*Anchor country*: money growth or inflation; *Others*: exchange rate peg to the anchor country	*Anchor country*: national; *Others*: national (limited by peg)
4—***Internal grid*** with inflation targets	National money growth or inflation targets, coexisting with limited flexibility of intra-EAC parities	National (limited by grid)
5—***Collective anchor***	Collectively managed money growth and/or inflation targets, possibly coexisting with limited flexibility of intra-EAC parities	Shared (possibly limited by grid)

Source: Authors.
Note: EAC = East African Community.

managed float system in which countries make no exchange rate commitments, to an external grid system in which each country unilaterally pegs to a global currency. The second is the allocation of monetary policy autonomy across the union, defined in terms of the de facto locus of policy sovereignty and the scope for directing monetary policy to internal objectives like inflation or aggregate demand. Here the options range from a managed float system, in which sovereignty remains fully at the national level and flexible exchange rates allow considerable autonomy for monetary policy, to a collective anchor system, in which a supranational institution acquires policy authority in advance of formal union, or an external grid system, in which sovereignty remains at the national level but an exchange rate peg receives priority over internal objectives. In what follows, we first describe the five alternatives and then assess their relative merits in the context of the EAC.

Option 1: A Managed Float

Our first option combines country-level managed floats with convergence criteria on inflation or, equivalently, jointly agreed inflation targets. This option is close to the status quo in the EAC (see the previous discussion), where all countries but Burundi maintain a fairly clear hierarchy in which reserve money growth is the dominant inflation anchor and exchange rate intervention is mainly limited to smoothing short-run volatility.[16] In a *managed float* system, therefore, the nation-

[16] Uganda is implementing a formal inflation-targeting system, which will ultimately place significantly greater emphasis on inflation forecasts than on money growth rates as intermediate targets, and on policy interest rates rather than reserve money as operational instruments. But its exchange rate policy remains a managed float.

al central banks would continue to operate their existing frameworks, basing their monetary programs on jointly agreed inflation targets that might in principle be country specific, but with minimal adjustments to existing national targets that could be set at a uniform 5 percent. Monetary autonomy would remain fully at the national level, and exchange rate flexibility would leave considerable room to direct policy to domestic ends (including prominently, the inflation target). The partner states would pursue fiscal convergence criteria as entry requirements and develop a set of union-wide fiscal safeguards to be operated postunion. They would work out the operational details of the postunion monetary framework and put structures in place to increase information sharing about the conduct of monetary policy. Explicit exchange rate commitments would be deferred until the final stage of the move to union.

Option 2: An External Grid

In an *external grid* system, each country specifies a central rate against a global currency, such as the U.S. dollar or the euro, and commits to keep its exchange rate within a predetermined band around this rate. Gulf Cooperation Council members operate such a system, in which each member has committed to maintaining its preexisting peg to the U.S. dollar during transition.

In its impact on exchange rates, an external grid system is the equivalent of a system of mutual pegging between the n member currencies, supplemented by an explicit link of any one of their currencies (or any basket) to global currencies. The external link is crucial to the anchoring properties of the system, because although a set of n external pegs and bands implies a grid of $n - 1$ bilateral cross-rates and bands within the community, the reverse is not true. Mutual fixity among n partners—what we will call an *internal grid*—determines only $n - 1$ exchange rates, leaving the relationship of the group to external currencies indeterminate (the so-called *$n - 1$ currency problem*).

By tying the system to external currencies, an external grid also provides an inflation anchor for individual countries and the system as a whole. Policy autonomy remains at the country level, although the pegs leave relatively limited scope for discretionary monetary policy.

Option 3: A Delegated Anchor

Neither of our first two options involves an explicit mechanism for stabilizing cross-rates among union partners. An external grid stabilizes these rates as a side effect of country-level links to the global currency, while a float leaves them tethered only by the commitment to a common inflation target. In a *delegated anchor* system, an internal grid emerges through individual pegs to the currency of a selected union partner. In this approach, the partners delegate one country from among them to maintain a strong domestic anchor. Each of the other countries then commits to keeping its own currency within a narrow (or narrowing) band of the delegated country's currency, with an arrangement for coordinated intervention when a member's rates go to the weak edge of the band. Within this system, the exchange rates of partner countries with respect to global currencies reflect those of the delegated currency.

While the European exchange rate mechanism is sometimes interpreted as a nonanchored internal grid system (such as by ECB, 2010), it in fact operated as a delegated internal anchor system. Germany, the largest economy of the community and the one with the strongest post–World War II inflation performance, provided the de facto delegated anchor.

Option 4: An Internal Grid

Option 4 combines a grid of central parities with inflation targets at the country level. This is the option the ECB report favors. Its exchange rate component mimics the internal grid system operated in Europe during the long transition to union. A centerpiece of the European transition was the establishment of a grid of central parities between national currencies and the European currency unit (ECU), the precursor to the euro. By committing to stay within a narrow band of the ECU, each country was in effect committing to keep its own exchange rate movements relative to external currencies close to those of its partners.

An internal grid system with country-level inflation targets is, in principle, overconstrained, in the sense of imposing $2n - 1$ constraints on nominal variables (n inflation targets and $n - 1$ internal exchange rates) when only n are independently feasible for any extended period. For consistency, therefore, inflation targets would have to be derived from the exchange rate commitments, or vice versa. But even with consistency across targets, the system lacks transparency. Policy autonomy would rest at the national level, but without clarity about how national responsibilities should be allocated between anchoring inflation and maintaining exchange rate commitments.

Option 5: A Collective Anchor

For completeness, we include as a final option a *collective anchor* system that would vest the authority for anchoring union-wide inflation in a supranational body composed of representatives of the national central banks. In principle, such an authority could devote either weak or strong attention to stabilizing cross-rates among union partners; the key is that the structure as a whole would be anchored indirectly through allegiance to money growth and/or inflation targets union wide. A collective anchor system with intraunion exchange rate commitments would come closest to mimicking the monetary framework that is likely to prevail under the union, in which intraunion exchange rate changes will be absent and union-wide monetary policy will be formed through a collective process over which all members have some influence. A system without intraunion exchange rate commitments would be similar to our managed float option, but with significant policy sovereignty ceded immediately to a supranational agency. The task of the supranational body would be to coordinate national policies that continue to employ internal anchors (money growth rates or inflation forecasts). Given the monetary frameworks currently in use in EAC countries, this might be accomplished by creating a zone-wide financial program to which the national reserve money programs are subordinate in some well-defined sense.

Assessing the Alternatives

Two of our options, the external grid and the collective anchor system, appear to lie at unsuitable extremes for the EAC countries. The external grid gives up all the benefits of exchange rate flexibility for a potentially extended period, and faces potentially existential challenges from speculative attacks in the context of open capital accounts and growing de facto capital mobility. Unlike the Gulf Cooperation Council countries, the three large countries of the EAC definitively abandoned their adjustable peg regimes and have been operating flexible exchange rate regimes, in most cases, since the mid-1990s. The reasons for this are various and include unfavorable experiences with exchange controls, vulnerability to substantial current account shocks, a desire for some degree of monetary autonomy in the context of an open capital account, and a desire to spur the development of domestic markets for exchange risk. Any disadvantages of reverting to fixed but adjustable exchange rates are greater, moreover, in a context of uncertainty about the duration of the transition.

The collective anchor system fails for a very different reason: it transfers sovereignty prematurely and ambiguously in the context of unclear political commitments to union by the partner states. If the authority of the union-wide agency is seen as contingent on unresolved political decisions by national governments, the agency may find itself either unable or unwilling to constrain national policies during the transition. The system may then evolve into a de facto delegated anchor or a managed float system, but with substantial policy uncertainty in the meantime and with damage to the credibility of the union-wide central bank.

Among the remaining three options, the delegated anchor and internal grid systems both feature strong convergence criteria on nominal exchange rates. The delegated anchor system has the advantage of greater transparency but the near-fatal disadvantage of demanding a highly asymmetric sacrifice of policy autonomy across the partners. In effect, four of the five partners acquiesce to the monetary policy choices of the fifth. It may be possible to contemplate a political bargain in which Kenya—the obvious delegated anchor in terms of economic size and long-term inflation history—retains monetary policy autonomy during the transition while the other partners operate peg-plus-band systems vis-à-vis the Kenya shilling. However, the content of such a bargain is unclear, and in its absence it is extremely difficult to imagine the larger partners, particularly Tanzania, accepting a subordinate role. A delegated anchor system seems almost as unlikely to emerge endogenously from an internal grid system as it did in Europe.

The list of plausible ex ante choices for the convergence period, therefore, narrows to two: a managed float system or an internal grid, in both cases supported by country-level inflation targets. We favor the managed float option, which minimizes the disturbance to monetary frameworks that are currently in use in the EAC and have performed successfully, in the larger countries, for over a decade. A managed float is not only robust to a potentially protracted convergence period, but also supports the continued development of domestic financial markets and the continued refinement of existing policy frameworks, including moves toward inflation targeting. In light of the tradeoffs reviewed earlier, the managed float also retains nominal exchange rate flexibility, a reality that traders and financial markets have become accustomed to in the larger countries of the community and that has probably had some protective effect with respect to speculative movements against national currencies. As we argued previously, intraunion exchange rate flexibility also has a continuing role to play in facilitating adjustments to asymmetric shocks to trade, aid, and longer-term capital flows.

We acknowledged previously that a managed float system could be subject to manipulation by partners seeking to enter the union with relatively weak exchange rates. More generally, flexible exchange rates can be a source of short-run real exchange rate misalignment, due to thin market effects or other sources of volatility unrelated to the fundamentals. Our view, however, is that the combination of convergence criteria on inflation and adjustments for misalignment at the conversion step handle these concerns adequately.

A final and potentially serious concern about a managed float system is the flip side of its strongest advantage. By comparison with the other options, a managed float is a minimalist option for the EAC, not just in the sense of leaving existing anchors largely unchanged, but also in the deeper sense of requiring the smallest sacrifice of monetary policy autonomy during the convergence phase. In a managed float system, the national authorities agree on an inflation target but do not subordinate domestic objectives to exchange rate commitments and do not coordinate policy instruments explicitly during the convergence period. Such a system would preserve the strengths of existing national frameworks (especially for the large countries), and in that sense would be highly robust to uncertainties about the timing of the move to union. It would do little, however, to create, legitimize, and strengthen the union-wide institutions that will be fully responsible for policy from the conversion point forward. By the same token, it would do little to confront national stakeholders with the costs of union in terms of the inevitable loss of policy sovereignty. Because this option demands so little sacrifice of sovereignty, partner states must be more purposive in their investment in and commitment to EAC-wide institutions and the delegation of at least advisory functions to the proposed East African Monetary Institute (EAMI) during the convergence period.

The Conversion Phase

Once the requisite macroeconomic convergence criteria have been satisfied, the final steps in the consummation of monetary union are the transfer of sovereignty to a supranational institution and the replacement of national currencies with a union-wide currency. In Adam and others (2012), we argue that these steps should be preceded by a *conversion phase* of fixed and short duration (perhaps about two calendar quarters or so) during which the partner states commit to maintain their exchange rates within narrow bands of a set of preannounced conversion parities. This phase is not strictly necessary; an unannounced "overnight" transition at prevailing market exchange rates could work equally well if it were prepared logistically in advance by the partner states, immediately understood and embraced by market participants, and preceded by adequate internal surveillance to prevent competitive depreciation. The implausibility of these conditions is what recommends our approach, which draws heavily on the successful final transition in Europe. In this section, we briefly review the nature of the transition, including the role of a new regional currency and the choice of conversion parities.

Introducing the East African Currency Union

Despite the current travails of the euro area, the successful replacement of the individual currencies of its 11 founding members with the euro on January 1, 1999, was acclaimed in all quarters and offers a valuable template for managing the final stages of the transition to monetary union in East Africa. Based on this model, the conversion phase should commence with a major, union-wide announcement of (1) a date for the creation of full monetary union, (2) a commitment by the partner states to the irrevocable conversion of their national currencies into a new East African currency on that date, (3) a set of final basket weights for the EACU, and (4) a set of irrevocable central parities between national currencies and the EACU at which conversion to the new currency will occur.

At the heart of this process is the EACU, which would be defined well in advance of the conversion phase as a fixed composition basket (like the ECU or the special drawing right of the five regional currencies). Weights would reflect initial GDP and/or trade shares, and could be subject to minor adjustments when appropriate, including at the outset of the conversion phase.[17] From its inception, the EACU would float vis-à-vis third-party (i.e., global) currencies, its value reflecting the third-party exchange rates of its constituent currencies. Figure 8.6 shows a hypothetical EACU, constructed using 2010 GDP weights and set equal to US$1 in December of 2010. Like any weighted average, the basket tends to be less variable against third-party currencies than its constituents, though its movements can be large when the exchange rates of the big three countries move together, as in the second half of 2011.

In Europe, the ECU served as a parallel unit of account during the transition period, and then, as the euro, the euro area's exclusive legal unit of account from the outset of union. Euro notes and coin were not actually circulated until two to three years after the consummation of union. The ECU had been intended to serve as a currency of denomination during the long transition—not just for official intraunion clearing purposes, but also for private commercial transactions and financial contracts including bonds and bank deposits—but it never accounted for a significant share of transactions in the European Union, despite

[17]The ECU's weights, set initially in 1979, were adjusted in 1984 and 1998.

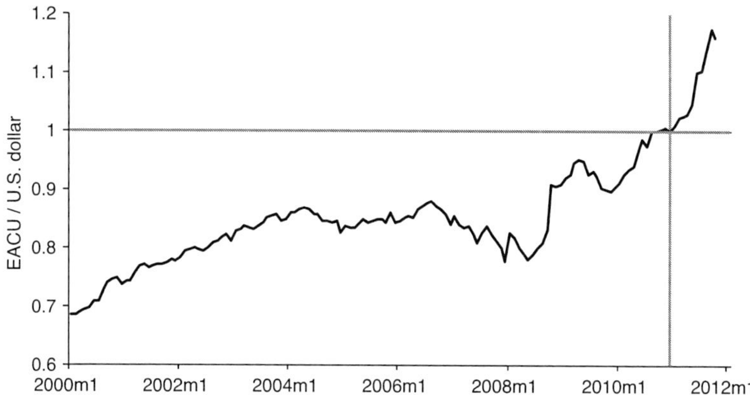

Figure 8.6 A Sample East African Currency Unit *(2010 GDP weights at official exchange rates)*

Source: IMF, International Financial Statistics database; and authors' calculations.
Note: This EACU is composed of 25.22 Burundi francs, 32.33 Kenya shillings, 42.50 Rwandan francs, 426.23 Tanzania shillings, and 498.84 Uganda shillings. These imply initial basket weights of 2.05 percent, 39.90 percent, 7.15 percent, 29.29 percent, and 21.61 percent, which are the GDP shares of the five partners based on U.S. dollar figures at official exchange rates in 2010. EACU = East African Currency Union.

the advantages of denominating in a stable unit of account. Eichengreen (2006) attributes this outcome to network externalities in favor of incumbent currencies. The same outcome seems highly likely for any EACU introduced solely as a unit of account during the transition. This situation implies no loss to the process, provided that other aspects of the transition support the acceptability of the EACU once the union is established.

Masson (2012) and Kigabo, Masson, and Masson (2012), however, have advocated a more substantial role for the EACU based on the introduction of notes and coin at a much earlier stage (see also Agarwala, 2003, on South Asia, and Mori and others, 2002, on Association of Southeast Asian countries). Their argument is that an early introduction of EACU currency provides a way to demonstrate partner states' political commitment to union and to involve the public in the process of monetary integration during a potentially protracted convergence period. The currency issue would be regulated by a currency board–type arrangement, in which a supranational body (such as the EAMI) would hold a 100 percent reserve of constituent currencies and would be committed to exchanging the EACU for these currencies on demand.

This proposal deserves serious consideration, although it raises concerns associated with competing media of exchange that were absent in the European case. The network externalities associated with exchange suggest that in the absence of strong legal restrictions there will typically be multiple locally stable equilibria with widely divergent market shares of the competing currencies (Dowd and Greenaway, 1993). These include equilibria like those observed in Europe, where the EACU fails to establish a foothold in actual usage—though in this case the stakes seem higher because they imply the outright rejection of EACU notes and coin. More appealing would be a set of equilibria in which the EACU establishes a relatively stable but nontrivial role in the local economies, perhaps even reducing the extent of transactions and liability dollarization in Tanzania and Uganda where it is currently substantial. More worrisome, however, are equilibria in which the weaker local currencies are driven out by the EACU, or in which a combination of credibility problems at the national currency and/or EACU level leads to an advance rather than a retreat of dollarization. These considerations, together with the potentially destabilizing effects of portfolio substitution on the effectiveness of national monetary policies, suggest that the advantages of the currency board approach should be carefully weighed against possible damages to the credibility of the overall process.

At the point of union, the EACU will convert at an exchange rate of 1:1 with the new East African currency unit. Following the European example, the new currency should initially be used for nonphysical transactions (i.e., electronic and interbank transfers), with national currency notes and coin continuing to circulate at their fixed parities within national jurisdictions for a period of time prior to the introduction of new notes and coin. From the moment of union, however, all public sector transactions, interbank payment system clearing activities, and new debt issues and rollovers would be obliged to be denominated in the new currency. Dual pricing in new and old local currency values will be both necessary and desirable during the changeover, for wholesale and retail goods and services including, for example, all invoicing, wage and salary notification, and bank statements. If the euro area blueprint is followed, the duration from formal union to the sole circulation of the new currency at the retail level could be in the order of two to three years (Adam and others, 2012).

Choosing Conversion Parities

The choice of conversion parities is subject to the familiar $n - 1$ problem of what will anchor the EACU vis-à-vis global currencies and also to the challenge of avoiding severe misalignments. In Adam and others (2012), we addressed the first issue by arguing that a coordinated set of national inflation targets could anchor the internal exchange rate grid during the conversion phase, provided that some degree of de facto sovereignty had been transferred to the East African Central Bank or its institutional predecessor (such as the EAMI) in advance of the conversion phase. The exchange rate commitment would have to be backed up in practice by the near equivalent of a set of external pegs, supported by mutual intervention where necessary; this underscored the need for a functioning supranational institution in advance of the conversion phase. We argued that the ambiguities inherent in such a situation argued strongly in favor of a short duration for it, as did the danger of speculative attacks in a system of open capital accounts.

Here, we focus on the second question: the choice of conversion parities. Once this choice is made, the partner states give up any prospect of using intraunion exchange rate adjustments to address asymmetric real exchange rate misalignments.[18] Countries that enter the union with relatively strong currencies will therefore be at a potentially persistent competitive disadvantage relative to those that enter with relatively weak currencies. The resulting macroeconomic strains may be substantial: the high-cost economies will tend to have lagging exports and employment, and the low-cost economies will tend to be strong exporters and may be favored destinations for FDI. Depending on national tax structures, these differences may affect relative fiscal performance as well.

These concerns suggest that the EAC partners should agree in advance that conversion parities will be chosen to avoid locking in severe real exchange rate asymmetries at the outset of union. In Adam and others (2012), we review alternative methodologies for real exchange rate assessment and argue that a combination of approaches should be employed, along the lines of the IMF's current assessment methodology (Lee and others, 2008). It is worth emphasizing that if our managed float proposal is adopted for the convergence phase, the advance commitment to a real exchange rate assessment may be as important as any parity adjustments such an exercise actually delivers. Retrospectively, of course, the assessment will have the protective effect of allowing conversion parities to differ from internal spot rates at the outset of the conversion phase. But even if adjustments are not required, the knowledge that such an assessment will take place should have the separate impact of reducing the incentive for the partner states to implement competitive depreciations late in the convergence phase. Europe was explicitly protected from the latter by the internal exchange rate grid and an explicit rule against devaluation in the final two years before union. National inflation targets should limit the scope for competitive depreciation in the EAC case, but with uncertain efficacy, particularly if convergence criteria on inflation are nondemanding or adherence to them is weak.

Are Nominal Rigidities a Barrier to Real Exchange Rate Adjustment?

The remainder of this section focuses on an empirical question that informs both the costs of initial misalignments and the strength of national incentives for late-stage depreciation: how severe are wage and price rigidities in the EAC? If the large informal sectors and relatively uncomplicated supply chains that are characteristic of these economies mean that price rigidities are largely absent, then the likelihood of extended real exchange rate misalignments—and the urgency of setting appropriate conversion parities—may be relatively limited. We use monthly data for 1995 to 2011 to assess the relative importance of exchange rate and price adjustment in resolving real exchange rate misalignment for the five EAC countries. For comparison purposes, we undertake the same estimation for

---

[18] They also give up the ability to reconcile divergent fiscal needs for devaluation, which may be associated either with different medium-term preferences for inflationary finance or with short-run fiscal solvency pressures that favor a de facto default on nonindexed domestic-currency liabilities of key actors (such as the public sector). With respect to misalignments, note that only asymmetric misalignments matter, because symmetric ones can be eliminated through movements in the union-wide currency. See Beetsma and Giuliodori (2010).

a sample of 19 countries that Reinhart and Rogoff (2004) classify as either "managed floating" or "freely floating" for the majority of the period.[19]

Observed reliance on nominal exchange rate adjustment may of course reflect a preference for letting the nominal exchange rate carry the burden of correcting misalignment, rather than the existence of structural rigidities to domestic price adjustment. Our analysis nonetheless suggests two main conclusions. The first is that the nominal exchange rate appears to play a decisive role in eliminating real exchange rate misalignments in the EAC. This effect is strongest in Kenya, Tanzania, and Uganda; domestic prices bear a larger share of the adjustment burden in Rwanda, and especially in Burundi. The second finding is that the EAC pattern is quite similar to what we observe in emerging market and advanced economies. In particular, we find only very weak evidence that domestic prices play a greater role in achieving real exchange rate adjustment in the EAC countries than they do in higher-income countries.

An Empirical Framework

The log of a trade-weighted real effective exchange rate, e_t, can be calculated as $e_t = p_t + (S_t - p_t^*)$, where p_t is the log of the consumer price index in the home country and S_t and p_t^* are the logs of partner trade-weighted indexes of nominal exchange rates and partner country (wholesale) prices. Increases in e_t and S_t are appreciations. Denoting the log of the unobservable *equilibrium* real exchange rate as $\tilde{e}_t$, the degree of misalignment of the real exchange rate is given by

$$m_t = e_t - \tilde{e}_t = \left[\left(p_t - p_t^*\right) + S_t\right] - \tilde{e}_t. \tag{8.2}$$

Theories of the equilibrium real exchange rate imply that misalignment is a stationary variable.[20] It follows that if the equilibrium real exchange rate is nonstationary, the real exchange rate itself must also be nonstationary and the two must be cointegrated. This in turn implies that one or both of S_t and $(p_t - p_t^*)_t$ must be not only nonstationary but also cointegrated with $\tilde{e}_t$. All three elements of $y_t = \left[(p_t - p_t^*), S_t, e_t\right]$ are in fact I(1) for the EAC countries and for the majority of the comparator group.[21] Stationarity of equation (8.2) therefore

[19] Our sample consists of countries that have maintained a broadly floating exchange rate regime and for whom the IMF reports trade-weighted nominal and real effective exchange rate indices over the 1995–2011 period. The Organization for Economic Cooperation and Development subsample consists of Australia, Canada, Denmark, Japan, New Zealand, the United Kingdom, and the United States. The emerging market subsample consists of Algeria, Bolivia, Brazil, Chile, Ghana, Malaysia, Mexico, Nigeria, the Philippines, Singapore, South Africa, and Tunisia. Of these, only Australia, Japan, South Africa, and the United States are characterized as freely floating. Within the managed float category, Algeria, Bolivia, Brazil, Burundi, Denmark, Malaysia, Rwanda, and Singapore are classified as maintaining a de facto crawling band around their reference currency for at least some of the period.

[20] In IMF parlance, $\tilde{e}$ is typically referred to as the "fundamental equilibrium real exchange rate." See Hinkle and Montiel (1999) for a survey of theory and evidence on equilibrium real exchange rates and misalignment.

[21] Details available on request.

implies that these variables should be cointegrated, with an equilibrium error given by the degree of misalignment.

Cointegration implies, in turn, that at least one of the components of Δy_t must respond in an equilibrating direction to the lagged equilibrium error, m_{t-1}. This could in principle include the equilibrium rate itself if policymakers adjusted underlying policy determinants like government spending to reduce misalignments. But in what follows, we assume that $\tilde{e}_t$ is weakly exogenous (i.e., it does not adjust) so that adjustment is confined to the actual real effective exchange rate. The real depreciation required by a situation of temporary overvaluation $(\tilde{m}_{t-1} > 0)$ can then be accomplished either through nominal depreciation $(\Delta S_t < 0)$ or through disinflation relative to trading partners $[(\Delta p_t - p_t^*) < 0]$. Our analysis asks how the burden of adjustment is shared between these two channels.[22] Notice that the EAC countries are small, open economies, implying that wholesale prices should be weakly exogenous and therefore that any adjustments in relative prices reflect movements in *domestic* prices.

To assess the relative importance of exchange rates and domestic wages and prices in real exchange rate adjustment, we embed both aspects of behavior within a partial vector error correction model of the form

$$\Delta y_t = \alpha \tilde{m}_{t-1} + \sum_{i=1}^{k-1} \Gamma_i \Delta y_{t-i} + u_t, \tag{8.3}$$

where $\Delta y_t = \left[\Delta S_t,\ \Delta(p_t - p_t^*)\right]$ and where α consists of the parameters of interest, measuring the adjustment respectively of the nominal exchange rate and relative prices to the realized real exchange rate misalignment, $\tilde{m}_{t-1}$. This adjustment can in principle be asymmetric, for example if wages and prices rise more readily than they fall. The vector Γ_i consists of the short-run parameters of the model, and u_t is a white noise error term.

As we do not directly observe the equilibrium real exchange rate, we must estimate it in order to infer the degree of misalignment. A standard approach is to model the fundamental rate as a linear combination of observable fundamentals such as aid, the terms of trade, and government spending. Here we adopt the alternative approach of decomposing the actual real exchange rate, e_t, into its stationary and nonstationary components using the Hodrick-Prescott filter. The nonstationary trend component of this decomposition serves as our proxy for the equilibrium real exchange rate, and the stationary component for misalignment, so that $\tilde{m}_t = e_t - e\_hp_t$ where e_hp_t is the Hodrick-Prescott estimate of the nonstationary

[22] Notice that we assume that policymakers seek to adjust the nominal effective exchange rate. In practice, policymakers in the EAC have tended to focus particularly on the U.S. dollar exchange rate. Although we have not chosen to do so here, we could in principle reflect this in our empirical work by decomposing the nominal effective exchange rate into the bilateral rate versus the U.S. dollar and a "correction" term that depends only on the exchange rates of partner-country currencies versus the U.S. dollar.

(equilibrium) component of the real effective exchange rate.[23] Lagging once and substituting the resulting expression for $\tilde{m}_{t-1}$, we finally estimate equation (8.3).

Results

Table 8.4 reports the estimated coefficient vectors α from equation (8.3) estimated for the EAC and our comparator country groups, along with a range of diagnostic tests. The model is estimated for January 1995 to August 2011.

Column [1] reports Johansen's (1992) weak exogeneity test of partner wholesale prices, p_t^*, which indicate that for the large EAC countries and for the two sets of comparator countries, partner wholesale prices play no significant role in eliminating real exchange rate misalignment. This justifies our focusing exclusively on the respective adjustment burden carried by nominal exchange rate and domestic price adjustment. Only for Burundi and Rwanda do we reject the null of weak exogeneity, although this result is caused by the heavily managed nature of these two countries' exchange rates over the estimation period.[24]

The central results of the analysis are contained in columns [2] to [7], which record the adjustment coefficients α_S and $\alpha_{(p-p^*)}$ for the nominal effective exchange rate and relative prices, respectively. In each case, we report the coefficients for both symmetric and asymmetric adjustment. Columns [8] and [9] then report F-tests against the null that adjustment to real exchange rate shocks is symmetric, that is, that the speed of adjustment is the same when the real exchange rate is overvalued as when it is undervalued.

A number of features emerge from the analysis. First, taking the EAC group as a whole, adjustment to real exchange rate misalignment occurs principally through movements in the nominal exchange rate rather than through domestic prices. The nominal exchange rate adjustment coefficients are, in the main, statistically significant while those measuring the adjustment of relative prices are not. This pattern is stronger for the three big partner states, Kenya, Tanzania, and Uganda than for Rwanda and, especially, Burundi, where the burden of adjustment is shared more evenly between nominal exchange rate and price adjustments.

Second, for Kenya, Tanzania, and Uganda exchange rate and price adjustments are symmetric between temporary overvaluation and undervaluation of the real exchange rate. There is weak evidence of asymmetry in Rwanda and Burundi, where the nominal exchange rate responds somewhat more strongly to

---

[23]The results in Table 8.4 filter the real exchange rate using a smoothing parameter of λ = 14,400. A potential drawback to our approach is that univariate filtering methods tend to track the actual evolution of the real exchange rate, and may therefore attribute "too much" of its observed movement to changes in the underlying equilibrium real exchange rate. We find, however, that varying the smoothing parameter does not fundamentally alter our results. Full results for alternative values of the smoothing parameter, and for estimation under the Baxter-King band-pass filter, are available on request.

[24]Johansen's likelihood ratio test entails testing the partial system restriction that $\alpha_{p^*} = 0$ on the rank-one vector error correction model shown in equation (8.3), where $\Delta y_t = [\Delta s_t, \Delta p_t, \Delta p_t^*]$. This restriction implies that the cointegrating vector is weakly exogenous with respect to Δp_t^*.

TABLE 8.4

Adjustment to Real Exchange Rate Shocks

		Adjustment Coefficients					
	Weak Exogeneity[1]	Unrestricted		Positive shocks[2]		Negative shocks[2]	
		NEER	RELP	NEER	RELP	NEER	RELP
Country	[1]	[2]	[3]	[4]	[5]	[6]	[7]
Burundi	0.01	–0.14**	–0.17***	–0.25**	–0.17***	–0.04	–0.18***
Kenya	0.16	–0.35***	–0.05*	–0.32***	–0.06*	–0.41***	–0.05
Rwanda	0.02	–0.37	–0.02	–0.57	0.06*	0.01	–0.04
Tanzania	0.29	–0.26***	–0.01	–0.34***	0.00	–0.21***	–0.02
Uganda	0.27	–0.24***	–0.03	–0.21**	–0.04	–0.27***	–0.02
Mean EAC-5		–0.27	–0.06	–0.34	–0.04	–0.18	–0.06
Mean EAC-3		–0.28	–0.03	–0.29	–0.03	–0.30	–0.03

Joint F test[3] (*p*-value):			
		[2]	[3]
	EAC-5	0.001	0.109
	EAC-3	0.006	0.060
Difference in means[5] versus OECD:		[2]	[3]
	EAC-5	0.023	–0.042
	EAC-3	0.011	–0.025*

Test of symmetric response[4] (*p*-values):	NEER	RELP
	[8]	[9]
Burundi	0.12	0.93
Kenya	0.44	0.82
Rwanda	0.12	0.06
Tanzania	0.30	0.45
Uganda	0.63	0.69

Source: Authors' calculations.

Notes: Real exchange misalignment is defined as the deviation of the real effective real exchange rate from its long-run trend, where the latter is estimated by a Hodrick-Prescott filter with smoothing parameter 14,400. The adjustment coefficients are the error-correction coefficients from a dynamic error-correction model. Asterisks denote significance levels of *10 percent, ** 5 percent and *** 1 percent. EAC-3 = Kenya, Tanzania, Uganda; EAC-5 = EAC-3 plus Burundi and Rwanda; NEER = nominal effective exchange rate; OECD = Organization for Economic Cooperation and Development; RELP = relative prices.

[1] The null hypothesis is that the trade-weighted world price index is weakly exogenous; *p*-values correspond to the likelihood ratio test proposed by Johansen (1992).

[2] Positive and negative misalignments indicate overvalued and undervalued real exchange rates, respectively.

[3] The null hypothesis is that all error-correction coefficients are zero.

[4] The null hypothesis is that the adjustment coefficients on positive and negative lagged misalignments are identical.

[5] The subtable reports the difference in average adjustment coefficients between the East African Community countries and the OECD countries. Asterisk indicates significance levels for a test of equality of means.

overvaluation than to undervaluation, but the difference is not statistically significant (the F-tests on symmetry are not rejected, but this reflects the low precision of the coefficient estimate on negative real exchange rate shocks).

Third, for the large EAC countries as a whole, the strength and pattern of adjustment is broadly comparable to that observed for our emerging markets comparator group. In both groups, the balance of adjustment is strongly skewed in favor of the exchange rate, and the adjustment pattern is broadly symmetrical with respect to over- and undervaluations of the real exchange rate. Within the arguably more homogenous Organization for Economic Cooperation and Development subsample, the balance of adjustment is even more decisively skewed in favor of movements in the exchange rate—to the point that for this group, we can comfortably accept the restriction that all the adjustment is through the nominal exchange rate. This is not the case for the emerging markets group, and is only just accepted for Kenya, Tanzania, and Uganda taken together.

In summary, our investigation strongly suggests that the larger EAC countries have tended to rely as heavily on exchange rate flexibility for eliminating real exchange rate misalignments as have other more developed floating-rate economies, and that wage and price flexibility has not shouldered a significantly larger share of the adjustment burden. It is not self-evident, therefore, that wage and price flexibility can be assumed to rescue the EAC countries from the oldest concern of the literature on optimum currency areas, which is that the loss of intraunion exchange rates increases the costs of asymmetric shocks. This underscores the value of an advance commitment to setting conversion parities that avoid severe initial misalignments.

REAL EXCHANGE RATES AND MONETARY UNION

We close the chapter by briefly addressing an exchange rate issue that relates to the postunion period rather than the transition: what impact will union have on real exchange rates and competitiveness across the union? Both theory and the experience of other African monetary unions suggest that national price levels will be tied together much more closely in the postunion period than before. Two very different mechanisms bring this about. One is the adoption of a union-wide exchange rate and monetary policy, which increases the comovement in nominal variables, such as the prices of internationally traded goods, regardless of the degree of intraunion trade. But the choice of nominal anchor cannot matter for the real exchange rate in the long run, because relative prices are tied down eventually by real rather than nominal factors. The second factor, therefore, and the factor we focus on here, is the increase in cross-border price arbitrage that follows a reduction in trading costs. We argue that monetary union will produce a convergence of *equilibrium* real exchange rates by stimulating an increase in intraunion trade. We provide evidence from sub-Saharan Africa that is consistent with this effect.

The essence of this argument can be understood by considering a pair of countries that form a currency union starting from a nonunion equilibrium in which they may or may not be engaged in bilateral trade.[25] The countries are identical, with the exception that one of them has a large oil export sector. The two countries face the same world prices for all traded goods and services, but the oil-rich country has a higher domestic price of nontraded goods and therefore a more appreciated real exchange rate. Reflecting the Dutch disease effect of its natural resource wealth, this country has a larger nontraded goods sector and a smaller manufacturing and cash crop sector than the resource-poor country.

Monetary union alters this situation by driving down the cost of intraunion trade. The size of this cost reduction is not known, but the trade-creating effects of monetary union appear to be large. Rose (2000) found that, all else equal, membership in a monetary union tripled intraunion trade. The subsequent empirical literature has reduced this substantially to an impact somewhere

[25] Annex 8.1 develops this argument in greater detail.

between 5 percent and 25 percent (De Grauwe, 2009; Dellas and Tavlas, 2009), but a consensus remains that regional trade will increase, and perhaps sharply. The impact on price arbitrage is of course more extensive than the impact on trade flows, because price competition can operate as long as trade is *feasible* on the margin, regardless of the volume of that trade. The evidence is very strong, in other words, that monetary union widens the scope for cross-border price arbitrage within the union.

Monetary union therefore widens the scope of intraunion price arbitrage. Previously nontraded goods become tradable: they flow from where their prices were initially lower, in the resource-poor country, to where they were initially higher, in the oil-exporting country. The real exchange rate differential between the two countries shrinks, and may disappear altogether. The oil exporter experiences a long-run real depreciation, which unwinds a portion of that country's Dutch disease and produces an expansion of noncommodity exports to the world economy (or a contraction of imports: its trade balance with global markets increases). The resource-poor partner, in turn, experiences a real appreciation and a shift in the composition of its exports from globally traded goods to regional goods that were previously nontraded.

In Annex 8.1, we undertake a set of regression-based tests of the hypothesis that monetary union narrows real exchange rate differentials. Sub-Saharan Africa provides a unique empirical lens on this hypothesis, because of the relatively large number of countries in the CFA franc zone and the substantial variation in natural resource intensity across the continent.[26] Using a difference-in-difference approach, we test our hypothesis by asking whether natural resource endowments have a smaller effect on equilibrium national price levels across the members of the CFA zone than across countries in sub-Saharan Africa with independent national currencies.

The empirical results for 1988–2008 and various subperiods are strongly consistent with our hypothesis. We find that the Dutch disease effects of national resource endowments are sharply lower among the CFA countries than among countries with independent currencies; in some specifications, in fact, we cannot reject the hypothesis that variations in resource rents have no impact at all on relative real exchange rates in the CFA zone.

These results suggest an answer to the question we posed at the outset of this section. Monetary union is likely to spur price arbitrage across the union, particularly with respect to goods that are not traded with global markets. Relatively resource-rich members will thereby tend to "export" some portion of their Dutch disease in global markets (the competitiveness problem faced by their non–commodity traded goods sectors) to relatively resource-poor members of the union. Holding overall trade balances constant, the trade balances of the latter

[26]The Common Monetary Area is a third monetary union in sub-Saharan Africa, but given South Africa's predominance in the union, it is best to think of South Africa as operating an independent national currency.

group will tend to deteriorate vis-à-vis global partners, as resources previously devoted to globally traded goods are shifted over to serve the expanded common-currency market. The same logic applies, of course, where the "resource endowment" is not minerals or another natural resource, but other ongoing sources of financing for a country's deficit in goods and services, such as large and persistent inflows of foreign aid or private capital.

It is important to emphasize that the welfare implications of these effects are far from obvious: for the non-oil or non-aid economy, for example, any Dutch disease impact of membership applies to the country's preunion export sector, and not to its overall exports. The latter are likely to rise, as we have emphasized, as previously nontraded goods find a favorable single-currency market. Our analysis in this section, moreover, is only partial, based on the pure trade-creation effects of currency union. The full impact of union on relative competitiveness and growth may depend on a host of additional factors that lie outside of the scope of this chapter. These include dynamic effects on factor markets, on the location of investment, and, importantly, on how resource revenues are spent, particularly in the areas of infrastructure.

CONCLUSIONS

What exchange rate arrangements are appropriate for the EAC in the transition to monetary union? After reviewing the feasible options, we have argued against tight exchange rate commitments based our interpretation of the EAC's policy history, its vulnerability to external shocks, and the openness of its capital account. The appropriate exchange rate regime during the transition to union, in our view, is a managed float in which national inflation targets—consistent with community-wide convergence criteria for inflation—serve as the nominal anchor. The advantages of a managed float are strengthened considerably by the uncertain horizon over which union will occur.

In developing this argument, we undertook a set of empirical exercises that may have applications beyond this chapter. The first is an adaptation of the time-honored literature on offset coefficients to low-income and potentially aid-dependent countries operating flexible exchange rates. For Kenya and Uganda, we find that domestic monetary expansions create a high degree of exchange market pressure, leading to a combination of exchange rate depreciation and reserve losses that are concentrated in the first three or four months in Uganda, and appear after a lag of about a quarter in Kenya. For these countries, exchange rate commitments would appear to harbor significant risks of speculative attack. Pressures emerge more slowly in Tanzania and are cumulatively much smaller, consistent with that country's relatively tight capital controls. These conclusions could not be drawn with any confidence from direct measures of the scale of private capital flows.

The partner countries will of course eventually face the irrevocable loss of intraunion exchange rates. In a second empirical exercise, we generated indirect evidence of the potential costs of this loss by assessing the relative importance of nominal exchange rate movements and domestic price adjustments in addressing real exchange rate misalignments in the past. We found only very weak evidence that wages and prices were more flexible in this sense in the big three countries of the EAC than in emerging market and advanced economies operating flexible exchange rates. This finding provides strong support for our argument that the partner states should agree, in advance, on an approach to choosing conversion parities that avoids locking in severe misalignments at the outset of union.

Our final contribution focused on the likely impact of union on equilibrium real exchange rates and national competitiveness. Considerable empirical literature suggests that monetary union brings a substantial increase in intraunion trade. Cross-border price arbitrage will increase even more, since prices can be disciplined by the possibility of trade even when the volume of trade is low. We argued that union-wide price convergence on previously nontraded goods would moderate equilibrium real exchange rate differentials in the union, producing a situation in which the relatively resource-rich partners export some portion of their Dutch disease to the resource-poorer partners. Sub-Saharan Africa provides an unusually favorable environment for testing this hypothesis, given the large number of participants in the CFA zone and the substantial differences in resource endowment across the continent. We found strong confirmation of our hypothesis: differences in natural resource endowment have much smaller effects on long-run differentials in real exchange rates across the members of the CFA zone than across countries in sub-Saharan Africa operating independent national currencies.

Our analysis suggests a number of areas in which further work would strengthen the basis for a successful transition. One is the early development of a regular, union-wide real exchange rate surveillance exercise. Given the vagaries of existing empirical methods, only substantial misalignments—such as 15 percent or more by a combination of approaches—would justify a departure from current spot rates when conversion parities are set. An internal, union-wide exercise would nonetheless be of very substantial value if undertaken regularly and subject to high-level review during the convergence phase. It would not only facilitate agreement over conversion parities, but also minimize exchange rate surprises for market participants at the outset of the conversion phase.

The possibility of new entrants into the union raises a second topic for study. Accession by new members will undoubtedly be dictated by macroeconomic and institutional convergence requirements, and in these arenas the European Union's recent enhancement of its fiscal convergence and coordination criteria deserve close study by EAC members.[27]

But what nominal exchange rate criteria should new entrants be required to satisfy, vis-à-vis the EACU, in advance of their entry into the union? Our

[27]The European Union's *Treaty on Stability, Coordination and Governance in the Economic and Monetary Union* came into force in January 2013, superseding the Stability and Growth Pact that accompanied the launch of the euro in 1999.

taxonomy implies that there is a tension between rules that are robust enough to be applied uniformly to all potential entrants and rules that are optimal on a country-by-country basis. If practical considerations favor a uniform rule, however, the leading contenders seem likely to be the two that emerged from our discussion. A version of our managed float approach would leave new entrants free from exchange rate commitments vis-à-vis the EACU until a final, brief stage; the alternative would be a grid-based approach that would require them (as with new entrants to the euro area) to maintain a narrow band with respect to the EACU two or three years before entry. Open capital accounts and other arguments in favor of exchange rate flexibility favor the first arrangement. The broader context of ultimate fiscal or even political union, however—the relevance of which has been illustrated by the recent experience of the euro area—suggests that incumbent members may wish to seriously consider imposing a grid-based criterion on new entrants to enforce greater macroeconomic discipline during the accession process.

ANNEX 8.1

Real Exchange Rates and Monetary Union in Sub-Saharan Africa

We argue in this chapter that monetary union will produce a convergence of *equilibrium* real exchange rates by stimulating an increase in intraunion trade. The structure of this argument appears in Figure 8.1.1, where rectangles denote the global market and circles denote countries. The left-hand rectangle shows a pair of potential partners before union. These countries are small relative to the global market, and they maintain identical trade policies and constant overall trade balances (financed by some sustainable level of aid, for example, or long-term capital inflows); for concreteness, we assume that they each run a small overall trade deficit. Their real exchange rates are defined as the ratio of the domestic price of nontraded goods to the domestic price of a composite basket of internationally traded goods. If the two countries were identical in preferences, factor endowments, net international asset positions, and other macroeconomic fundamentals, theory would predict identical real exchange rates in a situation of internal and external balance (i.e., identical *equilibrium* real exchange rates) regardless of the choice of exchange rate regime in the two countries or of whether they share a common currency.

To induce a difference in preunion real exchange rates, we endow country 1 with a natural resource that is not used at home, but can be extracted at zero cost and sold on world markets. Trade patterns now differ, despite the fact that the two countries are identical in all other respects. The resource-rich economy exports its natural resource (denoted by *R*) to the global market to pay for (most of) its deficit in all other traded goods (denoted by *T*), while the non–resource-rich economy runs a small deficit in the latter. The degree to which the two countries trade with each other in this equilibrium is immaterial: both are price takers in the global market, and purchasing power parity holds for traded goods in equilibrium, so their bilateral balance in *T* goods has no macroeconomic impact in either country. Behind the scenes, of course, both countries also consume nontraded goods, which (by definition) they produce themselves. By virtue of its commodity rents, the first country has a more appreciated real exchange rate in the initial equilibrium, along with a higher absolute price of nontraded goods when measured in a common currency. Its nontraded goods sector is larger, and its traded-goods sector smaller (excluding the commodity export), than that of country 2. Cross-border trade costs are high enough in the initial equilibrium to prevent trade from arbitraging away the price gap in nontraded goods.

Monetary union alters this situation by driving down the cost of intraunion trade. The right-hand box in Figure 8.1.1 therefore interprets union as a widening of intraunion price arbitrage. As discussed in this chapter, previously nontraded goods (denoted by *N*) become tradable, and flow from the resource-poor to the resource-rich partner. The real exchange rate differential between the two countries shrinks and may disappear altogether. The resource-rich economy experiences

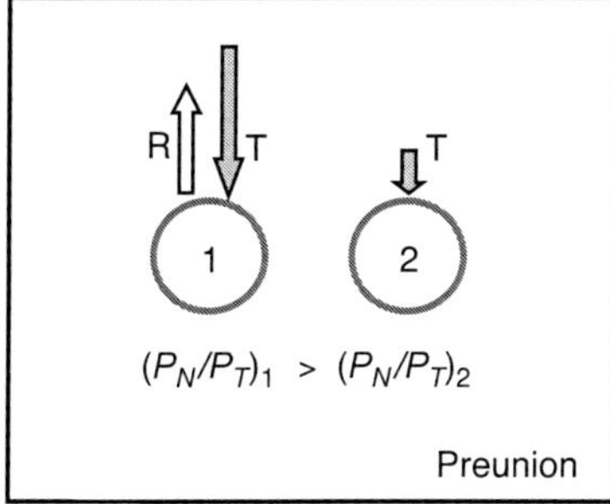

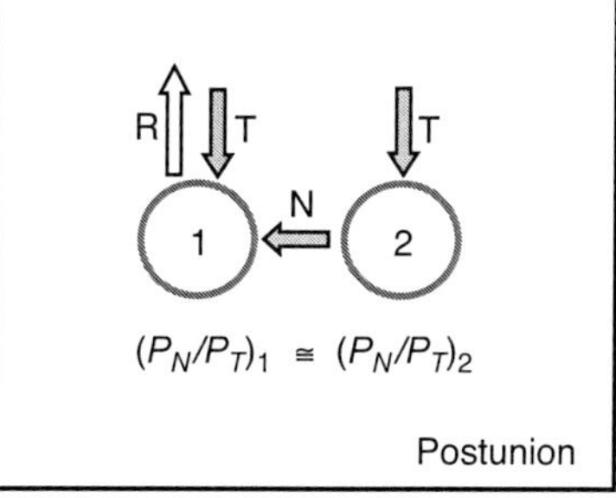

Figure 8.1.1 Trade and Real Exchange Rate Effects of Monetary Union
Source: Authors.
Note: R = natural resource export; T = traded goods; N = nontraded goods. Arrow lengths show the values of trade at international prices. Both countries have small overall trade deficits both pre- and postunion.

a long-run real depreciation, which unwinds a portion of that country's Dutch disease and produces an expansion of noncommodity exports to the world economy (or a contraction of imports; trade balance in T goods increases). The resource-poor partner, in turn, experiences a real appreciation and a shift in the composition of its exports from globally traded goods to regional goods that were previously nontraded.

Table 8.1.1 shows a set of regression-based tests of the hypothesis that monetary union narrows real exchange rate differentials. Our basic model is therefore a cross-sectional regression of the form

$$\log p_t = \alpha_0 + \alpha_1 \cdot CFA_i + \alpha_2 \cdot NR_i + \alpha_3 \cdot (CFA_i \cdot NR_i) + \alpha_4 \log y_{i,t-1} + \varepsilon_{i,} \quad (8.1.1)$$

where p_t is a measure of national prices converted to U.S. dollars for a comparable basket of goods across countries, CFA_i is a dummy variable taking the value of 1 if country i is a member of a CFA franc zone, NR_i is a measure of the natural resource intensity of country i, and $CFA_i \cdot NR_i$ is the interaction of the two effects. The coefficient on the interaction term provides a test of our hypothesis: a large, negative, and statistically significant value for α_3 would constitute strong evidence that the impact of national macroeconomic fundamentals on equilibrium real exchange rates is "shared out" among the members of a monetary union, and is therefore muted relative to what would emerge in the absence of union. The peripheral members of the Common Monetary Area (Lesotho, Namibia, Swaziland) are excluded, so the regression compares CFA zone members with countries in sub-Saharan Africa operating independent currencies.[28]

To control for the differing compositions of national expenditure, we draw on the Penn World Tables to benchmark national price levels against international

[28] The differences-in-differences design compares members of individual monetary unions with countries with independent national currencies. It is critical that each group be of sufficient size and that it contain appreciable variation in natural resource rents. The Common Monetary Area group is too small in these respects.

TABLE 8.1.1

Differences-in-Differences: Monetary Union and Equilibrium Real Exchange Rates

	NR = Indicator			*NR* = Rents
	1988–2008	1988–2002	2003–08	2003–08
Variable	[1]	[2]	[3]	[4]
CFA	0.104***	0.072*	0.184***	0.193***
	(3.06)	(1.68)	(3.82)	(4.14)
NR	0.126***	0.067	0.245***	0.480***
	(2.65)	(1.10)	(4.48)	(3.47)
*CFA*NR*	−0.197***	−0.143*	−0.302***	−0.779***
	(3.14)	(1.77)	(4.12)	(4.54)
log $y_{(i,t-1)}$	0.014	−0.014	0.078***	0.090***
	(0.70)	(0.56)	(3.18)	(3.89)
Number of countries	36	36	36	36
Number of observations	251	179	72	72
R^2 (adjusted)	0.3537	0.3587	0.4552	0.3885
F test on the sum of the coefficients on *NR* and *CFA*NR* (*p*-value)				
	0.126	0.214	0.259	0.016**

Source: Authors' calculations.

Note: The dependent variable is the log of the ratio of the official exchange rate in dollars per unit of local currency to the purchasing power parity exchange rate. Observations are nonoverlapping three-year averages. The sample includes all countries in sub-Saharan Africa with available data and population of at least one million in 2000, including South Africa but excluding other members of the Common Monetary Africa. All regressions include a full set of period dummy variables, and the earlier regressions include a dummy variable for Angola, due to a very large outlier observation. *T*-statistics based on robust standard errors are in parenthesis (asterisks denote significance at the *10 percent, **5 percent, and ***1 percent levels). CFA =African Financial Community, NR = natural resource intensity,

reference prices. Our dependent variable is the ratio of GDP measured at the official exchange rate to GDP measured at the purchasing power parity exchange rate.[29] An increase in this series denotes an increase in domestic prices relative to the foreign prices of similar goods, and therefore a real appreciation.[30] To focus on low-frequency movements, we take nonoverlapping, three-year averages of the data, for 1988 to 2008, and include a set of fixed time effects to capture developments in global markets. Because higher levels of real GDP per capita are associated with more appreciated real exchange rates across countries (the Harrod-Balassa-Samuelson effect), we control for the log of once-lagged real per capita income, log $y_{i,t-1}$, in all regressions.

[29] This underlying data series as reported in the World Bank World Development Indicators databse are: *GDP, PPP (current international $)* (NY.GDP.MKTP.PP.CD), and *GDP current US$* (NY.GDP.MKTP.CD). This is equivalent to the *inverse* of the *PPP Conversion Factor (GDP) to market exchange rate ratio* reported by the World Bank as series (PA.NUS.PPPC.RF).

[30] Recall that purchasing power parity ties the prices of traded goods together in a common currency, in the long run. Lower overall national price levels therefore mean lower prices of nontraded goods measured in a common currency, and therefore a more depreciated real exchange rate.

The sample consists of 36 countries, comprising all countries in sub-Saharan Africa with available data and with populations of at least one million in 2000, with the exception of the peripheral members of the Common Monetary Area. The MU dummy variable takes on the value "1" for members of the two CFA monetary unions—12 of these are in our sample, and we treat them as members of a single monetary union—and zero for the remaining 24 countries in the sample. Table 8.1.1 reports the results. In columns [1] through [3], we measure resource endowments using a time-invariant binary indicator for whether a country is a significant natural resource exporter; there are three such countries in the CFA group and eight in the non-CFA group.[31] Column [2] focuses on the subperiod from 1988 to 2002, a favorable one for assessing the equilibrium implications of resource abundance given the relative tranquility in global commodity markets. Column [3] considers the more recent subperiod from 2003 to 2008. Resource abundance surely mattered a great deal during this period given the quintupling or so of nominal global fuel prices, but the empirical test is less clean than in the earlier period because rigid nominal exchange rates are likely to have generated larger short-term real exchange rate misalignments in the CFA countries than elsewhere in Africa. In the final column, we report a regression for the later period that measures natural resource dependence as the lagged value of natural resource rents relative to GDP.

The results in Table 8.1.1 are strongly consistent with our hypothesis. For the full period and the period since 2003, the familiar "resource curse" effect is apparent among the non-CFA countries, because $\alpha_2 > 0$ implies that higher levels of resource wealth generate more appreciated currencies within this group. The point estimate remains positive for the relatively tranquil period before 2003, although it is smaller and statistically insignificant. The very strong results from the 2003–2008 period should of course be treated with caution, because this was a period of sharp cumulative increases in global fuel prices; the interaction term therefore provides a joint test of our hypothesis about equilibrium real exchange rates and a complementary hypothesis about greater short-run misalignments in the CFA zone due to the lack of nominal exchange rate adjustment. But our estimates of α_3 are negative and highly statistically significant for the full period, and for both subperiods. Differences in natural resource endowment therefore have much smaller impacts on real exchange rate differentials across the CFA zone than across countries with independent national currencies. In columns [1]–[3], in fact, we cannot reject the hypothesis that variations in resource rents have no impact at all on relative real exchange rates in the CFA zone.

---

[31] Countries' natural resource intensity is based on total natural resource rents as a share of GDP (World Development Indicators series NY.GDP.TOTL.RT.ZS). The indicator variable *NR* takes the value "1" for countries with a share of natural resources in GDP exceeding 10 percent on average between 1986 and 2008.

REFERENCES

Adam, C., C. Kombe, P. Kessy, and S. O'Connell, 2012, "Exchange Rates in the Transition to East African Monetary Union," International Growth Centre Working Paper 12/0458 (London: International Growth Center).

Agarwala, R., 2003, "Road to a Single Currency for South Asia" RIS Policy Brief #9 (New Delhi: Research and Information System for the Non-Aligned and Other Developing Countries, December).

Beetsma, R., and M. Giuliodori, 2010, "The Macroeconomic Costs and Benefits of the EMU and Other Monetary Unions: An Overview of Recent Research," *Journal of Economic Literature*, Vol. 48, No. 3, pp. 603–641.

Chinn, M., and H. Ito, 2008, "A New Measure of Financial Openness," *Journal of Comparative Policy Analysis*, Vol. 10, No. 3, pp. 309–322.

Debrun, X., P. Masson, and C. Pattillo, 2005, "Monetary Union in West Africa: Who Might Gain, Who Might Lose, and Why?" *Canadian Journal of Economics*, Vol. 38, No. 2, pp. 454–481.

Debrun X., P. Masson, and C. Pattillo, 2010, "Should African Monetary Unions Be Expanded? An Empirical Investigation of the Scope for Monetary Integration in Sub-Saharan Africa," *Journal of African Economies*, Vol. 20, No. 2, pp. 104–150.

De Grauwe, P., 2009, *Economics of Monetary Union* (Oxford: Oxford University Press, 8th ed.).

Dellas, H., and G. S. Tavlas, 2009, "An Optimum-Currency-Area Odyssey," *Journal of International Money and Finance*, Vol. 28, No. 7, pp. 1117–1137.

Dhungana, S., 2008, "Capital Account Liberalization and Growth Volatility," unpublished BA thesis (Williamstown, Massachusetts: Williams College).

Dowd, K., and D. Greenaway, 1993, "Currency Competition, Network Externalities and Switching Costs: Towards an Alternative View of Optimum Currency Areas," *Economic Journal*, Vol. 103, No. 20, pp. 1180–1189.

Eichengreen, B., 2006, "The Parallel Currency Approach to Asian Monetary Integration," *American Economic Review*, Vol. 96, No. 2, pp. 432–436.

Eichengreen, B., A. K. Rose, and C. Wyplosz, 1994, "Speculative Attacks on Pegged Exchange Rates: An Empirical Exploration with Special Reference to the European Monetary System," in *The New Transatlantic Economy*, ed. by M. Canzoneri, P. Masson, and V. Grilli (Cambridge: Cambridge University Press).

European Central Bank, 2010, "Study on the Establishment of a Monetary Union among the Partner States of the East African Community," ECB Staff Study (Frankfurt).

Hinkle, L., and P. Montiel, 1999, *Exchange Rate Misalignment: Concepts and Measurement for Developing Countries* (Oxford: Oxford University Press).

Johansen, J., 1992, "Testing Weak Exogeneity and the Order of Cointegration in UK Money Demand Data," *Journal of Policy Modeling*, Vol. 14, No. 3. pp. 313–334.

Kigabo R., T. Masson, and P. Masson, 2012, "Design and Implementation of a Common Currency Area in the East African Community," unpublished.

Lane, P., and G. M. Milesi-Ferretti , 2007, "The External Wealth of Nations Mark II," *Journal of International Economics*, Vol. 73, No. 2, pp. 223–250.

Lee, J., G. M. Milesi–Ferretti, J. Ostry, A. Prati, and L. A. Ricci, 2008, "Exchange Rate Assessments: CGER Methodologies" IMF Occasional Paper No. 261 (Washington: International Monetary Fund).

Masson, P., 2012, "A Simple Method of Introducing a Regional Currency," unpublished (Kigali: National Bank of Rwanda).

Mori, J., M. Kinukawa, H. Nukaya, and M. Hashimoto, 2002, "Integration of the East Asian Economies and a Step by Step Approach towards a Currency Basket Regime," Institute for International Monetary Affairs Research Report No. 2 (Tokyo: Institute for International Monetary Affairs).

O'Connell, S. A., B. O. Maturu, F. M. Mwega, N. S. Ndung'u, and W. R. Ngugi, 2010, "Capital Mobility, Monetary Policy and Exchange Rate Management in Kenya" in *Kenya:*

Policies for Prosperity, ed. by Christopher Adam, Paul Collier, and Njuguna Ndung'u (Oxford: Oxford University Press).

Porter, M. G., 1972, "Capital Flows as an Offset to Monetary Policy: The German Experience," *IMF Staff Papers*, Vol. 19, pp. 395–424.

Reinhart, C. M., and K. S. Rogoff, 2004, "The Modern History of Exchange Rate Arrangements: A Reinterpretation," *Quarterly Journal of Economics*, Vol. 119, No. 1, pp. 1–48.

Rose, A., 2000, "One Market, One Money: Estimating the Effect of Common Currencies on Trade," *Economic Policy*, Vol. 30, No. 1, pp. 7–45.

Willett, T. D., K. M. Al-Barwani, and S. M. El Hag, 2009, "The Gulf Cooperation Council's Fixed Exchange Rate: A Major Anomaly for OCA Analysis" (School of Politics and Economics, Claremont Graduate University, California).

CHAPTER 9

Financial Sector Stability: A Regional Approach

MARY ZEPHIRIN AND S. KAL WAJID

This chapter looks at the issue of financial stability in the envisaged East African Monetary Union (EAMU) and the responsibility for it among East African Community (EAC) authorities. Signatories to the EAC Treaty undertook to establish a customs union, a common market, a monetary union, and ultimately a political federation. With the ratification of the Customs Union Protocol in 2004 and the Common Market Protocol in 2010, work is now under way to draft a monetary union protocol. In this connection, the EAC Council of Ministers has adopted as a blueprint the European Central Bank study on the *Establishment of a Monetary Union among the Partner States of the EAC* (European Central Bank, 2010).

Under monetary union, the EAC would establish a regional central bank entrusted with the formulation and implementation of monetary and exchange rate policy and promotion of financial stability. This chapter presents a framework for financial stability within the EAC and the preparatory work needed to ensure regional and national authorities are well prepared to carry out their responsibilities in this regard.

The next section outlines the prerequisites of a financial stability framework, followed by reviews of the arrangements in place in the EAC states to identify areas that need attention, and a discussion of key elements of a framework, taking account of adaptations suggested by a regional rather than purely national setting.

PREREQUISITES OF A FINANCIAL STABILITY FRAMEWORK

A financial system must first be stable before it can be developed, implying certain preconditions and institutional arrangements. At the macroeconomic level, appropriate mechanisms for implementing and coordinating monetary and fiscal policies—alongside appropriate macroeconomic policies—are needed. Central banks must pursue price stability and governments' prudent management of fiscal policy, supported by appropriate institutional arrangements. A well-designed financial stability framework must also comprise the following:

- Effective financial sector regulation and supervision (microprudential oversight) is essential for limiting the risk of instability in the financial system.

- Macroprudential analysis and policy, focusing on system-wide risks and using prudential tools to minimize disruptions of financial services that can harm the real economy.
- Institutional arrangements and infrastructure and the capacity to conduct regular analysis and assessment of financial stability. This includes the legal frameworks and payment systems designed to mitigate risks and encourage proper coordination.
- Arrangements for crisis preparedness and management, including systemic liquidity arrangements, financial safety nets, and resolution mechanisms.

Such elements can prevent a crisis or manage and resolve one when it occurs. A financial stability framework is needed in a regional setting because of the financial market integration that follows from monetary union. The financial stability framework is aimed at controlling the systemic risk that arises from contagion between institutions or from macro-financial linkages. In a regionally integrated system, financial institutions and activities are permitted and encouraged to operate across borders, increasing the risk of systemic and spillover effects.

The challenges of cross-border operations in a range of legal, regulatory, and supervisory systems are well-known. Individual countries may promote their national institutions by providing less stringent regulation, including licensing policy, encouraging institutions to locate in the jurisdiction with the lightest requirements (regulatory arbitrage). Authorities are naturally more concerned with protecting their own institutions and citizens and are likely to give less attention to spillover from nationally based institutions that affect foreign jurisdictions.

With different supervisory systems, institutions operating cross-border can also face different requirements from home and host supervision, raising their costs (which will be passed onto clients) and potentially engendering perverse incentives. Although cooperation and information exchange are stressed in effective cross-border supervision, even in the presence of agreements, the incentives to supply information may be perverse when problems arise in the financial system. In addition, features of safety net arrangements in a regional setting would need to be carefully considered and reinforced by strong supervision given the potential for moral hazard.

The establishment of an appropriate financial stability framework for the EAMU will present significant challenges and opportunities. A number of the member states are still developing their frameworks and building capacity for the analysis and assessment of financial stability. Conceptually, the optimal design of a framework for financial stability in a monetary union is as yet undefined, especially given shortcomings revealed in the recent financial crisis. At the same time, still-evolving national arrangements in the region provide the opportunity to harmonize national frameworks for a coherent regional arrangement. Although financial market integration is still limited, the EAMU can help encourage the defining of a regional framework for financial stability, establishing harmonized minimum requirements, and promoting capacity building in this area. Specific areas for action include the following:

- *Common legal framework.* For the harmonization of supervision, both regulations and supervisory practice must converge. The European Union (EU) model of common directives is one way to do this. Common regulations, as well as manuals and toolkits, would help to bring about the common supervisory culture that would support financial stability in the region as a whole.
- *Coordination mechanisms.* Consolidated and cross-border supervision in banking and group-wide supervision in insurance with arrangements in place to ensure exchange of information and cooperation between supervisory authorities and central banks on macroprudential monitoring, responses to financial market developments, and crisis management.
- *Monitoring complex institutions.* As more complex financial institutions emerge in the region, they may expose financial markets and payment and settlement systems to greater risk. Effective monitoring of financial risks in such institutions would be crucial for maintaining systemic stability, and will require that data deficiencies in the household and corporate sectors be addressed.
- *Locating supervisory powers.* The location and distribution of supervisory powers in a monetary union require careful consideration. Several options are possible: centralized supervision in the regional central bank or in a separate regional body for financial supervision, and national-level supervisors with coordinating mechanisms or with more formal arrangements for joint action. Clarity on the preferred option is important, along with the process for updating regulations/arrangements governing cross-border cooperation in the areas of prudential supervision and crisis management.
- *Nonbank supervision.* Coherent arrangements for the supervision of nonbank financial institutions in a regional setting will be necessary to contain systemic risk emanating from this segment. Supervision of the nonbank sector is inadequate throughout the EAC region, in particular, in the regulation and supervision of insurance and securities markets and pension funds.

FINANCIAL STABILITY FRAMEWORKS IN EAST AFRICAN COMMUNITY PARTNER STATES

All five EAC states are building capacity for assessing financial stability, although their approaches differ. And they all face challenges in data availability and skills for the application of analytical tools. The EAC financial integration process allows the raising of supervisory effectiveness to international standards across all partner countries, consideration of appropriate crisis management, and safety net arrangements. It also encourages the harmonization of payments systems, which are crucial in a monetary union.

Regulation, Supervision, and Financial Stability Analysis in the East African Community

All the EAC central banks have explicit financial stability oversight arrangements with dedicated departments, or subunits, and four of the five countries issue financial stability reports. Some of these take account of the financial sector indicators for other member states. Coordination arrangements among the regulatory agencies and the ministry of finance exist in Kenya, Tanzania, and Uganda, and informal exchanges take place in Burundi. The National Bank of Rwanda is the single regulatory agency of the country, excepting the very limited securities market (Annex Table A9.1 summarizes the financial stability frameworks in the community).

Regular discussions and meetings between the staff of the central banks, with sharing of methodologies, could help in the development of a common framework for the region. An integrating regional market necessitates that the jurisdictions carry out a joint financial stability assessment, taking account of potential spillover arising out of the macroeconomic and institutional environments. Close collaboration in developing individual country frameworks would be of particular importance. Technical assistance from the IMF is helping to build these systems, and the EAC member states should be proactive in forging a common framework able to harmonize national systems.

Banking Supervision

The EAC countries have begun harmonizing their regulatory and supervisory frameworks, using compliance with international standards, such as the Basel Core Principles as the harmonizing mechanism (Basel Committee on Banking Supervision, 2012). In all five, central banks conduct banking supervision. Banking supervision assessments in recent Financial Sector Assessment Programs found there was almost full compliance with objectives, independence, powers and transparency, capital adequacy, and the supervision of credit risk. But abuse of financial services, country and transfer risk, and market risk all required considerable additional work for the jurisdictions to achieve uniformly adequate supervision.

Since the Financial Sector Assessment Programs in 2009–2011, the jurisdictions have worked to address the gaps identified in Basel Core Principle compliance, although challenges remain. Of the areas important for cross-border oversight, supervision of country and transfer risk remains a major challenge, consolidated supervision could be improved, and a better understanding of the links between institutions is needed. Financial institution ownership structures can be opaque, which could limit the understanding of the national, and even more so, the regional supervisors. These issues have given rise to proposals for regional supervisors—such as in Schoenmaker and Oosterloo (2007) and European Central Bank (2008)—but because understanding of banks often requires local knowledge, centralized supervision will still need to rely on local supervisors, and effective cooperation between the two will remain crucial.

All five central banks signed the EAC's 2009 memorandum of understanding (MOU) for cooperation in the supervision of financial institutions. It lays down a framework for information exchange and rules for sharing licensing and information between home and host supervisors with regard to concerns about cross-border establishments and enforcement actions. It also recognizes the benefits of coordinating onsite inspection, and central banks in the region have already carried out such joint inspections. The provisions of the MOU closely track the good practices recommended by the Basel Committee on Banking Supervision for MOUs. Additional content is likely to be helpful in two areas: (1) dealing with a problem cross-border institution and crisis situations, and (2) cost sharing in some situations, for example, where a supervisor needs to incur costs to conduct an investigation for a requesting supervisor.

Obtaining the benefits of a common supervisory culture, which would help ensure harmonized supervision, requires taking a common approach to supervision. The EAC jurisdictions are all moving toward risk-based supervision, but some do not yet have the supervisory arrangements and skills to implement this consistently. Four have similar risk-based supervision approaches and a similar approach to consolidated supervision, although gaps exist in the implementation of the latter.

Three jurisdictions subscribe to the Bank Supervision Application,[1] which provides a generic information system allowing institutions to report to their supervisors. It is intended to help harmonize banking supervision. The supervisors may wish to consider whether it would be helpful for EAC members to all adopt this platform for supervisory reporting. It would be important to adopt similar data definitions, though these should take account of the peculiarities of each jurisdiction. For example, comparison of capital adequacy is impaired by differences in measured capital—at least one EAC jurisdiction has a nonstandard definition of nonperforming loans, with implications for provisioning and capital measurement. Annex Table A9.2 demonstrates that the jurisdictions publish different financial soundness indicators, making for limited comparison at even this basic level.

Insurance Supervision[2]

The regulatory regimes in place in the region for other sectors reflect the development of the sectors. Insurance regulation and supervision in the EAC is generally lagging behind that for banking. Three countries have specialized insurance supervisors, and the other two have units in the central bank or ministry of finance. Insurance regulatory skills and supervisory capacity are lacking. Besides shortcomings in legal and regulatory provisions, there are differences in the provisions between jurisdictions. Examples include minimum capital requirements, the calculation of solvency margins, corporate governance requirements, and recognition of microinsurance. The scope for regulatory arbitrage and the

[1]This was initiated in 1997 by the Eastern and Southern African Banking Supervisors Group.

[2]Annex Table A9.3 provides an indication of the financial institutions and markets of the EAC.

difficulty comparing the financial health of insurance companies across the jurisdictions are evident.

Member states are using the International Association of Insurance Supervisors (IAIS, 2008) core principles for insurance supervision, but progress toward implementation of international standards of insurance oversight has been slower than in other sectors. Regulators in the five countries (all members of the East African Insurance Supervisors Association) signed a multilateral MOU for the regulation and supervision of insurance in August 2010.[3] But even though it establishes a framework for cooperation and coordination, national arrangements constrain its effectiveness. The Common Market Protocol is encouraging the cross-border establishment of insurance companies (in addition to banks). As insurance laws, regulations, and their implementation are very constrained, the sharing of information may be limited because the national regulators themselves may lack the necessary data and detailed knowledge of their industries. In several member states, weak or insolvent insurance companies continue to operate, illustrating the weak nature of insurance sector oversight.

Microfinance Institutions and Cooperatives

These institutions are growing in the region and welcomed as a means of increasing access to finance. That some have grown large enough to be registered as banks is evidence of their success. In general, the central banks oversee microfinance institutions, particularly the deposit-taking, under separate legislation, and separate bodies oversee microfinance institutions and cooperatives. Their similarities to banks (both are credit institutions) warrant central bank oversight, as does their potential to compete directly with banks as they grow. Their numbers, however, may stretch central bank resources. It is also likely that the oversight of microfinance institutions and cooperatives is lighter than optimal.

Pension Sector Oversight

Only three EAC jurisdictions have regulatory bodies for overseeing pensions, two of them only recently established, but only in Kenya and Tanzania does the sector appear important. The Tanzanian authority covers only social security funds. The capacity for oversight is consistent with this institutional structure, though even the longest-established regulatory body needs to strengthen its offsite analysis. Authorities should introduce minimum standards for actuarial evaluation and funding rules, and ensure that they have the capacity to analyze the effect of shocks on the financial positions of the schemes. Though they are largely government schemes, the fiscal impact of a failure could be serious.

---

[3] See http://www.eac.int/index.php?option=com_content&view=article&id=476:eac-insurance-regulators-sign-mou&catid=146:press-releases&Itemid=194.

Securities Regulation

Four of the five EAC partner states have organized securities exchanges and capital market regulatory authorities, though the market and its regulator are nascent in one case. Measures are required to improve market transparency. Processes have been agreed or are in train for the demutualization of the Dar es Salaam Stock Exchange, the Nairobi Stock Exchange, and the Uganda Securities Exchange. The EAC treaty calls for harmonization of capital market policies and legal frameworks, cooperation of the exchanges, and the promotion of cross-border listings and trades, as well as the development of a regional rating system. The four states' capital market regulatory authorities are all members of the East African Member States Securities Regulatory Authorities, a forum set up in 1997 to share information among regulators, provide for mutual assistance and cooperation, and to advance the integration of the capital markets. They are undertaking initiatives to regionalize capital markets while developing the regulatory framework.

As was done in the banking sector, regulators are harmonizing and coordinating oversight on the basis of the International Organization of Securities Commissions' objectives and principles. Member states are reviewing their legal and regulatory frameworks and have identified the amendments to bring them in line with the standards. Kenya, Tanzania, and Uganda have signed the International Organization of Securities Commissions multilateral MOU. The East African Member States Securities Regulatory Authorities is also planning a program of regional certification for industry professionals.

The member regulatory authorities of the East African Member States Securities Regulatory Authorities should, under its auspices, undertake other measures to coordinate regulatory oversight in the region. These include agreeing to an MOU to define home-host supervisory responsibilities for capital market intermediaries, exchanges, central securities depositaries, and institutional investors; implementing common licensing standards for market intermediaries; and adopting common prudential standards for institutional investors. Common standards for accounting and auditing and uniform requirements for reporting and disclosure are also needed.

Infrastructure

The overall legal and judicial framework for financial infrastructure in the region requires strengthening in the EAC member states, and most have reform programs in place. But implementation can be slow. In the area of payments, the EAC has established the East African Payments System Harmonization Committee and work is under way for interconnection of Kenya's, Tanzania's, and Uganda's real time gross settlement systems. Technical specifications have been agreed and submitted to vendors, and draft agreements, rules, and operational procedures circulated. Burundi still lacks a real-time gross settlement, although work has begun on developing this, and Rwanda implemented an integrated payment processing system in 2011. The authorities are implementing an integrated regional payments system that would allow regional payments to be settled in national currencies. It would be desirable to put real-time gross settlement systems in place, as rapidly as possible in all the partner states. Mobile payments system are growing throughout the region, and although none appear to be operating cross-border yet, a harmonized approach to their oversight should be instituted.

Crisis Management and the Safety Net

The financial safety net provided by deposit insurance and emergency liquidity assistance (or lender of last resort) helps the system avoid severe instability by preventing rumors of institutional difficulty from becoming self-fulfilling prophecy. In a regional context, ex ante cooperative agreements among supervisors can prove insufficient to deter supervisors from taking action in their own jurisdiction's narrow interest.

The arrangements for crisis management in the EAC are ambiguous and need to be developed. A comprehensive approach to crisis management seems to be lacking in most member states. For instance, in one country, lender-of-last-resort arrangements are governed by the central bank law, while the banking law establishes intervention modalities for bank insolvency situations. To better guide decision makers, additional regulations and definitions would benefit from clarification. For example, systemic establishments, which can benefit from exceptional facilities, are not defined. A second state has broad powers of intervention for the central bank in the banking act, deposit protection, and emergency liquidity assistance functions available to the central bank.

Safety nets and crisis management are still to be addressed in another country, but the introduction of deposit insurance (so far only allowed for in the financial institution law) will require effective supervision. In a fourth member state, the operational framework for lender-of-last-resort facilities functions appears adequate and a new legal framework for deposit insurance was adopted in 2006. A fifth has the basic elements of the financial safety net—deposit insurance and lender-of-last-resort facilities—but needs to do more on domestic and regional contingency planning for crisis management and arrangements for dealing with failed institutions.

The EAC can take a several steps in this area. Each jurisdiction could implement legislation and measures for prompt corrective action to extend the options available to the supervisor to deal with weak banks. A joint review of their emergency liquidity facilities should facilitate discussion of how to proceed if a cross-border bank were to experience difficulties, as well as an ex ante agreement. Finally, a joint crisis management plan should be worked out among the central banks, other supervisors, and the ministry of finance. Such planning is best done before periods of instability occur.

A FRAMEWORK FOR FINANCIAL STABILITY

Financial Stability Analysis

Financial stability analysis aims to identify threats to stability and devise appropriate policy responses. Its core elements include (1) macro-financial analysis, (2) assessment of the financial supervision framework, and (3) evaluation of the robustness of financial infrastructure and crisis management and safety net arrangements.

Macro-Financial Analysis

Macro-financial analysis is focused on the potential impact of macroeconomic factors on the soundness and stability of financial systems. It assesses the likelihood of shocks to the financial system stemming from financial market and macroeconomic developments, and of how changes in financial soundness may themselves affect macroeconomic and real-sector developments. Macroeconomic and financial market risk factors feed into the assessment of the soundness of the financial sector, including thorough evaluation of financial soundness and market indicators, stress testing, and analysis of the structure of the financial system (including its efficiency and competitiveness).

Stress testing is a common tool for assessing the vulnerability of a financial system to exceptional but plausible events. Stress tests gauge the sensitivity of a group of institutions (such as commercial banks) or even an entire financial system to a set of common shocks and to stressful scenarios. The analysis identifies the major risks and exposures in the system, defines the coverage and identifies the data required and available, calibrates the scenarios or shocks to be applied to the data, selects and implements a methodology, and interprets the results. In most countries, stress tests primarily focus on banking systems because banks form the core of the financial system. Close monitoring of banking sector financial soundness indicators, including capital adequacy, asset quality, management soundness, earnings and profitability, liquidity, and sensitivity to market risk, would be important for detecting potential vulnerabilities.

A very useful feature in implementing plausible stress tests is a macroeconomic model that can generate scenarios depicting varying macroeconomic conditions. An ongoing methodological challenge is to link such macro scenarios to the balance sheets of financial institutions in order to assess systemic risks. Most EAC countries do not employ macroeconomic models on a regular basis, and efforts should focus on capacity building in this area. Once adequately robust and flexible models are developed at the country level, attention should turn to developing a regional model to gauge the impact of common shocks on the financial system of the region as a whole.

Analysis of key balance sheets in the nonbank sector is an integral part of financial stability assessment. Monitoring the financial condition and vulnerabilities of the corporate, household, and real estate sectors can enhance capacity to assess risks to the financial sector, particularly where growing incomes and credit are fueling demand. More generally, the importance of the insurance sector for financial stability is increasing because of growing links between insurers and banks and the potential for contagion. These links can include cross ownership (or affiliation), credit risk transfers, and financial reinsurance. In most emerging markets, insurance tends to be a developing industry subject to only rudimentary supervision. Segments of this industry are often characterized by aggressive competition and even fraudulent behavior, such as third-party motor liability insurance. While this is unlikely to be of systemic importance on its own, the reputation risks and lack of confidence generated can have wider and longer-lasting effects.

The ease of movement between markets in a union heightens this risk. Cross-border market links are still very limited in the EAC, but collection of data that allows their development to be monitored is important. Similarly, while securities markets are likely to be systemic only in Kenya, Tanzania, and Uganda, as these markets deepen and develop in the region, households, corporations, and financial institutions can become exposed through investments in primary and secondary markets and trading of risk in financial markets. Monitoring and analysis of these exposures would become critical in the regional context.

A lack of data for systematic analysis is a key challenge in the nonbank sector. Data on financial stability indicators for the insurance sector and key nonbank balance sheets would need to be compiled within the EAC on a uniform basis to facilitate analysis of cross-sector and cross-country links at the regional level. A range of quantitative indicators measuring depth, tightness, and resilience of securities markets would need to be collected.

Regulation and Supervision—Microprudential

Effective microprudential (as compared with macroprudential discussed later) regulation and supervision is crucial to help gauge risks and vulnerabilities, protect market integrity, and provide incentives for strong risk management and good governance of financial institutions. At the national level, the assessment of compliance with the internationally agreed standards complements the quantitative macro-financial analysis. The standards provide a benchmark against which country practices can be compared, as the EAC is doing. The standards used are the Basel Committee's Core Principles for Effective Banking Supervision, the IAIS Insurance Supervisory Principles, and the International Organization of Securities Commissions' Objectives and Principles for Securities Regulation. These provide qualitative information, including on the effectiveness of institutions' risk management systems and, thus, on how well the system is positioned to respond to specific risks. Standards assessments also help to interpret financial soundness indicators by clarifying the definitions underpinning the data institutions provide.

Similarly, the analysis and interpretation of soundness indicators in insurance can be complemented by the assessments of compliance with the Insurance Core

Principles. These cover the effectiveness of supervision, qualitative information on regulatory thresholds, the structure and characteristics of companies in the sector, and other useful qualitative information.

Qualitative information from the assessments of the Securities Core Principles can also be helpful in assessing the resiliency of securities markets. This should allow some judgment of the effectiveness of the legal, judicial, and regulatory framework, and governance practices and provide information on the trading systems, price transparency, margining rules, and capital committed by the exchange to support trading.

The challenges for financial regulation and supervision in the region concern the ability of supervisory authorities to keep up with the proliferation of financial services; undertake consistent, risk-based supervision and prompt corrective action; implement consolidated supervision—including cross-border, group-wide, and conglomerate—and cooperate with other domestic and foreign supervisory agencies. The evolving nature of the understanding of financial risks and the international guidance to address them, in particular in capital adequacy and quality and liquidity buffers, compounds these challenges.

All three prudential standards offer guidance on international cooperation. The Basel Core Principles (Basel Committee on Banking Supervision, 2012) specify principles for the supervision of cross-border institutions—Basel Core Principle 3 requires that the laws, regulations, and arrangements provide for cooperation and collaboration, consolidated supervision, and the relationship between home and host supervisors in Basel Core Principles 12 and 13, respectively. Background and additional details are provided among others, by the Basel Committee on Banking Supervision (1992 and 1996), which provide for the division of responsibilities between home and host supervisors, MOUs, and guidance for improving information flows.

One mechanism for better coordination in consolidated supervision is the supervisory college. Such colleges consist of multilateral groups of supervisors from all countries where an institution has substantial operations (see Basel Committee on Banking Supervision, 2010a), and help to ensure host supervisory involvement in the process for banks that are systemically important in their jurisdiction. They allow the sharing of understanding on local conditions, the coordination of supervisory work, and, when necessary, the coordination of stability measures.

Practical decisions must be made about the supervisors to involve; for example, a college for a bank that has a presence throughout the region as well as substantial activities outside should also allow membership from that jurisdiction, even if it is not a member of the union. This allows supervision to benefit from their knowledge and allows a better division of work among the home and host. Box 9.1 summarizes the Basel Committee supervisory college recommendations.

From a regional perspective, IAIS guidelines for cooperation and cross-border supervision can also provide an important guide to regional supervisors. In addition to the principles on information exchange and group-wide supervision Insurance Core Principles 3 and 23, respectively, IAIS (2011/12) provides

BOX 9.1 Basel Committee on Banking Supervision Recommendations for Supervisory Colleges

- Enhanced information exchange and cooperation to support effective supervision of international banking groups.
- Establish a college structure that enhances effective oversight, taking account of scale, structure, and complexity of the banking group and ensuring that common functions related to communication, and a common approach to information sharing.
- The best efforts of college members to share appropriate information on the principal risks of the banking group.
- Communication channels within a college that ensure efficiency, ease of use, integrity, and confidentiality of information exchange.
- Collaborative work between members that improves the effectiveness of group oversight and is based on agreement between the supervisors, recognizing national legal constraints.
- Facilitate interaction between the college members and the banking group that complements oversight and information sharing between individual supervisors and the supervised entity.
- Work of the college that provides a building block for crisis management planning.
- Colleges should ensure that the supervision of large groups is tailored to their systemic importance, and facilitate the process of identification and dissemination of information relevant to macroprudential analysis.

Source: Basel Committee on Banking Supervision.

principles on supervisory cooperation and coordination, both group-wide and cross-border, with criteria that include guidance on forming supervisory colleges (ICP 25), as well as on cross-border cooperation and coordination on crisis management (ICP 26). They have also formulated a multilateral MOU to provide practical arrangements in cooperation and information exchange and a high standard of confidentiality.

The nature of securities markets suggests that the interests of securities regulators are better aligned for cross-border oversight. As Tafara (2007) notes, the protection of domestic markets turns on the ability to obtain and provide international cooperation, particularly in an increasingly global market. The International Organization of Securities Commissions' multilateral MOU sets an international benchmark for cross-border cooperation that is effective against violations of securities and derivatives laws.[4] It specifies the types of information a signatory may be asked to provide (such as bank records), the permitted uses of such information, and the confidentiality of nonpublic information.

[4]There are two levels for ascribing to the multilateral MOU classified by the Annex in which the member is listed. Annex A members are those whose legal systems have been evaluated and judged to allow them to fulfill the terms of the MOU (there were 94 members listed in March 2013). Those in Annex B have committed to fulfilling the necessary legal conditions.

Financial Infrastructure

The institutional arrangements and infrastructure required to support financial stability includes the legal infrastructure for finance and payments and securities settlement systems. Payment systems are critical because if one or more financial institutions are unable to settle claims against them, they may cause other participants in the system to fail. Financial market infrastructure, including trading systems and payment and clearing and settlement systems, affects financial institutions' access to funding and ability to liquidate positions. Liquidity and operational risks in the payments and clearing and settlement system can thus have systemic effects.

In this area, as well, international standards for national systems are used as the basis for harmonization: the 2012 Principles for Financial Market Infrastructures established by the Committee on Payments and Settlements Systems, and the International Organization of Securities Commissions cover systemically important payment systems, central securities depositaries, security settlement systems, and central counterparties. Sound cross-border payment infrastructure allows less risky and cost-effective international payment transfers. The June 2008 report of the Committee on Payments and Settlements Systems also recommends actions to address the challenges by interdependencies between systems. The key features of sound cross-border infrastructure for systemically important systems are:

- Harmonization based on national real-time gross settlement systems offering intraday finality for cross-border payments. This reduces the settlement risks associated with deferred net settlement systems and the cross-border structure offers payment speeds similar to cross-border transactions.
- A sound and transparent legal structure that ensures national laws leaves payments immune to challenges based on insolvency laws, including protecting payment transfers against foreign insolvency procedures.
- Effective, accountable, and transparent governance arrangements so that the responsibilities of different organizational levels are clearly defined and separate risk management, oversight, and audit functions are in place.
- Harmonization of rules and procedures that outline the roles and responsibilities of different actors and describe the system and the rules on access and exclusion of participants.
- Clearly defined procedures for management of liquidity and credit risk, avoiding liquidity risk through central bank provision of intraday liquidity with collateral.
- A high degree of security and operational reliability of the national system—the system will only be as strong as its weakest link, and national central banks should address this area together, involving system users. Adequate business continuity plans, including special arrangements to provide minimum services in case of severe disruption.
- Effective oversight of the national systems.

Arrangements for Crisis Management and Safety Nets

The challenges of crisis preparedness and management depend to some extent on the structure of supervision and regulation under the monetary union. Although centralization of supervision may simplify the issue, if resolution laws and regulations and deposit insurance systems remain heterogeneous, coordination issues will remain. In the event that the supervisory responsibilities remain primarily with national authorities, contingency planning would be more complicated and coordinating support and managing conflicts of interest will remain a challenge. The decision of whether to provide emergency liquidity to (part of) a cross-border banking group in one country can have a significant impact on developments in other countries.

Liquidity assistance in situations when solvency of a cross-border group is not assured would also have to involve the ministries of finance. It would seem useful to have ex ante decision making on some principles for burden sharing between countries to avoid delays in negotiations, which is often warranted in times of stress. Furthermore, burden sharing for which authorities plan and agree beforehand may be easier to achieve. To allow flexibility, the authorities in the region could agree on some general guidelines for emergency liquidity assistance (Box 9.2).

It would be desirable to regularly test the arrangements for crisis. Such tests could take the form of regular crisis management exercises that (1) function as a tool to detect any shortcomings in the current arrangements and (2) facilitate common understanding and effective practices in a changing environment.

BOX 9.2 Possible General Guidelines for Emergency Liquidity Assistance in the East African Community

- Not all banks need to be rescued, and public support should only be provided to systemically important banks that would threaten financial stability if they were to fail. Shareholders' equity in rescued banks should be wiped out and new management should be installed.
- In interventions in cross-border groups, decisions should be made on burden sharing among national authorities. Guiding criteria could include estimates of the costs and benefits of intervention for each country, the extent to which the bank is systemically important in each country, the size of exposure and deposits in each of the countries, the origin of the problem, and the size of the national economies and abilities to provide the necessary resources. It would be preferable if these decisions are made ex ante and agreed in a "crisis memorandum of understanding," for example.
- The injection of public funds should be reversed soon after the crisis has ended and the rationale for support has gone. To avoid further distortion of competition, state aid should hence be wound down.

Source: Authors.

The main challenge of safety net arrangements in an integrated market where deposit insurance is a national function, as seems common, will come from differences in insurance design, in addition to the potential for moral hazard. Typically, national authorities are responsible for deposit insurance for locally incorporated subsidiaries, whereas deposits in branches are covered by the home authorities. Design differences such as the definition of insured deposits, the coverage limits, premium, and funding arrangements can distort competition and would need to be consistent across countries. Such differences may influence the movement of deposits in an integrated market (made worse with a single currency), possibly even creating destabilizing flows at just a hint of difficulty in one jurisdiction. It is even possible that jurisdictions attempt to compete on the design of their deposit insurance (e.g., through low premiums) to attract entry. Cross-border arrangements for deposit insurance will need to be developed.

No international insolvency regime exists (Lastra, 2007), but the Basel Committee (2010b) has a set of recommendations on cross-border bank resolution and the IMF (2010) has suggested a framework for enhanced coordination. In times of systemic stress, governments often restructure distressed institutions (rather than closing them) and cost sharing becomes an important issue when institutions operate across borders. The outcome in the event of a failed bank will depend on the resolution frameworks of individual countries and the losses to uninsured creditors and to the deposit insurance scheme. Some countries have special bankruptcy laws for dealing with banks, but most appear to use the general corporate code.

A common approach to insolvency resolution is desirable in an integrated market—this would involve similar treatment of creditors, mutual recognition of partner jurisdictions' bankruptcy procedures, and coordination among the authorities. The common approach would diminish conflicts and allow a faster and less costly solution. It needs to recognize, however, that cooperation deteriorates under adverse conditions. Declaring a bank insolvent may impact the home and the host differently.[5] This is complicated by accounting rules for insolvency that may differ, particularly when the bankruptcy procedures are not specific to financial institutions.

To take account of the differences in bankruptcy legislation applied to financial institutions across jurisdictions and the costs of disorderly bankruptcy and fiscal rescues, special resolution regimes have also been called for (Cihak and Nier, 2009). Internationally, enhanced coordination arrangements would need to accompany these (IMF, 2010).

---

[5] Under Basel guidelines, solvency of branches is the responsibility of the home jurisdiction, whereas the solvency of subsidiaries or joint ventures is that of the host supervisor or country of incorporation. But the home (or parent) jurisdiction should take account of the exposure of their banks' foreign subsidiaries and joint ventures because the parent bank has a responsibility for their subsidiaries.

Lessons from the Recent Global Financial Crisis

The global financial crisis highlighted the inadequacies of supervisory frameworks in accounting for systemic risk arising from the interaction between institutions. This section considers two major areas of change arising from this realization: (1) the attention to macroprudential oversight, and (2) the lessons the EU has drawn for the structure and conduct of supervision and contingency planning in their monetary union. While EU arrangements should not be taken as a template or guide for the EAC, the lessons the EU has drawn from crisis should still be of value.

Supervisors are now seeking to adopt a macroprudential approach to regulation and supervision. The concept recognizes that supervision that focuses only on ensuring the soundness of the individual institution will miss the linkages and interactions between institutions, other market components, and the wider economy, and this may constitute the greatest threat to the financial stability. Sound individual institutions do not necessarily imply that the system is sound, as unforeseen interactions may produce systemic risk. Cross-border links are an important aspect of such interactions. The design of a harmonized financial stability framework allows the EAC to consider how the renewed focus on a macroprudential approach could benefit their own financial stability arrangements.

As is clear from the Committee on the Global Financial System's 2010 paper and Lim and others (2011), the operationalization of macroprudential oversight is still under development. Lim and others (2011) have provided initial inferences on the use of macroprudential instruments. Caps on the loan-to-value and debt-to-income ratios, and on credit or credit growth, as well as reserve requirements, countercyclical capital requirements, and dynamic provisioning, were all found to help dampen procyclicality. Limits on net open currency positions, currency, and liquidity mismatch help reduce exposure. The use of several instruments, and of targeted and time-varying instruments, were also all found to be more effective. Rules-based instruments, such as dynamic provisioning, were found effective, but potentially difficult to design. Potential costs exist, of course, mainly in the form of unintended consequences from inappropriate calibration of the instruments. The inability of macroprudential policy to compensate for poor fiscal or monetary policy is stressed.

To incorporate macroprudential policies into their toolboxes and permit effective arrangements to address systemic risk, countries have been reviewing and adapting their financial stability frameworks. Institutional arrangements should support the identification and monitoring of systemic risks (requiring information and expertise), provide incentives for timely use of policy instruments, and allow for cooperation such that policy functions (macroprudential, microprudential, monetary) can operate autonomously and are effectively coordinated (Nier and others, 2011). Some advanced economies are incorporating prudential functions into their central banks, with separate agencies responsible for conduct-of-business and securities market oversight. In some cases, dedicated overarching committees responsible for macroprudential policy, somewhat analogous to monetary policy committees, are being created. Emerging markets are also creating similar structures. The choice of institutional structure should depend on country-specific circumstances.

The arrangements the EU made following the crisis reflect the conclusions reached by de Larosière (2009). That is, that in a single financial market, diversity of rules leads to competitive distortions and regulatory arbitrage and that presumably common directives were too often transposed into national options with different provisions and interpretations. Within a single market, similar definitions must apply to institutions, and capital-consistent approaches to risk management and supervision are needed. While some countries may want stricter rules for their specific circumstances, all must observe minimum core standards. As financial support is provided on a shared level, appropriate incentives require that banking supervision must also be shared. Implementing this approach in a sustainable fashion has led the EU toward a banking union (Box 9.3).

EU arrangements in response to the crisis are clearly complex, and their governance and operational details are still being worked out. The EAC should look to the principles underlying these arrangements that are aimed at circumventing perverse incentives arising in a single market with diverse oversight, and establishing and policing appropriate incentives and actions. Similar rules, regulations, and supervision appear necessary in a single market. Harmonization of approaches is likely insufficient because strong national biases are likely to dominate in times of stress, creating negative externalities at a cost to all. As monetary union approaches, the EAC authorities should review their financial stability

BOX 9.3 European Union Lessons from the Global Crisis

A banking union is a single supervisory and regulatory framework, resolution mechanism, and safety net for the euro area (Goyal and others, 2013). A harmonized regulatory setup, harmonized national resolution regimes for credit institutions, and standards for national deposit insurance schemes was planned for 2013.

A single supervisory mechanism is to be implemented once legislation is passed. Technical standards on sectoral microprudential regulation are set by the European Banking Authority, the European Securities and Markets Authority, and the European Insurance and Occupational Pensions Authority (all established in 2011). They are tasked with overseeing national supervisors and settling supervisory disputes.

The European Central Bank is to be the principal supervisor for the European Union, accountable to the European Parliament, directly supervising at least the three largest banks in any member, with the power to bring any bank under its supervision. National authorities remain responsible for any banks under their direct supervision.

Macroprudential oversight is assigned to the European Systemic Risk Board, which is to ensure effective recognition of cross-border spillover through risk warnings and recommendations. A single resolution mechanism and authority (including legislation and regulations) deposit insurance and common backstops is also expected.

Source: Goyal and others (2013).

frameworks to arrive at a single framework for the union that takes explicit account of spillover, systemic risk, and externalities.

CONCLUSIONS

EAC financial integration needs a regional financial stability framework. Key aspects in this regard require considerable collaborative effort. This includes not only harmonization and a unified approach to supervision and regulation across the region, but also development of appropriate legislation and methods for effective consolidated supervision and home-host cooperation. Financial stability analysis could also be undertaken jointly by following review of data definitions and interpretations to assess the potential for cross-border contagion through regionally headquartered banks. A number of challenges will have to be addressed, including the development of macroeconomic models, information, and analytical capacity for the nonbank financial sector, harmonization of supervision and regulation, and arrangements for crisis management and safety nets. The process arising from these arrangements should be sequenced immediately after completion of the negotiation of the EAC Monetary Protocol.

ANNEX 9.1

TABLE A9.1

Financial Stability Frameworks in the East African Community

	Burundi	Kenya	Rwanda	Tanzania	Uganda
National coordination	Informal coordination with other regulators	Coordinated by the Ministry of Finance with responsibility shared by regulatory agencies, though leadership not formalized	BNR is the only regulator of financial institutions and is responsible for the financial stability framework	There are consultations and exchange of information among financial regulators, with an MOU in process	FSSC whose membership includes all financial sector regulators and the Ministry of Finance, MOU among domestic regulators
Sectoral regulators	Banking: BRB Insurance: Agence de regulation et de Contrôle des Assurances in Ministry of Finance Pensions: Ministry of Labor, Public Service and Social Security	Banking: CBK Insurance: IRA Pensions: RBA Securities: CMA Microfinance institutions and cooperatives: SASRA	BNR Securities: CMA	Banking: BoT Insurance: TIRA Pensions: SSRA Securities: Capital Markets and Securities Authorities	Banking: BoU Insurance: IRA of Uganda Pensions: Uganda Retirement Benefits Regulatory Authority established 2012/13 Securities: CMA
Responsibility and organizational arrangements	BRB: Banking Supervision and Financial Stability Department	Regulators' Forum with an MOU monitors financial stability through a Financial Sector Stability Committee of technical staff from the overseeing ministries and the 5 regulators, and an Information and Sharing Committee	BNR has a Financial Stability Directorate that houses the Financial Stability Analysis Division as well as bank supervision, nonbank (insurance, pensions) financial institution, and microfinance supervision departments. Directorate's work overseen by Financial Stability Committee.	BoT has a Financial Stability Department and is mandated as the responsible authority for macroprudential oversight and facilitates the TFRF whose members include BoT, SSRA, TIRA, Deposit Insurance Board, and Ministry of Finance. The MOU stipulates the mode of operation in normal and crisis times and members' responsibilities	Financial Stability Department (within the supervision function) coordinates policy on financial stability for the FSSC and coordinates meetings of the BoU's Financial Stability Committee.

(continued)

TABLE A9.1

Financial Stability Frameworks in the East African Community (*continued*)

	Burundi	Kenya	Rwanda	Tanzania	Uganda
FSR	None	FSR	FSR	FSR	FSR
Tools for risk identification	Financial soundness indicators	Financial soundness indicators, EWS-CAMEL	Financial soundness indicators, CAMEL	Financial soundness indicators, EWS-CAMEL	Financial soundness indicators, EWS, CAMEL
- Internal risks	No models	Stress testing models, 2	Stress testing	Stress testing	Stress testing
- External risks	No models	No models	No models	Development started	No models
- Contagion risks					
Crisis management arrangements	Liquidity: BRB provides ELA on condition that banks have eligible collateral (government securities and some performing loans). Intervention: Banking act empowers BRB to intervene banks in difficulty through naming a provisional controller who participates in and can override board; and through naming new managers for two months. Decisions regarding resolution taken by commercial court on request of the central bank.	Financial Regulator's Forum MOU allows for coordinated approach to crisis management. Liquidity: Central bank act provides that CBK can make loans for fixed periods with government securities as collateral, on terms and conditions decided by bank. Intervention: Laws allow for CBK to organize statutory management and liquidation of banks. Safety net: Deposit Protection Fund Board to provide insurance cover and act as liquidator	No formal crisis management framework. Liquidity: BNR Act gives wide ability to decide on its facilities, including penalty interest rates. Intervention: Banking law provides BNR with enforcement and resolution powers to address individual institutions, including through liquidity and solvency support. Safety net: Law also requires a deposit insurance fund, legislation for which is under way.	Liquidity: BoT is lender-of-last-resort facilities at penal interest rates to solvent but illiquid banks with adequate collateral or government guarantee. Intervention: BoT can appoint an advisor, remove managers, impose fines, merge a bank, transfer assets and liabilities, and reorganize. Safety net: Deposit insurance Fund managed by the BoT	Liquidity: Act allows BoU loans with collateral of securities specified by board Intervention: BoU can place bank in receivership, receiver can mandate merger, purchase and assumption, sale of bank, and liquidation of assets. Safety net: Deposit protection scheme managed by bank supervision department
Cross-border cooperation	EAC central banks' MOU, but it does not provide for crisis management.	EAC central banks' MOU, but it does not provide for crisis management.	EAC central banks' MOU, but it does not provide for crisis management.	EAC central banks' MOU, MOUs between BoT and central banks of Kenya, Cyprus, Zimbabwe, Comoros, Uganda, Burundi, Rwanda	EAC central banks' MOUs, but it does not provide for crisis management.

Source: Websites of the central banks of EAC countries.

Note: BNR = Banque Nationale de Rwanda; BoT = Bank of Tanzania; BoU = Bank of Uganda; BRB = Banque de la Republique de Burundi; CAMEL = capital adequacy, management capability, and liquidity; CBK = Central Bank of Kenya; CMA = Capital Markets Authority; EAC = East African Community; ELA = emergency liquidity assistance; EWS = early warning system; FSSC = Financial Sector Surveillance Committee; FSR = Financial Stability Report; IRA = Insurance Regulatory Authority; MOU = memorandum of understanding; RBA = Retirement Benefits Authority; SACCO = Savings and Credit Cooperatives; SASRA = SACCO Societies Regulatory Authority; SSRA = Social Security Regulatory Authority, Tanzania; TFRF = Tanzania Financial Regulatory Authority; TIRA = Tanzania Insurance Regulatory Authority.

TABLE A9.2

Financial Soundness Indicators in the East African Community, 2011

	Burundi	Kenya	Rwanda	Tanzania	Uganda
Capital adequacy[1]					
Regulatory capital to risk-weighted assets	19.8	19.4	25	17.6	20.3
Regulatory tier 1 capital to risk-weighted assets	17.3	17.3	22.9	17	17.9
Asset quality					
Nonperforming loans to total gross loans	7.7	4.4	8	6.9	2.2
Nonperforming loans net of provisions to capital	4.9	3.5	14.7	17.5	—
Earning and profitability					
Return on assets	3.2	3.3	2.9	0.5	4
Return on equity	23	32.2	14.1	15.1	27.4
Interest margin to gross income	175.6	38.6	47.3	52.6	—
Liquidity					
Liquid assets to total assets	—	33.3	30	37	—
Liquid assets to short-term liabilities	93.1	37	—	40.2	—
Total loans to total deposits[1]	—	77.4	88.1	64.2	78.4
Sensitivity to market risk					
Net open position in foreign exchange to capital	—	3.3	9.6	0	—
FX currency denominated assets to total assets	—	11.8	16.5	33.8	—
FX assets to FX liabilities	—	—	—	—	100.2

Sources: Burundi—Staff Report for the 2012 Article IV Consultation, posted 8/06/2012 at www.imf.org; Kenya—Staff Report for Fourth Review under the ECF, posted 11/05/2012 at www.imf.org; Rwanda—Financial Stability Report 2011, posted 11/15/2012 at www.bnr.rw; Tanzania—Fifth Review under the PSI, posted 01/17/2013 at www.imf.org; Directorate of Banking Supervision Annual Report, 2011 at www.bot-tz.org; Uganda—Fourth Review under the PSI, posted 6/08/2012 at www.imf.org and Fifth Review under the PSI, posted 1/25/2013 at www.imf.org.

Notes: Different sources were used to obtain the largest number of comparable indicators, while taking account of possible revisions to the data. FX = foreign exchange.

[1]For Tanzania, the denominator for capital adequacy is total risk-weighted assets and off balance sheet exposures; the ratio of loans to deposits is total loans to customer deposits.

TABLE A9.3

Financial Systems in the East African Community

	Burundi	Kenya	Rwanda	Tanzania	Uganda
	(Number, unless otherwise specified)				
Commercial banks	9	43	9	31	24
Ratio of assets to GDP (percent)	31.6	66.8	28.3	38.2	29.2
Other banking institutions	2	1	6	17	3
Insurance companies	6	47	8	27	22
Pension funds	—	23	40	—	—
Microfinance deposit-takers	—	6	11	—	4
SACCOs	—	123	486	—	—
Stock market capitalization to GDP (percent)	na	28.7	21.3	30.5	468.5
Bureaux de change	—	118	148	198	176

Sources: EAC central banks' annual reports; supervision and financial stability reports; websites of the stock exchanges (Dar Es Salaam, Nairobi, Uganda); regulatory agencies; and IMF staff reports.

Notes: The data in this table may not be strictly comparable because the definition of microfinance institutions and SACCOs may differ across countries. The data may not be complete because it is not always possible to locate an appropriate source. SACCO = savings and credit cooperative organization.

REFERENCES

Basel Committee on Banking Supervision, 1992, "Minimum Standards for the Supervision of International Banking Groups and Their Cross-Border Establishments" (Basel: Bank for International Settlements). http://www.bis.org.

———, 1996, "Minimum Standards for the Supervision of International Banking Groups and Their Cross-Border Establishments" (Basel: Bank for International Settlements). http://www.bis.org.

———, 2010a, "Good Practice Principles on Supervisory Colleges" (Basel: Bank for International Settlements). http://www.bis.org.

———, 2010b, "Report and Recommendations of the Cross-Border Bank Resolution Group" (Basel: Bank for International Settlements). http://www.bis.org.

———, 2012, "Core Principles for Effective Banking Supervision" (Basel: Bank for International Settlements).

Cihak, M., and E. Nier, 2009, "The Need for Special Resolution Regimes for Financial Institutions: The Case of the European Union," IMF Working Paper 09/200 (Washington: International Monetary Fund).

Committee of Payments and Settlement Systems, 2008, "Interdependencies of Payment and Settlement Systems." http://www.bis.org.

Committee on the Global Financial System, 2010, "Macroprudential Instruments and Frameworks: A Stocktaking of Issues and Experiences," CGFS Papers No. 38 (Basel: Bank for International Settlements).

deLarosière, J., 2009, "Report of the High-Level Group on Financial Supervision in the EU." http://ec.europa.eu/internal_market/finances/docs/de_larosiere_report_en.pdf.

European Central Bank, 2008, "Developments in the EU Arrangements for Financial Stability," Monthly Bulletin (Frankfurt, April).

European Central Bank, 2010, "Study on the Establishment on a Monetary Union Among the Partner States of the EAC" (Arusha, Tanzania).

Goyal, R., P. Brooks, M. Pradhan, T. Tressel, G. Dell'Ariccia, R. Leckow, and C. Pazarbasioglu, 2013, "A Banking Union for the Euro Area," IMF Staff Discussion Note 13/01 (Washington: International Monetary Fund).

International Association of Insurance Supervisors, 2008, "Principles on Group-Wide Supervision" (Basel).

International Monetary Fund, 2010, "Resolution of Cross-Border Banks–A Proposed Framework for Enhanced Coordination" (Washington). http://www.imf.org/external/np/pp/eng/2010/061110.pdf.

Lastra, R. M., 2007, "Cross-Border Bank Insolvency," *Law in Transition Online*, October. http://www.ebrd.com/country/sector/law.

Lim, C., F. Columba, A. Costa, P. Kongsamu, A. Otani, M. Saiyid, T. Wezel, and X. Wu, 2011, "Macroprudential Policy: What Instruments and How to Use Them? Lessons from Country Experience", IMF Working Paper No. 11/238 (Washington: International Monetary Fund). http://www.imf.org/external/pubs/ft/wp/2011/wp11238.pdf.

Nier, E. W., J. Osinski, L. Jacome, and P. Madrid, 2011, "Towards Effective Macroprudential Policy Frameworks: An Assessment of Stylized Institutional Models," IMF Working Paper No. 11/250 (Washington: International Monetary Fund).

Schoenmaker, D., and S. Oosterloo, 2007, "Cross-Border Issues in European Financial Supervision," in *The Structure of Financial Regulation,* ed. by David Mayes and Geoffrey Woods (London: Routledge).

Tafara, E., 2007, "Cooperation in the Securities Sector," in *Working Together: Improving Regulatory Cooperation and Information Exchange*, Chapter 13 (Washington: International Monetary Fund).

CHAPTER 10

Cross-Country Financial Linkages and Implications for Financial Sector Supervision

ETIBAR JAFAROV

The authorities of the East African Community (EAC) countries envision strengthening and integrating the banking and financial systems in the hope that greater regional integration will increase the scale of financial operations and competition. This would reduce the cost of financial services, increase the efficiency of financial intermediation, and stimulate investment. International donors have been supportive.

The beneficial effects of opening financial sectors are well documented (de Mello, 1999; Fry, 1995). Indeed, greater integration facilitates risk-sharing and diversification, allows better allocation of capital among investment opportunities, and helps deepen financial markets. One could also expect greater competition, which in turn might help lower margins and reduce prices for financial services. But it is not free. As the recent global financial crisis has shown, increased financial linkages also expose financial systems in individual countries to shocks originating elsewhere. Understanding and effectively managing these risks is the key to sustaining robust growth and encouraging financial deepening in the region.

This paper analyzes financial linkages and flows in the EAC region to understand the associated risks of greater interconnectedness and implications for supervision. In the absence of data on financial flows (including on cross-country lending in the EAC), it does so by analyzing flows of trade, foreign direct investment (FDI), and remittances—as financial flows usually correlate well with these flows, cross-country ownership in the banking sectors, and the so-called sigma-convergence and beta-convergence measures of interest margins (lending rates–deposit rates or lending rates–Treasury bill rates).

The following conclusions emerge from the analysis. First, the EAC banking systems are linked through cross-country ownership of banks. This leaves the region vulnerable to crises through contagion. Second, weaknesses in banking supervision in both home and host countries increase the risk of contagion. In particular, some home and host supervisors do not have the capacity to supervise complex financial institutions. Finally, the emergence of financial conglomerations requires closer cooperation among agencies supervising different types of financial institutions.

The chapter concludes that improved supervision would enhance the resilience of the financial sectors in each country, which would also facilitate greater regional integration. Specifically, the paper suggests a more regional approach to banking supervision and managing vulnerabilities, including through supervisory colleges to supervise regionally active banks, jointly undertaking risk assessments and conducting stress tests, and extending coverage of the existing and future memorandums of understanding (MOUs) to cover the management of a financial crisis. Other measures include conducting a crisis simulation, which could help identify weaknesses in communication channels and procedures and improve understanding of responsibilities within and between countries and clarify the nature of information and data needs. The chapter also argues for building constructive cooperative relationships with all home- and host-country supervisors, phasing out remaining capital controls (relevant to other EAC countries to benefit from better allocation of capital and economies of scale), and promptly implementing the recommendations of the recent financial sector assessment program updates, which would increase the resilience of EAC financial systems.

In the chapter, the next section analyzes trade linkages, FDI flows, and remittances. The following section analyzes financial sector linkages, and the final section summarizes the policy implications of the analysis.

TRADE LINKAGES, FOREIGN DIRECT INVESTMENT FLOWS, AND REMITTANCES[1]

Trade Linkages

While they have low export capacities, the EAC countries are moderately open.[2] In 2013, the import-to-GDP ratio averaged 30 percent, with Kenya recording the highest (45 percent) and Uganda the lowest (21 percent). The countries have small export bases. Kenya has the highest export-to-GDP ratio (14 percent), followed by Tanzania (12 percent), and Uganda (8 percent). Exports from Burundi and Rwanda are much smaller: about 4 percent of GDP and 6 percent of GDP, respectively. And trade openness increased significantly in the late 1990s and 2000s, perhaps related to structural reforms and liberalization efforts and the end of internal conflicts in Rwanda and Burundi.

The EAC countries trade mostly outside the region. The European Union (EU) is the largest export destination, accounting for about one-third of total exports (outside of the region), followed by Africa (18 percent excluding the EAC), and developing Asia (15 percent). Developing Asia accounts for about 28 percent of imports, followed by the Middle East (21 percent), the EU (19 percent), Africa (9 percent excluding the EAC), and developed Asia (8 percent, including Japan, Singapore,

---

[1] Trade, FDI, and remittance flows usually correlate well with financial flows. No data was available on portfolio investments and loans among the EAC countries, but anecdotal evidence suggests they are small.

[2] Donor investments have largely financed associated and sizable current account deficits.

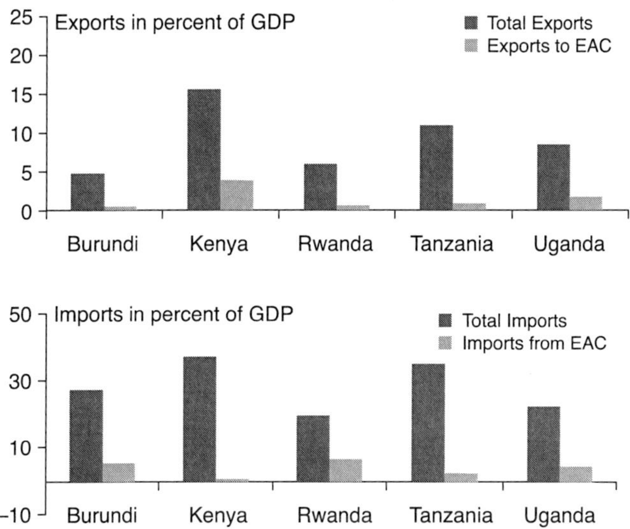

Figure 10.1 East African Community: Foreign Trade, Percent of GDP, average for 2005–13

Sources: IMF, Direction of Trade database; and IMF staff estimates.
Note: EAC = East African Community.

South Korea, and Taiwan Province of China). The largest individual trade partner countries include China, Germany, India, the Netherlands, Saudi Arabia, the United Arab Emirates, the United Kingdom, and the United States.

Official data suggest that trade linkages among the EAC countries are modest and imbalanced (Figure 10.1). In particular, intraregional trade is characterized by large exports from Kenya to the other countries, while Kenya's imports from its neighbors are small. This outcome broadly reflects the countries' industrial development, as Kenya has a larger and more advanced manufacturing sector, which exports to the region. Although agricultural products account for a significant portion of cross-border trade in the region, a large share of this is informal and not captured in official stastics (EAC Development Strategy, 2006–10, 7). This underreporting suggests that official data underestimate actual cross-country trade flows.

The implementation of the EAC customs union (in 2005) and the common market (mid-2010) that reduced tariffs and nontariff barriers may have significantly strengthened trade linkages among the EAC countries.[3] Indeed, exports from Tanzania and Uganda to the region more than doubled and tripled in the seven years of the union, although at low levels. However, increases in regional trade have been in line with increases in total trade flows. This outcome suggests

[3] Under the customs union, Tanzania and Uganda enjoy duty-free treatment in the EAC, and Kenyan exports were levied a 10 percent duty until 2010. Burundi and Rwanda joined the customs union in July 2009.

TABLE 10.1

Foreign Direct Investment Flows and Stocks
(Millions of U.S. dollars, unless otherwise specified)

	Inward FDI flows (average)		Inward FDI Stock in 2012	
	1990–2000	2001–12	Level	% of GDP
Burundi	1.6	0.9	9	0.4
Kenya	29.1	162	2,876	7
Rwanda	4.3	58	743	10
Tanzania	135.4	875	10,984	39
Uganda	89.3	615	8,191	39

Sources: United Nations Conference on Trade and Development, *World Investment Report* (2012); and IMF staff estimates.
Note: FDI = foreign direct investment.

that the region benefited from earlier, broad structural reforms and liberalization efforts alongside regional efforts.

Given problems with official trade data and potentially large underreported trade flows, an alternative methodology based on the law of one price is used to gauge trade linkages. In particular, an autoregressive model of bilateral real exchange rates is used to analyze price convergence in the region. The idea is that prices of traded goods across countries will tend to equalize if there are significant trade linkages.

Foreign Direct Investment Flows

Most FDI inflows in the EAC countries come from outside of the region. Available data suggest that Tanzania and Uganda have attracted significant FDI inflows, while Kenya and Rwanda lag behind. Burundi has attracted limited inflows (Table 10.1). Most of the inflows have gone to tourism and mining (EAC Development Strategy, 2006–10, vi). Kenya is the only country with significant capital outflows, most of which were invested in the region. However, outflows from Kenya are much smaller than inflows to the other countries in the region, suggesting that most inflows to the EAC countries come from outside the region (there is no data on FDI flows among the EAC countries). The authorities in the region have been trying to harmonize the investment incentives, which they hope will boost intraregional investments (IMF, 2008).

Remittances

While political tensions, wars, lack of job opportunities at home, and the possibility of earning higher income abroad force hundreds of thousands of people in EAC countries to migrate to other countries, official data suggest that the region is a net recipient of immigrants. In relation to total population, stocks of emigration have been the highest in Burundi (4.2 percent of total population) and Rwanda (2.6 percent) (Table 10.2). While emigration is higher than immigration in Burundi and Uganda, the other countries recorded large net inflows of

TABLE 10.2

Migration in East African Community Countries

	Burundi	Kenya	Rwanda	Tanzania	Uganda
Net emigration	295.2	−360.6	−202.1	−342.3	111
Stock of emigration	356	457.1	263.4	316.9	757.5
Stock of emigrants as percentage of population	4.2	1.1	2.6	0.7	2.2
Top 10 destination countries	Tanzania	United Kingdom	Uganda	Uganda	United Kingdom
	Uganda	Tanzania	Tanzania	United Kingdom	Tanzania
	Rwanda	United States	Belgium	Canada	United States
	Belgium	Uganda	Canada	Mozambique	Canada
	Canada	Canada	France	Malawi	Rwanda
	Netherlands	Germany	United Kingdom	United States	Sweden
	United Kingdom	Australia	United States	Australia	Germany
	France	India	Germany	Rwanda	Australia
	Australia	Netherlands	Italy	Germany	Zambia
	United States	Switzerland	Netherlands	Netherlands	Denmark
Inward remittances (in U.S. dollars, millions)	3	1,758	91	17	773
Stock of immigrants	60.8	817.7	465.5	659.2	646.5
Stock of immigrants as percentage of population	0.7	2	4.5	1.5	1.9
Refugees as percentage of immigrants	31	32.9	11	69.9	38.7
Top source countries	Rwanda	Uganda	Dem. Rep. of Congo	Burundi	Sudan
	Dem. Rep. of Congo	Tanzania	Burundi	Mozambique	Rwanda
	Tanzania	Sudan	Uganda	Kenya	Burundi
		Somalia	Tanzania	Rep. of Congo	Dem. Rep. of Congo
		Ethiopia	India	Rwanda	Tanzania
			Belgium	Zambia	Kenya
				Uganda	United Kingdom
				Malawi	United States
				India	Canada
				United States	Australia
Outward remittances (in U.S. dollars, millions)	0	81	71	54	463

Source: World Bank, *Migration and Remittances Factbook 2011*.

Note: This table reports officially recorded remittances. The true size of remittances is believed to be larger. Data on outward remittances are for 2009.

immigrants—reflecting large numbers of refugees to Kenya from Sudan, Somalia, and Ethiopia; to Rwanda from the Democratic Republic of Congo and Burundi; and to Tanzania from Mozambique, Republic of Congo, and Malawi.

There has been significant migration of people within the EAC region, including significant forced migration. For example, the other EAC countries are among top source countries for immigration to all EAC countries. Reportedly, about 40 percent of the immigrants in EAC countries are refugees (70 percent in Tanzania).

Data on transfers and remittances in the EAC countries are sketchy. Migrants often use unofficial channels to transfer money because of tax issues and the high cost of bank transfers. Available data suggest that net inflows of remittances (both from the EAC and the rest of the world) constitute an important component of foreign financing in Uganda (5.6 percent of GDP), Kenya (2.5 percent of GDP), Burundi (1.6 percent of GDP), and Rwanda (1.3 percent of GDP). The World Bank estimates (using migrant stocks, host country incomes, and origin country incomes) suggest that the largest flow of remittances are from Kenya to Uganda (about 1 percent of Ugandan GDP) and other flows are small or negligible.

Implications for East African Community Financial Systems

Modest intraregional trade, FDI flows, and remittances suggest that financial flows among EAC countries are not large. Thus, if EAC countries establish a currency union as they currently envision, impact on banks' income from foreign exchange operations will not be large. Modest intraregional trade and FDI flows and remittances mean that (1) an individual country's vulnerability to regional contagion through these channels is limited, and (2) there is room for strengthening trade links and boosting cross-country investments, which would create more business opportunities for banks' clients, and thus more financial flows. On the other hand, limited intraregional trade also means that gains from reduced transaction costs (for traders) in a currency union would be limited.

REGIONAL FINANCIAL LINKAGES AND INTEGRATION[4]

Overview of the Financial Sectors

The financial sectors in the EAC countries are small and dominated by the banking sectors. In all five countries, banks' credit to the private sector in percent of GDP is smaller than the average for sub-Saharan African countries. This remains the case even when South Africa and Nigeria, the two most financially developed African countries, are excluded from the average.

[4]As in European Commission (2005), integration here is defined as a process driven by market forces in which separate financial markets gradually enter into competition with each other and eventually become one market characterized by converging prices, product supply, and converging efficiency/profitability among the financial service providers.

Banks in the region pursue a traditional commercial bank business model. Funded mainly with retail deposits, banks provide loans and invest in government securities. On average, about half of total assets are loans, and 13 percent are invested in government securities. Compared with the averages, the share of loans is significantly lower in Uganda (37 percent), whereas the shares of government securities are significantly higher in Uganda (21 percent) and Kenya (20 percent). The shares of wholesale funding are only 4.4 percent in Tanzania, 9 percent in Uganda, and 12 percent in Kenya. Interest income is the major source of earnings, but banks also have significant income from fees and foreign exchange transactions.

Bank credit grew rapidly over the few years before the global financial crisis started, especially in Burundi and Tanzania, but had been financed mostly with deposits. Domestic banks had been growing rapidly, tapping into the low-income and rural markets. Nevertheless, loan-to-deposit ratios remain well below 100 percent, in part reflecting low wholesale funding (and a regulatory ceiling of 80 percent in Tanzania). Although most of this growth reflects the process of financial deepening, rapid credit growth can give rise to prudential and macroeconomic risks (see Iossifov and Khamis, 2009).

The banking sectors are characterized by a combination of wide spreads, high interest rates, and high profitability. While high interest rates are in part related to macroeconomic and country risks, including high fiscal deficits and credit risks, they also point to efficiency problems. In particular, continuing high spreads suggest that competition is not strong in the region, despite the entrance of many new banks. Also, banks have high liquidity ratios, reflecting high shares of investments in government securities and balances with foreign banks.

Recently, some banks started to form groups with nonbank financial institutions. Several such groups, where banks have invested in securities and insurance firms, can be detected in Kenya, the most developed of the five EAC countries. This business model, which raises the issue of coordination among different agencies supervising different sectors, could also be emulated in other EAC countries.

All countries except Burundi have introduced risk-based banking supervision. The authorities have also stepped up their efforts to comply with the Basel Core Principles for Effective Banking Supervision (BCPs). In the longer term, some authorities intend to adopt Basel II.

Nonbank financial sectors, typically associated with long-term financing, remain underdeveloped. Pension funds, mostly state-controlled institutions, suffer from investment policies determined largely by the needs of the state rather than the needs of beneficiaries (World Bank, 2007). Their investments are generally limited to government securities, real estate (often in state-sponsored projects), and locally listed shares. The insurance sectors have extremely low penetration rates. This outcome reflects a combination of factors, including low per capita income, income distribution, lack of understanding of insurance products, and traditional social structures that provide individuals with informal insurance; high operating costs, including high payment costs in the banking system; a lack of important elements needed for an effectively working insurance sector such as banking, capital markets, and legal infrastructure; and fraud cases that erode public confidence in the sector. On the other hand, weaknesses in supervision and gaps in the licensing regime have allowed the entry of many firms in the insurance sector in some countries.

Payment systems in EAC countries are expensive to use. For example, the average cost of making cross-border transfers, reportedly, is about 10–45 percent. As a result, individuals and small businesses use mostly informal transfer mechanisms and cash payments, which risk losses. Moreover, they tend to avoid financial companies' services, which facilitates tax evasion and deter economies of scale that could allow reducing the costs of providing financial services. In recent years, however, EAC countries have taken measures that will increase the efficiency of payment systems and may reduce the cost of transfers. In particular, all countries but Burundi have established national real-time cross-settlement systems. The founding members of the EAC have also integrated these systems with central securities depositors to achieve simultaneous delivery and payment for government securities (European Central Bank, 2010). Importantly, an East African Cross-Border Payment System (linking the real-time cross-settlement systems in Kenya, Tanzania, and Uganda) was due to be operational in 2012. In addition, recently, novel techniques such as mobile phone payments have become very popular.

Banking Sector Linkages and Associated Risks

Foreign-owned banks have a strong presence in the EAC. The shares of foreign-owned banks in the total assets of banking sectors are more than half in Uganda, Rwanda, Tanzania, Kenya, and Burundi.[5] To a large extent, the presence of foreign-owned banks reflects the colonial history of EAC countries and their trade linkages, and was facilitated by improvements in international communications (airline and telecommunications) and reform efforts in the host countries, including privatization of insolvent state-owned banks. For example, Barclays Bank and Standard Chartered have been present in Kenya for more than 90 years. The presence of banks owned by investors from India and the Middle East may be related to significant trade linkages between these countries and the EAC.

Subsidiaries of a few large foreign banks are of systemic importance in the region. In particular, Barclays and Standard Chartered (United Kingdom), Stanbic/Standard Bank (South Africa), and Citibank (United States) are prominent. For example, Barclays accounts for about 14 percent of banking sector assets in Kenya and Uganda, and about 5 percent in Tanzania. In addition, pan-African banks—such as Bank of Africa (Mali), Ecobank (Togo), Access Bank (Nigeria)—and from India (Bank of India and Baroda) and the Gulf countries have significant presence. All foreign banks in Burundi and Rwanda can be considered large given the small size of the banking sectors in these countries: in these two countries, the shares of individual foreign-owned banks in total assets of banking

[5]See the IMF's Financial System Stability Assessment reports for the EAC countries.

sectors vary between 6 percent (Ecobank in Burundi) and 28 percent (Bank of Africa in Burundi).

Some large multinational banks operate on a regional basis and have centralized key business functions. For example, the World Bank (2007) notes that Citibank manages its operations in East Africa (including Zambia) from its regional headquarters in Nairobi, Kenya, and has centralized its back office operations there. Stanbic Bank set up its regional processing center in Kampala, Uganda. When necessary, the bank syndicates credit to its other regional subsidiaries, and Standard Chartered Bank manages all its EAC operations from Nairobi, where it has also centralized its operations and credit control.

Foreign-owned banks in the EAC countries do not depend on funding from parent banks or from borrowing on international markets. Low-cost retail deposits have been the main financing source in the EAC countries. Moreover, banks keep sizable balances with foreign banks (8 percent of their total assets on average). The shares of assets with foreign banks are particularly large (exceeding 20 percent of total assets) for some subsidiaries of foreign banks. This practice limits the risk of rolling over the foreign debt of banks, as was recently observed in Eastern Europe and other markets. In terms of leveraging, loan-to-deposit ratios suggest that foreign banks have been more conservative than local banks.[6]

International banks tend to be more profitable than local banks. While this outcome largely reflects their better organization and cost control, it may also reflect market power.[7] In Uganda, for example, the share of income from foreign exchange operations was 19 percent for foreign-owned banks, compared with 3 percent for domestic banks, suggesting the former take advantage of their large networks (and sizes) to provide services for most foreign trade–related operations. Foreign-owned banks also have higher liquidity ratios than local banks, which mainly reflects the higher shares of government securities and assets abroad in their portfolios.

Nevertheless, foreign bank dominance in EAC financial systems exposes the region to capital repatriation or contagion. High profitability in foreign banks' EAC operations and the unlikelihood that they will withdraw from the region limit this risk, but problems in their home countries or third countries (where they also have operations) could force them to abandon their EAC subsidiaries. Bank of International Settlements (BIS) data, which covers bank exposure in 30 BIS reporting countries (including the United Kingdom, the United States, and India) illustrate the possible contagion channels.

- As of December 2012, the EAC countries had net claims on the BIS reporting banks of about $11 billion (Table 10.3): deposits (including deposits with subsidiaries of BIS reporting banks) were about $14.2 billion, whereas

[6]In some countries, high loan-to-deposit ratios for domestic banks are due to higher ratios for state-owned banks.

[7]Available data suggest that the ratio of operating expenses to income is smaller for foreign-owned banks.

TABLE 10.3

External Loans and Deposits of BIS Reporting Banks vis-à-vis All Sectors in the East African Community, December 2012

	Loans	Deposits	Net
		In millions of U.S. dollars	
Burundi	46	205	−159
Kenya	1,381	8,991	−7,610
Rwanda	10	642	−632
Tanzania	344	1,517	−1,173
Uganda	329	1,709	−1,380
Total	*2,110*	*13,064*	*−10,954*
		In percent of GDP	
Burundi	3.3	14.5	−11.3
Kenya	4.6	29.8	−25.2
Rwanda	0.2	12.8	−12.6
Tanzania	1.6	6.8	−5.3
Uganda	2.1	10.9	−8.8
		In percent of total for the region	
Burundi	2.2	1.6	1.5
Kenya	65.5	68.8	69.5
Rwanda	0.5	4.9	5.8
Tanzania	16.3	11.6	10.7
Uganda	15.6	13.1	12.6
Total	*100.0*	*100.0*	*100.0*

Sources: Bank for International Settlements (BIS); and IMF staff estimates.

borrowing was about $5.2 billion. In percent of the host country's GDP, Kenya's net claims were the largest (22.8 percent), followed by Burundi (11.4 percent) and Rwanda (7.6 percent). Net claims in Uganda were 7.3 percent of GDP and Tanzania 2.4 percent. These exposures suggest that any liquidity and solvency problems in large foreign-owned banks would have severe consequences.

- In liabilities to the BIS reporting banks, Kenya has the largest exposure, about $1.4 billion or 5 percent of GDP, and about half of its international reserves. Although the country also has large claims on the BIS reporting banks, it is clear that a liquidity shock in combination with any difficulty in realizing foreign assets could cause serious financial problems.
- On the other hand, the BIS reporting banks' exposures to the EAC relative to their home countries' consolidated balance sheets is far smaller. The EAC's largest exposure is to the United Kingdom (at 59 percent of total liabilities to all BIS reporting banks), which represents only 0.2 percent of its GDP. The region's second and third largest exposures are to the United States and France, respectively, which are also small in relation to consolidated bank balance sheets of the home countries. Hence, it is possible that

the parent groups and their home supervisors do not focus on the potential risks banks' activities may pose to the EAC countries.

- Risks of contagion from other countries should be considered in the context of serious weaknesses in the policies and processes for identifying, measuring, monitoring, and controlling country risk and transfer risk in the international lending and investment activities of banks in the EAC countries. In particular, none of the countries in the region is compliant with the relevant BCPs, such as BCP 12, which deals with country transfer and risks under the 2006 BCP methodology.[8]

Furthermore, risks of contagion for subsidiaries in the EAC of banks not reporting to the BIS banks should be considered in the context of serious weaknesses in banking supervision in some home countries and relative sizes of the subsidiaries. Assessments of BCP 3 (on bank licensing) for some African countries that have presence in the EAC banking sectors, for example, revealed weaknesses in the licensing criteria used in these (home) countries.[9] Assessments of BCP 24 (on consolidated supervision) suggest that operations of some foreign-owned banks may not be subject to supervision from home countries.

By size, the operations of most banks in the EAC not reporting to the BIS are significant relative to the worldwide operations of these banks. For example, deposits with subsidiaries of Ecobank (in Burundi, Kenya, and Rwanda) are more than 3 percent of total deposits of the group and more than 16 percent of capital.

Among local banks, several Kenyan banks and a Tanzanian bank have presence outside of their home countries:[10]

- Prime Bank, with the opening of a subsidiary (First Merchant Bank) in Malawi in 1995, was the first Kenyan bank to expand outside of Kenya. The subsidiary subsequently acquired 51 percent of shares of Capital Bank Limited in Botswana in 2008.
- The Kenya Commercial Bank is one of the country's oldest banks and has the most developed network in the region: it opened its subsidiary in Tanzania in 1997, in Southern Sudan in May 2006, in Uganda in November 2007, in Rwanda in December 2008, and in Burundi in 2011. The bank is listed on the Nairobi Stock Exchange, the Uganda Securities Exchange, the Dar-es-Salaam Stock Exchange, and the Rwanda Stock Exchange.
- The Commercial Bank of Africa has a subsidiary in Tanzania (through the purchase of the First American Bank of Kenya in July 2005).

[8]The *Core Principles for Effective Banking Supervision*, developed by the Basel Committee on Banking Supervision (the Committee) in cooperation with fellow supervisors, have become de facto the standard for sound prudential regulation and supervision of banks. The core principles are mainly intended to help countries assess the quality of their systems and to provide input into their reform agenda.
[9]Some of these assessments were made a long time ago and may be less relevant now.
[10]In discussions of these banks in the following text, they will be referred to as Bank A, B, C, D, E, F, or G, in no particular order, to avoid revealing market sensitive information.

- Equity Bank, which focuses on microfinancing, has subsidiaries in Uganda (it bought Microfinance Limited in June 2008), Sudan (established in October 2008), and Rwanda (2009), and plans to expand into Tanzania. The bank, previously a building society, was licensed as a bank in August 2006.
- Fina Bank has subsidiaries in Rwanda through the purchase of the insolvent BACAR that was under central bank supervision due to managerial issues. It also has subsidiaries in Uganda, with the opening of two branches in Kampala in October 2008 and plans to open three more in 2009. It also plans to expand into Burundi and Tanzania. It targets service to small and medium enterprises in the region.
- Investments and Mortgages Bank, in February 2008, bought 50 percent of the shares of the First City Bank of Mauritius, which was renamed Bank One Limited.
- Tanzania's FBME Bank has operations in Cyprus.

The balance sheets of Kenyan bank subsidiaries in other EAC countries are quite large relative to those of their parent banks and are significant compared with consolidated bank balance sheets for host countries. For example, the net assets of a subsidiary of Bank A were more than the capital of the parent company. The sum of net assets of Bank B subsidiaries, for which data are available, was about half of the parent bank capital.[11] Net assets of a subsidiary of Bank C were about 7.4 percent of the total net assets of all banks in the host country. No data are available on operations of a subsidiary of Bank D, but anecdotal evidence suggests that they are quite large compared to the parent bank's operations.

The balance sheets of some recently established subsidiaries (of Kenyan banks in other EAC countries) are small, but they are growing fast. For example, from end-2008 to June 2009, deposits and loans of a subsidiary of Bank B doubled, although from low levels. In the same period, deposits of a subsidiary of Bank E grew by about 40 percent.

While this analysis suggests that the region's bank sectors are well linked, analysis of integration using standard methodologies yields mixed results (Box 10.1).

- As can be seen from Figure 10.2, there was a trend decline in interest margins in Kenya, Tanzania, and Uganda, from 2000 to 2007, but there are no clear trends after 2007. Margins in Burundi and Rwanda were broadly stable with a shift in the level in 2006–07.
- *Sigma-convergence* measure of integration using data on (1) interest margins (between lending rates and deposit rates) and (2) margins between lending rates and three-month Treasury bill rates suggest that significant convergence took place in 2000–07, but this trend reversed somewhat after 2007. In particular, dispersion in margins across the EAC countries

[11]Measuring cross-border exposures helps assessing the extent of individual countries' susceptibility to regional contagion.

BOX 10.1 Measuring Financial Integration

Here, following Adam and others (2002), integration is measured using the sigma-convergence and beta-convergence measures. The former measures cross-sectional dispersion using *standard deviation*. More specifically, it is calculated as follows:

$$\sigma_t = \left[\frac{1}{n-1}\sum (R_{it} - R_t)^2\right]^{\frac{1}{2}} \tag{10.1.1}$$

where $R_{i,t}$ represents margin (lending rate-deposit rate) in country *i* at time *t*.

The beta-convergence measure is borrowed from the growth literature to measure the speed of convergence. It is calculated as follows:

$$\Delta R_{i,t} = \alpha_i + \beta R_{i,t} + \sum \gamma \Delta R_{i,t-1} + \varepsilon_{i,t} \tag{10.1.2}$$

where α_i stands for country dummies, and Δ is the difference operator. A negative β coefficient indicates that convergence takes place, and the size of β is the direct measure of the speed of convergence.

A. Interest Margins in the East African Community Countries (in percent)

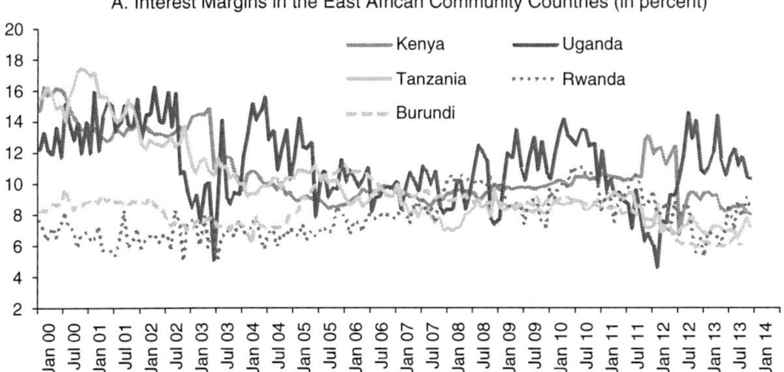

B. Cross-Country Dispersion of Margins (lending rate – Treasury bill rate)

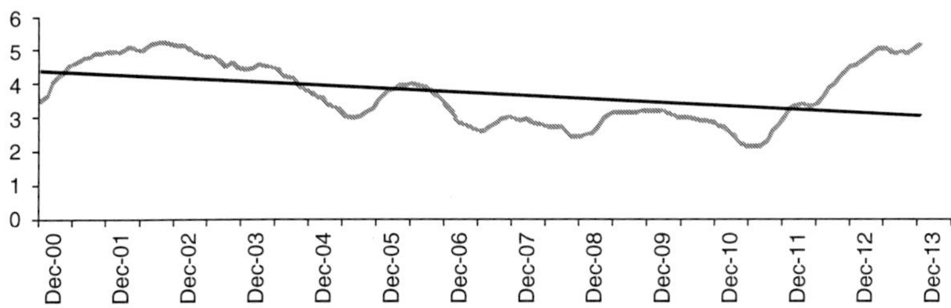

Figure 10.2 Interest Margins (A) and Their Dispersion (B) in East African Community Countries (in percent)

Sources: Country authorities; and IMF staff estimations.

declined until 2007, but since then it has remained unchanged or even increased (Figure 10.2B).

- *Beta-convergence* evaluates whether spreads have converged toward a mean. In particular, the estimation of equation (10.1.2) (Box 10.1) yields a counterin-

TABLE 10.4

Beta Convergence

	Simple OLS	Fixed-effect	Simple OLS
Beta	0.002	0.125	0.009
p-value	0.58	0.00	0.10
Country dummies	(not shown)		
Trend			−0.001
Adjusted *R*-squared	0.13	0.19	0.13
Number of observations	739	739	739

Sources: East African Community portal; and IMF staff estimates.
Note: OLS = ordinary least squares.

TABLE 10.5

East African Community Countries: Stock Exchanges in 2013

	Burundi	Kenya Dec-13	Rwanda Sep-13	Tanzania Dec-13	Uganda Feb-14
Number of listed companies	...	61	4	17	16
Market capitalization in millions of US$	...	22,334	1,919	10,306	8,137
Market capitalization in percent of GDP	...	49.1	25.8	31.7	35.7
Value traded in millions of US$ (year to date)	...	407.3	10.3	65.6	3.1

Sources: African Securities Exchanges Association; and IMF staff estimates.
Note: "..." indicates that data is not available.

tuitive sign for the coefficient of β, which is statistically not significant in most specifications. These findings may be related to the fact that regionally active banks operate in niche markets, and that competition among banks operating in different niche markets has been weak (Table 10.4).

SECURITIES MARKETS AND PENSIONS AND INSURANCE SECTOR LINKAGES

Securities markets in the EAC countries are small and illiquid. Kenya has the most developed securities market in the region, with 60 companies listed on the Nairobi Stock Exchange and the market capitalization of 49 percent of GDP in 2013 (Table 10.5). Its outstanding government bond market was about 17 percent of GDP, and the corporate sector bond market and derivatives markets are at nascent stages. In 2013, the stock exchanges in Tanzania and Uganda had only 17 and 16 listed companies, respectively, with market capitalization ratios of 31 percent of GDP and 35.7 percent of GDP, respectively. In Rwanda, there were four listed companies, with market capitalization of 24 percent of GDP. Burundi is at a nascent stage of developing capital markets.

The EAC's founding members are fairly advanced in coordinating securities market regulation. They created the East African Member States Regulatory Authority to coordinate capital market cooperation and integration. To facilitate the regional integration agenda, the legal and regulatory frameworks in Tanzania and Uganda were largely designed with the objective of minimizing deviations from the Kenyan securities law. The Uganda Stock Exchange has harmonized its listing rules with those of the Nairobi Stock Exchange (IMF, 2009a, 2009b, 2010, 2011, 2012). Cross listing is encouraged, but cost considerations have reduced interest from companies for cross listing (World Bank, 2007).

But a number of restrictions inhibit intraregional capital flows.[12] Among the founding members, Kenya and Uganda have the most liberalized regimes for capital flows. Tanzania has the most restrictive, with investing abroad constrained. Rwanda has made good progress toward harmonizing its legal and regulatory frameworks with those of Kenya and Uganda. Authorities in the EAC countries have agreed to eliminate controls on capital flows in the region by 2015.

A number of institution-specific restrictions also prevent financial institutions from investing abroad, including in other EAC countries, including the following:

- The national pension funds are either limited or prohibited from investing abroad, including other EAC countries. For example, in Kenya, the government recently decided to invest all future net cash flows of the National Security Scheme in government securities;[13] in Uganda, the internal guidelines of the National Security Scheme stipulate a 10 percent offshore limit that applies also to investments in other EAC countries.
- Insurance companies' cross-border activities are also constrained. For example, in Tanzania, insurance companies are prohibited from investing or lending abroad without the insurance commissioner's permission.

Furthermore, weaknesses in the basic infrastructure and operational environment of individual countries not only prevent financial institutions from expanding regionally, but also reduce demand for financial products. For example, weaknesses in the enforcement of contracts and expensive payment systems reduce demand for financial services across the region. Market abuses, including unauthorized trading of clients' securities and theft, have dented public confidence in financial institutions. Weaknesses in laws and regulations relating to financial activities also increase costs of operating in other countries. To date, only one Kenyan insurance company, APA Insurance, has expanded regionally. It has an associate in Tanzania and was preparing to launch a subsidiary in Uganda.

To summarize, significant cross-country ownership in the EAC countries' banking sectors suggest that their financial systems are increasingly interconnected while standard measures of integration suggest they are not yet well integrated. The latter outcome may reflect remaining barriers in capital

---

[12]As noted, there are no data on intraregional capital flows/stocks, but the analysis in this chapter's first section suggests that they are limited.

[13]This came after a long period of underperformance by the National Security Scheme.

flows, expensive payment systems, and the facts that regionally active small banks operate mainly in niche markets and small domestic banks are not in position to compete with multinational financial institutions with large networks and sizes.

IMPLICATIONS FOR SUPERVISION

Greater interconnectedness of the banking sectors through cross-country ownership makes the region vulnerable to crises, even if the markets are not well integrated, unless the regionally active institutions are not properly supervised. Indeed, as the recent global financial crisis has shown, greater financial linkages can increase the vulnerability of countries to external shocks and contagion. In particular, liquidity or solvency problems of foreign-owned banks could spread to their subsidiaries in the EAC. Furthermore, the predominance of large cross-border banks increases the vulnerability of the region to regulatory arbitrage.

That some multinational banks are of systemic importance in the EAC, but small in relation to parent banks, has both advantages and disadvantages. On the one hand, it would be easy for big parent banks to support their subsidiaries in the EAC in case of liquidity and solvency problems, if the problems are limited to the EAC region. On the other hand, parent institutions and their supervisors may not focus on the potential risks such banks may pose in the host countries, which have limited resources (both human and financial) to deal with the consequences should parent banks abandon their subsidiaries (such as in cases of problems with the parent banks). In this context, some large foreign-owned banks centralizing key business functions in home or third countries would make it difficult for host country supervisors to supervise these banks' subsidiaries in the host countries and ring-fence the subsidiaries to avoid asset stripping during a crisis.

Risks of contagion are heightened by weaknesses in banking supervision in some home countries and host countries. For example, the shares in consolidated balance sheets of EAC countries of banks whose countries do not fully comply with the BCPs for licensing, abuse of financial services, and consolidated supervision (Core Principles 3, 18, and 24 under the 2006 BCP methodology) are large. In some countries, these shares are large. Moreover, there are weaknesses in banking supervision in the host EAC countries, including in the areas of licensing, identifying country and transfer risks, internal control and audit, and accounting and disclosure. As Claessens and others (2008) note, when banks in countries with weak banking supervision enter other countries with similar problems, "they could introduce new risks and vulnerabilities, since they may be less well supervised both in their home and in the host markets."

The regionally active banks are not supervised on a consolidated basis. The existing frameworks gives the host country supervisor the ultimate responsibility for subsidiaries. Emergency liquidity assistance and deposit insurance schemes are also organized along national lines. Accordingly, supervisors are unable to accurately assess the risk posed to a regionally active bank's operations in one country by its operations in other countries. For example, supervisors are unable to accurately assess a bank's exposure to a single borrower with regional operations that also borrows from the bank's subsidiaries. In addition, as noted, the centralization of some key business functions makes separate assessments of individual subsidiaries more difficult. Also, supervisory agencies in some host countries may not have the capacity to exercise effective risk assessments over large financial institutions.

Up to now, the authorities in the region have dealt with these challenges through MOUs. The Bank of Tanzania signed an MOU with the central bank of Cyprus in 2003, the EAC countries signed an MOU in January 2009, and some central banks in the region have begun to explore the possibility of signing MOUs with the central banks of home countries. The signed memorandums cover a number of areas such as information sharing, licensing, and coordination of on-site inspections, but do not cover the very important area of crisis management.

Nevertheless, authorities need to step up efforts to establish contacts and forge similar MOUs with all homes and host supervisors. In light of the dominant position of some multinational banks in EAC markets, establishing good cooperation with their home supervisors is particularly important. It may be difficult for individual EAC countries to establish such cooperation, but together they may be able to do so. The authorities could pursue establishing MOUs with all home and host supervisors prior to granting permission for cross-border financial operations.

To benefit from economies of scale and better allocation of capital, the authorities need to phase out both general and institution-specific capital controls relevant to other EAC countries and improve supervision of capital market activities. This would allow making prices for financial products more responsive to supply and demand, and reduce inefficiencies in mobilizing savings. In the pension and insurance sectors, reforms at the national level to improve supervision, management of institutions, and upgrade skills should perhaps proceed either before or at the same time as regional efforts. To avoid tax arbitration and associated distortions, the authorities may need to narrow disparities in tax treatments of investments and dividends. For example, a unified or similar tax treatment of capital gains would reduce incentives to invest through one market rather than another.

Also, the authorities need to collect critical data on cross-country capital and financial flows and monitor the degree of financial integration. In particular, collecting and publishing data on cross-country loans (including bank and interbank loans) and debt, remittances, and FDI and portfolio investments, as well as data on interbank money market rates (including unsecured lending rates and repo rates), interest swap rates, forward exchange rates, yields on government bonds, and ratings of securities would allow monitoring financial integration in the EAC.

The ongoing upgrading of payment systems and declines in the cost of transfers are likely to increase demand for banks' services, including cross-country transfers. This will create economies of scale for the banking systems and may help deepen financial intermediation. The upgrading of payment systems is also likely to reduce system-wide risks. However, it is not clear how the newly established cross-border payment system will be supervised.

Finally, in individual EAC countries, the authorities should promptly implement the recommendations of the recent financial sector assessment program updates. These include those relating to regulatory frameworks, crisis management, coordinated early interventions, safety mechanisms, bankruptcy procedures, payment systems, credit information (credit bureaus), and court and arbitration mechanisms. These reform measures would not only make the financial systems in individual countries resilient to shocks, but would also facilitate regional integration.

REFERENCES

Adam, K., T. Jappelli, A. M. Menichini, M. Padula, and M. Pagano, 2002, "Analyse, Compare, and Apply Alternative Indicators and Monitoring Methodologies to Measure the Evolution of Capital Market Integration in the European Union," Report to the European Commission.

Claessens, S., N. Van Horen, T. Gurcanlar, and J. Mercado, 2008, "Foreign Bank Presence in Developing Countries. 1995–2006: Data and Trends," unpublished (Washington: World Bank).

de Mello, L. R., Jr., 1999, "Foreign Direct Investment-led Growth: Evidence from Time Series and Panel Data," *Oxford Economic Papers*, Vol. 52 (January), pp. 133–151.

East African Community Development Strategy, 2006–10, "Deepening and Accelerating Integration," (Arusha, Tanzania).

European Central Bank, 2010, "Study on the Establishment of a Monetary Union among the Partner States of the East African Community," unpublished ECB Staff Study (Frankfurt).

European Commission, 2005, "Financial Integration Monitor—2005," background document (Brussels).

Fry, M. J., 1995, *Money, Interest, and Banking in Economic Development* (Baltimore: The Johns Hopkins University Press).

International Monetary Fund, 2008, "Kenya, Uganda, and United Republic of Tanzania: Selected Issues," Country Report 08/353 (Washington).

———, 2009a, Burundi Financial System Stability Assessment (Washington).

———, 2009b, Kenya Financial System Stability Assessment (Washington).

———, 2010, United Republic of Tanzania: Financial System Stability Assessment Update (Washington). http://www.imf.org/external/pubs/ft/scr/2010/cr10177.pdf.

———, 2011, Rwanda: Financial System Stability Assessment (Washington). http://www.imf.org/external/pubs/ft/scr/2011/cr11244.pdf.

———, 2012, Uganda Financial System Stability Assessment (Washington).

Iossifov, P., and M. Khamis, 2009, "Credit Growth in Sub-Saharan Africa: Sources, Risks, and Policy Responses," IMF Working Paper 09/180 (Washington: International Monetary Fund).

United Nations Conference on Trade and Development, 2012, *World Investment Report* (Geneva).

World Bank, 2007, "Financial Sector Integration in Two Regions of Sub-Saharan Africa: How Creating Scale in Financial Markets Can Support Growth and Development" (Washington).

———, 2011, *Migration and Remittances Factbook 2011* (Washington).

CHAPTER 11

Financial Integration Ahead of East African Monetary Union

MASAFUMI YABARA

Well-functioning financial markets can accelerate economic growth and alleviate poverty. A large body of research has found a positive relationship between financial market development and economic growth, including in sub-Saharan Africa (Levine and Zervos, 1998; Adjasi and Biekpe, 2006a; Collins, 2004).[1] Developed financial markets promote growth by mobilizing domestic savings and investments, efficiently allocating mobilized resources to local companies, and allowing diversification of risks. In addition, deep and liquid local financial markets can lessen an economy's vulnerability to external shocks by reducing currency and duration mismatches in raising funds. Cross-country evidence shows that financial development can reduce income inequality by increasing the income of the poor (Making Finance Work for Africa, 2007).

Despite these merits, financial markets remain underdeveloped in most low-income countries because of structural constraints. Limited income and a small private sector make investors and issuers scarce. Running capital markets entails huge start-up and operating costs for both regulators and market participants. This can be prohibitive for countries with limited capacity and small markets: authorities are required to establish and manage regulatory frameworks and trading platforms, and issuers need to go through painstaking due diligence for initial public offerings and maintain detailed financial reporting afterwards. An empirical study suggests that a certain minimum-efficient size of bond markets exists, because large issuance and trading volumes are more economical (Eichengreen and Luengnaruemitchai, 2004).

Regional integration can help countries overcome these constraints. Integrated financial markets, if managed properly, will allow pooling of savings across the region, cost and information sharing among members, wider diversification of risks, enhanced competition and innovation across financial institutions, richer choice of financial products provided to regional and foreign investors, and more integration into the global economy facilitated by more attractive markets (Irving, 2005; Making Finance Work for Africa, 2007).

[1] Murinde (2012) provides a comprehensive survey of the literature in this field, from both theoretical and empirical perspectives, highlighting evidence specific to African economies.

East African Community (EAC) countries have been pursuing financial market development through regional integration. These countries face growing financing needs to build up infrastructure for sustained growth, making well-functioning local financial markets important. Financing through markets could complement commercial bank financing, which dominates EAC financial sectors, where competition is low (Sanya and Gaertner, 2012). Recognizing the benefits of financial markets and the limitations of individual country approaches, the EAC member states are committed to establishing a common market, which would include free movement of capital under the treaty establishing the community. Furthermore, integration of financial markets, in particular government debt markets, is essential for a monetary union to transmit common monetary policy effectively across the region and realize the full benefits.

This chapter empirically investigates whether actions taken under the EAC framework have succeeded in advancing financial integration. Few previous studies exist on this subject. IMF (2009) assesses comovements of government bond yields among Kenya, Uganda, and Tanzania. Wang (2010) measures deviations from covered interest rate parity in foreign exchange markets for the same countries. Both of these studies conclude that EAC financial integration is limited.

This paper contributes to the literature by comprehensively assessing the degree of integration of the financial markets (treasury, interbank, stock markets) of the five EAC countries where possible, and examining whether integration has progressed.

Although there is no universal definition of financial integration, in general, financial markets are said to be integrated when the law of one price holds. In perfectly integrated financial markets with no barriers to cross-border transactions, returns of comparable assets should be equalized across markets, as long as there is no difference in country and exchange rate risks as well as in transaction costs. In this sense, it should be noted that deep financial integration can be achieved without any institutionalized unification of markets: the markets of the United States and the United Kingdom are said to be highly integrated, although these markets are separate under different legal frameworks.

The literature relies on two broad categories of measures to assess financial integration: price-based and quantity-based measures. The former directly estimate whether and at what speed rates of return of comparable assets converge across borders. The latter investigate correlation between domestic savings and investment, building on the idea of Feldstein and Horioka (1980) that in a world of high capital mobility, there should be no relation between domestic savings and investments, because domestic investments are financed by a pool of global savings under a unified interest rate. This paper employs the price-based measures because they have a clear-cut interpretation; price data are simple and relatively reliable compared with savings and investment data in low-income countries, and the measures have high frequency, allowing assessment of progress in integration over a relatively shorter time series.

The next section briefly describes EAC financial markets, focusing on debt and stock markets, the following section reviews the EAC authorities' efforts to integrate their financial markets under the EAC framework, and the final section empirically assesses the depth and progress of financial market integration in the EAC using the methodology of beta and sigma convergence and cointegration analysis.

EAST AFRICAN COMMUNITY FINANCIAL MARKETS

Current Market Structure

Debt Markets

Each of the five EAC countries operates a government debt market, although at different stages of development. Central banks in each hold auctions under different frameworks (Table 11.1) to sell Treasury bills and bonds on behalf of the governments as instruments of monetary and fiscal policy implementation. These auctions are open to nonresidents, except in Tanzania, where nonresidents are prohibited from holding government securities. Issued securities are traded over the counter, on local stock exchanges, or both, although the secondary markets are largely inactive, as argued below.

Market size differs considerably among the countries (Table 11.2). Kenya leads the region, with government securities outstanding at 27.3 percent of GDP and with maturities of up to 30 years. Tanzania and Uganda follow with amounts outstanding at 10.3 percent and 8.1 percent of GDP, respectively. These two countries succeeded in extending the maturities of Treasury bonds to 10 years in the early 2000s. Markets in Burundi and Rwanda were recently instituted. The central bank of Burundi started auctioning government securities at the end of 2006, with maturities now up to 10 years. Rwanda launched its over-the-counter securities market in 2008 and started listing government securities there. A first five-year Treasury bond was marketed in Rwanda in 2010, and the over-the-counter market was converted to a full-fledged stock exchange in January 2011.

TABLE 11.1

Auction of Government Securities

	Burundi		Kenya		Rwanda		Tanzania		Uganda	
	T-bill	T-bond	T-bill	T-bond	T-bill	T-bond	T-bill	T-bond	T-bill	T-bond
Maturity	13–52 weeks	2–5 years	13–52 weeks	1–30 years	4–52 weeks	2–5 years	5–52 weeks	2–10 years	13–52 weeks	2–10 years
Auction frequency	Weekly	Weekly	Weekly	Monthly	Weekly	Monthly	Biweekly	Monthly	Biweekly	Monthly
Minimum bid amount	Fbu 100 million (US$81,200)		KSh 0.1 million (US$1,200)	KSh 0.05 million (US$600)	Rwf 0.1 million (US$200)		TSh 0.5 million (US$300)	Tsh 1 million (US$700)	Ush 0.1 million (US$400)	
Nonresident	Eligible		Eligible		Eligible		Ineligible		Eligible	

Sources: African Development Bank, *African Fixed Income and Derivatives Guidebook;* and central bank websites.

Note: Government securities are Treasury bills (T-bill) and bonds (T-bond). Fbu = Burundi francs; Ksh = Kenya shillings; Rwf = Rwanda francs; Tsh = Tanzania shillings; Ush = Uganda shillings.

TABLE 11.2

Treasury Bills and Bonds Outstanding at End-2010

	Burundi[1]	Kenya	Rwanda	Tanzania	Uganda[2]
			(Millions of US$)		
Treasury bills and bonds	126	8,612	120	2,080	1,230
Treasury bills	...	2,046	94	445	544
Treasury bonds	...	6,566	25	1,635	686
			(Percent of gross domestic product)		
Treasury bills and bonds	8.5	27.3	2.2	10.3	8.1
Treasury bills	...	6.5	1.7	2.2	3.6
Treasury bonds	...	20.8	0.5	8.1	4.5

Sources: East African Community central banks; IMF, World Economic Outlook database; and author's calculations.
Note: "..." indicates that data is not available.
[1] As of September 2010. Includes other debts held by nonfinancial institutions.
[2] As of June 2010.

TABLE 11.3

East African Community Corporate Bond Markets at End-2010

	Kenya	Rwanda	Tanzania	Uganda
Number of issuers	10	1	5	5
Amount outstanding (million US$)	743.8	1.7	51.6	44.3
Amount outstanding (percent of GDP)	2.4	0.03	0.26	0.29

Sources: Country stock exchanges; IMF, World Economic Outlook database; and author's calculations.
Note: There are no operational corporate bond markets in Burundi.

The size of the market is relatively large in Burundi, at 8.5 percent of GDP, but Rwanda's is small, at only 2.2 percent of GDP.[2]

Corporate bonds are issued in the EAC countries, except for Burundi, and traded at local stock exchanges. But the markets are in the early stages of development and are inactive, with local companies mainly relying on commercial bank financing. The amounts outstanding are negligible when measured as a percent of GDP (Table 11.3); issuers are limited to financial institutions, especially foreign affiliated institutions. Transactions in the secondary markets rarely take place, including in the much larger Nairobi Stock Exchange (NSE), in Kenya.

Stock Markets

Disparities across the region are larger in stock markets than in debt markets. The NSE, established in 1954, has the longest history and is by far the largest in the region. It has 55 listed companies, with market capitalization of 46 percent of GDP as of end-2010 (Table 11.4). The Dar es Salaam Stock Exchange (DSE) in Tanzania and the Uganda Securities Exchange (USE), established in the late

[2] The relatively large scales of securities outstanding in Tanzania and Burundi are partly due to central bank holdings of government securities.

TABLE 11.4

East African Community Stock Markets at End-2010

	Kenya	Rwanda	Tanzania	Uganda
Number of companies listed	55	2	15	13
Market capitalization (million US$)	14,498	...	3,253	1,810
Market capitalization (percent of GDP)	46.0	...	16.1	11.9
Turnover (million US$)	1,283	0.01	23.9	18.4
Turnover ratio[1]	8.8	...	0.7	1.0

Sources: Country stock exchanges; IMF, World Economic Outlook database; and author's calculations.
Note: There exists no operational stock market in Burundi. "..." indicates data is not available.
[1]The ratio of turnover to market capitalization.

TABLE 11.5

Bond Holding by Category of Investors (in percent, as of June 30, 2009)

Burundi[1]		Kenya		Rwanda[1]		Tanzania[1]		Uganda	
Commercial banks	65	Commercial banks	53	Commercial banks	83	Central bank	41	Commercial banks	77
Central bank	24	Pension funds	27	Pension funds	2	Commercial banks	30	Pension funds	15
Insurance companies	6	Insurance companies	11	Insurance companies	2	Pension funds	23	Central bank	5
Pension funds	4	Individuals	2	Others	13	Nonbank	2	Insurance companies	2
Others	0.2	Others	6			Insurance companies	2	Individuals	1
						Individuals	1		
						Others	1		

Source: African Development Bank, *African Fixed Income and Derivatives Guidebook*.
[1]Figures include only government security holdings, not corporate bonds.

1990s, have market values of about 15 percent of GDP. The Rwanda Stock Exchange (RSE) had only two companies listed as of end-2010,[3] with transactions seldom taking place. Burundi has no stock exchange and capital is raised mainly from commercial banks.

Challenges for Financial Markets in the East African Community

Despite differing levels of development, the EAC countries face the same challenges as other low-income countries in developing domestic financial markets: low capitalization and liquidity. Owing to the costs of issuing and listing securities, issuers in the markets are overly confined to government entities, former state-owned enterprises, and foreign-affiliated banks. Low income and savings prevent individuals from participating in the markets, leaving investor bases heavily dominated by commercial banks and pension funds (Table 11.5). Whereas foreign investors' transactions account for fair amounts of total turnover on the

[3]In January 2011, Bralirwa, a brewing company, became the third company listed on the RSE.

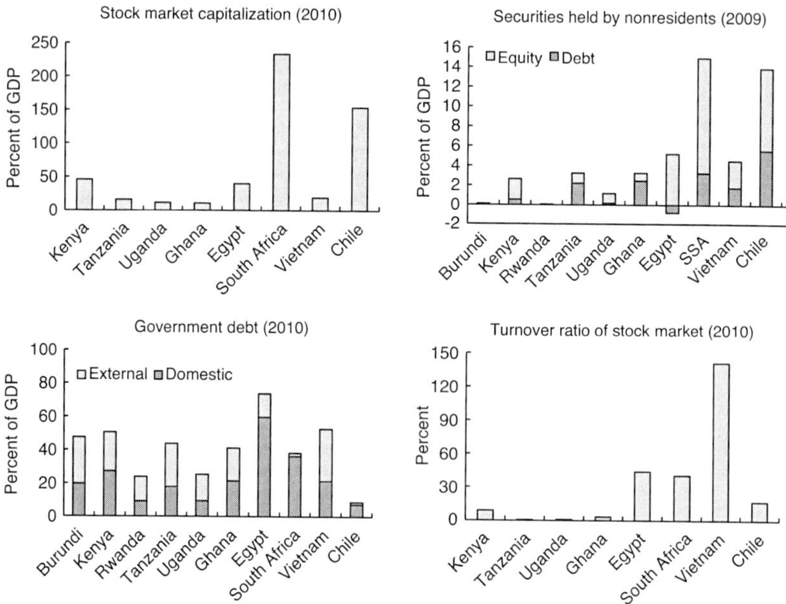

Figure 11.1 Comparison of Financial Markets

Sources: Country authorities; World Federation of Exchanges; IMF, World Economic Outlook database, *Regional Economic Outlook: Sub-Saharan Africa*, and Coordinated Portfolio Investment Survey; World Bank, World Development Indicators database; and author's calculations.

Note: Turnover ratio is calculated as the ratio of turnover to market capitalization.

stock markets,[4] available statistics, though coverage is restricted, indicate that nonresident holdings of securities are low in the EAC compared with the aggregate of sub-Saharan Africa (see Figure 11.4).[5] As a result, market size has remained small, and governments are largely dependent on external sources of financing, including concessional borrowing (see Figure 11.5).

Low liquidity is also due to shallow investor bases. Local commercial banks and pension funds, the dominant investors in the region, generally tend to hold securities until maturity. Market infrastructure is another impediment. While trading infrastructure consisting of real-time gross settlement systems, clearing houses, and central securities depositories are all operational, except in Burundi; these systems are yet to be connected outside the borders, rendering foreign investors' investments costly and time consuming.

These constraints create rather illiquid capital markets in the EAC. Figure 11.1 shows turnover ratios of nearly zero in the Tanzania and Uganda stock markets. There is no secondary market in Burundi: most investments are held to maturity.

---

[4] In 2010, foreign investors' transactions accounted for 28.2 percent on the NSE and 21.8 percent on the DSE of the total value traded (African Securities Exchanges Association, 2011).

[5] Data are compiled from the Coordinated Portfolio Investment Survey conducted by the IMF and are available at http://www.imf.org/external/np/sta/pi/datarsl.htm. About 75 countries voluntarily participate in the survey, reporting cross-border holdings of portfolio investment securities, classified by issuers.

REGIONAL INITIATIVES TO INTEGRATE FINANCIAL MARKETS IN THE EAST AFRICAN COMMUNITY

As noted, the EAC countries have pursued financial market development through regional integration. In the treaty establishing the EAC, the member states committed to establishing a common market with free movement of capital. Specifically, the treaty calls for (1) removal of controls on capital transactions among the member countries (Article 86) and (2) harmonization of capital market infrastructure including regulations, taxation, accounting, trading systems, and cross-listings of securities (Article 85).[6] The common market was officially launched in June 2010, awaiting full implementation by 2015. The Common Market Protocol requires legislation by each member to fully implement the common market by 2015. The annexes to the protocol provide timetables of actions to be undertaken by each state, including capital account liberalization.

Liberalizing capital transactions and harmonizing market infrastructure are essential and natural steps toward financial market integration. Regulations for cross-border capital transactions prevent domestic investors from freely participating in foreign markets and foreign investors from investing in domestic markets, making barriers to cross-border financial flows. Market infrastructure that is not harmonized hampers cross-border transactions and constitutes another barrier to financial market integration. Because financial transactions are affected by many factors such as regulatory frameworks, trading systems, and taxation, harmonization of these market settings is essential to realizing the law of one price. The ultimate form of financial market integration is the unification of the entire market infrastructure, in which all participants can engage in financial activities across borders in exactly the same way as they do in their home countries.

Capital Account Liberalization

Although liberalizing capital transactions across a region is the first step for integrated financial markets, experience indicates that capital account liberalization could cause crisis by making an economy vulnerable to external financial flows.[7] To minimize the adverse effects, countries are advised to sequence liberalization and advance it along with comprehensive promarket reforms to maintain the stability of an economy (Ishii and Habermeier, 2002).

Kenya, Rwanda, and Uganda have already liberalized capital transactions within the region. Uganda was the first to fully open capital accounts in 1997, as part of a broader package of market-oriented reforms. Rwanda achieved full capital account liberalization in 2010. Even though restrictions on nonresidents' investments in domestic markets remain in Kenya, East African investors are treated as local investors, meeting the commitment under the treaty.

---

[6] Adelegan (2008) and (2009) find positive effects of cross-listings of securities in deepening stock markets and increasing values of companies cross-listed in sub-Saharan Africa.

[7] For the history of capital account liberalization in the EAC, see IMF (2008) and (2009).

Plans for gradual removal of capital controls are under way in Tanzania, while Burundi is lagging behind. Tanzania partially liberalized capital transactions in the 1990s. The Bank of Tanzania, recognizing the risk of opening the capital account, is formulating a plan for the gradual lifting of capital controls, in accordance with the Common Market Protocol. In Burundi, where capital markets are the least developed, the authorities still have significant control over capital transactions, and regulatory frameworks are yet to be established in some areas.

Harmonization of Market Infrastructure

In the EAC countries, the intent to harmonize market infrastructure was evident even before the establishment of the community. The capital market authorities of Kenya, Tanzania, and Uganda established the East African Member States Securities Regulatory Authorities in 1997 to enhance cooperation and advance market integration. Rwanda and Burundi joined in 2008 and 2011. The Capital Markets Development Committee, consisting of chief executives of the regulatory authorities and security exchanges, was established in 2001. It is a standing committee of the EAC, making policy recommendations on regulation and integration of the capital markets.[8]

Cooperation and harmonization are fairly advanced in the EAC compared with other regional integration arrangements in Africa (United Nations Economic Commission for Africa, 2008; African Development Bank, 2010). The East African Member States Securities Regulatory Authorities agreed on an approval procedure for cross-border listings in the EAC in 2000 and compiled common debt-ratio criteria for those wishing to issue debt securities. The organizations are also taking the lead in taxation of financial transactions, financial reporting standards, trading systems, and financial education. The USE has harmonized its listing rules with those of the NSE, although only six companies were cross-listed on the EAC stock exchanges at the end of 2010. Kenya, Uganda, and Tanzania are working toward demutualizing their respective stock exchanges, and merging them into a single regional stock exchange in the future.[9] Regional initiatives are ongoing to integrate payment and settlement systems across the region.

MEASURING FINANCIAL MARKET INTEGRATION IN THE EAST AFRICAN COMMUNITY

The previous section noted that EAC authorities made salient efforts to integrate their local financial markets. To gauge the success of their efforts, this section measures the progress of integration in the EAC financial markets, employing the methods of beta and sigma convergence and cointegration analysis.

---

[8]The committee was reorganized into the Capital Markets Insurance and Pensions Committee, with an expanded mandate covering insurance and pension development.

[9]The Rwanda Stock Exchange has been demutualized since its inception.

Methodology

Beta and Sigma Convergence

Two concepts have been widely used in the literature to assess integration of financial markets. The first one, beta (β) convergence, is measured by the following regression with panel data:

$$\Delta S_{i,t} = \alpha + \beta S_{i,t-1} + \sum_{i=1}^{L} \gamma_l \Delta S_{i,t-l} + \varepsilon_{i,t} \tag{11.1}$$

where $S_{i,t}$ denotes a spread of yields on a relevant portfolio investment between country i and a benchmark market at time t, and l represents lag. If financial markets are perfectly integrated, this spread should be zero as long as securities traded have the same risks and maturity structures, following the law of one price (mean reversion). Therefore, a negative β coefficient indicates mean reversion taking place across the markets, and an absolute value of the coefficient represents the speed of convergence at which the spread is dissolved and investment returns on securities in country i converge with those in the benchmark market. The γ_l measures lagging effects of ΔS_i in previous periods.

In this analysis, the benchmark market is assumed to be Kenya, as in IMF (2009), given its dominant size and development in the region. Thus the analysis focuses on the spreads of returns between Kenya and the other countries. Three-month lags are uniformly taken, with lags beyond the duration not being statistically significant in any of the estimates.

The second concept, sigma (σ) convergence, employs the cross-sectional standard deviation of yields across countries at each time, calculated as follows:

$$\sigma_t = \left[\frac{1}{n-1}\sum (R_{i,t} - \overline{R_t})^2\right]^{\frac{1}{2}} \tag{11.2}$$

where n represents a number of the countries, $R_{i,t}$ represents a return on a portfolio investment in country i at time t, and $\overline{R_t}$ identifies an average return in the region at time t. Regressing the computed sigma on a time trend tells us whether and at what pace the dispersion is decreasing and thus whether financial integration is deepening over time. Perfect convergence is realized when the sigma stays at zero. Beta and sigma convergence capture different aspects of financial integration: while beta convergence measures to what extent integration has been achieved in a fixed time framework, sigma convergence illustrates whether markets are moving toward deeper integration. Beta convergence is a necessary but not a sufficient condition for sigma convergence: beta convergence could be associated with sigma divergence (Sala-i-Martin, 1996).

An extensive number of empirical studies use these concepts, especially in the context of financial market integration in the European Union (EU). Adam and others (2002) apply these indicators to 10-year bond yields and interbank rates, as well as the mortgage rates and corporate loans rates of the EU countries, concluding that EU financial integration has increased, particularly since 1999.

Babetskii, Komárek, and Komárková (2008) use these indicators to assess stock market integration of the new EU member states, such as Czech Republic and Hungary, and find positive evidence. For other regions, Espinoza, Prasad, and Williams (2010) measure interest rate convergence in the Gulf Cooperation Council interbank markets and see evidence of integration, although little progress has been made since 2000.

Cointegration Analysis

Another approach widely used in assessing stock market integration is investigating the long-run equilibrium of returns among stock markets using cointegration modeling. Specifically, the following error correction model with l lags is considered:

$$\Delta P_t = v + \Pi P_{t-1} \sum_{i=1}^{l} \Gamma_i \Delta P_{t-i} + \varepsilon_t \tag{11.3}$$

where P_t is a $(n \times 1)$ vector of stock indices at time t, v is a $(n \times 1)$ vector of parameters, $\prod$ is a $(n \times r)$ parameter matrix with rank $r < n$, $\Gamma_1, \ldots, \Gamma_l$ are $(n \times n)$ matrices of parameters, and ε_t is a $(n \times 1)$ vector of random errors. The essence of the approach is to identify r, a number of cointegrating vectors. If n variables with unit roots have r cointegrating relationships, they have $n - r$ common stochastic trends. Thus if r equals $n - 1$, stock markets are perfectly integrated under one common long-run trend. Alternatively if r equals zero, all data series are independent (Kasa, 1992). Johansen and Juselius (1990) derive two likelihood-ratio tests to infer on r, known as the trace statistics and the maximum-eigenvalue statistics.

A number of empirical studies implement this approach.[10] Serletis and King (1997) and Bley (2009) investigate stock market integration across the EU. Manning (2002), Click and Plummer (2005), and Yu, Fung, and Tam (2010) apply the technique to assess integration of Asian stock markets. However, there has been little empirical work on assessing long-run linkages among African stock markets. To my knowledge, only Wang, Yang, and Bessler (2003) and Adjasi and Biekpe (2006b) conduct cointegration analysis focusing on African stock markets. The former find no cointegration relationship among five African stock markets (South Africa, Egypt, Morocco, Nigeria, Zimbabwe) and the U.S. market between July 1999 and May 2002. The latter select seven African economies (Egypt, Ghana, Mauritius, Nigeria, Kenya, South Africa, Tunisia) and identify two cointegrations for November 1997 to August 2005.

Data

This chapter assesses integration of the three types of financial markets in the EAC—Treasury bill, interbank, and stock markets—using the methodology described previously. For the Treasury bill markets, monthly data on 91-day

[10] For a literature review, see Sharma and Bodla (2010).

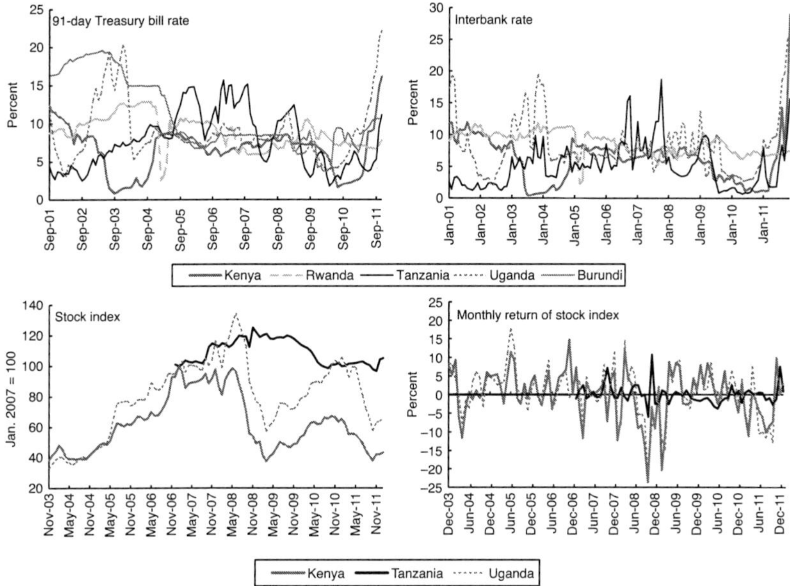

Figure 11.2 Interst Rates and Stock Indices in the East African Community

Sources: IMF, African Department database; Bloomberg L.P.; Thomson Reuters; and author's calculations.
Note: The Treasury bill rate for Rwanda is the weighted average rate of Treasury bills with maturities of 28, 91, 182, and 364 days. All stock indices are adjusted for exchange rates. Stock returns are computed as the log difference of the indices.

Treasury bill rates for Burundi, Kenya, Tanzania, and Uganda are retrieved from the IMF African Department database (Figure 11.2). For Rwanda, weighted average interest rates of 28-, 91-, 182-, and 364-day Treasury bills are alternatively employed because the data on the 91-day Treasury bill are available only after 2009. The database consists of data published or reported by the authorities. The data have, in total, 615 observations from September 2001 to November 2011, when data for all five countries were available. Monthly data on interbank market rates are also obtained from the same source. The data contain a total of 524 observations for January 2001 to December 2010, but Burundi is not included, reflecting its largely inactive interbank market (Figure 11.2).

For the stock markets, monthly averages of representative stock indices—the NSE 20 Share Index, the DSE All Share Index, and the USE All Share Index—are computed from daily data retrieved from Bloomberg L.P.[11] Rwanda and Burundi were not included in the analysis because the RSE has no stock index, with only

[11] Monthly frequency is adopted, taking the low liquidity of the markets into consideration, as shown in Figure 11.1. In the USE, for example, the number of deals and trading days were only 11 and 8, respectively, in November 2003, the beginning of the study period. Using weekly data in such a low-liquidity market is unlikely to appropriately reflect market fundamentals, biasing the analysis. Thus, monthly averages with less noise and more information to estimate a long-run relationship are employed in this analysis. Cointegration analysis using semimonthly data is conducted as a robustness check (discussed subsequently).

TABLE 11.6

Beta Convergence in the Treasury Bill Markets

	Pooled Regression			Individual Regression			
	OLS	Fixed effects	Random effects	Burundi–Kenya	Rwanda–Kenya	Tanzania–Kenya	Uganda–Kenya
β	−0.052*** (0.014)	−0.054** (0.015)	−0.052*** (0.017)	−0.021 (0.018)	−0.054* (0.024)	−0.096*** (0.026)	−0.061 (0.040)
Number of observations	476	476	476	119	119	119	119
R-squared	0.151	0.152	0.151	0.123	0.166	0.222	0.240
Half-life of deviations (months)	12.9	12.4	12.9	32.4	12.4	6.9	11.1

Sources: IMF, African Department database; and author's calculations.
Note: Robust standard errors are reported in brackets. *** denotes significance at the 0.1 percent, ** at the 1 percent, and * at the 5 percent levels. Coefficients on constant, lagged variables, and country dummies (for the fixed effects model) are not reported. Implied half-life of deviations is calculated as ln(0.5)/ln(1 + b). OLS = ordinary least squares.

two companies listed at end-2010, and Burundi does not have a stock market. The data set covers November 2003 to January 2012. The DSE All Share Index, however, is available only after December 2006, resulting in 260 observations in total. For this analysis, the stock indices are converted to a common currency, using spot rates between the local currencies and the U.S. dollar.[12] Stock returns are computed as the log difference of the indices (Figure 11.2).

Results

Treasury Bill and Interbank Markets: Beta Convergence

Beta convergence suggests a tendency for returns to converge across the EAC Treasury bill markets. The first three columns in Table 11.6 show the estimated beta coefficients using the panel data with ordinary least squares, fixed effects, and random effects models. The coefficients are negative and statistically significant, and robust to estimation method. The estimated beta indicates it takes more than a year before the magnitude of a deviation is reduced by half (a "half-life" of deviations).[13] Four columns on the right side of Table 11.6 present the results of ordinary least squares regressions using individual yield spreads of Burundi, Rwanda, Tanzania, and Uganda from the benchmark Kenyan market. These individual regressions show substantive variation in the magnitude of beta coefficients, ranging from −0.021 for Burundi (a 32.4 month half-life) to −0.096 for

[12] Converting to a common currency may not be necessary in relatively advanced financial markets, because investors may hedge foreign exchange risks using forward contracts. But that is not necessarily the case for the EAC, because the forward markets are at nascent stages of development (Wang, 2010). I conducted the analyses using data series both adjusted and not adjusted for exchange rates, resulting in the same conclusions (discussed subsequently).

[13] A half-life of deviations is calculated as $\ln(0.5)/\ln(1+\beta)$.

TABLE 11.7

Beta Convergence in the Treasury Bill Markets—Before Full Membership and After

	Pooled Regression			Individual Regression			
	OLS	Fixed effects	Random effects	Burundi –Kenya	Rwanda –Kenya	Tanzania –Kenya	Uganda –Kenya
β							
Before July 2007	–0.046**	–0.047**	–0.046**	–0.021	–0.058*	–0.072*	–0.057
	(0.015)	(0.016)	(0.015)	(0.017)	(0.025)	(0.028)	(0.043)
After July 2007	–0.111***	–0.114***	–0.111***	–0.158*	–0.036	–0.164**	–0.106
	(0.029)	(0.029)	(0.030)	(0.065)	(0.049)	(0.058)	(0.065)
Number of observations	476	476	476	119	119	119	119
R-squared	0.159	0.161	0.159	0.170	0.167	0.238	0.244
Test: β is the same before and after July 2007	4.57	4.65	3.32	5.24	0.23	2.14	0.43
	(0.033)	(0.032)	(0.069)	(0.024)	(0.635)	(0.146)	(0.514)
Half-life of deviations (months)							
Before July 2007	14.8	14.3	14.8	33.0	11.6	9.2	11.9
After July 2007	5.9	5.7	5.9	4.0	19.1	3.9	6.2

Sources: IMF, African Department database; and author's estimates.

Note: Figures in brackets are standard errors for coefficients and p values for Wald tests. *** denotes significance at the 0.1 percent, ** at the 1 percent, and * at the 5 percent levels. Coefficients on constant, lagged variables, and country dummies (for the fixed effects model) are not reported. Implied half-life of deviations is calculated as ln(0.5)/ln(1 + β). OLS = ordinary least squares.

Tanzania (a 6.9 month half-life), seemingly reflecting respective markets' degrees of integration with the Kenyan market.

The speed of convergence in the Treasury bill markets has significantly increased in recent years. To evaluate the developments of beta over time, separate beta coefficients were estimated before July 2007[14] and after by modifying equation (11.1) as follows:

$$\Delta S_{i,t} = \alpha + \beta_{bfr} D_{bfr} S_{i,t-1} + \beta_{aft} S_{i,t-1} + \sum_{l=1}^{L} \gamma_l \Delta S_{i,t-1} + \varepsilon_{i,t} \quad (11.4)$$

where β_{bfr} and β_{aft} denote beta coefficients before and after July 2007, respectively. Two dummy variables, D_{bfr} and D_{aft}, take values one before and after July 2007, respectively (and zero otherwise). Table 11.7 shows that speed of convergence has significantly increased since July 2007, reducing a half-life of deviations from 15 months to 6 months.

Looking at individual countries, the absolute values of beta coefficients have increased for all the countries but Rwanda. In particular, the beta convergence of Burundi has turned out to be statistically significant after July 2007, reducing a half-life of deviations from 33 months to 4 months. These results should be interpreted with caution as they are sensitive to the sample period, due to the small number of observations.

[14]The timing when Burundi and Rwanda joined the EAC is chosen for analysis.

TABLE 11.8

Beta Convergence in the Interbank Markets

	Pooled Regression			Individual Regression		
	OLS	Fixed effects	Random effects	Rwanda – Kenya	Tanzania – Kenya	Uganda – Kenya
β	–0.103**	–0.116**	–0.103***	–0.033	–0.139*	–0.139*
	(0.033)	(0.039)	(0.027)	(0.067)	(0.060)	(0.061)
Number of observations	381	381	381	127	127	127
R-squared	0.141	0.144	0.141	0.099	0.196	0.193
Half-life of deviations (months)	6.3	5.6	6.3	20.4	4.6	4.6

Sources: IMF, African Department database; and author's estimates.
Note: Robust standard errors are reported in brackets. *** denotes significance at the 0.1 percent, ** at the 1 percent, and * at the 5 percent levels. Coefficients on constant, lagged variables, and country dummies (for the fixed effects model) are not reported. Implied half-life of deviations is calculated as ln(0.5)/ln(1 + b). OLS = ordinary least squares.

TABLE 11.9

Beta Convergence in the Interbank Markets—Before Full Membership and After

	Pooled Regression			Individual Regression		
	OLS	Fixed effects	Random effects	Rwanda –Kenya	Tanzania –Kenya	Uganda –Kenya
β						
Before July 2007	–0.088*	–0.100**	–0.088***	–0.048	–0.126*	–0.097
	(0.034)	(0.039)	(0.014)	(0.056)	(0.062)	(0.064)
After July 2007	–0.165*	–0.187*	–0.165	0.004	–0.204	–0.402***
	(0.083)	(0.090)	(0.111)	(0.126)	(0.174)	(0.129)
Number of observations	381	381	381	127	127	127
R-squared	0.144	0.149	0.144	0.102	0.199	0.244
Test: β is the same before and after July 2007	0.74	0.94	0.53	0.24	0.18	5.08
	(0.391)	(0.334)	(0.468)	(0.622)	(0.673)	(0.026)
Half-life of deviations (months)						
Before July 2007	7.5	6.5	7.5	14.2	5.1	6.8
After July 2007	3.9	3.3	3.9	...	3.0	1.3

Sources: IMF, African Department database; and author's estimates.
Note: Figures in brackets are standard errors for coefficients and *p* values for Wald tests. *** denotes significant at the 0.1 percent, ** at the 1 percent, and * at the 5 percent levels. Coefficients on constant, lagged variables, and country dummies (for the fixed effects model) are not reported. Implied half-life of deviations is calculated as $ln(0.5)/ln(1 + \beta)$.

Beta convergence in the EAC interbank markets, shown in Table 11.8, also suggests mean reversion taking place: the coefficient is negative and statistically significant regardless of the models used. It also provides an intuitively sensible result that the speed of convergence is faster in the interbank markets (about a 6-month half-life) than in the Treasury bill markets (about a 13-month half-life). The estimated speed of convergence is comparable to that in the Gulf Cooperation Council markets (a half-life of deviations ranging from 3.6 to 5.5 months), estimated by Espinoza, Prasad, and Williams (2010).

Speed of convergence has increased in the interbank markets, as in the Treasury bill markets (Table 11.9). The implied half-life of deviations has declined from

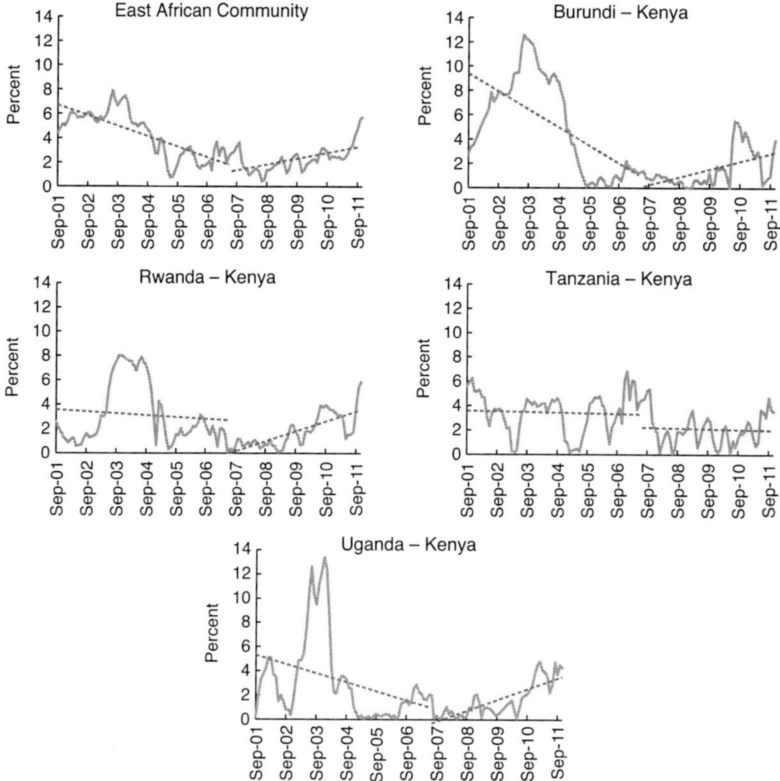

Figure 11.3 Sigma Convergence in the Treasury Bill Markets

Sources: IMF, African Department database; and author's estimates.
Note: Dotted lines denote linear time trends of sigma convergence, in periods before and after July 2007.

seven months before July 2007 to around four months since then. The individual regressions also show increasing beta convergence for the countries, except Rwanda. However, as mentioned for the Treasury bill markets, this result is to be interpreted with caution, as the number of observations is relatively limited and most of the estimated beta coefficients lack statistical significance.

Treasury Bill and Interbank Markets: Sigma Convergence

Sigma convergence reveals that integration of the EAC Treasury bill markets has deepened somewhat since 2001, but the progress has stagnated in recent years. Figures 11.3 and 11.4 show the calculated sigma convergence in the EAC Treasury bill and interbank markets, respectively, as well as the linear time trends before and after July 2007. The figures present sigma convergence both with respect to dispersion across the region and dispersion between Kenya and each of the other markets. The figures suggest a downward trend in the dispersion in the EAC markets since 2001; however, the trend has reversed since July 2007 in most markets.

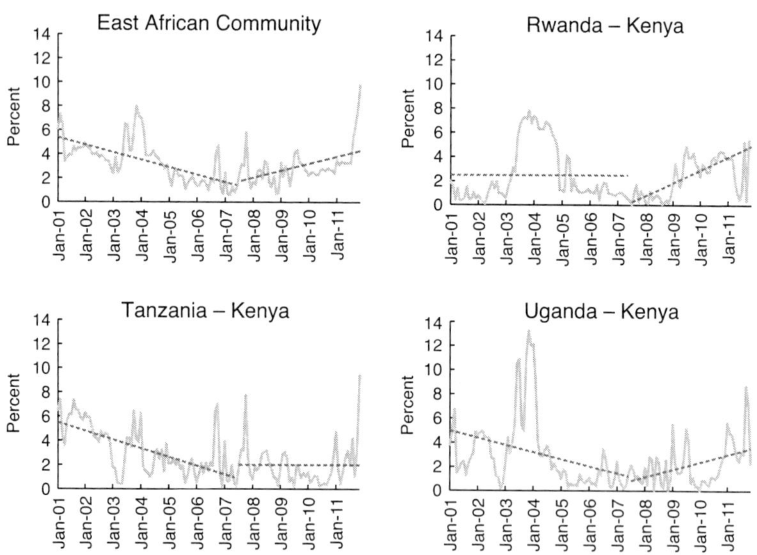

Figure 11.4 Sigma Convergence in the Interbank Markets

Sources: IMF, African Department database; and author's estimates.

Note: Dotted lines denote linear time trends of sigma convergence, in periods before and after July 2007.

Table 11.10 shows the results of regressions of σ_t on a linear time trend, summarizing the time trends arising in Figures 11.3 and 11.4. The coefficient of σ_t in the Treasury bill markets changed from –0.07 before July 2007 to 1.2 after, and the same reverse of the time trend can be found in the interbank markets. These changes are statistically significant. The widening of the dispersion has further accelerated since July 2011, especially in the interbank markets. This is due to high inflation in the region caused by global commodity price hikes and drought in the region: countries hit by these exogenous shocks responded by tightening monetary policy and increasing interest rates considerably (Figure 11.1), widening the dispersion of interest rates across the region. The rising trend of dispersion, however, cannot be solely attributed to these shocks, as the trend emerged before 2011, in particular in Rwanda and Uganda.[15]

Stock Markets: Beta and Sigma Convergence

Beta convergence implies mean reversion taking place among the stock markets of Kenya, Uganda, and Tanzania (Table 11.11). The beta coefficients, estimated at –0.55 in the panel regressions, are statistically significant regardless of the model employed. The results suggest surprisingly fast convergence in the stock markets, with less than a month of half-life. The beta coefficients remain

[15] Dropping observations in 2011 from the analysis does not change the declining trends of sigma convergence in the Treasury bill and interbank markets, although some of the time-trend coefficients lose statistical significance.

TABLE 11.10

Sigma Convergence in the Treasury Bill and Interbank Markets

	EAC	Burundi –Kenya	Rwanda –Kenya	Tanzania –Kenya	Uganda –Kenya
Treasury Bill Market					
Time trend of σ					
Before July 2007	–0.072***	–0.123***	–0.013	–0.004	–0.062***
	(0.007)	(0.018)	(0.011)	(0.010)	(0.014)
After July 2007	1.207***	0.054***	0.068***	–0.005	0.074***
	(0.327)	(0.011)	(0.010)	(0.015)	(0.009)
Constant					
Before July 2007	7.363***	10.493***	3.682***	3.616***	5.863***
	(0.336)	(1.035)	(0.668)	(0.474)	(0.935)
After July 2007	0.040***	0.081	–0.056	2.224***	–0.390
	(0.011)	(0.229)	(0.206)	(0.484)	(0.240)
Number of observations	123	123	123	123	123
R-squared	0.922	0.766	0.656	0.786	0.562
Test: trend of σ is the same before and after July 2007	74.23	68.42	29.52	0.00	65.74
	(0.000)	(0.000)	(0.000)	(0.983)	(0.000)
Interbank Market					
Time trend of σ					
Before July 2007	–0.052***	...	–0.001	–0.059***	–0.049***
	(0.005)	...	(0.008)	(0.008)	(0.009)
After July 2007	0.049**	...	0.090***	0.001	0.052**
	(0.018)	...	(0.027)	(0.021)	(0.016)
Constant					
Before July 2007	5.435***	...	2.484***	5.575***	5.040***
	(0.279)	...	(0.450)	(0.346)	(0.577)
After July 2007	1.693***	...	0.146	1.979***	0.770*
	(0.446)	...	(0.505)	(0.557)	(0.389)
Number of observations	131	...	131	131	131
R-squared	0.866	...	0.589	0.772	0.594
Test: trend of σ is the same before and after July 2007	29.34	...	10.60	7.01	31.17
	(0.000)	...	(0.001)	(0.009)	(0.000)

Sources: IMF, African Department database; and author's estimates.

Note: The regressions are estimated with OLS. Figures in brackets are robust standard errors for coefficients and *p* values for Wald-tests. *** denotes significance at the 0.1 percent, ** at the 1 percent, and * at the 5 percent levels. EAC = East African Community; OLS = ordinary least squares.

TABLE 11.11

Beta Convergence in the Stock Markets

	Pooled Regression			Individual Regression	
	OLS	Fixed Effects	Random Effects	Tanzania–Kenya	Uganda–Kenya
β	–0.551**	–0.556**	–0.551***	–0.521*	–0.792
	(0.182)	(0.179)	(0.058)	(0.203)	(0.182)
Number of observations	114	114	114	57	94
R-squared	0.385	0.385	0.385	0.395	0.426
Half-life of deviations (months)	0.87	0.85	0.87	0.94	0.44

Sources: Bloomberg L.P.; Thomson Reuters; and author's estimates.

Note: Robust standard errors are reported in brackets. *** denotes significance at the 0.1 percent, ** at the 1 percent, and * at the 5 percent levels. Coefficients on constant, lagged variables, and country dummies (for the fixed effects model) are not reported. Implied half-life of deviations is calculated as $ln(0.5)/ln(1 + \beta)$. OLS = ordinary least squares.

TABLE 11.12

Sigma Convergence in the Stock Markets

	EAC	Tanzania–Kenya	Uganda–Kenya
Time trend of σ	−0.011	−0.026	−0.007
	(0.016)	(0.023)	(0.005)
Constant	4.436***	5.343***	2.432***
	(0.673)	(0.932)	(0.326)
Number of observations	61	61	98
R-squared	0.006	0.019	0.013

Sources: Bloomberg L.P.; Thomson Reuters; and author's estimates.
Note: The regressions are estimated with ordinary least squares. Figures in brackets are robust standard errors. *** denotes significance at the 0.1 percent, ** at the 1 percent, and * at the 5 percent levels. EAC = East African Community.

significant if regressions are separately estimated using the individual spreads of returns in Tanzania and Uganda. These individual regressions suggest that integration between the Ugandan and the Kenyan stock markets (a 0.4-month half-life) is stronger than that between the Tanzanian and the Kenyan markets (about a month half-life), as suggested in Figure 11.2.

Sigma convergence suggests that divergence among the EAC stock markets has not diminished in the past few years. Estimated sigma convergence shown in Figure 11.5 seems to imply that the dispersion of stock returns among the NSE, the DSE, and the USE has declined slightly. However, regressing the estimated σ_t on a linear time trend reveals that the coefficient on σ_t is not statistically significant, although it has a negative sign (Table 11.12). This finding does not change if σ_t is computed as dispersion between the Kenyan market and each of the other two markets. Sigma convergence also shows that dispersion between the Tanzanian and Kenyan markets is larger than that between the Ugandan and Kenyan markets, consistent with the results of beta convergence. These results partly reflect that the global financial crisis had less effect on the Tanzanian stock market than on its neighbors (Figure 11.5), owing to its relatively limited integration with the global economy. These results of beta and sigma convergence in the stock markets are unchanged if the data are not adjusted for exchange rates.

Stock Markets: Cointegration Analysis

Two steps are necessary before conducting cointegration analysis: (1) verifying whether the data series are nonstationary, containing unit roots, and (2) selecting the number of lags used in the model. For the first step, augmented Dickey-Fuller and Phillips-Perron tests are conducted on the stock price data. The results uniformly confirm that all the data series are modeled as integrated of order one and appropriate for cointegration analysis. For the second step, four lags are chosen following the Akaike's information criterion and a likelihood-ratio test. Adjusting or not adjusting for exchange rates does not change these results.

The result indicates that there is no long-run relationship among the EAC stock markets. Given the nonstationarity and the number of lags identified, Johansen's

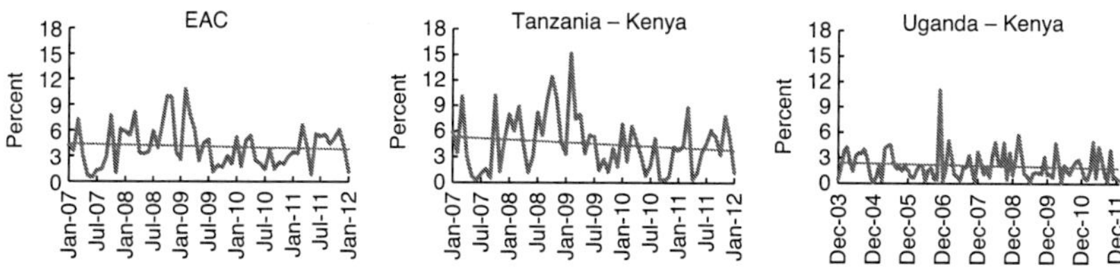

Figure 11.5 Sigma Convergence in the Stock Markets

Sources: Bloomberg L.P.; Thomson Reuters; and author's estimates.

TABLE 11.13

Cointegration Tests for the East African Community Stock Markets

	Trace Statistics			Maximum-eigenvalue Statistics		
Number of Co-integrating Vectors	Adjusted for Exchange Rates	Not Adjusted for Exchange Rates	5 percent Critical Value	Adjusted for Exchange Rates	Not Adjusted for Exchange Rates	5 percent Critical Value
$r = 0$	28.990*	28.261*	29.680	22.616	15.957*	20.970
$r = 1$	6.374	12.304	15.410	4.808*	9.199	14.070
$r = 2$	1.566	3.105	3.760	1.566	3.105	3.760

Source: Author's calculations.
Note: * denotes the number of cointegrating vectors suggested by the statistics.

trace tests are implemented to determine cointegration rank. The tests indicate that there is no cointegration vector in the EAC stock markets (Table 11.13). The maximum-eigenvalue statistics suggest one cointegrating relationship, but when the data are not adjusted for the exchange rates, both the trace statistics and maximum-eigenvalue statistics indicate no cointegration. I further conducted the same analysis following different information criteria for lags and using semi-monthly data, but found no cointegration vector among the EAC stock prices.

Summary and Interpretation of the Empirical Results

The results suggest that beta convergence is taking place, or even strengthening, in the EAC financial markets. This means that there is a foundation on which risk-adjusted yield spreads across local markets are arbitraged through cross-border financial transactions. This finding contradicts IMF (2009), which finds that such convergence is not taking place in the EAC Treasury bond markets. It is presumably because IMF (2009) has a much smaller number of observations (46), due to the infrequency of Treasury bond issues and transactions. Comparing estimated beta convergence across the EAC markets, the speed of convergence of returns is much faster in the stock markets (a half-life of less than a month) than in the Treasury bill markets (about a 13-month half-life) and the interbank markets (about a 6-month half-life). This is most likely because investors, especially foreign ones, actively trade stocks in the secondary markets.

Measured sigma indicates that cross-sectional dispersion of returns among the EAC financial markets has been unchanged or even widening in some markets, over the past few years. How is this result compatible with statistically significant beta convergence? Remember beta convergence is a necessary, but not a sufficient condition for sigma convergence. Estimated beta indicates that yield spreads across local markets tend to be arbitraged by cross-border financial transactions. Nevertheless, sigma convergence shows such dispersion of yields still remains. This suggests that the remaining dispersion is caused more by differences in underlying country economic conditions (such as inflation and interest rate) and risks (exchange rate and political risks) than financial barriers that prevent market participants from exploiting arbitrage opportunities. Different fundamentals and risks naturally result in different returns from investments, preventing realization of the law of one price. The decrease in dispersion before 2007, especially in the Treasury bill and interbank markets, is most likely the result of the more stable fiscal and monetary policies adopted by most African governments over the past decade, rather than of deepened financial integration in the EAC. This trend has since stagnated as national economies experienced asymmetrical impacts from shocks such as the global financial crisis, political turmoil in Kenya, and drought in the region. Cointegration analysis, which suggests that there has been no long-run relationship among the EAC stock markets since 2007, complements this observation.

CONCLUSIONS

EAC financial markets are underdeveloped, although with significant divergence of developmental stages among the countries. Whereas government debt markets are functional in all the EAC countries, market size ranges from 2.2 percent of GDP in Rwanda to 27.3 percent in Kenya. Kenya has the most advanced stock market, Rwanda only just launched its stock market, and Burundi has no stock exchange. Despite these differences, the countries face the same challenges—low capitalization and liquidity of the financial markets. Issuers are largely confined to public institutions and foreign-affiliated banks. Investors are dominated by commercial banks and local pension funds, leaving participation of individual and foreign investors limited. These constraints, as well as insufficient market infrastructure, result in small and illiquid financial markets.

To overcome these challenges, the EAC countries have been pursuing regional integration of domestic financial markets by removing capital regulations and harmonizing market infrastructure. Kenya, Rwanda, and Uganda have fully liberalized capital transactions across the region, while Tanzania and Burundi are obliged to do so by 2015. Momentum toward harmonizing market infrastructure was evident even before the launching of the EAC, and cooperation is fairly advanced. The outputs have included a common procedure for cross-border listings, while further progress in wide areas including taxes, financial reporting, trading systems, and financial education is expected.

The empirical results on financial integration in the EAC are mixed. Estimated beta convergence indicates that convergence of investment returns is taking place in all the three financial markets assessed in this paper—Treasury bill, interbank, and stock markets. It is even shown that the speed of convergence has increased in recent years in the Treasury markets (and to less extent in the interbank markets). This result suggests that the authorities' efforts at financial integration have reduced barriers to financial transactions across the borders, giving financial institutions motivation to take advantage of arbitrage opportunities across the markets. Nevertheless, estimated sigma convergence reveals that the mechanism of beta convergence has not succeeded in diminishing the dispersion of returns across local markets. On the contrary, the result shows increasing divergence in the Treasury bill and interbank markets for most countries. The cointegration analysis also indicates no long-run cointegration relationship among the EAC stock markets.

These results suggest that slow progress in the convergence of the EAC economies, rather than the existence of financial barriers, has impeded realization of the law of one price, or deepening of financial integration. Although the EAC states agreed upon a set of convergence criteria of economies in the context of establishing a monetary union, convergence of macroeconomic performance, such as inflation and fiscal balance, has been uneven. While it is imperative for the EAC countries to accelerate the momentum of removing barriers to financial transactions across the region, achieving a higher level of economic convergence and stability is essential in realizing integrated regional financial markets and reaping the full benefits of the monetary union to be established. Establishing effective mechanisms for conducting regional surveillance and enforcing sound national economic policies would help the countries achieve these objectives.

REFERENCES

Adam, K., T. Jappelli, A. M. Menichini, M. Padula, and M. Pagano, 2002, "Analyse, Compare, and Apply Alternative Indicators and Monitoring Methodologies to Measure the Evolution of Capital Market Integration in the European Union." Centre for Studies in Economics and Finance, Department of Economics and Statistics, University of Salerno, Italy.

Adelegan, O. J., 2008, "Can Regional Cross-Listings Accelerate Stock Market Development? Empirical Evidence from Sub-Saharan Africa," IMF Working Paper No. 08/281 (Washington: International Monetary Fund).

———, 2009, "The Impact of the Regional Cross-Listing of Stocks of Firm Value in Sub-Saharan Africa," IMF Working Paper No. 09/99 (Washington: International Monetary Fund).

Adjasi, C. K. D., and N. B. Biekpe, 2006a, "Stock Market Development and Economic Growth: The Case of Selected African Countries," *African Development Review*, Vol. 18, No. 1, pp. 144–161.

———, 2006b, "Cointegration and Dynamic Causal Links amongst African Stock Markets," *Investment Management and Financial Innovations*, Vol. 3, No. 4, pp. 102–119.

African Development Bank, 2010, *Financial Sector Integration in Three Regions of Africa* (Tunis, Tunisia).

African Securities Exchanges Association, 2011, "African Securities Exchanges Association Yearbook 2011." http://www.africansea.org.

Babetskii, I., L. Komárek, and Z. Komárková, 2008, "Financial Integration of Stock Markets among New EU Member States and the Euro Area," *Czech Journal of Economics and Finance*, Vol. 57, No. 7–8, pp. 341–362.

Bley, J., 2009, "European Stock Market Integration: Fact or Fiction?" *Journal of International Financial Markets, Institutions and Money*, Vol. 19, No. 5, pp. 759–776.

Click, R. W., and M. G. Plummer, 2005, "Stock Market Integration in ASEAN after the Asian Financial Crisis," *Journal of Asian Economics*, Vol. 16, No. 1, pp. 5–28.

Collins, S. M., 2004, "International Financial Integration and Growth in Developing Countries: Issues and Implications for Africa," *Journal of African Economies*, Vol. 13, AERC Supplement 2, ii55–ii94.

Eichengreen, B., and P. Luengnaruemitchai, 2004, "Why Doesn't Asia Have Bigger Bond Markets?" NBER Working Paper No. 10576 (Cambridge, Massachusetts: National Bureau of Economic Research).

Espinoza, R., A. Prasad, and O. Williams, 2010, "Regional Financial Integration in the GCC," IMF Working Paper No. 10/90 (Washington: International Monetary Fund).

Feldstein, M., and C. Horioka, 1980, "Domestic Saving and International Capital Flows," *Economic Journal*, Vol. 90, No. 358, pp. 314–329.

International Monetary Fund, 2008, *Regional Economic Outlook: Sub-Saharan Africa* (Washington).

———, 2009, "Uganda: Selected Issues," IMF Country Report No. 09/37 (Washington).

Irving, J., 2005, "Regional Integration of Stock Exchanges in Eastern and Southern Africa: Progress and Prospects," IMF Working Paper No. 05/122 (Washington: International Monetary Fund).

Ishii, S., and K. Habermeier, 2002, "Capital Account Liberalization and Financial Sector Stability," IMF Occasional Paper No. 211 (Washington: International Monetary Fund).

Johansen, S., and K. Juselius, 1990, "Maximum Likelihood Estimation and Inference from Cointegration—with Applications to the Demand for Money," *Oxford Bulletin of Economics and Statistics*, Vol. 52, No. 2, pp. 169–210.

Kasa, K., 1992, "Common Stochastic Trends in International Stock Markets," *Journal of Monetary Economics*, Vol. 29, No. 2, pp. 95–124.

Levine, R., and S. Zervos, 1998, "Stock Markets, Banks, and Economic Growth," *American Economic Review*, Vol. 88, No. 3, pp. 537–558.

Making Finance Work for Africa, 2007, "Financial Sector Integration in Two Regions of Sub-Saharan Africa." http://www.mfw4a.org/resources/documents/documents-details/financial-sector-integration-in-two-regions-of-sub-saharan-africa-how-creating-scale-in-financial-markets-can-support-growth-and-development.html.

Manning, N., 2002, "Common Trends and Convergence? South East Asian Equity Markets, 1988–1999," *Journal of International Money and Finance*, Vol. 21, No. 2, pp. 183–202.

Murinde, V., 2012, "Financial Development and Economic Growth: Global and African Evidence," *Journal of African Economies*, Vol. 21, African Economic Research Consortium Supplement 2, pp. i10–i56.

Sala-i-Martin, X., 1996, "Regional Cohesion: Evidence and Theories of Regional Growth and Convergence," *European Economic Review*, Vol. 40, No. 6, pp. 1325–1352.

Sanya, S., and M. Gaertner, 2012, "Assessing Banking Competition within the Eastern African Community," IMF Working Paper No. 12/32 (Washington: International Monetary Fund).

Serletis, A., and M. King, 1997, "Common Stochastic Trends and Convergence of European Union Stock Markets," *The Manchester School*, Vol. 65, No. 1, pp. 44–57.

Sharma, G. D., and B. S. Bodla, 2010, "Are the Global Stock Markets Inter-linked? Evidence from the Literature," *Global Journal of Management and Business Research*, Vol. 10, No. 1, pp. 29–39.

United Nations Economic Commission for Africa, 2008, *Assessing Regional Integration in Africa III* (Addis Ababa: Economic Commission for Africa).

Wang, Y. D., 2010, "Measuring Financial Barriers among East African Community Countries," IMF Working Paper No. 10 (Washington: International Monetary Fund).

Wang, Z., J. Yang, and D. A. Bessler, 2003, "Financial Crisis and African Stock Market Integration," *Applied Economics Letters*, Vol. 10, No. 9, pp. 527–533.

Yu, I., L. Fung, and C. Tam, 2010, "Assessing Financial Market Integration in Asia—Equity Markets," *Journal of Banking and Finance*, Vol. 34, No. 12, pp. 2874–2885.

CHAPTER 12

Themes and Lessons from the Financial Sector Assessment Programs

S. KAL WAJID

The recently completed IMF-World Bank Financial Sector Assessment Programs (FSAPs) for the partner countries of the East African Community (EAC) highlight the growing financial integration in the region.[1] The FSAPs acknowledge significant advances in expanding financial sector assets and services, removing barriers to intermediation, and strengthening regulatory and supervisory frameworks. At the same time, they underscore the considerable scope and challenges remaining on the road to further monetary and financial integration in the EAC.

Financial sector depth and soundness varies significantly in the EAC countries. And they also have common concerns, such as limited access to finance, shallow financial markets, challenges in consolidated supervision, and cross-border supervisory and crisis management arrangements, as well as the need for better liquidity management and financial infrastructure. Successfully addressing these issues would encourage financial integration and help to reap its benefits, such as greater competition, expansion of markets, reduced costs of intermediation, and more efficient allocation of capital.

The chapter looks at the main themes and lessons for financial sector integration in the EAC emerging from the FSAPs for the countries in the region. It discusses the findings on financial structure, soundness, and stability (Box 12.1), the financial sector policy framework in the region, as well as financial infrastructure and capital market development. It closes with a look at challenges and lessons.

This chapter is based on a paper prepared by an IMF team comprising George Anayiotos, Etibar Jafarov, Arto Kovanen, Bozena Radzewicz-Bak, and Wilson Varghese, and led by S. Kal Wajid.

[1]The EAC countries are Burundi, Kenya, Rwanda, Tanzania, and Uganda. Of these, only Burundi was a first-time FSAP, while the others were FSAP Updates. The FSAPs took place between 2009 and 2011 against a backdrop of the global financial crisis. In some cases, significant changes have taken place since the assessment. To the extent possible, this chapter takes these into account.

BOX 12.1 Key Lessons: Financial Sector Soundness and Stability

Progress has been made in reforming financial systems in the East African Community (EAC), but it has been uneven across countries. The EAC financial systems are still very small, shallow, and bank-centric. While measures of financial depth lag behind those of emerging markets and low-income countries, regional integration could provide opportunities for expansion and risk diversification. Profitability and soundness indicators of banks in the region are generally favorable and provide a good basis for regional banking even though banks face concentration, credit, and operational risks. Major nonbank financial institutions suffer from structural weaknesses and little public confidence, raising concerns about their stability. These institutions could provide long-term financing, but their weak finances and governance are a major constraint on the development of the EAC nonbank financial sector.

Source: Author.

FINANCIAL STRUCTURE, SOUNDNESS, AND STABILITY

Financial Sector Structure

Small, bank-centric financial sectors. The relatively small, bank-centric financial sectors in the EAC countries offer significant economies of scale through regional integration. Although commercial banks continue to play a dominant role and account for the majority of financial sector assets, nonbank financial institutions are gradually increasing in importance. Following the liberalization and opening of markets, ownership in the banking sector has seen greater involvement of foreign and private investors, while nonbank financial institutions remain largely domestically owned. Market concentration in both bank and nonbank sectors remains high (except in Kenya) and has tended to constrain competition, even though the entry of foreign banks over the last few years has had a positive impact in this respect.

- ***Low financial depth.*** Financial depth in the EAC is generally low, except in Kenya, where bank assets in relation to GDP are the highest in the region (at 50 percent). Banking sector assets are the lowest in Burundi, accounting for only 24 percent of GDP (Figure 12.1). Except for Kenya, EAC countries also lag behind emerging markets, other low-income countries, and peers in sub-Saharan Africa in deposit mobilization and private sector credit in relation to GDP. The factors impeding financial sector depth include (1) inadequate financial infrastructure, (2) lack of trust in the existing legal and judicial frameworks and creditor rights, (3) limited competition among banks, (4) an unfavorable business environment, and (5) low per capita income.[2]
- ***Centrality of banks.*** Financial systems in the region are highly bank-centric, with commercial banks accounting for 60–90 percent of total

[2]Total deposits in EAC countries amounted to 27.5 percent of GDP in 2013 compared with the sub-Saharan African average of 44 percent and the ratio of private credit to GDP was 21 percent compared with to the sub-Saharan African average of 28 percent.

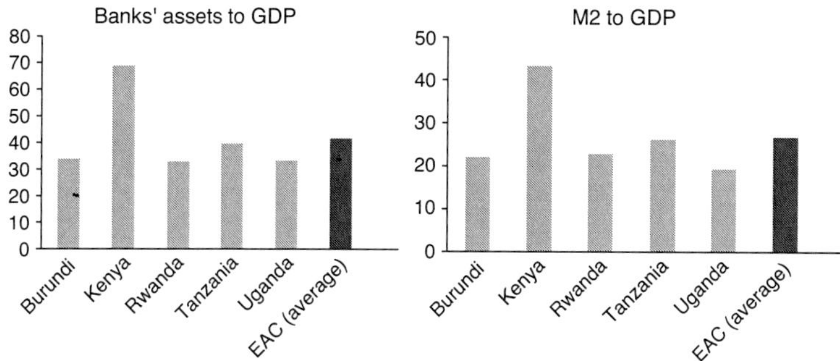

Figure 12.1 East African Community Banking Sector Depth in 2013

Sources: Central banks in the East African Community; and IMF staff estimates.
Note: EAC = East African Community.

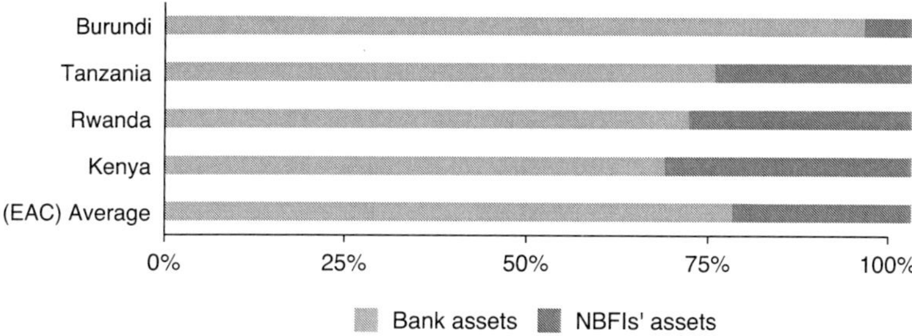

Figure 12.2 Structure of Financial Sector Assets in the East African Community, 2012 *(percent)*

Sources: Central banks in the East African Community; and IMF estimates.
Note: The chart does not include Uganda, for which information on financial sector assets was not available. EAC = East African Community; NBFIs = nonbank financial institutions.

financial sector assets (Figure 12.2). In terms of assets and deposits, Kenya has the largest banking sector, followed by Tanzania and Uganda. Together, these three countries account for more than 80 percent of total financial intermediation in the region. In Rwanda and Burundi, where financial sectors are much smaller, banks also account for a relatively smaller proportion of the region's total assets, loans, and deposits.

- ***Increasing foreign and private bank ownership.*** Ownership characteristics in the banking sector have evolved since 2005. Liberalization and changes in licensing criteria have spurred an influx of foreign banks into Rwanda, Uganda, and Tanzania. As a result, the share of foreign ownership has varied from 40 percent in Kenya to as high as 84 percent in Uganda (in 2009).[3] The region has also witnessed an expansion of pan-African banks, including

[3] In Uganda, the expiration of a moratorium on new licensing in 2007 triggered an influx of foreign banks. Nine banks were approved for operation, with four entering anew and four through an acquisition.

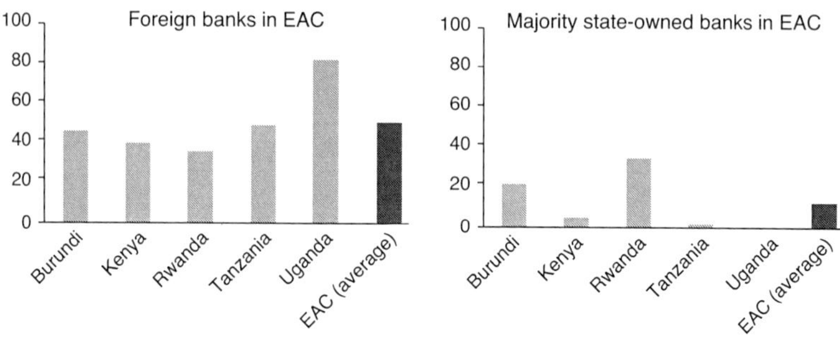

Figure 12.3 Ownership Structure in the Banking Sector in the East African Community (EAC), 2012 *(percent share of total banking sector assets)*

Source: Author's calculations.

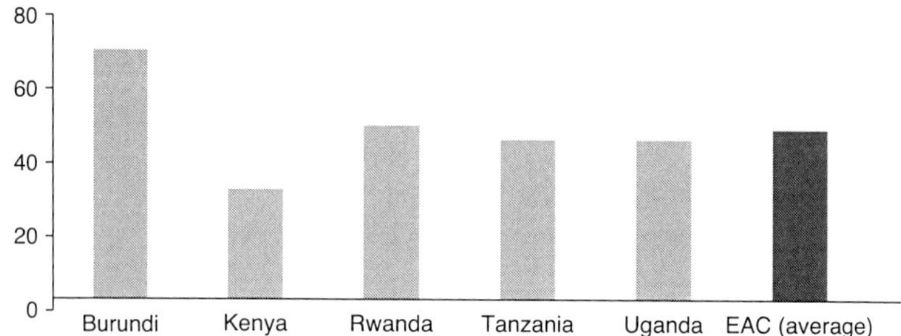

Figure 12.4 Concentration of Banking Sector Assets in the East African Community (EAC), 2012 (*percent*)

Sources: Central banks in the East African Community; and IMF staff estimates.
Note: Concentrations are measured as a share of total banking sector assets accumulated by the three largest banks in each country.

subsidiaries of Kenyan, Nigerian, South African, and Togolese banks. Government stakes in the banking sectors have been reduced and the majority of banks in the region now have private shareholders. State ownership in Kenya, Tanzania, and Uganda has declined to around 5 percent of total banking assets, while in Burundi and Rwanda it remains relatively high at 22 percent and 35 percent of bank assets, respectively (Figure 12.3).[4]

- ***Highly concentrated banking sectors.*** Concentration in the banking sector has generally declined over the last few years, but it remains relatively high in the EAC countries (Figure 12.4). The share of assets of the three top-tier banks in total bank assets ranges from 31 percent in Kenya to 70 percent in

[4]Among EAC countries, Rwanda has the highest direct state ownership of bank assets: 25 percent of bank assets are held by the largest bank, which is 100 percent owned by the state. In Burundi, the state is the majority shareholder in two banks, with over 55 percent of the capital, and also in the two financial institutions specializing in housing and development lending, with 80 percent of their capital.

Burundi. Measured by total deposits and loans in the three largest banks to all deposits and loans in the banking sector, concentration is even higher—an average of 79 percent for deposits and 74 percent for loans. In the EAC, the top-tier banks usually provide services, mainly to a small group of large corporate and institutional clients, leaving the retail market largely underserved.[5]

- ***Evolving business models.*** Intermediation through agencies and mobile banking is broadening access to financial services, reducing the cost of mobilizing deposits and transforming the banking business model in the region. Banks tend to compete vigorously for limited corporate business, notwithstanding the high degree of concentration. As a result, they are increasingly venturing down-market into lending to small and medium-sized enterprises (SMEs) and retail clients, and have extended their branch network and services to locations outside the main cities.

Nonbank financial institutions. The low depth of the financial systems in the region reflects relatively small shares of nonbank financial institutions typically associated with long-term financing. These include insurance companies, pension funds, and capital markets (stocks and bonds). While the insurance sector appears generally underdeveloped across all EAC countries, pension funds are of significant size and constitute the second largest segment of the financial sector. Insurance and pensions sectors hold the potential to provide long-term financing for regional infrastructure development, but need to be put on a sounder footing. Capital markets are more developed in Kenya, Tanzania, and Uganda, while they are in a nascent state in Burundi and Rwanda.

- ***Pension funds.*** Pension funds intermediate significant savings, but operate mostly domestically. On average, they account for 10 percent of total financial sector assets (Table 12.1). In Kenya, where the pension system is the most developed, pension funds manage assets equivalent to 16 percent of GDP. In other EAC countries, this varies from 1.4 percent of GDP in Uganda to 7 percent of GDP in Burundi.[6] The number of mandatory pension schemes ranges from only one in Rwanda to six in Tanzania. There are also a large number of voluntary occupational schemes. Cross-border pension fund activity, however, is virtually nonexistent.
- ***Insurance sector.*** The insurance sector remains small and largely underdeveloped. Insurance companies account for a small share of total financial sector assets and GDP (Table 12.2), with the number of companies varying from 6 in Burundi to 42 in Kenya. They hold assets equivalent to 0.3 percent of GDP in Uganda (the lowest in the EAC countries) and 10.9 percent in Rwanda (the highest). Market penetration (gross premiums/GDP) also remains low and ranges from 0.6 percent in Uganda to 2.6 percent in Kenya.[7] The insurance

[5]For example, in Uganda only about 21 percent of the population has formal access to banking services.

[6]Data for Uganda pertain to assets of only the largest pension fund National Social Security Fund.

[7]There is a lack of information on the penetration rate in Tanzania.

TABLE 12.1

Pension Funds Sector in East African Community Countries

	Burundi	Kenya	Rwanda	Tanzania	Uganda
Types of pension plans	...	Four main pillars: occupational pension system, individual schemes, define contribution, civil service pension scheme	40 occupational pension schemes dominated by one large government-run institution	Six types of pension schemes, in that five at the mainland and one in Zanzibar	Mandatory pensions are provided through three main schemes: (civil servants and members of military), National Social Security Fund (workers in formal sector)
Percentage of labor force covered by pensions	5% of population	10% of labor force	Poor population coverage	...	Less than 3% of the population
Pension fund assets to GDP	7% of GDP	16% of GDP	4.8% of GDP	3.3% of GDP	National Social Security Fund account for 1.35% of GDP; data for others are not available
Pension fund assets to total financial sector assets	10.3% of assets	10.1% of assets	13.1% of assets	9.2% of assets	...

Sources: Financial Sector Assessment Program reports; and IMF staff estimates.
Note: ... = not available.

TABLE 12.2

Insurance Sector in East African Community Countries

	Burundi	Kenya	Rwanda	Tanzania	Uganda
Number of insurance companies	6	42	8, including large government-run health care insurer	22	22
Insurance assets as percent of financial sector assets (as percent of GDP)	5% (3.2% of GDP)	8.6% (7.3% of GDP)	10.9% (4% of GDP)	3.6% (1.3% of GDP)	0.31% of GDP
Gross premiums to GDP (in percent)	1% of GDP	2.6% of GDP	RAMA—2.1% of GDP	...	0.6% of GDP

Sources: Financial Sector Assessment Program reports; and IMF staff estimates.
Note: ... = not available.

business is concentrated in non-life insurance, with motor insurance as the dominant business line. Notwithstanding the relatively large number of insurers, the sector is highly concentrated and cross-border activities are limited.

- ***Capital markets.*** Capital markets are nascent, with a limited range of securities. Stock and bond markets in Tanzania and Uganda are limited in scope and

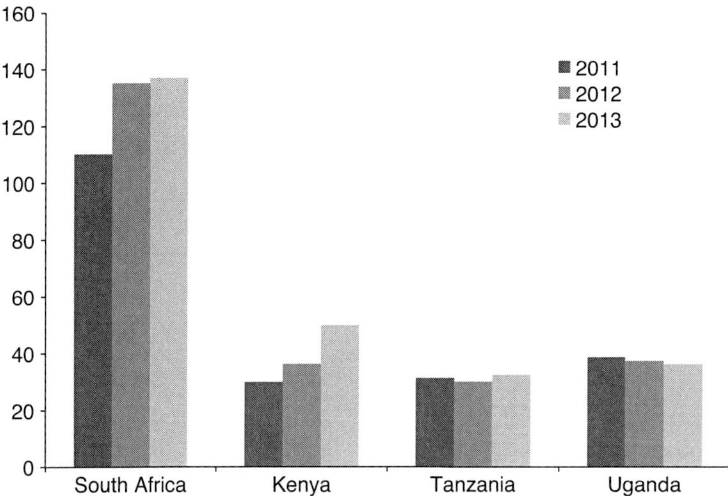

Figure 12.5 Stock Market Capitalization in the East African Community and South Africa *(percent of GDP)*

Sources: Stock exchanges' websites; and IMF staff calculations.

volume, while they are nonexistent in Burundi and Rwanda. Activity levels are modest, with total turnover and market capitalization substantially less than those of the Johannesburg stock exchange (Figure 12.5). The number of listed securities and corporate bonds is also small and concentrated in the banking, construction, transport, and telecommunication sectors.[8] Cross listings in the context of EAC regional integration has helped boost activity levels in markets other than the Nairobi Securities Exchange, and considerable scope exists for further economies of scale and integration of market infrastructure. It is expected that ongoing liberalization of capital flows and implementation of supporting policies may boost activities in these markets.

Banking Sector Soundness and Risks

Soundness indicators. Banking sectors across the region generally report favorable financial soundness indicators and provide a solid basis for region-wide banking (Box 12.2). Banks typically maintain capital levels in excess of the regulatory requirements, although there are variations across institutions and undercapitalization mainly pertains to smaller banks. Asset quality and earnings vary more across countries, with uncertainties about provisioning rules and policies, but liquidity is generally adequate. However, cost structures are heavily skewed toward operating costs, thereby contributing to high net interest margins.[9]

[8] Corporate bonds are mostly issued by banks or large state-owned companies for financing infrastructure and housing finance.

[9] The FSAP confirmed that the macroeconomic, bank industry, and bank-specific factors have been the main drivers of persistently high interest rate spreads and margins in the EAC countries.

BOX 12.2 Key Lessons: Harmonizing Regulatory and Supervisory Frameworks

Considerable effort is needed to strengthen and harmonize regulatory and supervisory frameworks and practices in order to foster regional financial integration.

Substantial staffing and capacity constraints in individual countries impair the adequacy of bank examinations and delay the transition to risk-based supervision.

Significant improvement is needed in the oversight of nonbank financial institutions and capital markets to enhance and sustain public and market confidence. Supervisory frameworks need to be upgraded to deal with increasing cross-sectoral and cross-country operations of financial institutions and any outstanding memorandums of understanding between home and host supervisors need to be finalized and become effective.

The main instruments of crisis management are in place in most countries, but a formal, comprehensive framework specifying the roles and responsibilities of key stakeholders in a crisis is lacking.

The efforts of East African Community authorities to build a common market would require harmonizing licensing, regulation, supervisory practices, and safety net arrangements.

In addition, a framework spelling out the broad principles for emergency liquidity assistance, home-host burden sharing, and resolution will be needed at the regional level.

Source: Author.

Cross-border exposures are an increasing source of risk, reflecting capital inflows and the increased presence of foreign banks, including those from within the region.

- ***Capital adequacy and asset quality.*** Banks in the region are well capitalized, often substantially exceeding regulatory requirements, especially in the larger systemic institutions. Weak capitalization typically afflicts smaller banks. Asset quality has generally been improving with the cleanup of nonperforming loan portfolios. However, there is some variation and, in some countries, nonperforming loans remain elevated, with uncertainties regarding loan classification and provisioning rules.
- ***Profitability.*** Bank profitability in the region is high by international comparison, reflecting high-risk premiums and limited competition. However, earnings trends across countries are mixed, with banks in Kenya and Uganda enjoying profits significantly above the regional average, and in Burundi and Tanzania profits are declining to below average. At the same time, bank costs have been increasing across all EAC countries, mainly due to the expansion of branch networks and limited skilled labor.[10]

[10]Employee costs account for the largest portion of overheads and have increased across the EAC countries over the last few years, mostly because of labor market pressures resulting from new entrants and increased lending activities.

- ***Liquidity.*** Banking systems are typically flushed with liquidity, reflecting (1) a captive retail deposit base, (2) limited long-term lending due to risk aversion and the lack of adequate financial infrastructure, and (3) holdings of sizeable precautionary reserve balances and short-term government securities.

Risk assessments. EAC FSAPs have focused on the implications of the global economic environment, potential sector-specific shocks, political uncertainties, and supervisory weaknesses. With generally moderate to high likelihoods of such risks materializing, their impact on financial stability was assessed to be moderate in most cases. Stress tests indicate that credit, concentration interest rate, liquidity, and operational risks are potential sources of vulnerability in the region, although these are more pronounced in some countries than others.

- ***Credit risk.*** Credit problems for countries in the region could arise from terms-of-trade shocks and a sharp drop in external assistance. This could lower some banks to below the minimum requirement, especially of small and medium-sized banks. Credit risk stemming from housing loans was seen to be particularly high for Rwanda, while the concentration of credit exposures to a few large borrowers was a major risk in Burundi, Tanzania, and Uganda. Although the concentration of credit exposures reflects economic structure to some extent, the availability of government guarantees for some industries, and the use of cash collateral, banks appeared to be highly vulnerable to potential shocks affecting their major customers. At the same time, indirect credit risk for banks seems to be relatively contained since the majority of foreign currency loans are concentrated in the tradable sectors and individual borrowers' exposures are typically hedged by their foreign currency incomes.
- ***Interest rate and liquidity risk.*** Banks are vulnerable to interest rate risk, particularly in Kenya and Tanzania. In both countries, banks hold a large share of assets in government securities and a sharp change in short-term rates could have a serious impact on their balance sheets. At the same time, liquidity risk appears to be contained in these two countries (mainly due to large holdings of government securities and a reliance on retail deposits), while it is quite significant for banks in Burundi, Rwanda, and Uganda. Liquidity risk was found most pronounced for banks in Uganda, with significant concentration of large deposits in a few banks.
- ***Operational risk.*** The growing complexity of operations and rapid expansion has increased the exposure of banks to operational risk, particularly in Kenya and Uganda. Domestic banks have been tapping more frequently into low-income and rural markets and reaching out to new market segments and product lines; while this is desirable, it also entails new risks.

Caveats. The stress testing analyses contained in the EAC FSAPs are subject to important caveats about data. In particular, the quality of data in some countries was impaired by shortcomings in the reporting and auditing infrastructure (Burundi), inconsistencies in data on nonperforming loans and provisioning (Tanzania), as well as the lack of detailed information on some smaller banks where weaknesses were concentrated (also Tanzania).

Macroprudential policies. To deal with financial sector systemic risks in a cohesive and comprehensive manner, the EAC countries need to embark on designing macroprudential tools and policy frameworks. As in many other countries, macroprudential policies in the EAC countries are at an early stage of development and further work in this area is desirable. Explicit coverage of this area in FSAPs has been limited, as they took place between 2009 and 2011, when the international guidelines and principles in this area were still nascent.

Nonbank Financial Sector Risks and Vulnerabilities

- ***Financially weak pension funds and insurance companies.*** The pension funds and insurance segments are financially weak in most EAC countries, which is a major impediment to the regional intermediation of long-term savings. A number of FSAPs judged public confidence in the pension fund sectors to be low (for instance, the Ugandan FSAP discusses the issue of past arrears and irregularities, which led to erosion of the public's faith in the National Social Security Fund. In a similar vein, the health of the insurance sector is seen as a reason for concern, and the FSAPs have identified a range of issues that need attention. These issues include (1) the limited availability of long-term assets and the need to develop investment guidelines (Rwanda); (2) the need to upgrade the legal framework and enhance the information produced by insurers (Kenya); (3) the lack of disclosure requirements for insurance brokers (Tanzania); and (4) the poor financial health of insurers and lack of compliance with regulations on share capital, solvency margins, and technical provisions (Burundi). Addressing the structural weaknesses and nonadherence to common regulatory guidelines and standards is an essential prerequisite for an EAC-wide pensions and insurance industry. Pension reforms have been adopted in some cases, and a sole regulator for the sector has been established in Rwanda, Tanzania, and Uganda.
- ***Stress testing of pension funds.*** The FSAP for Kenya highlighted the key risks on the balance sheets of the pension funds. Stress tests on the assets side of the balance sheets of a sample of 16 occupational pension schemes, representing about 45 percent of the market, indicated that they were exposed to concentration risk in government securities, equities, and real estate. On the liability side, the test found that longevity risk was the most important vulnerability, compounded by the absence of solvency standards and regulations.
- ***Pension funds' solvency concerns.*** The financial health of pension funds was judged to be at risk in a number of FSAPs. In addition to the low public confidence in Uganda mentioned previously, the FSAP for Burundi noted that the pension system had been in deficit since 2007, with implications for reserves, which were expected to be exhausted by 2015. Similarly, actuarial studies in Rwanda indicated that the large government-run pension fund will be in deficit by year 2030, while in Tanzania the investment portfolios of pension funds were found to be undiversified and illiquid.

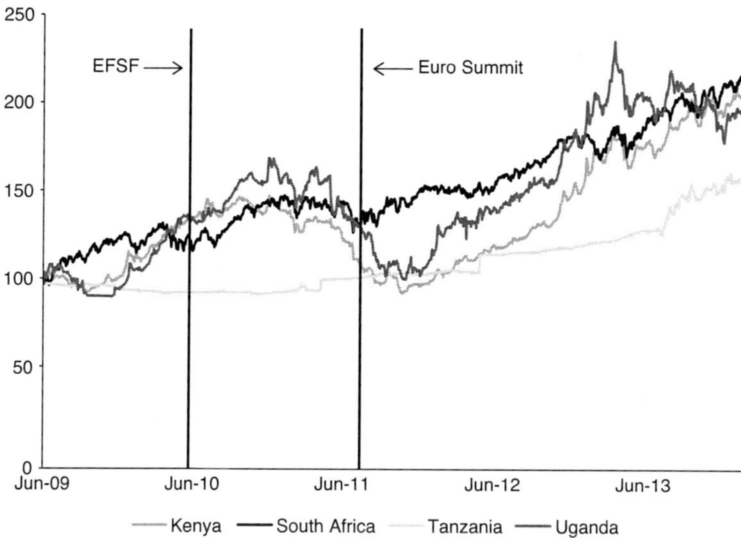

Figure 12.6 East African Community: Stock Market Index (June 29, 2009 = 100)

Sources: Bloomberg L.P.; and IMF staff estimates.
Note: EFSF = European Financial Stability Facility.

- ***Insurance sector health.*** A number of FSAPs underscored the poor financial health of insurance companies. The FSAP for Kenya, in particular, noted expansion of underreserved motor insurance companies that were at risk of not being able to meet their future liabilities. Similarly, a lack of compliance with regulations on share capital, solvency margins, and technical provisions were discussed for Burundi, while the low minimum required capital for both insurers and brokers was raised as an issue in the cases of Tanzania and Uganda. The insurance sectors in Rwanda and Tanzania were also found to be highly dominated by government-owned institutions.

Volatile financial markets. Capital markets remain susceptible to global market developments, particularly in Kenya where there are no restrictions on capital flows. As a result of the crisis in Europe, stock markets suffered substantial declines in Kenya (25.5 percent) and Uganda (14.8 percent) (Figure 12.6). In Kenya, the market remains vulnerable to loss of investor confidence and clearing and settlement failures. The brokerage industry remains concentrated, with five brokers accounting for 55 percent of equity trading, and internal controls and professional standards are weak. In the run up to the FSAP, market abuses, including unauthorized trading of clients' securities and theft, required the closure of three brokers. These offenses focused attention on the Capital Market Authority's (CMA) weak enforcement. The CMA is currently overhauling capital market legislation. Management of clearing and settlement risks is also a concern. The clearing and settlement agency should move to a structure where it does not bear settlement risk.

FINANCIAL SECTOR POLICY FRAMEWORK

Regulation and Supervision

Stronger common standard. Strengthening supervision and regulation to a common standard will be critical for establishing a robust financial policy framework supporting regional integration. While noting significant progress in this area, the FSAPs in the region focus on challenges in improving regulation and supervision. Regulatory and supervisory frameworks in Kenya, Tanzania, and Uganda are assessed favorably, with a higher degree of compliance with international standards. The FSAPs for these countries stress the need for further transition from compliance-based to risk-based supervision in banking and the importance of strengthening nonbank supervision. Significant scope for improving banking supervision is seen in Burundi and Rwanda given substantial staffing and capacity constraints. Overall, less-than-full compliance with the Basel Core Principles is common in the areas of abuse of financial services, corrective and remedial powers, consolidated supervision, market risk, and home-host relationships.

Banking

Progress in legislation and prudential guidelines. Banking supervision assessments underscore progress in updating relevant legislation and strengthening prudential guidelines. Appropriate amendment of key legislation, adoption of risk management and prudential guidelines, full implementation of risk-based supervision, and better onsite and offsite procedures have been highlighted in the EAC FSAPs, especially for the larger countries (Kenya, Tanzania, Uganda). In Rwanda, while legislation and prudential guidelines have been strengthened, the FSAP notes the need to further augment capital adequacy requirements and bolster provisioning rules. In Burundi, in light of the weaknesses in the legal and judicial framework and governance of financial institutions, significant reform of the supervisory framework is needed to conform to international standards.

Challenges in implementation. The FSAPs point to greater challenges in effective implementation and day-to-day conduct of supervision. Notwithstanding improved onsite and offsite supervision, staffing and skill constraints are a recurrent theme, limiting the frequency and quality of bank examinations and making the implementation of risk-based supervision more difficult. In most cases, the skills shortage goes beyond the official sector and extends to the banking industry more broadly, constraining banks' risk management capacity.

Variation in Basel Core Principles compliance. Assessments of compliance with Basel reveal significant variation both across countries and principles in the degree of compliance. Not unexpectedly, countries with relatively more sophisticated banking systems are generally more successful in meeting the standards than those with less developed systems, although full compliance eludes even these countries. In terms of principles, material or outright noncompliance is clustered around (1) licensing criteria; (2) transfer of significant ownership; (3) market, country, and transfer risks; (4) abuse of financial services; (5) consolidated supervision; and (6) home-host relationships. Significant shortcomings are also evident in corrective and remedial powers of supervisors.

Insufficient supervisory coordination. The FSAPs draw attention to insufficient supervisory coordination and lack of consolidated supervision. In light of cross-border expansion of banks and establishment of domestic financial groups, this was seen as a major challenge. Some efforts have been made to strengthen the framework of cross-border supervision, but these have fallen short of what is needed. The EAC countries signed a multilateral memorandum of understanding (MOU) in 2008 among the supervisory authorities and a joint onsite inspection has been carried out in Rwanda. However, in most cases, understandings (in MOUs) with the home supervisors of all foreign banks operating in the country remain to be reached.

Nonbank Financial Institutions

Weak regulation and supervision. The regulatory and supervisory framework for nonbank financial institutions is weak compared to that for banking, and there does not seem to be an effective mechanism for regional harmonization. This may be due to their small share in overall financial activity and significant public sector involvement, especially in the pension and insurance sectors (in some countries). Capital market oversight is more advanced in the larger countries with more developed and deeper markets (Kenya, Tanzania, Uganda), although there is much scope for strengthening in specific areas, even in these countries. A growing concern is the regulation and supervision of other small-scale intermediaries such as microfinance institutions and savings and credit cooperatives.

- ***Pension sector oversight and solvency.*** In the pension sector, long-term solvency and oversight are the main concerns. Among EAC countries, the pensions sector is important in Kenya and Tanzania and is very small in other countries. Regulation of the sector is not uniform across the region, and there are significant deficiencies in oversight. In Kenya, while there is an established regulatory body (the Retirement Benefits Authority), it needs to strengthen its offsite analysis of vulnerabilities, particularly of defined benefit schemes. Minimum standards for actuarial evaluation and funding rules need to be introduced and the capacity to assess the impact of shocks on the financial positions of the schemes needs to be enhanced. In Tanzania, while a regulatory agency for the sector (Social Security Regulatory Authority) had been set up by the time of the FSAP, it was not operational, and effective oversight framework was lacking. In the other three countries, the sector is in the early stages of development and reforms are needed to improve solvency, promote long-term savings, limit governmental involvement, and strengthen supervisory capacity.

- ***Insurance sector oversight weak.*** Progress in the oversight of the insurance sector remains limited. Original FSAPs in most EAC countries highlighted the underdevelopment of this source of long-term savings and investment. Only limited progress, mostly on the legal and institutional front, has been made since then and there remains a need to strengthen solvency rules and supervision. The FSAP Update for Kenya, for instance, notes the establishment of the Insurance Regulatory Authority as an autonomous body but expresses some concern about its regulatory capacity and scarce specialized skills. It welcomes the increased minimum capital requirements and the establishment of a policyholder's protection fund, but underscores the lack of a modern solvency test, early intervention mechanisms, and risk-based supervision. Such concerns are also underscored in the FSAPs for Tanzania and Uganda as well as for Burundi and Rwanda. The latter stresses the small size and undeveloped potential of the sector, in addition to the regulatory and supervisory deficiencies.
- ***Progress in capital market oversight.*** Some EAC countries are strengthening oversight of capital markets. Capital markets are most developed in Kenya, followed by Tanzania and Uganda, and are embryonic or nonexistent in Rwanda and Burundi. Issues of oversight are thus addressed more prominently in the FSAPs for the largest three countries and focus on stronger legislation, more rigorous oversight and enforcement, and risks in clearing and settlement. In the FSAPs for countries with smaller markets, greater emphasis is placed on regional integration initiatives and related oversight issues.
    - ***Kenya.*** The FSAP observed the CMA's efforts to overhaul the governing legislation and strengthen enforcement in response to weaknesses revealed by cases of market abuse. The FSAP called for a comprehensive enforcement strategy, encompassing regulations governing market participants; their licensing, fit, and proper tests for securities firms and individuals; and better disclosure of enforcement actions. More broadly, it suggested strengthening the CMA's supervisory processes through risk-based supervision, close monitoring of weak intermediaries, and better recruitment practices. The management of clearing and settlement risks also needed to be strengthened.
    - ***Tanzania.*** The FSAP recommended overhauling relevant legislation to grant greater independence to the Capital Markets and Securities Authority, empower it to undertake inspections and investigations, and collaborate and share information with other domestic and international regulatory agencies. It also recommended enhancing risk management in the settlement system by requiring guarantees from brokers' settlement banks of their obligations, initial and variation margin payments from settlement banks, and introducing a guarantee fund.
    - ***Uganda.*** The Uganda FSAP underscored the limited market depth and drew attention to the need to address the funding and staff resource

constraints of the CMA. It also stressed the required improvements in domestic market infrastructure and recommended that the Bank of Uganda (BOU) and the Uganda Securities Exchange implement full dematerialization of private sector securities. It suggested specific measures to ensure settlement through proper delivery-versus-payment arrangements.

- ***Small-scale financial services.*** Expansion of small-scale financial services providers poses regulatory and supervisory challenges. While improving access, new financial services and institutions, such as mobile payments and banking, microfinance institutions, and savings and credit cooperatives, entail new risks and call for appropriate regulation and supervision. Most EAC FSAPs—especially for Kenya, the leader in the region in mobile payments and banking—drew attention to the need for addressing the regulatory gap in this area. Concerns about the oversight of mobile payments were also prominent in Uganda where enactment of a National Payments System Law was recommended. The FSAPs for Burundi, Rwanda, and Uganda focused more on the regulation and supervision of microfinance institutions and savings and credit cooperatives. For example, the establishment of an apex institution, owned by the savings and credit cooperatives and providing training to its member institutions and ensuring that they meet their regulatory requirements was seen as a promising approach in this context.

Cross-Sector and Cross-Border Coordination

Consistency and coordination. Consistency of approaches to cross-sector regulatory and supervisory coordination will be important for regional integration. These issues received relatively limited attention in most EAC FSAPs, except for Kenya, where they are more germane. The latter stressed the need to bring regulatory agencies at par in terms of supervisory methods, staff skills, and regulatory capacity. It argued that prudential standards should seek to prevent significant regulatory inequalities and supervisory gaps through uniform definitions of eligible capital instruments, types of risks, minimum capital levels, and other relevant prudential risk limits. The MOU among domestic financial supervisors covering a wide set of issues, including information exchange, licensing, ongoing supervision and onsite inspections, and confidentiality, was seen as a positive step that needed to be reinforced by prompt implementation.

MOUs step forward. The signing of a multilateral MOU among regional supervisory authorities is seen as a welcome step to address home-host issues. In this connection, the FSAP for Kenya calls for a process for exchanging information and mapping local and regional groups, including relevant nonfinancial groups, their ownership structures, and parties related to significant ultimate beneficiary owners. There remains a need for MOUs to include an explicit protocol for communication and coordination in crisis situations (discussed in the following). For systemic cross-border banking groups, the establishment of formal supervisory colleges to undertake supervisory programs and assess risks is suggested.

Crisis Management Arrangements

Need for overarching framework. An overarching crisis management framework would be important in an integrated EAC market. The FSAPs find that, for most countries in the region, the main instruments of crisis management are in place and the central banks have adequate capacity to deal with individual bank failures. However, a formal comprehensive framework for dealing with systemic crisis is generally lacking. This is also the case in the larger countries—Kenya, Tanzania, and Uganda—where the legislation grants the central banks broad powers to intervene in order to prevent bank failures and to provide emergency liquidity assistance. Nonetheless, at the time of FSAPs, there were no formal protocols for a systemic crisis resolution, which would clearly define the roles of the main stakeholders (central banks, supervisory agencies, ministries of finance, home supervisors of foreign-owned institutions), and their respective responsibilities in a crisis. Deposit insurance schemes are also in place as a safety net, except in Burundi and Rwanda.

- ***Emergency liquidity assistance.*** Procedures for emergency liquidity assistance in a systemic crisis should be formalized. EAC FSAPs indicate that the central banks have adequate mechanisms for meeting the liquidity needs of banks in normal conditions and for dealing with an individual solvent bank with transitory liquidity problems. Most central banks maintain standing facilities for lending against eligible collateral (typically government securities) although the maturity varies. However, the framework for emergency liquidity assistance during systemic stress is not fully articulated. In such situations, it is often difficult to distinguish between illiquidity and insolvency, and support may need to be extended to institutions outside the banking system. A number of FSAPs (Burundi, Kenya, Tanzania) recommended explicit protocols for such situations.
- ***Provisions for systemic bank failures.*** Although provisions for dealing with individual bank failures seem adequate across EAC countries, they remain untested under a systemic stress. Most EAC FSAPs assessed the framework for bank intervention and resolution to be broadly adequate for a single nonsystemic bank failure. They found sufficient legal authority for supervisory action in cases of unsound bank operations, illiquidity, and insolvency. In most countries, there is relevant experience with supervisory intervention. However, there are questions about intervention efficacy and dealing with nonbank financial institutions in a systemic crisis. For instance, while noting the BOU's considerable experience in resolving failed institutions, the FSAP for Uganda doubted the capacity for timely bank intervention in a systemic crisis, reflecting staffing constraints. The FSAP for Burundi recommended establishing a special legal arrangement for liquidating insolvent banks (i.e., bank resolution regime), as the bankruptcy law was not designed for the banking system.
- ***Nonbank financial institutions resolution.*** Experience in resolving nonbank financial institutions is generally lacking in the region. The FSAP for

Kenya in particular stresses that nonbank financial regulators have little experience in the resolution of institutions they supervise. For instance, the Kenyan Insurance Regulation Agency is empowered to be named as either a conservator or receiver to administer resolution, but has no experience in doing so. On the other hand, the CMA in Kenya has gained some experience in dealing with market abuses in the brokerage industry and is strengthening its supervisory and enforcement capacity. Similarly, the FSAP for Tanzania calls for explicit logistical arrangements for communication and cooperation among the Bank of Tanzania, the Ministry of Finance and Economic Affairs, and other supervisory agencies in a systemic crisis to widen scope for discretionary action, if needed.

- ***Safety net arrangements.*** Safety net arrangements are narrow, are strapped for resources, and differ across EAC countries. At the time of the FSAP Updates, deposit insurance schemes in Kenya, Tanzania, and Uganda had a relatively narrow mandate and limited role in bank supervision, but since then were being reformed in Kenya and Tanzania. In Kenya, the Kenya Deposit Insurance Corporation has been created, independent of the Central Bank of Kenya. Further reforms are expected to enable the Kenya Deposit Insurance Corporation to become involved in problem banks at an earlier stage. In Uganda, while the previous FSAP recommendation to establish Deposit Insurance Fund as a separate legal entity within the BOU was being implemented, the FSAP Update noted that staffing limitations in the BOU constrained administration of the scheme. In Tanzania, while the role of the Deposit Insurance Fund has been restricted to repaying depositors, the Deposit Insurance Board has liquidation responsibilities and can participate in onsite examinations. There is no deposit insurance scheme in Burundi and Rwanda, although one was being considered in Rwanda. The FSAPs also underscore that available resources for deposit insurance funds are limited in certain cases (Tanzania) and coverage and participation premium varies from country to country (Table 12.3).

Stepped up efforts. Authorities in the EAC countries have stepped up their efforts to address risks from growing cross-border activity, but key aspects of a regional crisis management framework remain to be spelled out. The authorities have dealt with the supervisory challenges through MOUs among supervisors. An MOU among the EAC countries was signed in January 2009, and some central banks in the region have begun to explore the possibility of signing MOUs with the central banks of other home countries. The MOUs to date cover a number of areas such as information sharing, licensing, and coordination of onsite inspections, but do not cover the very important area of crisis management. In particular, the broad principles for emergency liquidity assistance to cross-border entities and home-host burden sharing remain to be addressed. Most FSAPs also recommended that the authorities conclude MOUs with all non-EAC supervisory authorities, whose banks are represented in EAC countries, clearly spelling out cooperation and coordination on crisis contingency planning and crisis management issues.

TABLE 12.3

Comparison of Deposit Insurance Schemes in East African Community Countries

	Burundi	Kenya	Rwanda	Uganda	Tanzania
Fund	No DIS. There is an implicit state blanket guarantee. The FSAP recommended studying the desirability of establishing a DIS.	The Deposit Protection Fund Board was created in 1985. In 2011, the Deposit Protection Fund Board was reorganized as an independent institution.	No DIS at the moment. As mandated by the LOB, the authorities intend to prepare a separate legislation on a DGF. If such a law moves forward, it is important that an effective process is in place for resolving banks, and the scheme will need to be carefully designed to ensure its effectiveness. In particular, the coverage should be limited to household deposits. Given current supervisory capacity, it is not advisable to extend the DGF to cover depositors in other financial institutions, such as microfinance institutions and savings and credit cooperatives.	Deposit Protection Fund, started operating in 1997.	Deposit Insurance Board, instituted in 2006.
Membership		All commercial banks, financial institutions, mortgage companies, and building societies.		All deposit taking institutions.	Commercial banks and nonbank financial institutions.
Coverage		K Sh 100,000 or about US$986		U Sh 500,000,000 or about US$1,759	T Sh 1,500,000 or about US$883
Memorandum item: Local currency/ US$ exchange rate (as of October 14, 2011)		101		2,842	1,700

Sources: FSAP reports for EAC countries; websites of respective authorities; and Bloomberg L.P.

Note: Since the conclusion of the FSAP missions, the funding and coverage of deposit insurance schemes have been increased in Kenya, Tanzania, and Uganda. DGF = deposit guarantee fund; DIS = deposit insurance scheme; FSAP = Financial Sector Assessment Program; K Sh = Kenya shillings; LOB = Law Concerning Organization of Banking; T Sh = Tanzania shillings; U Sh = Uganda shillings.

FINANCIAL INFRASTRUCTURE AND CAPITAL MARKET DEVELOPMENT

Payment and Securities Settlement Systems

Upgrading payment systems. Payment systems are being upgraded and adapted to regional needs, but scope remains for achieving greater regional synergies. In the more developed countries in the region, real-time gross settlement (RTGS) systems have been operating for a few years, but recent FSAPs call for enhancements and stronger legislative underpinning and oversight, especially of mobile payments. In particular, they stress the need to link the RTGS system with central securities depositories to achieve delivery-versus-payments and promote market development. Payments efficiency can be enhanced in some cases by linking small value automated clearing houses with the RTGS and by promoting interoperability of automated retail payments.

Mobile phone payments. A notable development in the region is the emergence of payments using mobile phones as an alternative to traditional banking and retail payments products. Providers of payments services and products involving mobile phones and nonbank correspondent networks remain largely unregulated and lack interoperability with other payments infrastructures. This reflects the lack of comprehensive payments legislation that renders the central bank vulnerable to legal challenges, handicaps its oversight function, limits the resolution of potential systemic risks in payments, and creates regulatory uncertainty (as stressed in the Uganda FSAP).[11] FSAPs in the region typically called for better regulation and supervision of these payments mechanisms.

A regional payment system. The central banks, and to a limited extent the banking industry, share a common vision to make the payment systems work for all segments of the population. At the regional level, the East Africa Cross Border Payments System aims to integrate national RTGS systems by linking the RTGS systems in Kenya, Tanzania, and Uganda. The integrated system, which was expected to become operational in 2012, will allow cross-border financial transactions to be settled in local currencies. Based on the FSAPs in EAC countries, further regional synergies can be achieved by adopting policy initiatives that support system modernization, enhanced cost and process efficiency, and realize improved access. These policies could include:

- Developing a regional payment system vision and strategy and bringing together various stakeholders and providing legislative and regulatory clarity, including by establishing central banks' regulatory and oversight roles over national payments infrastructures.

[11] For example, the lack of basic norms related to the finality and irrevocability of payments settled through the RTGS system or the automated clearing house has the potential to trigger a gridlock in the systems and a systemic crisis, in case of judicial disputes related to bankruptcy or insolvency of one of the participants.

- Developing an integrated payment processing system, integrated processing infrastructure comprising the RTGS system, automated clearing house, and the central securities depository.
- Implementing other measures such as dematerialization of government and private sector securities and establishment of an electronic link between the stock exchanges securities depositories and the RTGS system.

Systemic Liquidity and Debt Management

Coherent liquidity management. Effective and coherent systemic liquidity management across EAC countries will be essential for the development of a regional money market. EAC FSAPs generally consider proper liquidity management an important precondition for deepening the domestic money markets. Particular emphasis was placed on the transparency of monetary and exchange rate policies. Price stability is the principal objective of monetary policy in all the EAC countries, and central banks pursue this by relying either on monetary aggregates (Burundi, Rwanda, Tanzania) or on interest rates (Kenya, Uganda). Countries face varying degrees of implementation challenges, which tend to be more acute for countries with underdeveloped and shallow financial markets. For example, in Burundi, managing short-term liquidity has been problematic due in part to lack of securities for collateral in interbank operations.[12] Similarly, the FSAP for Rwanda calls for the National Bank of Rwanda to improve the issuance of government securities and automate the payment and settlement infrastructure in order to improve liquidity management.

Managing surges in liquidity. This is the principal focus of central banks in Kenya, Tanzania, and Uganda. The BOU, in particular, has adopted a more flexible approach by seeking to achieve relatively stable money market rates through the operation of the standing rediscount and Lombard facilities available at the counterparties' discretion against collateral—generally 91-day Treasury bills—at penalty rates. More generally, in these countries there is growing recognition that effective systemic liquidity management is essential for monetary and financial stability as well as for the development of the financial sector.

Public debt management. Some FSAPs (such as Burundi) considered effective public debt management important for the development of the financial sector. EAC FSAPs did not uniformly address public debt management and separate assessments of Medium Debt Management Strategy frameworks were undertaken in some cases. However, against the backdrop of exchange rate and interest rate volatility, developing a comprehensive debt management strategy is seen as a priority. Efforts to build capacity in public debt management and develop medium-term debt strategies should help the other EAC countries to contain the cost and risk of borrowing as well as smooth-out debt repayment schedule and ensure timely repayments. In some countries, the stock of government securities is small and concentrated in short-term maturities, while a secondary market

---

[12]To align rates with market realities, following the 2009 FSAP mission, Burundi Central Bank removed interest rate ceilings on its monetary operations.

BOX 12.3 Key Lessons: Upgrading Financial Infrastructure

Attention to regional consistency in upgrading financial infrastructure and systemic liquidity management will be important for regional financial integration, especially in developing a regional money market.

There is a need to articulate a vision and strategy, including legislative and regulatory framework and the role of central banks in the oversight of regional and national payments infrastructure.

Greater coherence in liquidity operations and instruments and increased availability of marketable securities for liquidity management are also needed.

Finally, a regional approach to capital market development, including stronger legal and regulatory frameworks, can contribute greatly to regional integration.

Source: Author.

trading is almost nonexistent. A larger stock of government paper with longer maturities and development of secondary markets in the context of sound public debt management as well as fiscal policies could help deepen the market and develop a yield curve as a benchmark for pricing of risk. In addition, better institutional coordination is needed between monetary and debt management policies to facilitate the development of money and government securities markets.

Capital Market Development

Capital markets and long-term funding. Capital markets in EAC countries can be further developed and deepened (Box 12.3). Most EAC FSAPs considered the development of stock and bond markets essential for increasing access to long-term funding and broadening investment opportunities, especially for institutional investors. They generally saw regional integration as a promising avenue for deepening bond and equity markets, but also focused on the need to strengthen oversight, improve clearing and settlements infrastructure, and, in some cases, liberalization of the capital account. Considerable attention was also paid to the governance of key institutional investors, such as pension funds and insurance companies. For instance, the weak governance arrangements of the National Social Security Fund, their weak investment management, and the lack of adequate custodial arrangements, received considerable attention in both the Kenya and Uganda FSAPs.

Specific capital market measures. A number of measures could promote capital market progress toward a regional EAC market. The primary market issuance framework in the region is biased toward equity, and more flexible regulations are needed to promote development of the nongovernment bond market.[13] Consideration could be given to mutual recognition of intermediaries and collective investment

[13]Though pension funds are the largest holders of corporate bonds, corporate bonds are a small percentage of their portfolio because of insufficient issuance. Onerous issuance requirements are imposed to protect retail investors in equity but impede bond market development. Bond instruments are more suitable for institutional investors so regulations being drafted by the CMA to provide a full disclosure approval process would assist institutional investors' ability to invest, and facilitate bond financing by infrastructure and project finance companies.

schemes among EAC partner states. Demutualization of the stock exchanges can also prove useful for enhancing competitiveness and overall soundness of the market. In addition, it would be important to ensure tax neutrality between different capital market products. Another promising avenue for deepening the securities market is greater government issuance activity, particularly in longer maturities.

Legal and regulatory framework. A stronger legal and regulatory framework could pave the way for regional harmonization and market integration. Key priorities are (1) demutualization of the stock exchange and the establishment of the central securities depository as a separate entity; (2) removal of limitations on foreign investment in listed corporations; (3) elimination of restrictions on foreign participation in the domestic government and corporate bond market; (4) adoption of regulations implementing common licensing standards for market intermediaries in the framework of the East African Member States Securities and Regulatory Authorities; (5) adoption of regulations implementing common prudential standards for institutional investors, to be agreed in the framework of the East African Member States Securities and Regulatory Authorities; (6) passage of double-taxation treaties with other partner states; and (7) prudent and sequenced capital account liberalization, supported by sound macroeconomic policies.

FINANCIAL INCLUSION AND DEVELOPMENT

Common challenges. EAC countries face several common challenges in financial development. These are not covered exhaustively in this chapter as the implications of many topics for regional integration are ambiguous. Nonetheless, two themes were recurrent and prominent in EAC FSAPs: (1) increasing inclusion and access to financial services and (2) promoting long-term financing.

Financial inclusion. Despite progress, broadening financial inclusion remains a critical policy challenge for the authorities in the EAC (Box 12.4). Large segments of the population in these countries have no access to financial services, in

BOX 12.4 Key Lessons: Financial Inclusion

- Broadening access to financial services remains an important challenge for the East African Community countries, and success in this would contribute to furthering financial integration.
- Microfinance institutions are likely to play a central role in this process, supporting growing small and medium-size enterprise sector. Capacity, governance, and regulatory issues with microfinance and small and medium-size enterprises have to be properly addressed.
- The success in developing longer-term financing requires government involvement, for instance, through development finance institutions. However, institutional and regulatory weaknesses need to be addressed to ensure their long-term soundness. Housing sector and infrastructure investment depend critically on the availability of longer-term financing.

Source: Author.

the formal or informal markets, especially in the rural areas. The share of underserved population is lowest in Kenya and Uganda, where only about one-third of the population is without access. In Rwanda and Tanzania, about one-half of the population has no access, while in Burundi access to financial services is very limited (the share of population having access, through formal or informal arrangements, is only a few percent).[14]

Informal services. Informal markets are crucial in providing the public access to financial services in the region. For instance, more than 40 percent of the population in Uganda uses the informal market, because coverage of the formal banking sector in terms of loans and deposits is still limited. In Kenya and Uganda, slightly more than 20 percent of the population has access to formal banking services, while in Rwanda and Tanzania the share is 10–15 percent.[15] Nonbank services are also offered, but these do not represent a significant part of financial services in most EAC countries, with the possible exception of Kenya, where almost 20 percent of the population uses them.

Improving access. Improving access to financial services, therefore, remains unfinished business. Sustained effort is necessary to reach rural areas. Microfinance institutions and savings and credit cooperatives have served to broaden access to deposit and credit products in some EAC countries (such as Burundi, Kenya, and Uganda), but these are not without problems. Advances in technology offer alternatives to traditional banking services (branch network). For instance, mobile banking can expand access to services to those who own a mobile phone. In Kenya and Uganda, mobile phones are increasingly used for remittances and bill payments. Important obstacles remain, however, as noted in the FSAPs:

- ***Inadequate capacity.*** Weak management capacity and poor accounting practices, lack of understanding of key products, pricing mechanism, information technology system, and risk management continue to contribute to poor business performance, governance problems, and insolvency. These issues seem most pressing in Burundi and Rwanda. Government involvement in the financial sector (such as in Rwanda and Kenya) has tended to create an uneven playing field and undermine efficiency in the financial sector.
- ***Lack of creditor protection.*** The absence of reliable credit information and weak creditor rights (collateral recovery) is contributing to high borrowing costs and poor repayment records (such as Burundi and Tanzania). The establishment of credit reference bureaus together with legislative reforms, under way in Uganda, Rwanda, and Tanzania, is likely to help address these concerns. Inability to provide collateral (for example, in Burundi) also remains an obstacle.
- ***Weak regulation and oversight.*** Strengthened financial sector regulation (e.g., Kenya has recently introduced microfinance and pension laws) would enhance efficiency in the microfinance institutions and savings and credit

---

[14] FinScope.

[15] For comparison, in South Africa, over 60 percent of the population has access to formal banking services.

cooperatives sectors. Strong supervisory oversight will be critical for ensuring financial soundness. Given the large number of microfinance institutions and savings and credit cooperatives, the authorities need to avoid overextending the limited supervisory resources (leads to creation of an apex bank).

Long-term financing. Promotion of long-term financial intermediation is a common concern in all EAC countries. In this connection, the importance of developing and strengthening capital markets and insurance and pension sectors received much attention in the FSAPs (as noted). Limited availability of longer-term investment products reflects the underdevelopment of national equity and debt security markets, as well as a shortage of development financing in the region. Adequate supply of longer-term debt financing, however, would be essential to provide investment alternatives to pension funds and life insurance companies.

Limited longer-term financing is an important obstacle for the development of housing markets in the EAC countries. In Uganda, for instance, in the absence of longer-term loans, microfinancing for housing has not developed and as a result lenders are increasingly moving to shorter-term home improvement loans that can be rolled over.

Housing markets would also benefit from better land code and land registry. The legal status of land as collateral needs to be clarified and its utilization for loans need to be made simpler (often too many requirements and permissions are needed to make the title as a solid collateral). Improved property registration systems would make it easier for banks to register mortgage liens and transfer the title. The authorities also need to develop standards for the valuation of land and other properties, and provide training for people on these matters. Developing a database for land and other property prices would benefit both the lenders and buyers of properties.

Developing a vibrant SME sector would also require better access to credit. Inability to obtain credit, including at longer maturities, hampers the operations and growth of SMEs. In part, this is due to weaknesses in financial reporting, the low capacity of SMEs to keep records, availability of good collateral, and weaknesses in the juridical system to protect creditors.

Institutional and regulatory concerns. Institutional and regulatory concerns are hampering the development of longer-term funding markets. In Kenya, for instance, progress in developing longer-term financing has been hindered by the unsound financial position of development finance institutions, while subsidized lending has prevented the emergence of private sector alternatives. Underdevelopment of a corporate debt market in Kenya has reflected regulatory weaknesses (favoring equity issuance over issuance of debt securities) and tax distortions. In Rwanda, the government is merging existing guarantee and refinance facilities into a single development institution to provide funding for the SMEs, while significant governance issues remain to be addressed. In Uganda, improving domestic market infrastructure for trading and facilitating the leveraging of regional opportunities through the EAC integration will over time contribute to deepening capital markets in the country. An effective risk management system and supervision of the capital markets will be essential for developing the longer-term markets in Tanzania.

Contributors

Christopher S. Adam is Professor of Development Economics and Research Associate of the Centre for the Study of African Economies, University of Oxford. He is currently the Research Director for Tanzania for the Oxford-London School of Economics International Growth Centre. He is a Fellow of the European Development Network; Visiting Professor at the University of Clermont-Ferrand, France; and a Visiting Scholar in the Research Department of the IMF.

Nabil Ben Ltaifa is a Senior Economist in the Middle East and Central Asia Department of the IMF. He has extensive experience in macroeconomic policy and reforms, IMF program design, monetary and financial sector reforms cross-country analysis, and IMF technical assistance. His wide-ranging experience extends to several IMF programs and low-income countries in the Middle East and sub-Saharan Africa.

Hamid R. Davoodi is a Senior Economist in the IMF's Institute for Capacity Development. He has been with the IMF since 1997 working on countries in Europe, the Middle East, Central Asia, and Africa. Prior to joining the IMF, he worked as an independent consultant at the World Bank, taught at Georgetown University's Economics Department, and worked in the research department at the Federal Reserve Bank of San Francisco. His work has been published in books and academic journals. He holds degrees from the London School of Economics (BSc Economics), the University of California (MS Applied Economics), and the University of Wisconsin at Madison (PhD Economics).

Shiv Dixit, an Indian national, is a PhD student in economics at the University of Minnesota. Prior to this, he was a Research Assistant in the African Department at the IMF.

Paulo Drummond, a Brazilian national, is a Deputy Division Chief in the African Department of the IMF. Mr. Drummond holds a PhD in economics from the University of Illinois at Urbana-Champaign. Prior to joining the IMF, he worked for the holding company of the group Bunge & Born and for Coopers & Lybrand. At the IMF, he has worked on a range of industrial, emerging market, and low-income countries in the European Department and the Policy Development and Review Department.

Sanjeev Gupta is the Acting Director of the Fiscal Affairs Department of the IMF. He has also worked in the IMF's African and European Departments. Mr. Gupta has led IMF missions to some 25 countries in Africa, Asia, Europe, and the Middle East, and represented the IMF in numerous international meetings and conferences. Prior to joining the IMF, he was a Fellow of the Kiel Institute of World Economics, Germany; Senior Faculty in the Administrative Staff College of India, Hyderabad; and Secretary (Economic Affairs) of the Federation of Indian Chambers of Commerce and Industry. Mr. Gupta has authored or coauthored over 100 papers on macroeconomic and fiscal issues and authored, coauthored, or coedited 10 books.

Richard Hughes is Division Chief of the Public Financial Management Division of the IMF's Fiscal Affairs Department. He has led the IMF's efforts to support reform to budgetary institutions in crisis-hit countries in Europe including Iceland, Ireland, Greece, and Portugal. In 2010, he helped launch the IMF's work with the East African Community Secretariat and member countries to help them to establish the regional and national fiscal prerequisites for East African Monetary Union.

Etibar Jafarov, a national of Azerbaijan, is a Senior Economist in the Monetary and Capital Markets Departments of the IMF. He holds a PhD in economics from Keio University (Tokyo, Japan), and a master's degree in international banking from Marmara University (Istanbul, Turkey). His latest research has been mostly in the areas of macroprudential policy, monetary policy framework, monetary union, financial-real sector linkages, cross-country trade and economic linkages, and fiscal management.

Pantaleo Kessy is Assistant Manager of the Research Department at the Central Bank of Tanzania. He is also a Senior Country Research Fellow for the International Growth Centre in Tanzania. His research interest is in macroeconomic policies in developing countries. Most recently, his work has been on the analysis of monetary and exchange rate policies in the economies of East Africa. He holds an MA (Economics) from the University of Dar Es Salaam, Tanzania, and a PhD (Economics) from Colorado State University, specializing in monetary and financial economics.

Camillus Kombe is a Manager in the Economics Department, Bank of Tanzania, Dodoma Branch. He is also a member of the Bank of Tanzania, Technical Research Committee. His main areas of research interest include monetary policy, economic growth in developing countries, regional economic integration, and exchange rate issues. His most recent work has been the analysis of the current account and real exchange rates in Southern African Development Community countries. He holds an MA (Economics) and a PhD (Economics) from the University of Geneva, Switzerland, specializing in international economics.

Catherine McCauliffe is currently Assistant to the Director in the Communications Department at the IMF. She was previously Mission Chief for Liberia,

Rwanda, and Guinea Bissau in the IMF's African Department. She also has extensive experience working as an economist on other African countries. She received a master's degree in international economics from Tufts University's Fletcher School of Law and Diplomacy.

Jimmy McHugh is Senior Economist in the IMF's Fiscal Affairs Department. Previously, he has worked as the IMF's Resident Representative in Armenia and the Kyrgyz Republic. He has also worked in the Directorate-General for Economic and Financial Affairs (European Commission). He holds a PhD from St. Antony's College, Oxford University.

Armando Morales, a national of Peru, is a Senior Economist in the IMF's African Department. He was Resident Representative in Indonesia, and Mission Chief for Financial Sector Assessment Programs and technical assistance missions to Latin American and African countries. Before joining the IMF, he worked in Peru as head of research at Macroconsult and as advisor at the Central Bank. He holds degrees from the Kiel Institute of World Economics, Germany, and Northeastern University, Boston.

Stephen A. O'Connell is Chief Economist at the U.S. Agency for International Development and Gil and Frank Mustin Professor of Economics at Swarthmore College. He coedited *The Political Economy of Economic Growth in Africa 1960–2000* (vol. 1, 2007; vol. 2 2008; Cambridge University Press), and has written extensively on monetary policy issues in Tanzania and the East African Community. In 2013, he was a Visiting Scholar in the Research and Strategy, Policy, and Review Departments of the IMF.

Gabor Pinter is an Advisor in the Bank of England's Centre for Central Banking Studies. He holds a PhD in economics from the University of Cambridge and an MSc in economics from the University of Cardiff. Previously, he was a visiting scholar at Princeton University and a summer intern at the IMF.

Sweta C. Saxena is a Senior Economist in the IMF's Research Department. She joined the IMF in 2009, working on African countries. Prior to joining the IMF, she worked in the Emerging Markets Unit at the Bank for International Settlements in Switzerland and at the University of Pittsburgh in the United States. Her research focuses on policy-relevant macrofinancial issues, namely, crises and recoveries, contagion, and exchange rates. She has published in academic journals. She holds bachelor's and master's degrees in economics from Delhi University, and a PhD from the University of Washington.

S. Kal Wajid has served as Division Chief in the African and Monetary and Capital Markets Departments of the IMF. He has extensive experience in macroeconomic, monetary, and financial sector policies, including at the IMF, the Institute of International Finance, the Board of Governors of the Federal Reserve System and

Bank of America. He has led IMF missions to numerous countries, including as part of the leadership team for the Financial Sector Assessment Program (FSAP) for the United States and leadership of FSAPs for South Africa, Denmark, Croatia, Pakistan, Barbados, and the Nordic-Baltic Regional Financial Integration Project.

Oral Williams is a Deputy Division Chief in the African Department of the IMF. He is currently Mission Chief for Burundi, previously led missions to Oman, and worked in the IMF's Fiscal Affairs, Western Hemisphere, and Middle East and Central Asia Departments. Prior to joining the IMF, he was a Deputy Director in the Eastern Caribbean Central Bank. He has published in academic journals and at the IMF on topics including fiscal and monetary policy, the economics of resource-rich countries, international finance, and development macroeconomics.

Masafumi Yabara is a Deputy Director of the Ministry of Finance, Japan, responsible for macroeconomic policy planning including monetary policy coordination with the Bank of Japan. He previously worked for the African Department of the IMF on Rwanda, South Sudan, and Lesotho, as well as research projects on sub-Saharan Africa such as financial integration and growth take-offs of the region.

Mary Zephirin is a Deputy Division Chief in the Technical Assistance Division of the Monetary and Capital Markets Department of the IMF. Prior to joining the IMF, she was an advisor in the Central Bank of Barbados and has also worked as a consultant, and with the United Nations Children's Fund and the United Nations Development Programme. Ms. Zephirin has a PhD in economics from the University of Warwick.

Index

[Page numbers followed by *b, f,* or *t* refer to boxed text, figures or tables, respectively.]

F

H

I